Making Marketing Happen: How great companies make strategic marketing planning work for them

Making Marketing Happen: How great companies make strategic marketing planning work for them

Dr Brian D. Smith

ELSEVIER
BUTTERWORTH
HEINEMANN

AMSTERDAM • BOSTON • HEIDELBERG • LONDON • NEW YORK • OXFORD
PARIS • SAN DIEGO • SAN FRANCISCO • SINGAPORE • SYDNEY • TOKYO

Elsevier Butterworth-Heinemann
Linacre House, Jordan Hill, Oxford OX2 8DP
30 Corporate Drive, Burlington, MA 01803

First published 2005

British Library Cataloguing in Publication Data
A catalogue record for this book is available from the British Library

Library of Congress Control Number: 2005924634
A catalogue record for this book is available from the Library of Congress

ISBN 0 7506 6248 4

For information on all Elsevier Butterworth-Heinemann publications
visit our website at http://books.elsevier.com

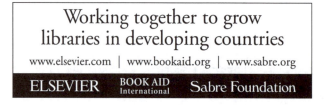

Typeset by Newgen Imaging Systems (P) Ltd., Chennai, India
Printed and bound in Great Britain

For Lindsay, Eleanor and Catherine

Foreword

I had the great privilege of supervising Brian Smith's doctoral thesis on marketing planning. His finished work was one of the most outstanding theses I have come across in over a quarter of a century in academia.

But it doesn't end there. I have been a senior marketing practitioner most of my working life and still work with the Boards of many of the biggest and best companies in the world. In this capacity, it is rare to find any research emanating from a business school that is directly applicable to and capable of being implemented by companies in a world which has become increasingly tough and more hostile since my days as Marketing Director of a fast moving consumer goods company in the late seventies.

In my view Brian Smith's work on marketing planning sets a new standard for research in business schools because, not only does it tackle head on the most difficult task in the domain of marketing, but it brings to it a refreshingly challenging, original and creative approach.

Now Brian Smith has translated his work into this book in a way which will catch the imagination of all experienced marketers. For everyone touched by the problems and issues associated with strategy-making, this book is a MUST read. Not only is it intellectually challenging, but it is urbane, pragmatic and entertaining in a way which most marketing books fail to achieve. Brian Smith is one of a new breed of marketers who are capable of original thinking.

I have read and enjoyed every word. If you want to improve your knowledge and wisdom and hence your success as a marketing practitioner, I beseech you to read and note carefully what Brian Smith has to say. Your ability to implement all that is best in marketing will be greatly enhanced.

Professor Malcolm McDonald
Cranfield University School of Management

Contents

List of figures

List of tables

Preface

> Now, here, you see, it takes all the running you can do to keep in the same place. If you want to get somewhere else, you must run at least twice as fast as that!
>
> (The Red Queen, in *Through the Looking Glass* by Lewis Carroll)

This book is written with a very specific target audience in mind. It is written for the practising marketer rather than for the marketing academic or student, although I hope it is of some use to those two groups. More particularly, *Making Marketing Happen* is written for the marketer who has already read books or attended courses on marketing planning, and it is not meant as an introduction to that subject. (For those readers seeking guidance on traditional marketing planning, I recommend the excellent *Marketing Plans, How to Prepare Them, How to Use Them*, by Professor Malcolm McDonald.) Most marketing practitioners now are qualified, either formally or through experience, and are familiar with the basic tools of the discipline, which this book does not attempt to cover. More particularly still, this book is intended for what the late Donald Schön referred to as the 'Reflective Practitioner' (Schön, 1999); that is, the practising professional who appreciates the complexity of the real world and is prepared to dedicate some significant thought to understanding it. By contrast, this book is not intended to appeal to those who prefer airport books of the genre 'How to Solve All Your Business Problems Whilst Waiting in the Departure Lounge'. Finally, this book is targeted at those qualified, reflective marketing practitioners who are frustrated by the difficulty of applying strategic marketing planning in practice, those who might empathize with Chuck Reid's statement that, 'In theory, there is no difference between theory and practice; In practice, there is'. It is for those qualified, reflective, frustrated marketing practitioners that this book is written.

The quotation from Lewis Carroll's eccentric masterpiece which heads this preface could have come from the mouth of a practising marketer. The cause of our exercise is not hard to see. Even more so than our colleagues in other functions, marketers are torn between two important groups of customers whose wants are, in short, contradictory. Primarily, of course, we see ourselves as struggling to meet the needs of the external, paying customers with their shifting needs and, whatever we like to think about loyalty, continual search for optimal value. Most marketers need no reminding that these people are important. Not quite so obvious is that whilst we sell our products and services to external customers, we sell ourselves to shareholders. However disguised by chains of command and ownership structures, we all sell ourselves to the people who fund the business. In short, they buy our skills and give us as little loyalty as, or less loyalty than, the external customer. They will move on, with their money, as soon as they perceive another marketer is better at creating a return on their investment. Neither group owes us, or each other, much in the way of loyalty. And therein lies our problem. Customers want the most value and utility for the least cost; shareholders want the biggest return on the lowest investment and risk. Between the two sit we, the marketing practitioners, our living dependent on reconciling these conflicting and unforgiving demands.

The challenge is, of course, one of resource allocation. Although, day to day, we concern ourselves with product design, distribution channels, pricing structures and advertising, marketing strategy is really just resource allocation. The skill shareholders pay us for is our ability to allocate their funds better than another marketer. What external customers reward us for with their custom is the end result of our resource allocation. As marketers in a business unit, we sit inside a complex web of resource allocation decisions. Far above us, corporate strategy is the allocation of resources between industries or sectors, which determines how much of the corporate pot, if any, our business unit gets to use. Immediately above us, business unit strategy makes broad decisions about how to allocate the business unit funds across the value chain, and therefore between functions. Those decisions will dictate whether most of the value we create will come from the management of product development, of operations or of customers.

Wherever the emphasis is placed, value creation depends on a set of interlinked and, hopefully, coherent resource allocation decisions by each function. It is the resource allocation decisions made by marketing which we call the marketing strategy. For all its potential complexity and confusion with marketing objectives and marketing tactics, marketing strategy has only two components: what we are going to offer, and to whom.

It is these decisions (and the concomitant negative decisions) that then dictate our marketing mix, the classic four (or perhaps seven) Ps of product, price, promotion, place (people, process and physical evidence). If we accept that marketing strategy is that set of management decisions regarding which customers to go after and what value propositions to offer them, then it is difficult to overstate its importance. Not only does it lead, or at least heavily influence, all other functional strategies; the quality of those decisions is also a major determinant of our business success.

It is not taking it too far even to draw wider societal implications. In a sense, our entire liberal capitalist economy is driven by the marketing strategies, the resource allocation decisions, of its constituent firms. It seems sensible, therefore, that we make the best strategies we can, and use the best tools we have to do it.

It is the marketing strategies we make, and the way we make them, that are the concern of this book. Its aim is to help marketing practitioners make the best marketing strategies possible. Part of its thesis is that our current process of strategic marketing planning, as taught by business schools and expounded in text books, is not good enough. That is to say, there is plenty of evidence that it *can* work and, when it does, that it contributes to organizational effectiveness. However, there is still more evidence that strategic marketing planning *does not work* in practice. This is not because of any fundamental weakness in its component tools and techniques, but because it can't be used by ordinary practitioners in a real world context. In a sense, marketing is merely a technology, based on the sciences of economics, psychology and sociology, just as medicine and engineering are based on their core sciences of biology and physics. However, it is a poorly developed technology, hard to apply practically and, more often than not, poorly applied and producing poor results. For such an important part of the business process, we need to do better.

This book is the result of many years of practice and research into marketing-strategy making. Its thesis is not that strategic marketing planning is wrong – far from it – but that it is not sufficient. To work, strategic marketing planning must be seen as one component of a hybrid marketing-strategy making process that also incorporates leadership and incremental development. Further, that hybrid process should not be prescriptive and applied universally. Instead, each company must learn to develop the specific hybrid of planning, leadership and incrementalism that fits its own market and its own organizational culture. Do this, and strong strategies are made. Apply planning blindly, and weak strategies, given false credibility by process, emerge. Those are the marketing strategy lessons of great companies.

Part I

The failure of strategic marketing planning

Part 1 of *Making Marketing Happen* looks at what we currently know about strategic marketing planning, or at least what we knew before the research for this book began. It concludes that the approach we currently take, largely rational and prescriptive, doesn't work well in practice. Part 2 describes the findings of five years of research into how companies make marketing strategy in practice. From the detailed pattern of success and failure, a common theme emerges – what works is what fits. Part 3 develops that theme. From the experiences of companies who make strong marketing strategies, we learn not how to make marketing strategy in exactly the way they do, but how to create a process for making marketing strategy in a way that works for your company.

The aim of Chapter 1 is to make sure that author and reader are talking about the same thing. Marketing strategists have the misfortune to work in an area where words are used very loosely. Both 'marketing' and 'strategy' would rank highly amongst any list of most abused words. Worse still, the process of strategic marketing planning is easily lost under a pile of jargon and acronyms in which nothing has a single definition and each definition is vague and misleading. We, author and reader, can't converse clearly until we are speaking the same language. Thus Chapter 1 tries to summarize what strategic marketing planning is, pooling the collective knowledge of many textbooks and adding some clarity. What emerges is actually a relatively simple story, confused and complicated by retelling. In the process of clarification, Chapter 1 also helps to remind us, amid the noise of a thousand authors, what strategic marketing planning is for.

The aim of Chapter 2 is to carry out a sanity check on the whole idea of planning. The research upon which this book is based began with the question: 'Does strategic marketing planning work?' In fact, researchers have been asking this question for only a slightly shorter time than marketers have been planning. The answer is 'yes, but'. The 'but' is that whilst strategic marketing planning works, it is not a panacea. No business process in the world can be said to cause profitability; business is just too complex to make that simple statement. However, strategic planning, and the marketing version of it, has a much better claim to usefulness than many other management tools. In the process of looking at the effectiveness of strategic marketing planning, Chapter 2 also provides useful ammunition to marketers who need to justify their existence to their non-marketing colleagues.

The aim of Chapter 3 is to introduce reality into our conversation about strategic marketing planning. If we know that strategic marketing planning works, why do so few people actually do it? This chapter reveals that planning fails in an organization when it doesn't fit. Either planning fails to cope with the conditions of the marketplace, or it doesn't fit the organizational culture, or both. In whichever case, the result is some adulterated version of planning that results in weak strategy at heavy cost of management time. This is an important conclusion, because neither the market nor the culture can be changed easily to fit the planning process. In the process of understanding why planning fails, we begin to understand what we must do to make strong strategy.

Chapter 4 provides pause for thought. Having agreed that strategic marketing planning is, in essence, a simple process and that it is worth doing, we've also discovered that it probably won't work for us, at least not in its current form. Strategic marketing planning is like a poorly designed tool that is effective in the hands of an expert and in the right conditions, but fails to deliver results in the hands of many practitioners. Chapter 4 describes the research work carried out to understand the failings of strategic marketing planning and how it is that great companies manage to make strong strategy without following the textbook. In the process, it demonstrates what it is about business processes that leads them to work in one organization but not in another.

Chapter 1

We know what strategic marketing planning is . . .

There are very many books about business strategy and they all say much the same thing.

(Professor Richard Whittington, *What is Strategy and Does it Matter?*)

Introduction

The movie *Indiana Jones and the Last Crusade* reaches an exciting climax when the hero, after surmounting three fiendish traps, reaches the cave that houses the Holy Grail. As he enters the cave, however, he sees not one but dozens of grails, each of a different design and level of grandeur. Jones' final test is to work out which is the true grail. He does, of course, and it all ends happily ever after. The story has some parallels with that of the reflective marketing practitioner, searching for a Holy Grail of strategic marketing planning. The practitioner's problem lies not in finding a way to do it, but in discerning which of the many different ways to do it is best.

A few minutes of web-browsing illustrates the problem. The phrase 'strategic marketing planning' throws up 299 results on Amazon. Entered into an electronic literature database, 17 388 articles are found. The same three words inserted into Google™ for an Internet search produce no fewer than 3.28 million results. By comparison, Indiana Jones' choice seems a simple one. When we set out to find the best way to make a strong and effective marketing plan, we are understandably confused by the options.

The message of this chapter is that the confusion, although understandable, is as unnecessary as it is harmful. The bewildering variety of processes, jargon and tools that characterize strategic marketing planning does not represent real and substantive differences between different planning approaches. Instead, the variation arises from the vanity of writers and attempts at differentiation by publishers, as each new book tries to make its interpretation of the core process more attractive than the others.

This chapter builds the argument that, in fact, there is only one core process of strategic marketing planning, and that the endless variation, whilst well meaning, is confusing and dangerous for practitioners. The different approaches confuse practitioners needlessly by pretending substantive differences. Worse, they hinder and slow down implementation, as marketers waste time comparing what are essentially similar approaches.

The rest of this chapter makes the argument that the core process of making marketing strategy is simple in principle, and that the difficulty of practical implementation is reduced if we understand the core process better. Further, although marketing planning shows a clear path of development from the tactical to the strategic over the last forty years, it now appears to be a stable entity. New marketing ideas, whilst useful, are largely developments of well-established concepts rather than revolutionary new thoughts. Marketers' time is therefore better spent understanding that core process and working out how to apply it in their organization, rather than endlessly assessing variations on a theme. To this end, this chapter looks at the development of strategic marketing planning, and its core process and concepts, in order to help the reader understand what it is that we are trying to make work.

Where did strategic marketing planning come from?

Understanding the origins of strategic marketing planning requires some little appreciation of history and how thinking in any discipline develops. In particular, we need to be conscious of two things that historians consider fundamental to the application of their subject. First, we need to understand that any concept arises from its social and historical context. Ideas and theories are not spontaneously formed in a cerebral vacuum. Secondly, linear progression and clear, discrete, concepts are the product of hindsight, rarely existing at the time. In other words, real history is messy. The development of strategic marketing planning is a good example of both these things. Although the following paragraphs try to clarify the picture, the reality of marketing history is messy.

Marketing as a discipline can be traced back to 1901, when Edward David Jones at the University of Michigan taught the first university marketing course. It seems to have evolved from studies in how products are distributed and sold. The earliest textbooks for marketing date from the 1920s (Converse, 1921). The American Marketing Association and the UK's Chartered Institute of Marketing were both formed in the 1930s, although each can trace their lineage back a further twenty years (Converse, 1952).

This historical context is significant, as it explains the continuing fascination the discipline has with tools, techniques and structured processes. Marketing evolved in a specific socio-historical context as the ideas of science and the positivistic confidence of that era influenced the study of management. This was the era of 'scientific management', as exemplified in Frederick Taylor's renowned studies of labour efficiency (Taylor, 1911). Marketing, at that time barely distinguishable in subject matter from advertising and sales management, was an example of attempts to rationalize and formalize the process of finding, satisfying and keeping customers. Not only did it arise from the historical context, therefore; it was already overlapping with related concepts like selling and physical distribution.

By 1941, the history of marketing thought had already justified a PhD thesis which later developed into an excellent book, to which readers are directed if they are interested in the early history of the subject (Bartels, 1962). However, despite its rapid growth in popularity, marketing in the first sixty years of the twentieth century remained an umbrella term for advertising and selling, and was not well defined in its own right.

This lack of distinct definition of the subject is well illustrated by one early text on the subject, *Marketing Management*, written by D Maynard Phelps in 1960. The fact that the book was a revised edition of *Sales Management Policies and Procedures*, a book by the same author written in 1951, is evidence of the nature of marketing at that time. In the late 1950s marketing was still a largely tactical discipline, not very distinct from selling and distribution. However, that was about to change.

The concept of strategic marketing as we know it today seems to have emerged around 1960. The milestone is usually recognized as Theodore Levitt's *Harvard Business Review* paper of that year (Levitt, 1960), although this publication date suggests that the ideas were forming prior to that time. In that article we see, for the first time ever, the concept of being 'market led' (i.e. making what the customer wants) as opposed to 'product led' (i.e. selling what we make). In retrospect we can see this as the emergence of marketing as a distinct subject, differentiated from (but still encompassing) advertising and selling and denoted by its emphasis on identifying and understanding customer needs. However, the processes and techniques that we now call strategic marketing planning did not yet exist. These seem to have developed during the 1960s as the marketing concept began to overlap with ideas of strategic planning.

In another example of ideas emerging from their socio-historical context, strategic planning in its business sense is generally seen as a product of the post-war period, presumably influenced by the military experience of most managers. Henry Mintzberg observes that in its early days it was mostly a budgeting exercise rather than a strategy making process (Mintzberg, 1994). Only later did it develop the tools and processes for creating and selecting strategy options with which we are now familiar. Its evolution is complex, but four seminal books by Drucker (1954), Ansoff (1965), Andrews (1971) and Porter (1980) mark this evolution of strategic planning from a budgeting and logistical exercise to a strategy creation process. In doing so they developed the tools that now characterize it, such as Ansoff's Matrix, Porter's Five Forces, and the various incarnations of portfolio management, beginning with the Boston Matrix.

Most of these tools are now familiar to marketers, even though their roots lie in strategy rather than marketing. This is because, as marketing planning has evolved, it seems to have conflated with strategic planning to create strategic marketing planning. To this day, strategic planning and strategic marketing planning continue to be hard to separate and share many of the same tools. However, they do concern themselves with different levels of strategy, as outlined in Chapter 5.

Application point: Has your organization adopted the marketing concept?

As with all of the Application Points in this book, the aim here is to pause for thought and give readers a chance to shift their thinking from the theory to the applied, from the page to the real world. Each box therefore challenges readers to put the ideas of the preceding few paragraphs into the context of their own situation.

The preceding section has described how marketing as a discipline underwent a huge transformation in the late 1950s and 1960s. The starting point for strategy shifted from 'we make this, how do we sell it?' to 'they want this, how do we give it to them?' Even today, it is clear that not all companies have kept pace with this fundamental shift in management thinking. One only has to experience air-travel to see that what the customer wants does not always drive a company's activity.

What about your organization?

How much does it start thinking about customer needs and work backwards to what its value proposition needs to be? Or does it start with what comes out of development and try to persuade the customer to take it?

Consider for a moment how your company defines its market (as a product category, or a group of people with needs) and what it knows about that market (do you research products or customer needs?).

To the extent that your organization has not yet adopted the marketing concept, it is an illustration that strategic marketing planning is not working. Why this is so is discussed later.

Whatever the origins of strategic marketing planning, it had by the late 1960s become a recognizable term in is own right. Further, it had begun to be codified into textbooks. In a sense, therefore, the history of strategic marketing planning dates from the late 1960s. The selling and distribution work before that can be thought of as its prehistory – the ancestors from which strategic marketing planning evolved.

Understanding this evolutionary turning point is important for two reasons. First, it helps us to see that issues of sales management and advertising policy are not synonymous with marketing strategy as we know it today. An understanding of those topics is necessary but not sufficient for the making of marketing strategy.

Secondly, understanding how the ideas about strategic marketing planning have developed and evolved since the 1960s is important and useful. We can see how core concepts have remained and new ideas have been assimilated. Most importantly, understanding a little about the evolution of strategic marketing planning allows us to differentiate fundamental ideas from fad and hype. To stay with the evolutionary metaphor for a moment, the history of marketing ideas allows us to differentiate important new species from transitory local variations.

The evolution of strategic marketing planning is recorded indirectly in the textbooks written to teach new practitioners. Each textbook attempts to capture the state of the art and, with each new edition and each new author, coincidentally creates a history of the subject. Reading them is like reading old newspapers, in that they tell us about marketing thinking at the time they were written.

Characteristically, many marketing textbooks fail to make it beyond one or two editions; these are like ancient insects trapped in amber. They give an interesting snapshot of strategic marketing at the time they were written. More useful to us, however, are those classic books that survive for many editions, over decades. These are like a continuous fossil record, charting the evolution of marketing thinking over time. Only three leading marketing authors have achieved sufficient longevity in their writing for their texts to be considered useful historical records. Philip Kotler, David Cravens and Malcolm McDonald are well-known to generations of marketers, and their books cover the decades over which strategic marketing planning has evolved.

The following section looks at how the content of their books has changed and how it has stayed the same over time. In doing so, it attempts to draw implications for marketing practice by identifying the evolution of a core process for making marketing strategy and separating out the fads and evolutionary dead-ends that occurred on the way.

Application point: How fad-prone is your organization?

Organizations are groups of people and, as such, reflect the idiosyncrasies of their members. Organizations therefore, like people, are more or less prone to seizing new ideas and spending time on them. As in all things, seizing new fads or being resistant to new ideas is neither good nor bad in principle. What matters is selecting ideas on the basis of the value they offer to the organization. Fad-prone organizations are simply less good at judging the real value of an idea, and are therefore liable to be seduced by new buzzwords and hype with little substance.

- What is your organization like at judging the value in new ideas?
- Does it do so rationally (for instance, by placing the idea in the context of its overall situation) or non-rationally (for instance, based on the enthusiasm of a single executive)?
- Does it look for evidence of the idea's value, or does it make a leap of faith?

As you will see later in this book, being too fad-prone seems to be a barrier to good strategy making.

How has strategic marketing planning developed?

As we have discussed, marketing seems to have emerged as a distinct discipline, as a result of the application of 'scientific management' to advertising and sales practice. This occurred during the first half of the twentieth century but, for all its value, did not create an idea of marketing that was truly distinct from distribution, selling and advertising. For those trained in late twentieth and early twenty-first century marketing, what was called marketing then was more or less what we now call marketing communications, together with some physical distribution.

The evolutionary breakpoint seems to have occurred in the late 1950s, with the development of the marketing concept – the idea that customer needs drive the design of the value proposition rather than *vice versa*. This idea spread rapidly but not instantaneously through companies, although the experienced reader will recognize that the marketing concept has still not reached a great many product-led companies.

On a parallel path, during the post-war years strategic planning developed from a budgeting and logistics exercise, gradually becoming a rational process for identifying and selecting strategic options and then translating them into action plans. During the 1960s, the ideas of strategic planning and the marketing concept intermingled to create, by the late 1960s, something approaching strategic marketing planning as we know it today. It shared many of its tools and concepts with strategic planning, but was more limited in scope. As will be discussed in Chapter 5, strategic marketing planning considered which customers to target and with what products (or services), but left the choices about which industry to be in and the fundamental basis of competition to the strategic planners.

The way strategic marketing planning has developed since the 1960s is recorded in the textbooks written by leading exponents like Kotler, Cravens and McDonald, and this history helps us to understand the core process of strategic marketing planning, as distinct from the froth and fads created by those trying to sell their books and services.

Arguably, the most internationally famous marketing author is Philip Kotler, of North Western University's Kellogg School of Management. As well as being prolific, he has an unmatched longevity as an author; no other marketing academic has as long a record in strategic marketing. In particular, his book *Marketing Management: Analysis, Planning and Control* is perhaps the most widely used marketing book at graduate level. It has been in continuous print since 1967, and is now in its eleventh edition (Kotler, 2002), albeit dropping its subtitle.

The thirty-six years between the first and latest editions cover a huge period in the terms of modern business. This is especially true when we consider the social, political and IT-enabled changes of the last three or four decades. As a continuous record of the development of marketing thinking, therefore, Kotler's work provides a unique resource to look for changes in the way we do strategic marketing planning. He has assiduously updated his work every three to four years, adding the results of his own research as well as that of others. He has also striven successfully to keep the book topical and relevant. Yet what strikes anyone who compares all the editions of his book is not huge, fundamental change, but the relative stability of the core subject matter, albeit overlaid with detailed changes.

As can be seen from Figure 1.1, comparing the structure and content of several different editions, Kotler has kept the same basic structure for all this period. Over time, new chapters were added and later removed, often reflecting current interests of marketers. Strategies for inflation, recession and shortages were added in the early 1980s,

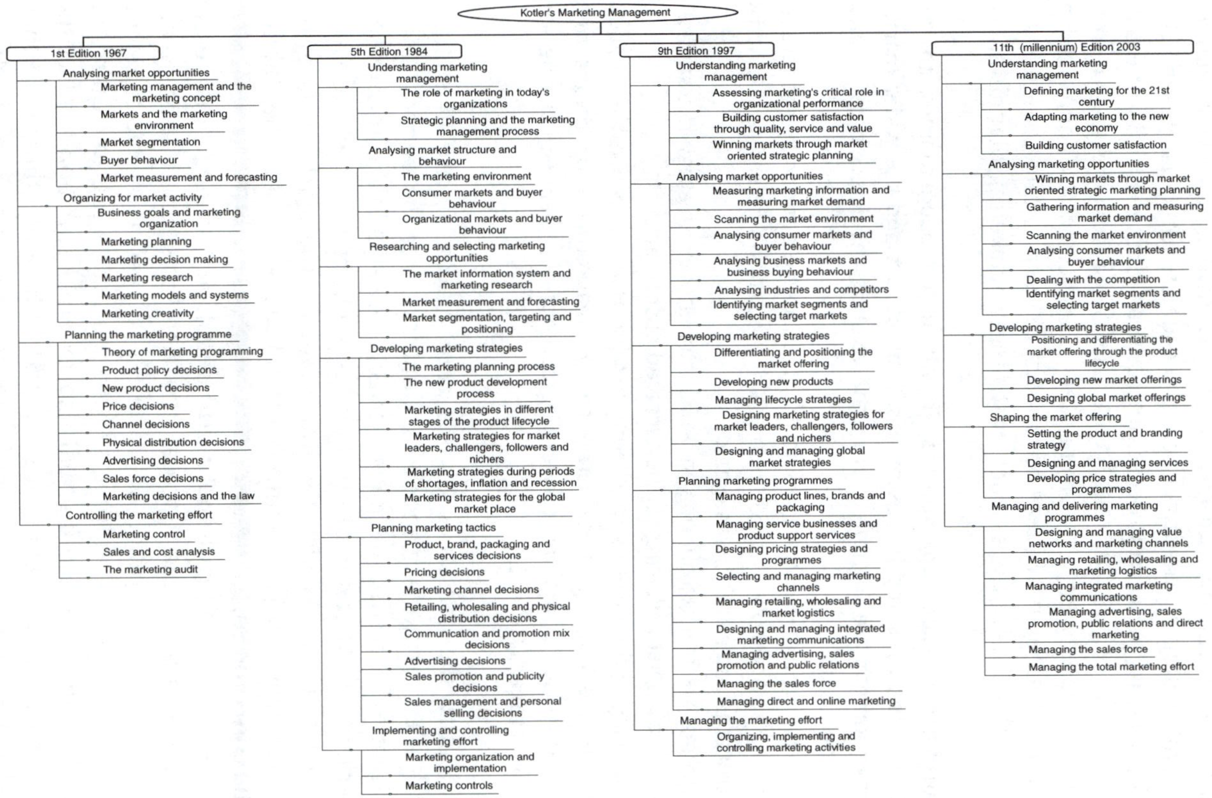

Figure 1.1 The content of Kotler's *Marketing Management*

for instance, whilst the eleventh (millennium) edition in 2002 took on a particularly 'new economy' slant. In between, new research is woven into the core framework, including the use of information and telecommunications technology, supply chain management and relationship marketing. Each of these new topics is presented in the context of the core process, and not as changes to its underlying principles. Over thirty-six years, this classic text has grown from twenty-three to twenty-seven chapters, then been consolidated down to twenty-four as new ideas are shown to overlap and coalesce into what Kotler sees as the essence of strategic marketing planning:

1. Analysing market opportunities, in which the opportunities, threats and context created by customers, competitors and the wider market environment are identified from the explicit and implicit data which surrounds us.
2. Developing market strategies, in which strategic options are generated and narrowed down, based upon the organization's objective, distinctive strengths and relative weaknesses.
3. Shaping the market offering, in which the chosen strategy is translated into a complete offering to the targeted customers.
4. Managing and delivering marketing programmes, in which the product or service offering is delivered to the marketplace by means of a coherent set of actions concerning promotion, channels, pricing and product management.

To identify the constancy of this core process is not to suggest that Kotler has not advanced his thinking over the period we are examining. Each edition shows extensive revision in the light of new experience, market conditions and research, but they are all variations on a theme. Whilst it is important for the marketer to grasp these changes, it is just as important not to lose sight of the stability of the core process.

Kotler shows, in great and useful detail, that strategic marketing planning is a matching process, in which the strengths and weaknesses of the organization are carefully aligned with and matched to the opportunities and threats of the market. Doing so requires us to understand both the internal and external situations, select the strategic option that represents the best fit between them, and then translate that option into a set of management decisions and actions. Beneath the complexity and detail, that is what Kotler has been telling marketers for thirty-six years.

Philip Kotler's work is marked by its comprehensiveness. In addition to his core text, he has written many other books on specialized areas of marketing such as the arts and not-for-profits. However, his *Marketing Management* is very much a reference text; its comprehensiveness makes it a huge tome that is perhaps best referred to rather than read cover to cover. It is not hard to see in Kotler's work his origins as an economist and mathematician.

An alternative approach is taken by the UK's equivalent of Kotler – Malcolm McDonald, now Emeritus Professor of Marketing at Cranfield School of Management, but at one time a practising marketing director. His most well-known work (again, one of many tens of books) takes the form of a marketing planning manual, and is accurately titled *Marketing Plans: How to prepare them, how to use them* (McDonald, 2002). McDonald's book has been in print for over twenty years, and during that period has more than doubled in size. However, it provides an even starker example of the stability of the core process for making marketing strategy. Throughout this period, the structure of the book has remained virtually unchanged, as shown in Figure 1.2. Again the core structure has been augmented and deepened as each new edition has added further research into areas such as customer relationship marketing, key account management and multichannel marketing.

As for all marketing professors, supervising PhD students provides a constant stream of new research and McDonald has been especially active in joint research with practitioners. However, these new ideas augment rather than replace the core process that McDonald stays with from the first edition to the fifth. He bases everything around his definition of the marketing concept:

> The central idea of marketing is of a matching between a company's capabilities and the wants of customers in order to achieve the objectives of both parties.

To this end, his book outlines how to make sense of the opportunities and threats that arise from the market environment (a process he calls the marketing audit) and how to achieve a fit between them and the organization's resources. As with Kotler, the alignment process is implemented by a set of management actions concerning product, pricing, distribution and promotion. Hence McDonald's book supports the idea that the core process of marketing is both clear and, at a fundamental level, quite stable.

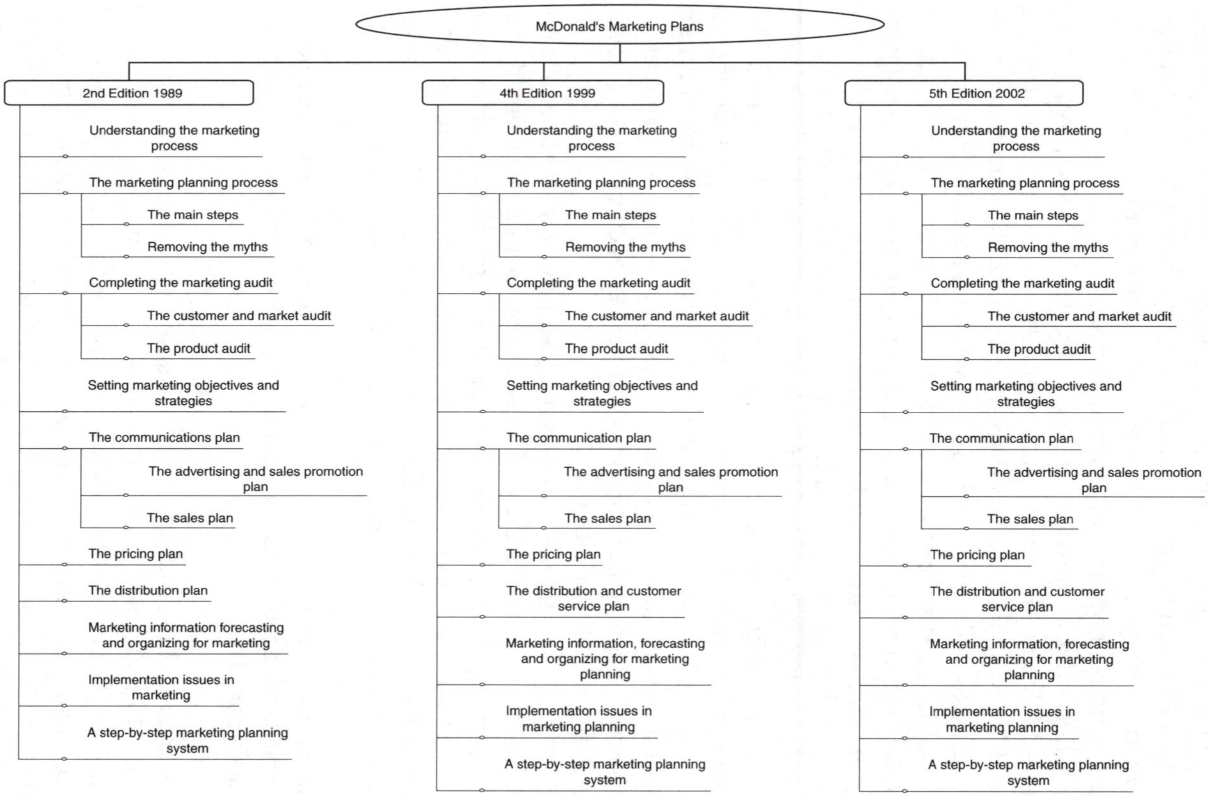

Figure 1.2 The content of McDonald's *Marketing Plans*

Understandable as it is to want to seize on new thinking, marketers should not confuse the latest ideas with important changes in the principles of marketing-strategy making. Nor should they think that they need to choose between several fundamentally different approaches to strategic marketing planning. Kotler, McDonald and, next, Cravens demonstrate the basic consensus that leading marketers hold about how to make marketing strategy.

Our third example, David Cravens, is another prolific and long-standing author. Professor of Marketing at Texas Christian University, his primary text is *Strategic Marketing* (Cravens, 2000), now in its sixth edition since 1982. Superficially, Cravens has a different slant on strategic marketing planning from either Kotler or McDonald. His perspective is much closer to strategic planning, and his work is more useful at putting marketing strategy in the context of corporate and business unit strategy. He is also much more explicit about creating 'market-driven' strategies, in which the emphasis is on the organization changing to fit the market, rather than the other way round or some form of mutual accommodation. Despite this different perspective, however, Cravens' work can be seen to reinforce the consensus illustrated by Kotler and McDonald.

As shown in Figure 1.3, Cravens' content has remained unchanged in its basic structure over the twenty years that it has been a leading text. Again, this belies great changes in detail. For instance, the third edition in 1991 added four new chapters, and each subsequent edition has accentuated a global perspective. However, the core process of matching or aligning the internal and external situations to each other remains the same, and is essentially identical to that of the other two writers.

The same conclusion is reached by looking critically at most other textbooks over the past thirty years. Although disguised by language and different perspectives, the core marketing process is agreed by all leading writers on the subject. Further, that core process has not changed significantly during that time period. It has been developed and augmented, but only in an evolutionary way. These are detailed changes in how to perform the core process, not changes in the process itself.

This is of more than historical interest to marketers. It means we need waste little time choosing between different approaches to strategic marketing planning, and should remember to see each new idea as an evolutionary step – not a revolutionary new concept. With the time saved, we can afford better to understand the core process and how to make it work in our organization.

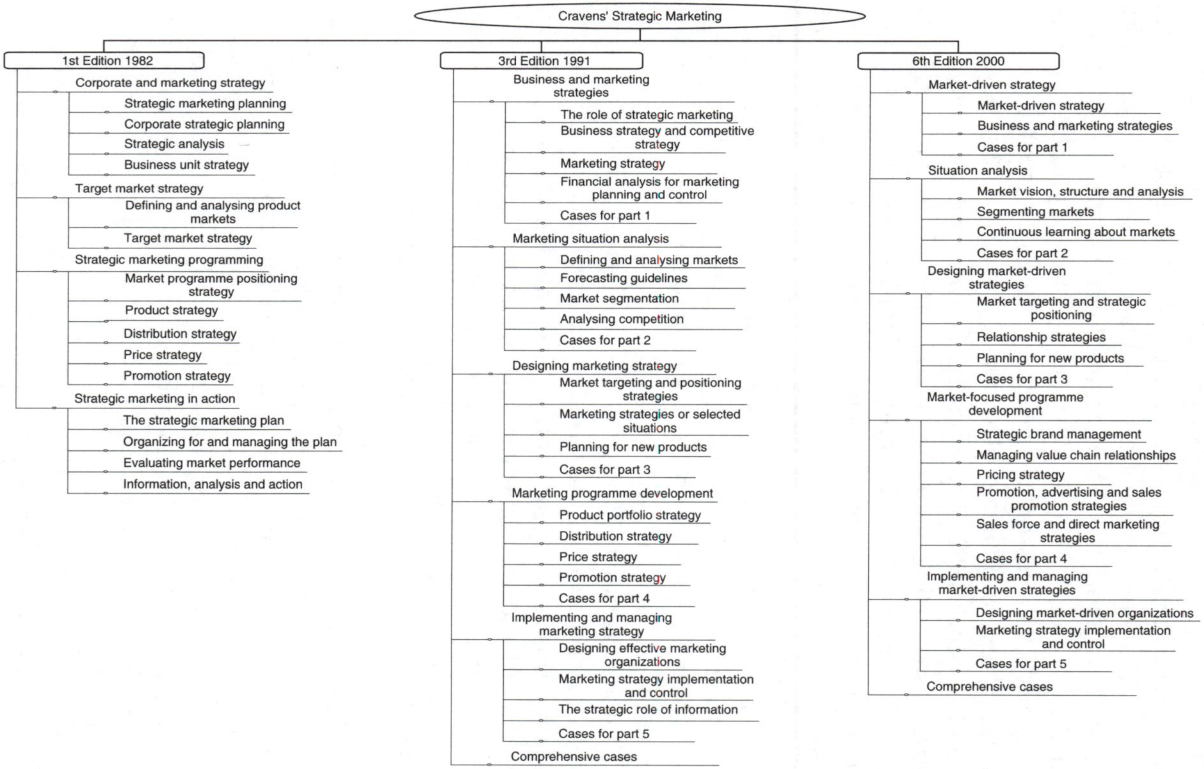

Figure 1.3 The content of Cravens' *Strategic Marketing*

Application point: How much time does your organization waste?

In the preceding section, the work of leading and longstanding authorities is used to make two points – that the core process of strategic marketing planning is stable and agreed, and that new ideas in marketing have been relatively minor adaptations of the core process rather than major changes in the principle. It follows that we can waste time giving each new adaptation a level of attention that is only deserved by a major new breakthrough in thinking. This time could be used instead to improve our application of the core process.

- How much time does your organization waste in this way?
- Is it inclined to view every new concept as fundamental and requiring major emphasis, or does it place new ideas in context and in proportion?

It can sometimes feel more valuable to play with a new idea than to follow through on old ones – and company cultures that encourage innovation can exacerbate this trend.

The history of strategic marketing planning suggests that we can reduce the time we waste by trying to put new ideas into the context of a stable core process.

What is the core process of strategic marketing planning?

So far in this chapter we have considered the potential for confusion faced by the practising marketer. The innumerable different approaches, each with its own jargon and acronyms, threaten to overwhelm the time-poor marketer. There is a real danger of jumping from fad to fad and not developing real expertise in anything. To avoid falling into this trap, we have looked at the development and history of strategic marketing planning. That history tells us that real (i.e. market-led) strategic marketing planning has its origins in the 1960s. Further, although the subject has matured and deepened, it has not changed in its fundamentals. This is not to belittle the useful refinements that have taken place over the past thirty-plus years, but to put them into perspective. In essence, the core process of strategic marketing planning is stable and agreed by the leading thinkers in the field.

This stability and consensus is important to practising marketers. It means that they can spend less time worrying about fads and the latest developments, and more time becoming excellent at the core process. The core process is clarified in the next few paragraphs, in the belief that a clear understanding of the basics will, later in the book, help us to better adapt it to our own organization.

Against the trend to elaborate and complicate the process of making marketing strategy that is evident in many texts, it is valuable to begin by simplifying it. Such simplification helps us to see what we are trying to do, and this is the objective of Figure 1.4.

Figure 1.4 is the process of strategic marketing planning reduced to its basics. It is useful to understand that it is this process that underlies all of the textbooks and the confusing array of terminology and approaches. A form of this process also occurs in organizations which don't seem to plan at all. As we will see in later chapters, organizations often perform this process with very little in the way of structure, rationality or formality. There is nothing intrinsically wrong with this, or right with rigorous planning. Whatever approach

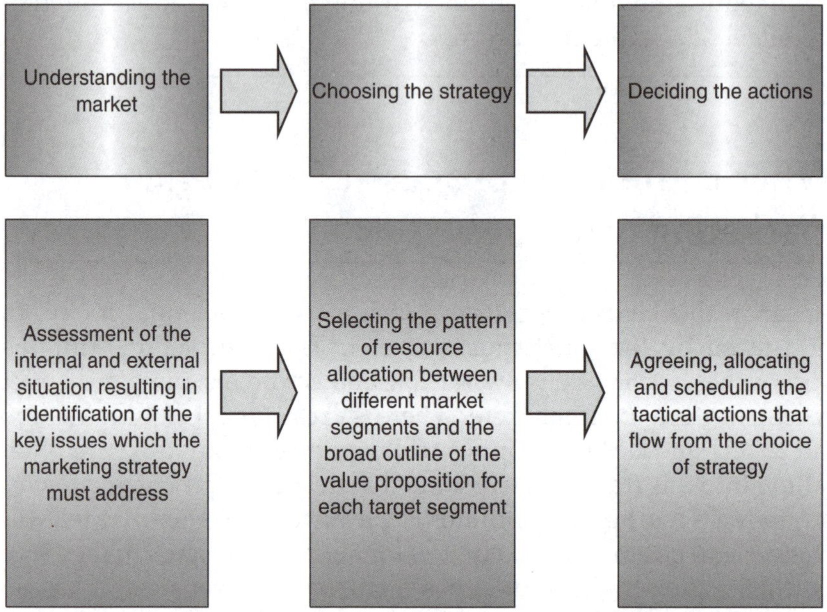

Figure 1.4 The core process of marketing-strategy making

to strategy making we take, what is important is to remember that we are trying to do the three things in the core process:

1. *Understanding the market.* The process for understanding the market takes as its inputs information about the market and the company. Market information is that concerning customers, competitors and channels to market, as well as that which concerns the wider market environment of social, legal and economic factors. Characteristically, it is information about the world outside our organization. The information about our company is mostly internal and concerns the capabilities and constraints implied by our resources, both tangible and intangible. Whatever the methods used to gather and analyse this internal and external information, the objective is the same: to see the wood for the trees, to identify the important facts (positive and negative, internal and external) that the marketing strategy must address. These key issues that are the outputs of understanding the market then become the inputs of the next stage – choosing the strategy.

2. *Choosing the strategy.* The process for choosing the strategy takes as its inputs the key issues identified in the previous stage, understanding the market. As a result, the effectiveness of this second stage is often enhanced or compromised by the quality of the first stage. At its simplest, marketing strategy choice means making two broad sets of related decisions: who to target and what to offer them. In effect, this is an alignment process which attempts to leverage our strengths against market opportunities and minimize the implications of our weaknesses in the face of market threats. Again, the methods employed to do this can vary from the methodical to the apparently intuitive or even haphazard. In any case, the objective is to decide the broad marketing strategy (i.e. who to target and what to offer them) that best aligns our company to the market. The best alignment is taken to be that strategy which best addresses the key issues arising out of our understanding of the market. The broad marketing strategy resulting from this second stage then becomes the starting point for the third stage: creating the action plan.

3. *Creating the action plan.* The process of creating the action plan takes as its inputs the broad strategy that is the output of the preceding stage: choosing the strategy. As a consequence, the effectiveness of this third process is dependent on the effectiveness of the first two. Creating action plans is the detailed extrapolation of broad strategy. It involves the decisions about product, pricing, service, promotion and channels to market that will turn the value proposition aimed at

each target into reality. The outputs of this process are the detailed instructions that will be acted upon. This is the tangible output of the strategic marketing planning process. It becomes the input for those departments responsible for delivering the description proposition.

So, the core process of strategic marketing planning is both stable and, at a fundamental level, quite simple. This helps us to put fads and detail into perspective. Not only are the different approaches to strategic marketing planning merely variations on this theme, but so too are all the ways of making marketing strategy that do not involve formal planning. The new and sometimes bewildering ways to approach the market do not contradict or replace this core process; rather they improve and elaborate upon it.

Armed with this 'big picture' view of what strategic marketing planning is, we are better able to consider questions like 'Does it work?' and 'How might we make it work for us?' It is those questions that the rest of this book goes on to address. Before we do, however, it is worth considering for a moment where the tools of strategic marketing planning fit into this core process. Understanding the place and utility of the tools both helps us understand the core process and informs our use, adaptation or deliberate neglect of the tools.

Application point: What does the core process look like in your organization?

For those of us enmeshed in the strategic marketing planning process, it is hard to see what is really happening. Often, our perspective only allows us to see the mechanistic parts of the process such as standard formats, head-office requirements and formal approval stages. Sometimes these processes are ritualistic, with their original aim and value lost in the mists of time.

- How does your company execute the core process?
- What steps do you take in each of the three sub-processes?
- Are there any things that you do that are now useless or offer little value?
- Are you not doing some things that you need to do?

Putting the reality of your process in the context of the core process will help you understand what it is your organization actually does and prepare you to make it work better.

The tools of strategic marketing planning

Part of the confusion faced by marketing executives is the panoply of tools available. There appear to be many of them, each claiming superiority and requiring an amount of learning and application time that precludes using its alternatives. However, as with strategic marketing planning, the number of different tools is misleading. There are only a few core tools, each with numerous useful, but not fundamental, variations. We understand our discipline better if we understand this difference between a few core tools and the innumerable variations on each of them. Further, it helps if we appreciate where each of the tools fits into the core process of strategic marketing planning.

Naturally it is impossible to list all of the different tools here, but the most commonly mentioned ones, placed in context below, are intended to help readers to put their own collection of tools into an organizing framework.

Understanding the market

Understanding the market usually begins with understanding the implications of the wider, uncontrollable market environment, on the basis that what can't be controlled has to be allowed for. The environment consists of social, legal, economic, political and technological factors, and its analysis is aided by numerous tools with mnemonic acronyms such as SLEPT, PEST, STEP and PESTLE. These are all essentially the same thing. The process involves capturing all the relevant facts (aided by the mnemonic) and translating each fact into an implication for the market. These implications are then synthesized into a smaller number of combined implications which can be positive (e.g. market growth) or negative (e.g. increased foreign competition). As external factors, they are classed as opportunities or threats accordingly.

The order of the other stages of understanding the market is not critical, particularly since the process is usually partly iterative. If customers are to be analysed next, the most critical technique is market segmentation.

There are literally thousands of approaches to segmentation, and the resultant confusion is amplified by the criticality of understanding the segmentation in a market. It helps us to understand the process if we remember that there is only one way to segment a market: by customer need. Segments are groups of customers who behave similarly because they are motivated to meet similar needs. Further, market segments exist in the market – we uncover them, rather than create them. The reason for the plethora of segmentation tools is because needs are complex, multilayered and difficult to measure. In short, all of the tools use different ways to substitute intangible customer needs with more practically useful measures, such as age, gender, company size or whatever. These are simply operational proxies for customer needs. Once that is understood, the relevance and utility of alternative segmentation methods becomes clearer. As market segments appear, grow, shrink and disappear under the pressure of market forces they create opportunities and threats for the company, which can be added to those uncovered in the SLEPT (or PEST, STEP, PESTLE etc.) analysis.

Competitor analysis involves trying to understand who the competitors are, what threat they represent and how that is likely to change. Of the countless approaches possible, most consider only the direct competitive set – other companies with comparable value propositions. All consider the relative (to our company) strength of the competition on various dimensions of the proposition, such as price, performance, availability, reputation and so forth. The critical point to bear in mind in this case is that strength is in the eyes of the customer, and not all customers want the same thing. Direct competitor analysis therefore only works in the context of a good understanding of market segmentation. By contrast, many competitive threats come from indirect competitors. The classic tool for understanding the magnitude and trends of both indirect and direct competitive forces is Porter's Five-Forces analysis. This uses discernible market factors, such as growth rate, barriers to entry and relative size of competitors, to predict the direction and magnitude of the competition. Whatever tool is employed, competitor analysis yields threats and, less commonly, opportunities arising from the competitive environment. These outputs can be added to those of the customer and macroenvironmental analysis.

After customers and competitors, market channels represent a source of opportunities and threats. Not all markets have channels to market, but when they do the most ubiquitous tool is market mapping. This involves plotting the flow of product or service from the different sources, via the different channels and sub-channels to the different market segments. As with competitor analysis, therefore, it requires a good appreciation of market segmentation to make market mapping work effectively. The positive opportunities and negative threats that emerge from market mapping or other channel analysis techniques are then added to the growing list of factors that characterize our market.

The final stage in understanding the market is that of considering the positives and negatives arising from our own organization. These are the result of the tangible and intangible resources that the company possesses. The value chain concept is a good tool for elucidating where to look for these, whilst tools like VRIO (**V**aluable, **R**are, **I**nimitable and **O**rganizationally aligned) allow us to judge the relevance and potency of the factor (Barney, 2001a). Benchmarking can be used to gather real data that inform this internal analysis and are important, since both strengths and weaknesses are not absolute but relative to the market and the competition. The positive strengths and negative weaknesses that come from this stage complete our audit of the market situation.

Gathering together the implications of the market situation (strengths, weaknesses, opportunities and threats) is a necessary but insufficient step in understanding the marketplace. What remains is to understand the strategic implications of these for the business. As the name suggests, SWOT analysis was invented for this purpose. Again, other techniques (e.g. the TOWS analysis) are simply variants, and involve the same process of matching up strengths with opportunities and weaknesses with threats. Hence SWOT analysis takes as its inputs the outputs of the previous processes, and is dependent upon their rigour for its effectiveness. Its outputs are usually a small number of key issues that the marketing strategy, whichever is chosen, must address. These usually take the form of a particular strength that must be leveraged against a particular opportunity or a weakness that must be protected or corrected in the face of a threat.

Hence, various tools of strategic marketing planning help us to understand the market. Typically, they identify the implications of the market situation – positive and negative, internal and external – which become the raw material for a SWOT analysis. This, in turn, synthesizes these inputs into key issues which are fed into the strategy choice process.

Choosing the strategy

Choosing the strategy involves making two sets of related resource allocation decisions: which customers to target, and what to offer them. In simple situations, these decisions are straightforward and do not require any particular tool to aid thinking. Even in more complicated situations, a well-executed SWOT analysis will identify a set of key issues that is so constraining that the choice of which segments to target is self-evident. For instance, the requirement to leverage technological superiority against a premium segment and to guard high relative costs against low-cost imports makes the choice of target segment very easy. However, in many markets the choice of target segments is more problematic. Moreover, the choice is less black and white, with the need to make some sort of allocation to all segments and hence the requirement to prioritize rather than simply accept or reject.

There is a whole category of tools for doing this, known as portfolio management matrices. The first of these was the Boston Matrix, in 1965. There has since been a steady flow of variants, such as the Arthur D. Little Matrix and, more recently, the Directional Policy Matrix (also known as the Shell, McKinsey or General Electric Matrix). All of the techniques have their origin in corporate strategy and have been adapted by marketers to use markets and segments, rather than industries, as their subject. All of these tools work to the same idea. They calculate the potential target's position within a grid defined by two axes. The Boston Matrix used market share and market growth rate whilst, for instance, the Directional Policy Matrix uses relative market attractiveness and relative competitive strength. Despite the variations in detail, all are in fact trying to assess the same two things: how much we want them, and how much they want us. The position of the target segment in the grid implies a broad policy of resource allocation toward it. This usually takes the form of building, investing in, maintaining or exiting (or perhaps ignoring) the segment.

Once the broad approach to a segment is chosen using a portfolio management grid, the second half of the strategy decision (what value proposition to offer them) is relatively straightforward. This is because the needs of the target have already been well characterized by the segmentation analysis undertaken previously. The combination of well-characterized needs and clearly defined resource allocation makes the broad nature of the value proposition quite obvious in most cases. More complex is the task of translating the broad strategy decision into a detailed action plan. This is the subject of the third stage, the input into which is the broad strategy decision.

Creating the action plan

Creating the action plan to deliver the broad strategy entails first designing the detail of the value proposition and then the activity needed to deliver that specific offer to the customer. The first stage is enabled by the concept of the marketing mix, whilst the second relies less on strategic marketing tools and more upon the devices of project management and traditional management by objectives.

The marketing mix concept hardly justifies the term 'tool' or 'technique'. It is little more than a mnemonic to prompt the marketer to remember that the value proposition is more than the product. Traditionally, it is codified as the four Ps of product, price, promotion and place, with the last term being an author's device to include distribution. More recently, the list has been extended to add people, process and physical evidence. This is a tactically useful addition, especially in service businesses. However, it is not a fundamental shift in the concept of the marketing mix.

A variation on the marketing mix theme is the idea of the core/extended/augmented product, in which the value proposition is represented as three concentric circles. These circles contain the successive component parts of a complete value proposition, including the product, pricing, service, brand image, etc. It takes little examination to see that this and other variants are useful but relatively trivial developments of the marketing mix concept. As such, they aid the marketer in extrapolating the broad strategy into a detailed value proposition. The management process of identifying and enabling the actions to deliver that proposition mark the boundary between strategic marketing management and tactical implementation.

Application point: What tools does your company use?

The tools of strategic marketing planning should not be given more credibility than they deserve. They are useful aids to thinking, resulting from the codification of good practice by other marketers facing the same problems as your organization. As such, they shouldn't be applied slavishly, or as substitutes for thinking. However, not using them might be said to imply a level of confidence in one's own judgement that is bordering on arrogance.

- What tools does your organization use at each stage of the core process?
- Does it apply them across the process, or is a level of rigour at one stage (for instance, financial budgeting) disproportionate to the lack of rigour at another (for instance, understanding customers)?

An intimate understanding of how your organization uses or abuses the tools of strategic marketing planning is useful preparation for improving the way it makes marketing strategy.

We know what strategic marketing planning is

The title of this chapter explains its aims. In order to make strategic marketing planning work, we need to understand what it is. This understanding is hindered by the bewildering number of different approaches and terms. This confusion is understandable but unnecessary. When we consider the history and development of strategic marketing planning, we can observe a stable and mature body of thought. Beneath the detailed variations lies a core process that is relatively simple to grasp, if not to apply. Supporting the core process are innumerable tools, but these too are variations on a few easily comprehensible themes.

In summary, we know what strategic marketing planning is, and it is not good use of our time to worry about which detailed variant to use. Instead, we are better served by concentrating on understanding this core process and how to make it work for us. As a step towards that, however, we should ask the question 'does it work for anybody?' That is the subject of the next chapter.

Power points

- Although marketing has its origins in the first decade of the twentieth century, for the first half of the century it was approximately synonymous with advertising, selling and physical distribution.

- The marketing concept of working out what the market needs and giving it to them, as opposed to selling what we have to sell, emerged in the late 1950s.
- Strategic marketing planning dates from the 1960s, when the marketing concept converged with the rise of formal strategic planning.
- Although there is a preponderance of slightly different approaches and jargon, the process of strategic marketing planning is fairly stable and has changed little since its inception.
- In essence, strategic marketing planning has three not necessarily sequential stages: understanding the market, choosing the strategy and creating the action plan.
- Although there are innumerable tools to aid the process of strategic marketing planning, they are in fact minor variations on a few basic themes.

Reflection points for marketing practitioners

- What is the strategic marketing planning process in your company?
- Can your strategic marketing planning process be understood in terms of the three stages discussed in this chapter?
- Does your company use the tools and techniques of strategic marketing planning well, or is it prone to leap from one new fad to another?
- Based on your answers to the questions above, what might be the strengths and weaknesses of your company's approach to strategic marketing planning?

Chapter 2

. . . And it does work

Proof is the idol before whom the pure mathematician tortures himself.
(Sir Arthur Eddington, *The Nature of the Physical World*)

Introduction

This book has been written with one audience and one aim in mind. It is written for the reflective marketing practitioner, and it aims to improve strategic marketing planning in her or his company or organization. To that end, Chapter 1 tried to see the wood for the trees and ensure that when we say 'strategic marketing planning' we are all thinking the same thing. The gist of that chapter is that there is a relatively simple core process and, whatever the latest fad or new three letter acronym, it is agreed and stable in the eyes of the leading thinkers in the field. That core process has three principal subdivisions: understanding the implications of the market situation, choosing which target customers to go for with what value proposition, and spelling out the steps needed to realize that strategy. There are relatively few tools and techniques (albeit with innumerable variations) that are commonly used to support the process, but we must not let the tools get in the way of the task. Armed with the knowledge of what we're trying to do, we can focus on making it happen rather than 'fad surfing', to borrow the irreverent title of Eileen Shapiro's excellent book (Shapiro, 1995).

But wait. To put our efforts into making strategic marketing planning is to accept the implicit assumption that the process works, that companies that do it perform better than those that do not. As the philosopher Bertrand Russell once said, 'it is unwise to accept a proposition without grounds' (Russell, 1935), and we have not yet given any consideration to the value of doing strategic marketing planning. Since it undoubtedly has both direct and opportunity costs, it is worth spending some time considering the resultant benefits, if any, of formal planning. Even if you are a marketing planning zealot with no need of further evidence, you are probably going to have to convince your colleagues it is worth their time and effort to take part. Marketers often have to convince stereotypical sales or finance colleagues, for instance. The former sometimes believe that sheer energy and effort can move markets, whilst the latter may believe disciplined cost control is the answer. It is a truism that almost every function thinks it has the answer to the challenges of the market.

Whether you need to convince yourself or colleagues, this chapter aims to review the evidence that strategic marketing planning is worthwhile. Of course, if you are in the fortunate position of being a zealot surrounded by convinced and supportive colleagues, you might be tempted to skip this chapter. However, as I've yet to meet anyone truly in that position, a chapter justifying strategic marketing planning seems a necessary step in our discussion of how to make marketing happen.

Application point: How sceptical is your organization?

It is a characteristic of many organizations that interpersonal and interdepartmental politics influence behaviour and management processes. One side effect of this is that some management processes, such as strategic marketing planning, are allowed to proceed with neither the active commitment nor the explicit dissent of the management team. Whilst this may be a necessary and acceptable compromise in some cases, it is sub-optimal for processes that need cross-functional support, as does strategic marketing planning.

- How does your management team feel about strategic marketing planning?

- Where does it sit in the spectrum from active support to passive compliance to passive resistance to active resistance?
- To what extent might this view be shifted by the provision of evidence about the usefulness of strategic marketing planning?

To look at the evidence for whether or not strategic marketing planning works, we need to answer two questions. First, what do we mean by 'work', exactly? Secondly, does the research prove that it works? Those two questions form the structure of the rest of this chapter.

What do we mean by 'work', exactly?

For many managers reading this book, this will seem like a silly question. For perhaps the majority of practising marketers success equals sales, and therefore 'Does it work?' equates to 'Do companies that do strategic marketing planning sell more than those that don't?' More sophisticated and senior managers might translate this into the same question but substitute profits for sales. However, using either sales or profit as a pure measure of business success is, of course, naïve, because it is perfectly possible to grow sales whilst shrinking profit or to destroy a business whilst growing profit. All we need to do is slash prices or milk the assets. Sales and profits are only contributory factors to company performance.

For most companies, the objective is neither sales nor profit but shareholder value. There are various methods for calculating shareholder value creation, and many readers will be familiar with ideas like Net Present Value (NPV) and Economic Value Added (EVA). To those that are not, Keith Ward's book *Marketing Finance* (Ward, 2003) is recommended. Simply put, most commercial organizations measure success as the degree to which they create profits above the cost of the capital employed. This applies to both publicly quoted companies and private ones, which differ only in the way that the shareholding is distributed.

So the first point that this section makes is that 'Does it work?' involves a lot more than simply looking at growth in sales or even profit. We live in a market economy and, as Mikhail Gorbachev said, markets were not invented by capitalism; they are the invention of civilization. If we choose to measure success by financial measures, it is the efficient use of capital, expressed as the creation of shareholder value, which we need to measure.

This book, however, was written in the early twenty-first century, not the late twentieth, and one of the big steps forward in management science has been the so-called 'performance management revolution', in which academics and managers realized that even relatively sophisticated financial measures like EVA were only a simplistic measure of organizational effectiveness. In short, good financial results can be achieved relatively easily by destroying the other, less tangible, assets of the firm and therefore its future competitiveness. Put simply, we can get more golden eggs if we work the goose to death. We could for instance, erode brand equity, or make cost reductions that reduce customer loyalty, or change working practices and remuneration so as to undermine employee commitment. Any of these steps would boost financial returns, at least in the short term, at the cost of reducing the firm's longer-term competitiveness.

The realization that this has been done often, to the detriment of shareholders, is what lay behind the performance management revolution. This transformation was characterized by a shift from narrow and short-term financial measures to broader and longer-term measurement of both financial and non-financial measures. The most famous example of this shift away from using only financial measures is the 'Balanced Scorecard' work of Kaplan and Norton (Kaplan and Norton, 1992), but their approach is only one example of a number of attempts to measure overall business performance more effectively. This is a complicated area, beyond the scope of this book. However, readers who are interested in knowing more about this particular area are recommended to read the work of Andy Neely (Neely, 1999). The second point to make, then, is that 'Does it work?' should involve a lot more than simply considering financial measures of success.

The third point regarding the effectiveness of strategic marketing planning requires a small diversion into the world of management research. Practitioners who have not been trained in social science research (of which management research is a subset) often confuse association with causation. In simple terms, the fact that a company that does strategic marketing planning is more successful than one that does not doesn't prove that planning works. Nor would failure prove the ineffectiveness of planning. These are simply associations between one thing and another. There is no evidence of causation, so we can't, scientifically, say that the data prove anything. The difference between association and causation becomes more important as the situation we are examining becomes more complex. In a simple situation, association can usually be held up as proof. If yellow widgets always outsell blue ones, we can, all other things being equal, say that we have proven that colour causes sales. Evidence of association is enough to give us a practical level of proof. However, the real business world is not like that.

The performance of a company is not simply correlated to the amount of strategic planning we do. Performance is affected by a huge number of different factors inside and outside the company. Internal factors include how well the strategic planning process has worked and how well the resultant strategy has been implemented. External factors include the macroeconomic environment, the competitive environment and political, social and technological factors, all of which are beyond the company's control. Weak companies can succeed just because the market is roaring.

At the time of writing, the global market for mobile phone ring tones is shooting past $3.5bn and a marketer would have to try very hard to fail in that market. By contrast, the combined marketing skills of the global airline business could do little to ameliorate the effects of a global recession combined with SARS and the threat of terrorist attacks.

In complex situations association is not enough to claim proof, so the third point this section makes is that 'Does it work?' is a harder question to answer than it is to ask. Given the complexity of the influences on organizational performance, anybody who answers an unequivocal 'yes' to that question is either naïve or misinformed. At best, our answer is likely to be a qualified one.

As practitioners, however, we need an answer, even if it is qualified. When faced with economic advisers who constantly said 'well, on the one hand ... and on the other ...', President Truman famously asked for a one-handed economist. As the quotation that heads this chapter suggests, it is easy for academics to spend a lifetime seeking incontrovertible proof. As managers, we need to reach a conclusion about the effectiveness of strategic marketing planning and act accordingly. So let us accept the qualifications that we need to measure shareholder value created as part of a broader set of measures, and that we must consider the effects of other influences, besides strategic marketing planning, on our performance. Let us make the reasonable assumptions that sales and profit growth does usually lead to shareholder value, and that most companies don't do it by destroying their intangible assets. Finally, let us assume that we can control for the effects of outside influences by taking larger samples over longer periods and doing carefully controlled experiments. Let us look, if not for scientifically incontrovertible proof, for a reasonable judgement about whether or not strategic marketing planning works.

If we take that pragmatic stance, can we say if strategic marketing planning works or not? The targeting of this book implies that the reader neither wants nor needs an exhaustive review of the published research. However, a quick tour of the literature seems appropriate, both to understand the topic better and to provide a small supply of ammunition for when we run up against those who think planning is a waste of our time.

Application point: What is proof to your organization?

Many, if not most, organizations take a pragmatic stance towards scientific proof. Most business cultures are positivistic, in that they believe things can and should be measured and that decisions should be based on proven fact. Yet the same organizations often accept that gathering incontrovertible proof even for major decisions is not always possible. They therefore bend positivistic theories to pragmatic realities.

- What does proof mean to your organization?
- Does it require evidence to support all major choices, or is much of its decision-making intuitive?
- In the absence of definitive proof, how does it assess the value of strategic marketing planning?

Does research prove that strategic marketing planning works?

Despite the limitations discussed in the previous section, research into the effectiveness of planning has a long history – not much shorter than that of planning itself. Not all of that research concerns strategic marketing planning specifically, and the overlap of different levels of planning confuses the picture. However, most of the work carried out over those thirty-plus years is useful in answering our questions about strategic marketing planning, so the next few paragraphs look at how these researchers approached the question of planning effectiveness.

Looked at as a whole, this research can be seen to be made up of three phases, roughly corresponding to the decades of the 1970s, 1980s and 1990s. As often happens in academic debates, it begins with an assertion (in this case, that planning works) followed by counter-assertion (in this case, that there is no incontrovertible proof that planning works), and then settles down to a broad if slightly qualified consensus (that nothing can be indisputably proven to work but the weight of evidence is that planning contributes to effectiveness).

Although there were earlier studies, the first really significant paper, and the prototype of the first of the three phases of research, was carried out in the late 1960s by Stanley Thune (a practising manager) and Robert House (an academic) (Thune and House, 1970). This work was very influential. Over the next couple of decades, various researchers tried to prove, disprove and extend or limit the findings of Thune and House. Almost every piece of research into planning effectiveness since then quotes their work.

What Thune and House did was to survey ninety-two different companies in six disparate industries (drugs, food, steel, oil, machinery and chemicals), all of which could be classed as large by the standards of the day. They found that about three-quarters of the firms were formal planners and the rest were informal planners. For each of these firms, they assessed five different measures of financial performance (sales growth, increase in earnings per common share, increase in stock price, increase in earnings on common equity, and increase on earnings on total capital). They found that 'formal planners significantly outperform informal planners with respect to [the] five economic measures'. Further, they found that planners improved their performance in comparison to the period before they began formal planning. Beneath that headline they found variations in the degree of improvement, both between industries and between firm sizes, but the general conclusion of their work supported the case for planning. By the standards of most practitioners the work of Thune and House would have answered our question, but academics make their living by proving or refuting the work of other academics, so the story doesn't end there.

In 1972, David Herold (Herold, 1972), a colleague of Robert House, reported an attempt to extend the original work by looking more closely at five pairs of formal and informal planners over a period of seven years. He looked only at the chemical and drug industries, but found, over this significant period, that the formal planners extended their lead over their less formal rivals. Both sets of work have their limitations, notably that they only really measure association (successful firms plan and *vice versa*) and don't say much about causation (does planning cause success, or is it the other way around?). They also look only at financial performance and not at intangible factors, so the successful firms may have been working the golden goose to death. Nevertheless these two early pieces of research make a reasonable case for planning, at least by the pragmatic standards of practitioners.

Other work came at the problem from different angles, some of it measuring planning formality and some of it looking at attitudes to planning. All of this early phase, however, related planning to financial performance and came to broadly the same conclusion. For instance, Joseph Eastlack and Philip McDonald (Eastlack and McDonald, 1970), surveyed 211 CEOs across a wide range of industries and compared growth rates to what the CEOs thought was important. They found that faster-growing companies had CEOs who thought planning was more important (and presumably therefore did more of it) than did their slower-growth counterparts.

In 1975, Delmar Karger and Zafar Malik (Karger and Malik, 1975) surveyed ninety companies in the clothing, chemicals, drug, food and machinery sectors and made the wonderfully worded observation that 'the top management of any growth seeking firm is delinquent if they do not engage in fully integrated long-term planning'. A narrower but more in-depth analysis was carried out by Robley Wood and Lawrence LaForge (Wood and LaForge, 1979), who carried out both surveys and interviews with twenty-nine of the fifty biggest US banks in 1979. They found that planners outperformed non-planners and a randomly selected control sample.

The list of research goes on, across numerous industries, looking at various parameters of planning and performance and using various methods. Although every piece of work is imperfect in some way by the standards of academics, together they form a coherent pattern that supports the 'planning works' school.

By the 1980s there were enough studies for meta-analysis – that is, synthesizing the work of numerous researchers and drawing conclusions from the aggregated findings – rather than carrying out more original data collection. In 1982, Armstrong (Armstrong, 1982) reviewed no less than fifteen different studies of the benefits of formal planning. He found that ten of the fifteen found in favour of strategic planning, whilst two found informal planning superior and three found no significant difference. Interestingly (and consistent with the discussion later in this book), Armstrong concluded that planning is usually a good thing but called for more research into the situations in which it is more or less valuable.

Hence, in the research we find both support for planning in general and also a hint that the answer to our question is not a simple, unqualified 'yes'. This idea of trying to qualify exactly when and where planning works led to a variety of research projects looking at relatively specific contexts. Jeffrey Bracker, Barbara Keats and John Pearson, for instance looked at small firms in growth industries (Bracker and Pearson, 1986), but concluded again that planners outperformed non-planners.

This first phase of research was as unequivocal as academic research gets in supporting the belief that planning works, but was already hinting at a 'contingency approach' – that is, they were suggesting that the question should not be about whether or not planning works, but about when and how it works.

For instance, Leslie Rue and Robert Fulmer (Rue and Fulmer, 1973) suggested that planning seemed to work better for goods than for services (although they noted that, at the time, service industries had only just begun to plan), and Lawrence Rhyne began to unravel important mechanisms of planning, such as long-term orientation and external focus (Rhyne, 1986). The tone of this work was that planning works, given certain qualifications. This hedged conclusion is best captured by two different papers published in 1987 by John Pearce and his colleagues (Pearce and Robbins, 1987; Pearce *et al.*, 1987). In one, after looking at ninety-seven companies they concluded that there exists:

> a strong positive correlation between the degree of planning formality and firm performance. Additionally, interactive analysis disclosed that this relationship pervaded the various grand strategies; the implication being that formalized strategic planning was consistently a positive factor associated with high levels of performance.

In their next paper, however, they reviewed eighteen different pieces of research and concluded that there was not enough evidence to support the universal recommendation of strategic planning. In short, it works, but don't assume it is a panacea in all cases.

As we described earlier, the nature of academic research is such that any firm conclusion acts as a magnet for those who wish to refute it. By this means, academics make the 'contribution to knowledge' that is their *raison d'être*. Hence, the second phase of work in the effectiveness of strategic planning can be seen as something of a reaction against the absolute positivism of the first phase. In this reactive second phase, researchers carried out both original work and meta-analysis (re-analysis of previous research) in an attempt to contrast the complexity of the problem with the relative simplicity of the early work. In doing so they quite rightly illuminated the two principal limitations of the work that had been carried out to date, both of which we raised earlier but need clarification here.

First, the planning/performance link is highly dependent upon a multitude of other factors, and the methodologies employed were often not sufficiently rigorous to allow for this complexity. Such criticisms were made by a number of researchers. Charles Shrader, Lew Taylor and Den Dalton (Shrader *et al.*, 1984) looked at the previous work and decided that the link between planning and performance was so tenuous as not to be amenable to the methods used by earlier research. They reinforced the contingency idea, that the question should be not 'Does strategic planning lead to improved performance?' but rather 'How, when and why does strategic planning lead to improved performance?'.

Barbara Keats and Michael Hitt (Keats and Hitt, 1988) tried to untangle the various complicating factors by looking at firm size, structure and market environment. They concluded that different market conditions and company situations seem to favour different ways of making strategy, rather than universally supporting planning, another way of calling for a contingency approach. It is interesting, however, that they did not manage to nail down the variables that decide whether or not planning works.

The picture that emerges from the research literature at this stage is complex and confusing. It takes a lot of in-depth reading and perspective to see a pattern emerging. The second phase of research doesn't refute planning or say it is a bad thing; it merely qualifies the evidence in favour of planning and warns against the idea of planning as a simple panacea, applicable in all cases. It is well summarized by Gordon Greenley (Greenley, 1994), who said:

> Many differences were found among the methodologies of these studies, while the rigour of each study is seemingly limited. Consequently their results cannot be legitimately combined, and therefore it cannot be concluded that an association is evident.

In other words, we are asking too simple a question of a complicated situation.

If the second generation's first critique of the early research was about method, their second was about constructs – the academics' word for an idea or concept that we try to measure. The construct of the earlier work that was criticized by the second-wave researchers was the whole idea of organizational effectiveness itself. As described in the previous section, researchers began to realize that company performance was much more complex than sales and profit and even more multifaceted than a comprehensive set of financial measures might allow for.

This was the beginning of the performance measurement revolution alluded to earlier. Kim Cameron (Cameron, 1986), for instance, pointed out that financial measures did not allow for the fact that performance has many aspects; it has to relate to lots of things the firm does and it has to reflect the sometimes conflicting goals of managers, shareholders, employees, customers and other stakeholders.

Chakravarthy (1986) took the criteria from Tom Peters' famous *In Search of Excellence* and used it to demonstrate that traditional profit measures don't demonstrate excellence, whilst Venkatraman and Ramanujam (1986) made the more radical case for perceptual measures of performance being as good as anything.

There are many more examples in the research about organizational effectiveness, but perhaps it is sufficient for our needs to note that whilst simple measures were discredited, no agreed and criticism-proof method of measuring firm performance arose from this debate either. What we mean by 'works' remains specific to a particular firm, and irreducible to a few simple numbers.

Note, however that this reactionary second phase in the research never did find that strategic planning did *not* work; it only went as far as saying that the case for strategic planning was not proven, and perhaps could never be, given the complexity of the problem. In addition, this refinement of the original, simple work seemed to suggest that the effectiveness of marketing planning might not be a black and white issue, but various shades of grey, depending on the company and the market.

Make a mental note of that, since it is an idea we will develop later in this book.

The third and most recent phase of work looking at the effectiveness of planning combined two developments in management research. By doing so, it suggested a position somewhere between the unbridled positivism of the first phase and the inconclusive relativism of the second.

First, it picked up on more sophisticated ideas about what organizational effectiveness is. We have already mentioned the work of Kaplan and Norton, and of Neely. A further good example of this was Peter Drucker's idea that we need to consider five factors: market standing, innovative performance, liquidity, cash flow and productivity. These new ideas led researchers away from simply measuring financial performance.

Secondly, the third wave tried to take account of the many complicating factors that might be getting in the way of the relationship between planning and performance. It did this by using bigger samples, longer studies and more sophisticated methodologies. Two New Zealand academics, for instance, surveyed 522 companies in a single study (Lysonski and Percottich, 1992) and looked at strategic marketing planning formalization, comprehensiveness, environmental stability and financial performance. They number-crunched the data using regression analysis and concluded that planning was correlated to performance and, further, that it was independent of environmental stability.

Similarly, Cindy Claycomb, Richard Germain and Cornelia Droge (Claycomb *et al.*, 2000) studied 200 firms in a variety of industries, looking at a complex mixture of internal and external measures including planning formalization, performance and market conditions. In their paper, they concluded that:

> Strategic marketing formalization also associates with improved market and financial performance. These findings hold when controlling for a range of contextual variables including firm size, industry growth rate and uncertainty in demand.

In plain English, planning works, and not just in special cases.

These conclusions were borne out by the work of other researchers in the third wave. Charles Schwenk and his colleagues (Schwenk and Shrader, 1993) carried out a meta-analysis of work that considered small firms and identified 'small but significant correlation between planning and performance'. Others synthesizing two decades of research deduced not only that planning contributes to organizational effectiveness but also that 'substantive external contingencies have little impact' (Miller and Cardinal, 1994), which is academic speak for 'It seems to work in most cases'. The more recent findings, therefore, seem to support rather than refute the effectiveness of planning.

Priem and his colleagues argued that 'more sophisticated methodologies have produced stronger links than earlier work' (Priem *et al.*, 1995). Furthermore, this more sophisticated work contends that the advantages of strategic planning are not only financial but lie also in less tangible 'process' benefits such as team-working (Appiah-Adu *et al.*, 1996).

In other words, planning seems to make us work better, not just more effectively. Taken as a whole, the third wave of research answers a lot of the qualifications raised by the second wave. In doing so, it reinforces the conclusions reached by the early research but makes it clear the answer is not simple. Planning works, but that simple answer hides a lot of important details.

Application point: Is this enough evidence for your organization?

It is a truism that sceptics sometimes demand proof and then refuse to accept that which is provided to them. The complexity of even quite simple businesses provides enough hiding places for those that don't want to accept the argument that planning works. However, as far as sceptics can be persuaded by research, the evidence helps.

- How amenable to evidence are the sceptics in your organization?
- Can they accept that proof can never be incontrovertible in a business situation?
- Do they accept that research in other companies and markets can be generalized to your situation?

To the extent that they will accept the evidence, the work reviewed in the preceding section may help your management team to form a stronger consensus about the value of strategic marketing planning.

So planning works

If, in a sense, this chapter looks at the research that put strategic planning on trial, we need to think about what it would take to convince us one way or the other. There is an issue in management research about the standard of proof required. Academics, driven by peer review and with the relative luxury of time, can and do set very high standards before a theory is accepted. Practitioners, the intended recipients of most management research, have less time but less criticism to contend with. As a result, the latter group has justifiably developed lower standards of proof than the former.

By the standards of most practitioners, the evidence that strategic marketing planning works was provided if not by Thune and House in 1970 then by their apologists a few years later. If, then, we consider as a whole the thirty years of research that followed them, the short answer to our question is 'yes, strategic marketing planning works'.

The slightly longer answer is reminiscent of Douglas Adams' *Hitchhiker's Guide to the Galaxy*, in which the entry for Earth ('harmless') was revised (to 'mostly harmless'). Strategic marketing planning works, mostly.

We get from the research some indication that there are limitations to its effectiveness, which we will discuss in the next chapter. From this work we also get an understanding that no management process 'works' in the sense that it is unequivocally and demonstrably proven to cause better results than if we did not do it. So it is for strategic marketing planning. It isn't possible to prove it works in a pure, undisputable sense, but within the limits of practitioner standards of evidence there is no doubt that it works and that we should do it.

This pragmatic answer to our question leaves us, like all the best answers, with another question. If we know, as described in Chapter 1, what strategic marketing planning is, and we know, from this chapter, that it works, then what's the issue? Surely we're all doing it and it has become just a necessary 'hygiene factor', like accounting standards, health and safety issues or legal controls – something that we must do to survive, but which can't be the source of advantage.

As Chapter 3 explores, nothing could be further from the truth. Strategic marketing planning remains, after almost forty years, remarkable in its absence. Most companies say they do it but don't; and in that observation lie two of the keys to competitive advantage that we, as managers, seek. First, if only the minority of companies do it then we can gain relative advantage from making strategic marketing planning happen in our company. Secondly, from the detail of why most companies fail to make it happen we can learn the secrets of how to not be one of them.

Chapter 3 therefore looks at the extent to which strategic marketing planning is carried out in practice, and what we can learn from that for our own organizations.

Power points

- It is naïve to try to correlate any single business process with the success of the business in any simple way.
- Organizations define success in different ways, and between strategy and outcome lie many intervening variables.
- There is a long history of research into the effectiveness of strategic marketing planning.
- When the academic debate is clarified and a pragmatic view is taken, it is clear that strategic marketing planning contributes to the success of an organization.

Reflection points for marketing practitioners

- How does your organization define success, and what are the pros and cons of that method?
- What factors intervene between your marketing strategy and the success of your organization, defined in your own terms?
- How well do you think your strategic marketing planning process works?
- Based on your answers to the questions above, how might you judge the effectiveness of your strategic marketing planning process?

Chapter 3

... But most of us can't use it.

The beginning of knowledge is the discovery of something we do not understand.

(Frank Herbert)

Introduction

To labour a point, this book has a purpose. It is intended to make practising marketers (or at least those who spend time thinking about their professional discipline) better at strategic marketing planning. To this end, we set out to be clear about what strategic marketing planning is and then considered the evidence as to its efficacy. In Chapter 1, we tried to clear away the confusion caused by different terms and jargon and to identify a core process. Strategic marketing planning, we resolved, was a process for aligning the company to the market in order to achieve its commercial or other objectives. We saw that this process can be divided into three not necessarily sequential parts: understanding the implications of the internal and external situation, selecting a strategy that best addresses that situation, and explicating a set of actions to make that strategy happen.

Having agreed what the core process of strategic marketing planning is, we looked in Chapter 2 at the thirty-odd years of research into whether or not it was worth doing. In doing so, we came across the different standards of proof required by academics and practitioners and the pendulum of argument in the research literature. By taking a pragmatic view, however, we settled on the view that strategic marketing planning works. It isn't a panacea, and companies can succeed without it and fail with it. All other things being equal, however, planners will outperform non-planners. To adapt a phrase, the market may not always go to the planner, but that's sure the way to bet.

These two conclusions – that we know what strategic marketing planning is and that it works – lead us to the logical conclusion that strategic marketing planning must be extensively used by all competent managers and therefore that there is little need for this book. Sadly (or happily, depending on your point of view), this is not the case. As this chapter will describe, strategic marketing planning is 'more honoured in the breach than the observance', to steal from Shakespeare. This needs explaining. In the course of the research for this book, one thing we did not come across was the nihilistic manager who got out of bed each morning with the intent of deliberately making a weak strategy. So this is something we don't, or didn't, understand – bright managers in good companies apparently choosing not to use strategic marketing planning, despite the fact that they know what it is and that it works.

As the quotation at the top of this chapter indicates, not understanding something is a good place to start in any quest to create new knowledge. In this case, discovering that good managers don't use a proven technique will help us understand how to improve the process. To this end, this chapter first of all looks at the evidence for how much, or how little, marketing practitioners use strategic marketing planning. Then it looks at what we know about why they don't use it much. Finally, this chapter concludes with a discussion about how our knowledge about failing to plan might help us succeed in planning.

How much do we use strategic marketing planning?

To many managers reading this book, the answer to this question is a pretty obvious 'not much'. Anecdotally at least, the average marketer is frustrated by his or her company's reluctance to use their strategic marketing expertise. However common that anecdote, however, real learning comes from looking at the research. There has been a lot of research into this question, and it began in the 1960s. Remember, from Chapter 1, that this was the decade in which the idea of strategic planning met the newly transformed idea of the marketing concept. From this union arose strategic marketing planning and, in academic research, new practices are rapidly followed by an earnest researcher seeking to contribute to the new field. Today's wonderful web-based literature search engines are much better for recent research, and struggle a little with work published a generation ago, but the earliest example of research into this area we could find was from 1965. In that year, Richard Hise reported a study of US manufacturing firms and concluded:

1. To a large extent, both large and medium manufacturing firms have adopted the marketing concept.
2. The greatest degree of acceptance is found in the customer orientation of marketing programmes and in the organizational structure of the marketing department, particularly in the status provided to the chief marketing executive.
3. Large firms are more fully committed to the marketing concept than medium ones. Although the difference is only slight as to some factors, a distinct pattern does exist.

So, even this early, the apparent uptake of the concept was tempered with signs of unevenness in the degree to which it was used between firms of different size. A few years later, McNamara (1972) did a similar study but compared consumer and industrial companies. He found another dimension of unevenness:

> The empirical evidence in this study clearly supports the hypothesis that consumer goods companies have tended to adopt and implement the marketing concept to a greater degree than industrial goods companies. Thus the existing fundamental differences between industrial goods and consumer goods businesses may explain the lag in the development of the concept in capital goods companies.

These and other early studies suggested that the marketing concept was becoming central to business planning, although there were clear variations across industry sectors and companies of different sizes. Interestingly, these variations seem to remain, in an attenuated manner, even today, suggesting that whatever caused the differential rate of adoption was fairly fundamental and not simply a matter of timing. We have to be properly sceptical when reading this work, however. At the time, marketing was the sexy new fad and there seems a fair chance that managers would overstate their commitment to the new religion. The research supports the idea that marketing was taking hold but was sometimes a matter of window-dressing and new jargon rather than an actual transformation in principles and practice. In 1970, for instance, Charles Ames, a director of McKinsey, wrote a *Harvard Business Review* paper called 'Trapping vs substance in industrial marketing' (Ames, 1970), and headed it with the claim that:

> Whilst executives are quick to say that they understand and believe the marketing concept, their actions show otherwise.

Ames' central argument was that whilst companies were adopting the outward paraphernalia of marketing, they weren't really making it happen. This bears all the signs of what we will later recognize as cultural persistence, in which the new, superficial, cultural artefacts like plans and mission statements are implanted into what remains a non-marketing oriented culture. Like other transplants, the appendage is gradually but effectively rejected by the host. Ames was far from the only one. A year later, Bell and Emory (1971) characterized the marketing concept as 'faltering' and called for a more humanistic, less mechanistic, approach to making marketing happen. Once again, their work suggested not that there was anything wrong with the marketing concept *per se*, but that it was failing to embed into the organization. In these and other pieces of research from the infancy of strategic marketing planning we can already see the signs that practising marketers and their companies could not make it work, even when it had the momentum and impetus of being the latest craze.

The failure of marketing to take root might be interpreted as just teething troubles in an earlier, less rigorously professional age, but the weight of research evidence continued to build. By the end of the 1970s, by which time managers in middle and senior positions had 'grown-up' with planning, we might reasonably have expected to see planning taking root, at least in bigger organizations. However, John Martin (1979), an experienced strategist writing in the respected peer reviewed journal *Long Range Planning*, still felt it necessary to be quite scathing about the gap between theory and practice.

In a context where authors often qualify and moderate their views, he pulled no punches when he said:

> Corporate planning as advocated by the theorists is not practiced in any developed form by large corporations.

Moreover, he felt very strongly about the reasons for this. He asserted that:

> Business planning in Britain (and I suspect the USA) is the victim of punditry.

He then went on to lambaste the lack of professionalism and rigour amongst those whose job it was to make strategy:

> All too often bad planning impedes or imperils a business: and gifted entrepreneurs who are at the heart of all successful businesses – and hence the generation of real wealth – know it.

On its own, Martin's tirade might be seen as merely an opinion, even if a well-informed and well thought out one; but other researchers looking from different perspectives said much the same thing. The academic Valarie Zeithaml looked at the problems of service marketing and found that few organizations really understand and carry out sophisticated marketing activities (Zeithaml *et al.*, 1985). By 1990, some thirty years after Levitt had written the paper that marked the birth of the marketing concept, Graham Hooley and his colleagues (Hooley *et al.*, 1990) still found it worthwhile (and the review editors concurred) to discuss the limitations in its implementation. After thirty in-depth interviews and statistical analysis of over 1300 questionnaires from senior marketers, they concluded that the marketing concept was still not embedded in the large majority of those companies.

A broad review of how far (or how little) strategic marketing planning had progressed by 1996 was written by Malcolm McDonald (McDonald, 1996). He concluded not only that the process worked but was little used, but also went on to point out the main reasons for failure to do marketing planning, which he summarized as cognitive (i.e. the organization doesn't know how to plan) or cultural (i.e. the organization knows how to plan but is prevented from doing so by its culture). Of course, it can be (and is) argued that an organization's knowledge base is part of its culture and, in that sense, culture is the umbrella cause for the failure of strategic marketing planning.

As we will discuss later, the situation is rather more complex than that, but as a defining point in describing, rather than prescribing, strategic marketing planning, McDonald's paper was seminal and provided insight into what really happens in practice. If this book can be said to have a single point of origin, that 1996 paper is it.

So, we can see a pattern in thirty years of research. Shortly after strategic marketing planning was born out of strategic planning and the marketing concept in the 1960s, researchers reported its avid uptake. Pretty soon, however, it became clear that the reality was less impressive and was often traditional product-led selling disguised by use of the jargon, without actually enacting a market led process. It began to seem, too, that this pretence at strategic marketing planning was the way that marketing-resistant cultures absorbed and neutralized a fad without absorbing its basic principles. In other words, companies who had not truly adopted the marketing concept were not actively resisting strategic marketing planning. Instead, they paid lip service to it and changed some superficial things like their vocabulary whilst, in reality, their core behaviour remained as product-led as before.

By this stage, researchers had taken the failure of companies to use strategic marketing planning as a given. Consequently, they moved their interest to understanding and describing the realities of marketing planning, as compared to the espoused activity of what managers said they did. The actuality uncovered by this later stage of research was not that strategic marketing planning was ignored, leaving a void of nothingness in the strategy making process. What in fact happened was that the rational, formal processes were subverted and diluted by less rational strategy making processes.

Walker and Ruekert (1987) found that marketing contributed to strategy implementation in more or less formal ways depending on the type of business unit strategy it was subordinate to. Others found that the rational process was subordinated to strategic vision (Carson and Cromie, 1989) in small firms, even when that vision was implicit. In an interesting experiment, Mary Curren and her colleagues watched managers playing a marketing-strategy simulation game and observed what she called their 'self-serving biases', as irrationality crept into what was supposed to be a completely rational process (Curren *et al.*, 1992). Her findings were reinforced by two studies across several company types that found strategic marketing planning heavily diluted by other decision-making processes that seemed embedded in the organizational culture (McColl-Kennedy and Keil, 1990; Abratt and Bendixen, 1993).

In short, the research into what companies were actually doing when they said they were doing strategic marketing planning all came down to pretty much the same conclusion. Even when we think we're being rational, we're often being irrational.

This was nicely summarized by Mowen and Gaeth (1992), who looked in more detail at the early stages of the strategic marketing planning process:

> In summary, we argue that the evaluation stage of the decision process consists of the marketing manager making judgements involving prediction and valuation. In any decision-making situation such decisions may be systematically biased through the application of heuristics.

By this stage in exploring the research, we might reasonably call a halt and decide that there is a consensus. How much is strategic marketing planning used? Not much, and certainly nowhere near as much as managers say they use it. As if to support that consensus, researchers in the broader area of strategic planning say similar things about their field. In the wonderfully understated style adopted by many academics, Eisenhardt and Zbaracki (1992) point out that the prescriptions for planning in the literature are a 'poor description of reality'.

This area of the research literature that concerns itself with how we make strategy is replete with criticisms of the textbooks as a description of what happens in reality. So exhaustive is this field that, in 1994, Henry Mintzberg felt moved to write an entire book on the subject, *The Rise and Fall of Strategic Planning* (Mintzberg, 1994), in which he firmly concluded that the rational, formal approach was neither a good prescription for, nor a description of, the real world. The case that strategic marketing planning is more honoured in the breach than the observance seems closed. However, we haven't heard the case for the defence yet.

Not all of the research says that marketers don't use strategic marketing planning much. One relatively recent piece of research suggested the opposite (Glaister and Falshaw, 1999). In a survey of 113 British companies, Glaister and Falshaw claimed:

> We have found a reasonable and increasing level of the use of several older and simpler planning techniques, with apparently little use of more sophisticated or new techniques. Despite this relatively unsophisticated

approach to strategic planning, there is generally a very positive attitude expressed by respondents to its benefits for their organizations.

This work is open to much criticism. It was, for instance, based on self-administered questionnaires, which are notoriously poor for understanding complex issues. That said, it does reveal a sort of defence for managers accused of not using a proven process. The defence which is used frequently by marketers who do not seem to be using strategic marketing planning goes something like this: 'True, we are not following the textbook to the letter and, true, we're not using all the tools and techniques. But we are analysing the market, choosing strategies and defining tactics. Just because we're not doing it your way doesn't mean we're not doing it at all.'

It is true that some of the academic criticism can be said to be pedantic and that those criticisms are sometimes of a semantic nature. What we really need to know, if we are to improve planning in practice, is who is right. If we strip away the academic pedantry, are real marketing practitioners using strategic marketing planning in all but name, or are they making marketing strategy by some other method?

To test this, we need to get down to the basics and what differentiates strategic marketing planning from, say, an inspired leader making strategy, or a process of trial and error. We need to look at the one or two fundamental things that we think strategic marketing planning must include, and assess their use. If they are used, the defending practitioners are right and they are planning in all but name. If not, the criticizing academics are right and the practitioners are pretenders.

There are two clear contenders for 'acid-test' parts of strategic marketing planning: segmentation and SWOT. The former is fundamental to understanding the implications of the internal and external situation, whilst the latter is the basis for selecting a strategy that best addresses that situation. It is hard to argue that an organization that is not using these two tools is doing strategic marketing planning. It may still be making strategy some other way, but its managers can't claim to be formally and rationally planning.

The textbooks are clear about what segmentation is. It is (to synthesize the definitions of several authors) dividing a market into groups of customers who have similar needs and therefore react similarly to different value propositions. It is followed in the strategic marketing planning process by the selection or prioritization of segments and the design of value propositions that are segment-specific.

Researchers have looked intensively at what real companies do when they segment and target markets. What they describe is not what the textbooks prescribe. Segmentation is meant to be both needs based and reflected in organizational structure. That is, the groups should be defined in terms of differing customer needs and the organization should reflect those differences. The reality is that most companies rely on customer categorization in terms of product categories, channels or sometimes descriptors like size (Jenkins and McDonald, 1997). This pale imitation of segmentation does not then permeate the company, but is bolted on to the customer-contact parts of the organization like sales, marketing and customer service.

Other researchers have emphasized the lack of focus on customer needs in many firms' segmentation in industrial (Albert, 2003), business-to-business (Freytag and Clarke, 2001) and consumer marketing (Stone, 2004; unpublished). The examination by researchers of companies' segmentation approaches has not only pointed out the fact that they are not using segmentation, but also given some insight into why. In essence, companies have difficulty translating strategic segmentation into operational plans (Piercy and Morgan, 1993) because they struggle to correlate customer needs (which are hard to understand) with the hard data of descriptor variables (such as age and income, or size and sector) with which they are comfortable (Mitchell, 1996). Whatever the reason, it seems pretty clear that the limited extent to which segmentation is really used supports the idea that strategic marketing planning is little used in practice.

The second piece of evidence concerns SWOT analysis, the central technique for aligning the internal and external environments and, therefore, defining the key issues to be addressed by the marketing-strategy making process. The process is supposed to involve collating verified relative strengths and weaknesses and aligning them to similarly validated external opportunities and threats. The result of this alignment is to reveal the key issues and so inform (and often define) the necessary strategy.

Again, the researchers found that reality differs hugely from this ideal world. Two pieces of work come to the same depressing conclusion regarding the use of SWOT, and none could be found holding contrary views. Nigel Piercy and William Giles (Piercy and Giles, 1989) found that although the technique is widely cited, it is often reduced to a 'subjective listing exercise' identifying none of the key issues that are the intended output of the technique. Even more damning, Hill and Westbrook (1997) suggested that SWOT was so ineffective in practice that, had it been a product, it would have been time for a recall. Although they found that 40 per cent of their sample claimed use of the technique, they pointed out that:

> All the applications showed similar characteristics – long lists (over forty factors on average), general (often meaningless) descriptions, a failure to prioritise and no attempts to verify any points. But the most worrying general characteristic was that no-one subsequently used the outputs within the later stages of the strategy process. The continued use of SWOT, therefore, needs to be questioned.

The use, or rather abuse, of two central planks of strategic marketing planning seems to confirm the academics' case that many managers really do not use it, rather than it being a matter of semantics and pedantry.

Of course, picking two techniques from the many possible characteristic symptoms of strategic marketing planning is open to criticism. Even though most authorities would find it hard to imagine a valid strategic marketing plan that doesn't use segmentation or SWOT, it would add weight to the argument if the same inference were supported by looking at the extent of use of other tools. That is exactly the result of some work carried out by Greenley and Bayus (1994), who rigorously reviewed the research in this area to conclude:

> Except for a small number of sophisticated decision makers, few companies seem to use these techniques which are advocated in the prescriptive literature.

The work of Greenley and Bayus draws together about fifteen years of research into the extent of strategic marketing planning (and strategic planning) use (see Table 3.1). That work looks at what tools are used, and to what extent. Its findings support and reinforce the conclusion that, despite being stable and proven, most companies don't do the sort of formal planning that both the textbooks prescribe and they themselves espouse. When we allow for sensitive managers overstating the degree to which they use well-known techniques for fear of looking amateur, we might guess that the reality is, if anything, even less use of strategic marketing planning than the research data imply.

Perhaps the point has been laboured, but in the face of denial it is important to gather the evidence – and the failure of companies, generally, to use strategic marketing planning is a central plank of this book's argument about how to make marketing happen.

Table 3.1 The observed use of marketing planning techniques (from Greenley and Bayus, 1994)

Study	*Country*	*Focus*	*Outline of results*
Buzzell and Wiersema, 1981	USA	Strategic planning	Limited use of formal planning methods
McColl-Kennedy and Keil, 1990	Australia	Marketing planning	Awareness and usage of methods – low
Greenley, 1985	UK	Marketing planning	Only 24 per cent use portfolio analysis; half use product life cycle analysis
Haspeslagh, 1982	USA	Strategic planning	Only 45 per cent use portfolio analysis regularly
Hopkins, 1981	USA	Marketing planning	A quarter use portfolio analysis, only 13 per cent use product life cycle analysis
Hooley *et al.*, 1981	UK	Marketing planning	Half use SWOT analysis, one-third use product life cycle, only a few use portfolio, profit impact of marketing strategy, perceptual mapping and conjoint analysis
Reid and Hinckley, 1989	UK/ Hong Kong	Strategic planning	Little awareness of PIMS, portfolio and product life cycle analysis
Ross and Silverblatt, 1987	USA	Strategic planning	Half use portfolio analysis regularly, and a quarter use profit impact of marketing strategy regularly
Verhage and Waarts, 1988	Netherlands	Strategic planning	15 per cent use portfolio analysis, 27 per cent use product life cycle with 62 per cent using SWOT
Wittink and Cattin, 1989	USA	Marketing planning	Limited use of conjoint analysis by market research consultants
Wood and LaForge, 1986	USA	Strategic planning	Portfolio analysis used by 67 per cent of sample

We can now close this part of the argument with an interim summary. In general, most marketers don't use strategic marketing planning much. Whatever the reasons for this, it cannot be that it is new (it is as old as most of its current potential practitioners) or that it is not yet stable (the textbooks haven't changed much in decades) or that it is unproven (it has more supporting evidence than almost any other process managers use).

Please note, however, that this negative-sounding conclusion is not a criticism. It is an observation rather than a judgement. We are not saying that these companies do not make strategy, or that they necessarily make weak strategy. As we will cover later, companies that don't plan still make strategy, and often make good strategy. Nor are we insisting that they do strategic planning. If a proven stable process is not used by the majority of intelligent and well-intentioned managers, there may be a good reason (arguably, *must* be a good reason) why this is so.

At this stage, all we can say is that strategic marketing planning is not used much, and that seems odd. Like Fleming with his mouldy Petrie dish, we can't explain this yet. We need to explore further why so many bright people and good companies appear to neglect a proven source of competitive advantage. In that exploration, we might hope to find a way of creating new knowledge and thereby improving the way we make marketing strategy.

Application point: How much strategic marketing planning does your organization do?

The preceding section demonstrated that many companies do not really do strategic marketing planning. They rarely refute the process, and usually espouse a formal process for making marketing strategy, but close observation reveals that they don't do what the textbooks recommend. This is not necessarily a bad thing but, given the evidence for the effectiveness of planning, it is something we need to explain. If we understand why companies don't use strategic marketing planning, we might learn something that is practically valuable.

- How much strategic marketing planning does your organization do?
- Does it follow the textbook or is it less formal?
- Does it use the tools, or does it simply dress up in the jargon and acronyms?
- Does the organization have a realistic understanding of how much formal planning it does, or is it deluding itself?

The answers to these questions are useful in improving the way an organization makes its marketing strategy.

Why isn't strategic marketing planning used more?

In one sense, there is nothing special about strategic marketing planning. It is a management process, one of many that go to make up the value chain of any company of a significant size. If we were discussing another of our processes (say quality assurance, or recruitment, or order processing) which we had found to be more honoured in the breach than the observance, we would want to understand why. In most organizations, troubleshooting failing processes is, if not routine, then certainly unexceptional. By contrast, strategic marketing planning is often left failing with little attempt to understand and correct that failing. Perhaps that anomaly is the biggest difference between it and other management processes.

As a start in correcting this anomaly and a beginning to improving the application of strategic marketing planning, we can follow the sort of method that troubleshooters of other management processes might adopt. We can start by asking if the basic process is sound, if it works in some circumstances but not in others, or if it is just a bad process. In effect, we have done that in Chapter 2. We know that strategic marketing does contribute to organizational effectiveness, so it seems safe to assume that it can work. The breadth of the work covered in Chapter 2 also suggests that the effectiveness of the process is not limited to a certain industry sector or type of market. No, all of the prior research tells us that strategic marketing planning, when used, is a good process. However, there's the rub, to borrow from Shakespeare again – *when used*. Just as Chapter 2 concluded that strategic marketing planning worked, the first half of this chapter is just as clear in indicating that it is not used much.

The focus of our troubleshooting, therefore, shifts from the basic process to the context in which it fails to be applied. Our question changes from 'When does it work and not work?' to 'When is it applied and not applied?' – what is going on at the time that strategic marketing planning fails to be applied, despite the fact that we know what it is and that it works?

As with the other questions that have arisen so far in this book (i.e. what is strategic marketing planning, does it work, and how much is it used?), the researchers have beaten us to this question. Management researchers are a little like cattle grazing, seeking new knowledge instead of nutrition. They stay until they have grazed out the field and then move on. Having exhausted the fields of defining strategic marketing planning, its effectiveness and its usage, they have already moved on to what helps or hinders it, or, in academic terms, 'moderates' it.

There are therefore many years's worth of research into what helps or hinders strategic marketing planning. As ever, it is a complex field and there is a danger of oversimplifying the results of the research. However, we do need to know what is going wrong as a first step in making it right, so an overview of this field is necessary. As a first iteration at getting to grips with problem, we can divide the thinking in this area into two broad categories. In simple terms, what moderates strategic marketing planning has been found to lie in two areas: inside the company, or in the marketplace.

Strategic marketing planning inside the company

Compared to some of the research we have looked at earlier in this book, this area is especially messy and doesn't follow a straightforward path to enlightenment. That is because the question (what goes on inside the company to moderate the effectiveness of strategic marketing planning?) is what the mathematicians refer to as an ill-posed problem – i.e. the same end result can be the result of multiple causes. The strategic marketing planning process, if done well, reaches into every part of the company, so there are potentially lots of possible mechanisms by which the internal context gets in the way of planning. As a result of this causal complexity, researchers have come up with various explanations for what is going on inside a company when it fails to apply planning. These different research perspectives don't disagree, however. Instead, by looking at the problem from different angles they give us a better understanding of what is happening in reality. The different perspectives and their findings can be loosely grouped under four headings:

1. Tangible barriers
2. Belief systems
3. Social practice
4. Entrenched cultural values.

Tangible barriers

The first perspective to consider is that of tangible barriers. Many marketing researchers have catalogued the different things about a company that can appear to incapacitate strategic marketing planning. For instance, Veronica Wong (Wong *et al.*, 1989) and her colleagues identified four broad factors that will be familiar to any marketing manager: lack of financial resources, departmental pre-occupation with functional problems, lack of skills, and unclear marketing objectives. This list overlapped noticeably with those of other writers. For example, it is hard in this area to get away from the prolific and valuable writing of Malcolm McDonald. He listed ten barriers to strategic marketing planning (McDonald, 1989):

1. Confusion between strategy and tactics
2. Isolating the marketing function from operations
3. Confusion between the marketing function and the marketing concept
4. Organizational barriers
5. Lack of in-depth analysis
6. Confusion between process and output
7. Lack of knowledge and skills
8. Lack of systematic approach to strategic marketing planning
9. Failure to prioritize objectives
10. Hostile corporate cultures.

Working with Hugh Wilson, McDonald went on to expand on the barriers as including management roles, management cognition (i.e. knowledge of marketing techniques), systems and procedures, resource allocation and data availability (McDonald and Wilson, 1999). The same sorts of factors occurred when researchers looked at the particular case of planning in small companies (McKiernan and Morris, 1994). Other researchers have looked at the way that organizations are structured, and found that structure hindered planning (Stampfl, 1983). The research contrasts the implementation of marketing (often very cross-functional and requiring open discussion) with the way organizations are built (often siloed and structured).

Ruekert and Walker (1987) summed this up as:

> Much of the horizontal interaction among departments is informal. Consequently, it is outside the prescribed structures of the organization chart, the substantive content of the marketing plan and the formal authority of the marketing and other functional managers.

Systems, procedures and structures keep recurring as barriers to strategic marketing planning. Some researchers doubt if the process can work in some settings and refer to the 'dysfunctional effects' of strategic marketing planning, fearing that 'formal planning may cause internal contradictions and endanger an organization's viability' (Bishop and Bresser, 1983).

Ruekert (1992) again says a similar thing from another perspective:

> The degree to which an organization can increase its market orientation is inextricably linked to the organizational structures, systems and processes created to sustain them.

This investigation into tangible barriers is useful but not enough. It helps us to see where the problems of strategic marketing planning implementation lie. However, whilst it is rich in data it is weak in insight. We now know that structure, processes and lack of knowledge all tend to hinder planning, but that knowledge doesn't help much.

At this stage of reading the research, the pragmatic marketer would be forgiven for feeling depressed. The tangible barriers to strategic marketing planning are so numerous and so endemic within the company; it almost looks as if strategic marketing planning can't work in some (perhaps most) companies without turning the company upside down to fit the process. The realists among us know that can't happen, so begin to wonder if we should even bother trying to make marketing happen. We need another perspective, one that complements but is different from that of marketers simply cataloguing their woes.

Belief systems

More recently, a second perspective has developed that looks less at the tangible barriers to strategic marketing planning within an organization and more at the reasons those barriers exist. Geoff Lancaster and Ian Waddelow, for instance, looked at small firms and concluded that although barriers manifested themselves in tangible factors, like knowledge and resources, they actually reflected deeper differences in the culture of those organizations (Lancaster and Waddelow, 1998).

Liu (1995), looking at the same area, reckoned that different degrees of market orientation could be attributed to fundamental differences in the beliefs firms have about themselves. In larger firms, some researchers have found that belief systems influence the way firms make decisions (Marginson, 2002). This work thus suggests that something much less tangible than systems and structures underlies the problems with implementing strategic marketing planning – it may be something to do with the underlying beliefs of the firm. This begins to give us valuable insight, but two more perspectives are needed before we try to make conclusions.

Social practice

A third perspective seems to reinforce and complement the idea that a company's belief systems can moderate the effectiveness of their strategic marketing planning. Some researchers look at the strategy making process as a social exercise, driven by the interactions between different managers and groups. From this point of view, strategy making is 'a technological and appropriative social practice' (Hendry, 2000) and strategic episodes are 'the effective locus of strategic practice and the interaction between strategic and operating routines' (Hendry and Seidl, 2003). This is complex stuff and, to many marketers, a little esoteric. It isn't necessary for the reader to grasp all this, however; simply to understand that this approach (known as social discourse theory) comes down to a conclusion pretty much the same as the researchers talking about belief systems.

Maitlis summarized it well (Maitlis and Lawrence, 2003):

> We argue the failure in organizational strategizing can be understood as resulting from the interplay of certain elements of organizational discourse and specific kinds of political behaviour.

So far, then, it seems that there are three perspectives on what it is about the internal company environment that moderates (usually hindering rather than helping) strategic marketing planning. The first lists the tangible factors like structure, systems and resources. It helps us see the facts but provides no practicable solution. The second views the problem as to do with the basic beliefs of the people that make up the company. That gives us more insight but still offers no solution. A third perspective considers the sociology of the strategy making process and again provides insight but offers little in the way of a solution.

It feels as though we are walking around a big, complex problem, and as we look at it we understand it better but we are not much closer to solving it. Why do organizations seem to hinder the application of strategic marketing planning?

Entrenched cultural values

The fourth and final perspective is that of organizational culture. One person has been pre-eminent and prolific in looking at how culture (of the company, rather than national, variety) interacts with marketing planning. In a series of papers, Lloyd Harris has looked at the problem and concluded that cultural context is critical to the implementation of marketing (Harris, 1996, 1999a, 1999b, 1999c, 2000, 2002; Harris and Ogbonna, 1999a, 1999b, 2001, 2002; Ogbonna and Harris, 2002). In particular, he points to a number of entrenched values that seem to be responsible for preventing marketing from happening:

> The study finds that six entrenched values appear to have impeded the initiation of planning within the company. These are: reactiveness, management activities and practice, compartmentalization, short term cost orientation, internal focus and stability.

So now we have a fourth possible explanation of why marketing fails to be applied inside organizations. In addition to structure, systems and other tangible factors, belief systems and social discourse, entrenched cultural values seem to explain the failure to implement a process proven to improve effectiveness. All four perspectives help us understand the problem better, but say little about how, practically, to solve it.

Organizational culture

We need an explanation for how the internal environment gets in the way of strategic marketing planning that somehow synthesizes these four perspectives into a usable piece of knowledge. The answer lies in a field often talked about by marketers but in fact very rarely understood by them: organizational culture. Theories of organizational culture explain the observations of tangible barriers, belief systems, organizational discourse and entrenched values, and offer a way to think about solving the problem. To steal a metaphor from physics, it is a kind of grand unifying theory of what goes on inside companies to moderate the implementation of planning. To improve strategic marketing planning, therefore, we are going to have to deepen our understanding of organizational culture.

Application point: What moderates strategic marketing planning in your organization?

The preceding sections have described different perspectives on how the internal environment within a company can moderate (usually hinder) strategic marketing planning. No single perspective solves the problem, but each provides some insight. By 'walking around the problem', we begin to understand it.

- What is it about your company's internal environment that seems either to help or hinder planning?
- What tangible factors can you observe?
- What intangible factors can you observe?
- Do these seem to have their origins in the fundamental beliefs or entrenched values of your company?

Understanding these factors is a necessary prerequisite to making marketing happen in your company.

Organizational culture is both much more complex and much more useful than most managers realize. In part, this is because culture is a very good example of where academic boundaries and semantics confuse rather than clarify the picture for practitioners. There are at least two camps of organizational culture researchers: the positivists (e.g. Kotter and Heskett, 1992; Denison and Mishra, 1995), who think that culture can be measured and characterized, and the relativists (e.g. Pettigrew, 1979; Smirchich and Calas, 1987), who think that culture is all intangible and relative. The two camps write from such different perspectives and use such different methods, it is hard to synthesize their different contributions. It requires a level of in-depth critical reading that makes their work inaccessible to anyone but other academics. Despite this difficulty, it is possible to draw out a number of key findings about organizational culture that are commonly held by both academic camps and are relevant to making strategic marketing planning work inside real organizations.

First, both positivists and relativists see culture as being 'a means by which the organization aligns itself to the external environment' (Smirchich, 1983) and that it 'regulates internal transactions' (Wilkins and Ouchi, 1983). This is important, for the former and, to an extent, the latter is what we attempt to do when we create and implement marketing strategies. If culture is doing the same thing as planning, there are important implications. We might expect the two things to interact and perhaps conflict with each other. It looks as though firms that attempt strategic marketing planning may be installing a new and explicit alignment process on top of an existing but implicit one. Imagine if we installed a new order processing or recruitment process without uninstalling the old one. We would surely expect to double order, or confuse applicants, or otherwise foul things up. Looked at this way, it is no wonder that culture seems to get in the way of planning. We are trying to do the same thing in two different ways at the same time.

Secondly, both schools see organizational culture as multilayered. This is best illustrated by the work of Edgar Schein, one of the elder statesmen of this field (see, for instance, Schein, 1984, 1991, 1999). Simply put, Schein described organizational culture in three layers. Its foundations lie in the underlying assumptions held by the organization (often coming from the founder or leader) about what it takes to succeed. These assumptions translate into values, the extent to which certain behaviours and attitudes are valued by the organization. In turn, these values translate into cultural artefacts, things we can see such as structures, systems and processes.

This multilayering is of more than academic interest. It explains the observations from all four perspectives discussed above. Tangible barriers are usually cultural artefacts, as is political behaviour. Belief systems and entrenched values can each be seen as different layers of Schein's model of organizational culture. Figures 3.1 and 3.2 are examples of parts of an organizational culture for two contrasting organizations. These examples, from real companies, are simplified but illustrate the point. Company A will clearly find it much easier to execute strategic marketing planning than Company B.

So what we know about organizational culture helps us to understand how the internal context of an organization might help or hinder the strategic marketing planning process. First, if culture is an existing and competing alignment process, we might predict conflict with a planning process trying to do the same thing at the same time. Secondly, if culture consists of artefacts which flow from values that are rooted in assumptions, this would explain and draw together the various different observations of how the internal environment hinders strategic marketing planning.

A third point of consensus exists between the positivist and relativist schools of organizational culture. This is that culture is, as Drucker (1993) puts it, 'persistent and pervasive'. Whilst managers

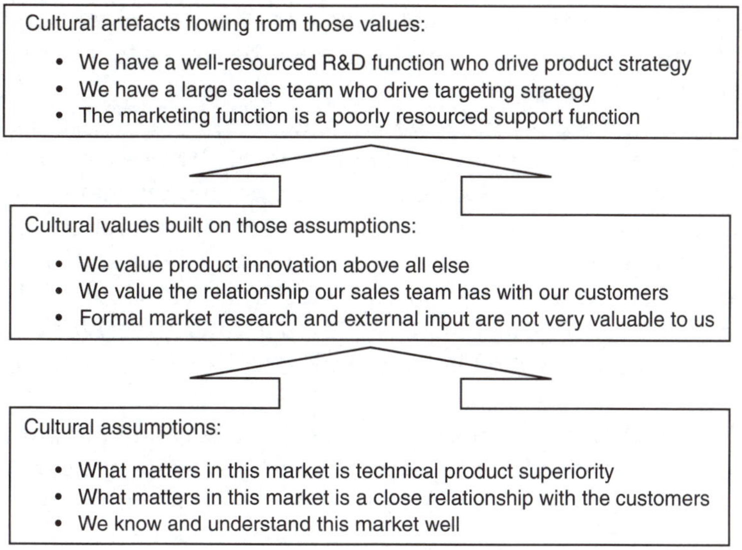
Cultural artefacts flowing from those values:
• We have a well-resourced R&D function who drive product strategy
• We have a large sales team who drive targeting strategy
• The marketing function is a poorly resourced support function
Cultural values built on those assumptions:
• We value product innovation above all else
• We value the relationship our sales team has with our customers
• Formal market research and external input are not very valuable to us
Cultural assumptions:
• What matters in this market is technical product superiority
• What matters in this market is a close relationship with the customers
• We know and understand this market well

Figure 3.1 An organizational culture that hinders strategic marketing planning

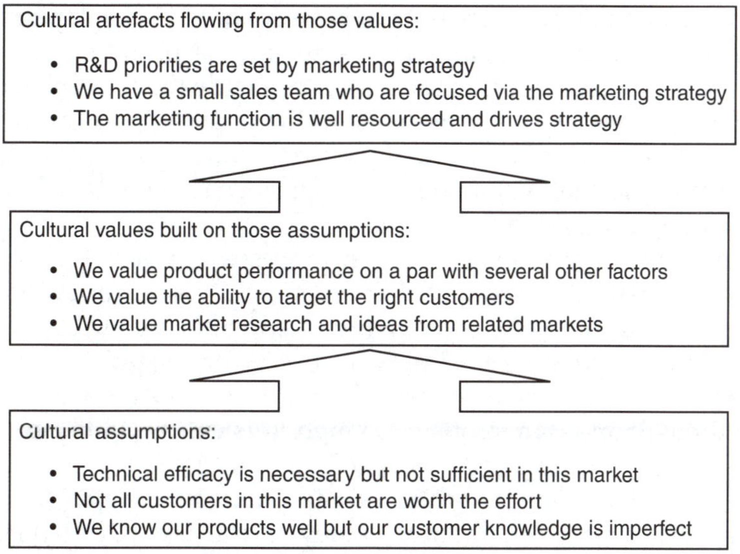
Cultural artefacts flowing from those values:
• R&D priorities are set by marketing strategy
• We have a small sales team who are focused via the marketing strategy
• The marketing function is well resourced and drives strategy
Cultural values built on those assumptions:
• We value product performance on a par with several other factors
• We value the ability to target the right customers
• We value market research and ideas from related markets
Cultural assumptions:
• Technical efficacy is necessary but not sufficient in this market
• Not all customers in this market are worth the effort
• We know our products well but our customer knowledge is imperfect

Figure 3.2 An organizational culture that supports strategic marketing planning

(and especially leaders) often pontificate about 'cultural change' in an organization, the researchers hold the view that 'the empirical evidence supports the difficulty of cultural change' (Legge, 1994), and that many attempts at changing a company culture 'largely fail to appreciate the deep seated values, beliefs and assumptions underlying a culture can rarely if ever be engaged by such an approach' (Fitzgerald, 1988).

Amusingly, it seems that some managers can be fooled into thinking they have achieved cultural change simply because they want to believe in it. Ogbonna tells the tale of a supermarket chain in which the managers were convinced of their newly customer-oriented culture, but in which interviews with the checkout staff revealed the old culture was still in place and driving behaviour (Ogbonna and Wilkinson, 2003). Ogbonna argues that much perceived cultural change is in fact 'resigned behavioural compliance' and not cultural change at all.

All of this is not to say that organizational culture is static. Quite the opposite; it seems to be in a permanent, if slow, state of flux. Where cultural change is achieved, it is usually the result not of dramatic change but of managing this 'natural dynamic flux of culture' (Hatch, 1999). Even if organizational culture were open to easy manipulation, attempts at wholesale cultural change ignore the fact that the existing culture must have had some value in order for the organization to have come this far. Researchers have found that companies that try extensive cultural change risk reducing the positive aspects of their existing culture (Lorsch, 1986) and increase the intangible costs of internal transactions (Wilkins and Ouchi, 1983); this can have a variety of unintended consequences (Harris and Ogbonna, 2002). All of this suggests that wholesale cultural change is not only difficult; it can be dangerous as well.

Thus it is not systems, structure, processes, knowledge, beliefs, politics or entrenched values that we should blame for the failure to make strategic marketing planning happen in a company. All of those things, it seems, are simply aspects of organizational culture, rooted in the basic assumptions held by the organization, which are both difficult and dangerous to change. It is culture to blame, and, realistically, we can do little do change the culture.

However, that is not to say that this new understanding of how culture hinders strategic marketing planning is useless. Indeed, this new understanding of culture suggests two ways of improving strategic marketing planning, which we will develop later. First, it suggests that, to the extent that culture is unchangeable, we have to learn to fit in around it. Secondly, to the extent that we can perhaps change some parts of the culture, it tells us that fiddling with the artefacts isn't enough. We need to change the assumptions that lead to those artefacts.

Application point: What is the culture of your organization?

The preceding section has described organizational culture as having three characteristic features: it is an alignment process, it is multilayered, and it is difficult and dangerous to change. Each of these characteristics is useful in understanding how our culture may hinder and might help us make marketing happen in our company.

- What are the cultural artefacts of your company that appear to moderate strategic marketing planning?
- What deeply held beliefs and values do these artefacts stem from?
- To what extent, if at all, are these underlying assumptions amenable to change, and what unintended consequences might flow from such change?

Later we will develop both the idea of strategic marketing planning fitting in around the culture and that of 'tweaking' bits of the culture where we can and must. First, however, we need to remember that internal factors are not the only things that prevent the application of strategic marketing planning. External factors moderate its use, too. The following section considers what we know about the external challenges faced by our planning.

Strategic marketing planning in the marketplace

We have established that organizational culture is the underlying internal factor affecting why strategic marketing planning is not used, despite all the factors in favour of a rational, formal approach. In the process, we developed the first inkling that culture is not something we can simply change, as if it were a piece of the corporate furniture. From what we can see so far, it looks as though the best thing to do is work with the grain of the culture, perhaps carefully adjusting it in parts where we can and where we must.

What about the other influences on the application of strategic marketing planning? The literature also finds that other, external, factors render planning more easy or less easy to apply. These external factors differ from culture in that they do not so much facilitate or prevent the application of rational tools and techniques; rather they make them more or less effective when applied.

As Harris (1996) noted, reluctant planners use a number of tactics to avoid or prevent planning. Typical among these are claims that planning is 'OK, but not for us because we're different' – the cited difference usually being that the firm is too small or the market so special as to make formal planning irrelevant. Interestingly, the research doesn't support these limitations of planning. Firm size and industry sector *per se* are not the issue. Instead, the effectiveness of strategic marketing planning seems to be related to two external factors that cut across divisions of firm size and industry sector, namely market complexity and market turbulence.

To the marketer working at the metaphorical coalface, all markets seem hopelessly complex and turbulent. In relative rather than absolute terms, however, there are clearly differences between markets in both dimensions. If we take markets to consist of customer segments, channels, competitors and macroenvironmental forces (SLEPT factors we discussed earlier), different markets clearly have different levels of complexity.

Some markets (for instance, retail grocery) have many segments while others (such as publishing in academic astrophysics) presumably have fewer. Competitive forces can be limited to only one significant direct competitor (for instance, in office software suites) while others have multiple direct competitors and all the threats of supplier power, buyer power, substitutes and new entrants (*in vitro* clinical diagnostics, perhaps). In many markets the channel to market is direct; in others there is a confusion of retail, wholesale, web and other channels. Between all markets, the extent to which SLEPT factors complicate the segmentation, channels and competition vary.

The same logic applies to market turbulence. If we loosely define market turbulence as the extent of change per unit of time in customers, channels and competition, then markets again differ in relation to each other. In industries like pharmaceuticals, where it takes ten to fifteen years to develop a product, change is relatively slow. The same is true where regulation stabilizes the market, as it does in some areas of financial services. In other sectors, driven by either fashion or embryonic technology, the rate of change is much faster. In both cases, the rate of change can accelerate or decelerate as the market matures over time.

Clearly, we might expect to find that differences in market complexity and market turbulence would impact on the effectiveness of any outward-facing business process, and that is exactly the case for strategic marketing planning. As Hodgkinson and Sparrow put it, our strategic competence depends on our ability to 'acquire, store, recall, interpret and act upon information of relevance to the longer term survival and well being of the organization' (Hodgkinson, 2002). Strategic marketing planning, it seems, can either enhance or diminish that ability to process relevant information, depending on the complexity and turbulence of the market.

Taking market complexity first, the literature supports the intuitive view that planning helps us to cope with market complexity. Even though this fits our intuition, it is worth spending a moment to ensure we understand not just the fact but also the mechanism behind it. It has its roots in the field of managerial cognition, that subset of psychology that deals with how managers understand their environment. The seminal work on which much of our understanding of managerial cognition is based is Simon's *Administrative Behaviour* (Simon, 1947). In this and subsequent works (March and Simon, 1958) Simon developed the concept of bounded rationality – the idea that, although managers try to make decisions rationally, their rationality is constrained by their capacity to process information. To try and get around the limitations imposed by our information processing ability we employ heuristics, or ways of simplifying our thinking. These make decision-making easier at the cost of sometimes reducing the quality of the decision. This is because the heuristics we use may introduce biases. Schwenk (1995), for instance, noted three broad types of bias in strategic decision-making:

1. *Causal attribution*: for instance, saying good results were planned and bad results were accidental
2. *Escalating commitment*: that is, increasing commitment to a failing strategy
3. *Biases in recollection*: that is, using memory selectively to support an established idea.

The managerial cognition literature tells us that without some sort of tools it is difficult for us to cope with anything more than a very simple market. If we attempt to, our inherent biases render our rationality very bounded indeed. In other words, we need some way of helping us understand the complexity of customer needs, channels and competitors and aligning it to our internal situation, which is itself a complex mixture of strengths and weaknesses. Strategic marketing planning is, of course, designed to do just that. Its value in coping with market complexity is illustrated well by the work of Fredrickson (1984), who found that planning works better the more comprehensive and rational it is.

So the research suggests that market complexity favours strategic marketing planning effectiveness. It does not say that planning does not work in simple markets, of course, but since planning has a cost (in time if nothing else), it probably is not worth it in markets so simple that they can be understood without planning. However, it may be that the number of markets that are so simple as to be understood without the aid of strategic marketing planning, at least in a simplified form, is very small.

The second dimension of the market that seems to influence the usefulness of strategic marketing planning is market turbulence. As we have seen already, Bishop and Bresser (1983) noted some 'dysfunctional' effects of planning. In particular, they noted that planning worked less well in uncertain or inefficient (in the economists' sense of not working well) markets.

This ties in well with a whole stream of work by Eisenhardt, who looked at planning in what she called 'high-velocity' environments. In such cases, she thought that 'planning formality may be negatively associated with performance' (Eisenhardt, 1989).

It also fits with the work of Fredrickson on planning comprehensiveness, who followed up his earlier work to suggest that the good effects of planning formality applied much more to stable markets and were less true in unstable markets (Fredrickson and Mitchell, 1984). The underlying mechanism for this seems obvious and simple; planning takes information and time, both of which are in short supply in turbulent markets. By the time information has been gathered and analysed, a turbulent market has moved on and our analysis has lost some or all of its value.

Thus this part of the literature suggests that although planning helps us cope with complexity, it copes less well with market turbulence. There is a lot of other research that fits in with this general conclusion that the external market environment affects the usefulness of strategic marketing planning. Speed, for instance (Speed, 1994; Pulendran *et al.*, 2003), found that 'external context affects decision character, decision process and decision outcome'. Similarly, Slevin (Slevin and Covin, 1997) and Covin (Covin *et al.*, 2001) found that planning worked best in hostile environments and in what they called 'mechanistic' (i.e. formal) structures; and non-planning ways of making strategy worked better in benign environments and what they termed 'organic' (i.e. informal) structures.

The same themes were at the basis of a heated academic debate between two giants of the field, Igor Ansoff (Ansoff, 1991) and Henry Mintzberg (Mintzberg, 1990). As is often the case, the debate seemed to generate more heat than light, but a careful reading of the argument shows that the two actually agreed on two core points: complexity is seen to favour rational planning, whilst turbulence is seen to favour less rational approaches.

All of this carries an important implication. Market conditions are not in our control. If textbook strategic marketing planning is moderated by market turbulence and market complexity, we may need to consider working around what we can't change. And we must do this at the same time as working around our persistent, pervasive and multilayered culture.

Application point: What is your market like?

The preceding section described the ways that markets vary in terms of their complexity and turbulence. Further, these factors seem to impinge on the effectiveness of strategic marketing planning. Understanding the relative complexity and turbulence of your market is a useful contribution to understanding the effectiveness of strategic marketing planning in your context.

- What does an objective assessment of your market reveal?
- Is the combination of customers, channels and competitive forces sufficient to classify the market as complex?
- Are those factors changing within the strategic timescale, or is the market relatively stable?
- What does the complexity and turbulence of your market imply about the effectiveness of strategic marketing planning in the particular context of your market?

How does that knowledge help us?

We have come a long way in this chapter. We have moved from a relatively simple and well-understood picture of knowing what strategic marketing planning is and that it works, to seeing that, despite this, it isn't used much. We've also gained a better understanding of what it is that goes on when strategic marketing planning does or doesn't happen. The culture either supports the process or it gets in the way. When applied, strategic marketing planning helps us cope with complexity in the market, with less chance of involving our bias-ridden judgements. When the market is turbulent, we have neither the time nor the information to make planning work well.

It is fundamentally important that both organizational culture and market conditions are practically out of our control. This implies that one form of strategic marketing planning might not work equally well in all cases. Further, this implies that we might have to adapt the strategic marketing planning process to fit what we can't change.

On Karl Marx's tomb, he is quoted as saying 'Philosophers may explain the world; the point, however, is to change it'. We have now done enough explaining of strategic marketing planning, its effectiveness and its application. We must now use those explanations to change the process. As a first step, we need briefly to pull together the strands of knowledge we have uncovered so far and then apply them to improving the effectiveness of strategic marketing planning. That is the aim of the next chapter.

Power points

- Almost all companies say they do strategic marketing planning, but most don't.
- For the most part, a superficial layer of jargon and misused tools is overlaid on top of budgeting and tactics that do not derive from the marketing concept.
- Even the most fundamental tools of strategic marketing planning, like segmentation and SWOT, are poorly used.
- The underlying reason for this lack of planning is organizational culture, which can support but more often hinders planning, and which it is difficult and dangerous to change.
- When applied, strategic marketing planning works differently in different market conditions. Planning is most valuable in complex markets, but is limited by its capacity to cope with market turbulence.
- Taken together, these findings hint at an important implication for marketers. If we can't change our culture or our market, we may have to adapt strategic marketing planning to fit the context in which it operates.

Reflection points for marketing practitioners

- To what extent does your organization really employ strategic marketing planning?

- What are the principal cultural artefacts that support and hinder the process?
- What are the underlying values and assumptions that lead to these artefacts?
- How complex and turbulent is your market?
- How does the complexity and turbulence of your market moderate the effectiveness of your planning process?

Chapter 4

Pause for thought – strategic marketing planning as a failed technology

Wonderful theory, wrong species.

(E. O. Wilson)

This short chapter is aimed at helping readers to assimilate what they have read so far. Rather than introducing new ideas, Chapter 4 pulls together and connects the broad spread of research findings reviewed in Chapters 1 to 3. It is not the aim of this book to review the literature exhaustively, but it is important, before we attempt to improve strategic marketing planning, to gather the facts about what it is, and how and when it works. Besides, the bookshelves of reflective practitioners are already groaning under the weight of half-read books about strategic marketing planning that are not much more than extended diatribes with little or no basis in research.

If, after almost forty years, most of us still aren't using strategic marketing planning, it suggests that improving the technique isn't going to be easy and is going to need some well-founded thought, not lightweight anecdote and opinion. The aim of this chapter therefore is to sum up what we know about strategic marketing planning and, more importantly, to draw implications for practice. In doing so, it forms a bridge between what we know and what we need to find out.

The first three chapters each came to clear conclusions which, coincidentally, refute the positions held by many managers who won't, don't or can't plan strategically for their markets.

In Chapter 1, we found that we know what strategic marketing planning is. This is far from a statement of the obvious. The antithesis of solid, practical, planning is fad surfing, leaping from fashion to craze and sometimes back again. In doing so, we often go through the time-costly learning stage but leap off just before we enter the reward-earning follow-through stage. Chapter 1 disabused us of the idea that each new fad is the essential and long awaited panacea for sustainable competitive advantage.

Instead, we saw that creating a marketing strategy is essentially a three-stage process of understanding the market, choosing the most appropriate strategy and translating that strategy into an action plan. This core process has not changed in its fundamentals for decades. Every new fad is simply a variation on this theme and, whilst it may be useful in detail, it is not an excuse for abandoning the core process. Whatever the reasons might be for failure to execute strategic marketing planning, not being able to identify an agreed process to implement is not one of them.

In Chapter 2, we found that strategic marketing planning works. This, again, is not as obvious as it seems. Many anti-planners hold the view that planning is, at best, a waste of resources for no benefit. Many practitioners who advocate planning do so as an act of faith, without being aware of the research evidence that supports it. In looking at the evidence, Chapter 2 took pains to avoid the simplistic proofs sought by some naïve managers.

It isn't possible to derive a quantitative proof that planning is directly proportional to performance; nor is it possible to prove the inverse. Businesses are too complex for that sort of analysis to be meaningful. What success means, and the linkages between planning and success, is not only complex but also varies between companies. That said, it is perfectly valid to draw a pragmatic, consensus view from the decades of research. In a nutshell, strategic marketing planning does contribute to organizational effectiveness. This seems to be true in almost all contexts, contrary to the unsubstantiated position of anti-planners who say that it won't work in their special business or that it only works for companies that are bigger/smaller/different from their own. It might be possible to make arguments against planning, but lack of proof that it works cannot rationally be one of them.

In Chapter 3, we found out that strategic marketing planning isn't used much. Not only is this a *non sequitur* with the combined logic of Chapters 1 and 2, it is also at variance with what many practising marketing managers espouse. It isn't that most marketing managers actively eschew strategic marketing planning (although some do) but that they do something that, although they call it planning, isn't. What passes for a strategic marketing plan in many companies is little more than product-led budgets and tactics, albeit dressed up in the jargon of the textbooks. Beneath the jargon dressing, what they do is not very different from what their grandparents might have written a generation before strategic marketing planning was born.

In uncovering this conundrum that planning isn't done, even when we know what it is and that it works, we uncover two areas of knowledge that will be important to us later. Strategic marketing planning is moderated by two things: organizational culture and market conditions. These two things are practically immutable, and their specifics are particular to each company. Whatever the defence given by non-planners for their inaction, 'we do it really' doesn't hold much water. There does, by contrast, seem some merit in the argument that lots of practitioners simply can't make it work in their context, and we'll explore the implications of that later.

If we want to resolve the ideas of Chapters 1, 2 and 3 into a single, concise sentence, it is this: strategic marketing planning is a well-defined tool that can and does work but seems to be too difficult to use in practice. That sentence is the crux of Part 1 of this book, and is worth dwelling on for a moment. It is more humorously and memorably expressed in the quotation at the top of this chapter from the renowned socio-biologist E. O. Wilson, although he was talking about Marxism's applicability to ants rather than humans. However we express it, the conclusion of Part 1 of this book can be viewed as a rather unsatisfactory one, made all the more so by the solid research base upon which it is built. Practising marketers need not only understand the failings of strategic marketing planning, they also need a way to improve the science or art of their profession.

There has long been an argument about whether marketing is a science or an art (see, for instance, Brown, 1996). The research reviewed in Chapters 1 to 3 suggests that this debate is rather pointless, and that it is neither. Marketing is a technology. Technologies are tools, based on but not identical to sciences. Medicine, for instance, is a technology based on the life sciences of biology, physiology and so on. Engineering is a technology with its underpinnings in physics and other physical sciences. In the same way, strategic marketing planning is a technology constructed from a social-scientific knowledge base in areas like economics, sociology and psychology.

This is not merely a semantic argument. If we think of strategic marketing planning as a technology, tool or device, it helps us to understand our problem. From what we can see, it is not that the basic science is poorly understood or that it is flawed in some way. Like many scientific concepts, it has its limits but it is certainly capable of sufficient generalization to be useful – an argument supported by Chapter 2. We don't need to go back to the drawing board; our problem lies in the practical utilization of the tool, not in the science upon which it is based.

Those academics and consultants who continue to refine incrementally the science underlying marketing offer little new value to marketing practitioners. What we need is an improvement in the technology, its user-friendliness and applicability in different organizational and market environments. Not only does the mountain of previous research suggest that we need to improve the practicality of the tool (and worry less about its fundamental principles), it even suggests where we might look for those improvements.

The research implies that any modified version of strategic marketing planning that we want to work better in practice must be better than the current approach in two important respects. The first is how it fits with organizational culture, and the second is how it copes with a range of market conditions, especially market turbulence and market complexity. Pause for a moment and reflect what this means in comparison to most current business school teaching. If textbook strategic marketing planning is a failed technology, it implies that we are failing students when we teach it. Further, if organizational culture and market conditions are company-specific, then any single, prescriptive process of strategic marketing planning will fail in many or most contexts. If the context is essentially out of our control, it implies that we must work around it and adapt the way we make marketing strategy to fit the specific internal and external environment of our company. By and large, this is not what we teach marketers.

Even though marketing textbooks do not prescribe it, the idea of adapting strategic marketing planning to fit its context better is not new. In 1982, a PhD thesis endorsing the use of strategic marketing planning was careful to point out that it should not be applied uniformly in all contexts, and that the process used should be 'requisite' to its context (McDonald, 1982). What was less clear was what the 'requisite' strategic marketing planning process actually *was* in any particular environment, and what aspects of it needed to be varied to suit a particular context.

Research before and since that work has expanded our knowledge in this area hugely, although the various strands of this knowledge have remained scattered in different academic silos. As will be discussed in Chapter 7, however, these various streams of learned thought come together to give us a practically useful explanation of why a strategic marketing planning process must fit with its internal and external context.

This first part of *Making Marketing Happen* has therefore reached a tentative, preliminary conclusion. Strategic marketing planning is a failed technology. It has failed not in the sense that it never works (it patently does), but in the sense that most of us mere marketing mortals can't make it work in practice. We start off with good intentions and end up deluding ourselves into thinking we are doing strategic marketing planning, whilst in reality we are just dressing up our old product-led budgets and tactics. This does not mean the whole idea of marketing is flawed; there is nothing much wrong with the theory and science that strategic marketing planning is built upon. The problem lies with its applicability in the messy real world of hostile organizational cultures and markets that are rarely simple and not always stable.

As with any preliminary conclusion, however, the value of the failed technology view lies in where it directs us next. Part 1 tells us that we make weak strategies when we use a strategy making process that doesn't fit either the company culture or the market conditions. Although this tells us what the problem is, it does not yet give us a solution. It only hints at it; we somehow need to adapt the process to fit our own particular and largely immutable context. This isn't a totally new idea; previous researchers have advocated 'requisite' strategic marketing planning but have not helped us to understand what requisite means.

Clearly, this leads the pragmatic, reflective marketing practitioner to demand answers to other questions: What does a strong marketing strategy look like? What do real companies actually do when they try to make strategy? What kind of strategic marketing planning fits with what context?

If we are really to improve how we make marketing happen, we need the answers to all three of these questions. It is these questions that prompted the research behind this book and which are answered in Chapters 5, 6 and 7 respectively. Taken together, they form a picture of how great companies make strategic marketing planning work for them, the subject of Chapter 8, and allow us to suggest ways that other companies might emulate them, the subject of Part 3.

Part 2

What great companies do

Part 2 of *Making Marketing Happen* looks at how those few companies that do make good marketing strategies achieve that difficult goal. Having clarified in Part 1 what strategic marketing planning is, and illuminated its shortcomings, we now look at how this clever but impractical technology is adapted in practice to create strong, competitive marketing strategies. What becomes clear is that good strategies result from hybridizing rational planning with visionary leadership and incremental experimentation. More to the point, no one hybrid is ideal in all contexts. What great companies do, often unconsciously, is to create a hybrid that fits them, their market and their organizational culture.

The aim of Chapter 5 is to clarify what we mean by a strong marketing strategy. The complexity of business means that we can't measure how good our planning is simply by the bottom line, or by any other end result. There are so many other factors in between the planning and the outcome that we need some more closely correlated measure of strategy making effectiveness. We need to measure the strength of the strategy itself. Fortunately there are decades of research about this – research that looks at what the marketing strategies of successful companies have in common and where they differ from those of lesser companies. As well as providing a yardstick by which to measure how good our strategy making processes are, Chapter 5 also provides a clear picture of what we are trying to achieve at the end of our planning.

Chapter 6 sets out to understand how companies, good and bad, go about making their marketing strategy in real life. It isn't by following a textbook, or by any other single process in fact. In reality, marketing strategy is made by a complex mixture of processes, both explicit and implicit. More to the point, every company has its own peculiar mixture, a hybrid of rational and non-rational processes that is shaped by its culture and external influences. Chapter 6 aims to create an understanding of marketing-strategy making as explicit processes that are broader than just textbook planning and more subtle than rational. In doing so, it equips us to think about marketing-strategy making in a more sophisticated way.

Chapter 7 explores the effectiveness of different ways of making marketing strategy, based on observations of companies that make strong and weak strategies. It describes how strong strategies can emerge from virtually any hybrid process, and how exactly the same process, in a different organization, can lead to a fatally flawed strategy. The explanation lies in the way in which the hybrid process fits or clashes with its context. Both the conditions in the marketplace and the prevailing organizational culture interact with the process, either facilitating it or hindering it. In short, what works is what fits, and a strong strategy comes from fitting the strategy process to its context. In uncovering this phenomenon we move from seeking a prescriptive panacea process for making marketing strategy towards the goal of creating our own company-specific, hybrid process.

In Chapter 8, we look at how great companies exemplify the idea of 'what works is what fits'. We consider what sort of hybrid process fits with what type of market environment, and how aspects of organizational culture hinder or support each type of hybrid. Further, we look at how companies gradually lose their fit, so that changes in the market and the inertia of company culture gradually erode a company's ability to make strong strategy. Finally, Chapter 8 gathers together the findings of Part 2 to create a process for achieving fit and therefore strong strategy. In doing so, it makes clear how the complexities of marketing-strategy making can be harnessed to create real organizational strength.

Chapter 5

We know what a strong marketing strategy looks like

Happy families are all alike; every unhappy family is unhappy in its own way.
(Leo Tolstoy, *Anna Karenina*)

Introduction

In Part 1 of this book, we took a helicopter trip over the years of research and millions of words that have been written about strategic marketing planning. We concluded that strategic marketing planning is a weak technology, not because it is ineffective when used, but because it is hard to use in practice. Real marketers, working in unsupportive company cultures and in turbulent markets, find that it does not work for them. As a result, it is mostly unused or abused.

We need to find a way not of replacing strategic marketing planning (which would be throwing the proverbial baby out with the bathwater), but of developing it to be usable in practice. The problem facing us resolves into a simple question: How can we adapt strategic marketing planning to make strong marketing strategies in the real world?

As the old saying goes, if you don't know where you're going, any road will take you there. If we want to get to a strong marketing strategy, we need first of all to agree on what a strong strategy looks like and, especially, how it differs from a weak one. This is easier said than done, since both 'marketing' and 'strategy' are words that have been used so loosely as to lose much of their original meaning. For many, 'marketing' is synonymous with 'promotion' and 'strategy' with 'important'.

Clearly, strategic marketing planning is about more than making the important promotional decisions. These might, and indeed usually are, part of the decision set that flows from marketing strategy, but they are not marketing strategy. To be clear about where we are heading we need to do two things: define marketing strategy and differentiate strong from weak. Fortunately this has already been done, albeit this valuable knowledge being widely dispersed and heavily camouflaged in the marketing and strategy literature. The aim of this chapter is to consolidate this knowledge in a way that is useful to the practising marketer.

Application point: What do your colleagues call a marketing strategy?

Marketing is not the only business process that is poorly understood by those outside its home department. The detail of many business processes is a mystery to many managers who need only its outputs and do not execute the process themselves. How much does the average marketer know about the outbound logistics process? Where strategic marketing planning differs from other processes is that it is particularly dependent on the buy-in and cooperation of functions other than marketing. This means that their lack of understanding becomes important.

Before you move on to the next section, it will benefit you to consider a few simple questions:

- How do your non-marketing colleagues define marketing strategy?
- Is it confined to promotion, or do they see it as wider than that?
- To the extent that marketing strategy impinges upon their roles, do they see the marketing strategy as central to their work, or merely a way to sell what the company makes?

Understanding the answers to these questions is an important part of making marketing happen in your organization.

What is marketing strategy?

Let's start with defining marketing strategy. A good definition of anything has four important properties:

1. It includes all cases of the object; our definition must be applicable to all marketing strategies.
2. It excludes cases that are not the object; it allows us to differentiate from other things that we might confuse with marketing strategy, such as marketing objectives and marketing tactics.
3. It describes the object; it helps us to understand what a marketing strategy is and recognize it when we set it.
4. It is non-circular; it doesn't depend on another definition such as 'marketing strategy is the output of the marketing plan' and 'marketing planning is the process of making marketing strategies'.

There are many definitions of marketing strategy in the literature, but most of them don't meet these criteria. Often they confuse marketing strategy content (what it is we are trying to make) with process (how we make it), and define the process but not the content. Like a cookery book without a photograph, such definitions leave practitioners wondering if, having followed all the steps, the end result is as intended, or whether they have gone horribly wrong at some stage. Alternatively, the definitions are very broad, including all of the objectives that lead to and tactics that flow from marketing strategy. Such broad definitions don't help the practitioner focus on what is to be achieved, and make it difficult to compare strong and weak marketing strategies.

To define marketing strategy, we need first of all to be clear about what strategy is, and then refine it into marketing strategy, as distinct from other kinds of strategy. From all the conflicting and sometimes contradictory attempts to define strategy, two management thinkers stand pre-eminent.

Michael Porter, as late as 1996, still felt it necessary to write a paper called *What is Strategy?* (Porter, 1996). This is really quite a seminal paper in defining and characterizing strategy, but the key point is that he defined it as a set of activities undertaken by the company.

At the same time, Henry Mintzberg was describing strategy as a 'sustained pattern of resource allocation' (Mintzberg, 1996). Since, in any organization, activity requires resource allocation, it's easy to draw these two perspectives together. We can think of strategy as that set of management decisions about where to allocate resources to enable our activity – in plain English, where we will spend the money. Of course, the money is spent to achieve the organization's objectives, such as creating shareholder value, but it is still a spending decision.

Thinking of strategy as resource allocation decisions is a useful perspective. Later, we'll discuss how it allows us to differentiate between strong and weak strategies. Before that, however, it's useful in allowing us to differentiate between different levels and types of strategy. Think of your company as a huge pyramid of resource allocation (i.e. spending) decisions. At the very top is corporate strategy, which can be thought of as the 'which industry will I spend my money in?' decision.

The corporate strategy decision is usually driven, of course, by which industry will create the greatest return on investment, when adjusted for risk. However, considerations like business cycles, synergy and risk management are also important. In conglomerates, this decision is explicit and aided by techniques of portfolio analysis, which formalize the process of spending choices. In single industry companies, the decision has already been made at some time in the past and is now implicit.

Whether explicit or implicit, the corporate strategy decision results in an amount of money and other resources being handed to a group of managers who are told to achieve the organization's objectives in that industry. Simply put, that group of managers and the organization they lead comprise a strategic business unit. Within the constraints imposed by corporate strategy, they are a self-contained unit. Business unit strategy therefore flows from corporate strategy, which itself flows from the investment strategy of the company's backers.

Business unit strategy can be thought of as 'which areas of the business will I spend the money on?' and, of course, is driven by the need to achieve the business unit objectives. At first, this seems like a bewildering set of choices to make, but in fact the choices are quite limited. A good way to think of it is in terms of the value chain – that chain of activities that the company does to make its outputs more valuable than its inputs. At a detailed level, there are hundreds or thousands of separate activities that a company does, from sourcing materials, people and finance to servicing products and customers after the sale. This is, of course, for a manufacturing company, but the same idea applies to all other organizations, including services, which take in one thing and deliver another. At a strategic level, these many activities can be grouped into three main subdivisions of the value chain. In other words, all companies basically do three things:

1. *We invent things.* These can be products, or services or some hybrid of both. They can be original or derivative, but in either case some value has been added in thinking them up. This is the product development part of the value chain.
2. *We make things.* This is the whole process of turning the ideas and concepts created in product development into a usable product and putting it into the hands of the customer. Because it involves inbound and outbound logistics as well as actual manufacture or service delivery, it is called supply chain management.
3. *We sell things.* This is the process of finding and understanding customers, selling to them and repeating the process continually. It includes the whole gamut of sales and marketing activity, but is appropriately known as customer relationship management.

In recent years, the term 'customer relationship management' has been hijacked by the IT industry and used to describe the systems that enable this process. Don't confuse the enabler with this part of the value chain.

This is a simplification, of course, but a useful one. Sometimes it's hard to put one or other department or function into one of the three categories, and some activities overlap (a sales and service engineer, for instance), but the general idea that there are three principal components to what we do is useful when it comes to understanding business unit strategy.

This idea comes from the work of Treacy and Wiersema (1995), although it has its roots in Michael Porter's concept of generic strategies (Porter, 1980). Each of the three stages creates value (i.e. makes the product or service more valuable to the customer) whilst consuming resources in the process. Competitive advantage for the business unit comes from creating more value and/or consuming fewer resources than the competition.

Incidentally, Treacy and Wiersema attribute differences in the competitiveness of different businesses to the way in which they differentially allocate resources between these three sets of activities. They argue that success is associated with focusing resources on one and giving the other two just enough to be 'good enough' for the customer. Their work certainly suggests that this is one contributory factor to strong strategy, but not the only one. In any event, strategy at business unit level can be usefully thought of as the pattern of resource allocation (business school speak for spending) between the product development, supply chain management and customer relationship management parts of the company. When resources are focused on one or other of these three processes, Treacy and Wiersema called the resultant strategy types product excellence, operational excellence and customer intimacy, respectively. Note, however, that they can be seen as derivatives of Porter's three generic strategies. Porter also recommended focusing spend, although he referred to it as trade-off, so we can see Treacy and Wiersema's work and Porter's work as being closely related. They both advocate focusing spend so as to create superior value in one part of the value chain, whilst providing satisfactory but not superior value in the other areas.

Business unit strategy clearly provides the context for subsequent strategy allocation decisions. The important thing from the marketers' point of view is that business unit strategy nestles within corporate level decisions, while functional strategies, such as marketing strategies, sit within the context of business unit strategies.

This discussion of strategy as a pattern of spending decisions, and of corporate leading to business unit leading to functional level strategies, is a useful perspective for marketers. It helps us to see where we sit in the scheme of things. In reality, marketing strategy doesn't involve choices of which industry to focus on, or even whether to be a cost-leader, product-excellent or customer-intimate company within that industry. Marketers only really get involved in those decisions when they reach board level, or at least business unit management team level, and even then their predecessors' resource allocations have often made their decision for them. Functional strategies, like marketing, usually begin within the context of already agreed business unit strategies, and are about the allocation of resources within that context.

Application point: What is the context of your marketing strategy?

Marketing strategies do not operate in a vacuum. They are part of a web of resource allocation decisions, connected vertically to corporate and business unit strategies and horizontally to other functional strategies. Understanding this context is important to making marketing happen in your organization.

- What is the context of your marketing strategy?
- What is the broad pattern of resource allocation decisions (implicit and explicit) that define your corporate and business unit strategies?

- How does this constrain and direct the various functional strategies within the business unit strategy?

Before we move on to look at exactly what marketing strategy is, it might be helpful to think about other functional strategies. On the assumption that most readers of this book are marketers, they are likely to be able to be more dispassionate, and therefore more open to learning, about other managers' strategies than their own.

Take, for instance, the strategy of the research and development department. It involves allocating resources to product development so as to create as much value as possible. It may be a lot of resources (in the case of a product-excellence company) or a little (in the case of an operationally-excellent or customer-intimate company), but the overall goal is the same. Depending on the situation, the research director (who may be a procurement or licensing director in firms that do not see themselves as research led) may choose to do all of the research in-house, contract some of it out (to clinical research organizations, for instance, in pharmaceuticals) or, in effect, contract all of it out and license products in.

If choosing the in-house option, the research may be any combination of focused or diversified, cooperative or not, *ab initio* or derivative. Whatever the management decisions made, it is a strategy, a pattern of allocation of resources (and therefore of activity), in this case the research resources.

Similarly, the operations or manufacturing strategy may be to build from scratch or to assemble, or somewhere in between. It could be flexible and relatively expensive cellular manufacturing, or fixed and highly efficient production lines. It could be capital or labour intensive. These are all resource allocation (i.e. spending on activity) choices that represent the manufacturing or supply chain strategy.

Whatever the function, a set of decisions is made about the best way of allocating resources – that is, the way that creates most value per unit of resource employed. In each case, the decisions are made to match the internal situation (the organization's competencies, constraints, resources) to the external situation (suppliers, competitors, the economic environment) in such a way as to achieve the objectives of the organization. These are, of course, simplified pictures, but they serve to give the picture of what happens as we proceed down the resource allocation pyramid from corporate to business unit to functional.

So what is the marketing equivalent of these? What choices does the marketing strategist make that are equivalent to where to do research or how to manufacture? The answer is confused by the unusual position of marketing in the organization and the fact that most marketing departments have two roles, the strategic and the operational. The strategic role is driving the decision about what to offer the customer. Marketers are then responsible for communicating the offer, an operational role. In some cases the strategic 'what to offer the customer' decision is made in the boardroom, but that's just a matter of structures and labels. Strategic marketers decide what offer to make to the market, even if the strategic marketing role doesn't reside in the marketing department and they are called something else.

Compare this to, say, manufacturing or finance. Here, they make what they are told to make, or count what they are told to count. They have an operational role but don't really get involved in the strategic 'what to offer the customer' decision until they are part of the executive team. Similarly, operational level marketers have to promote the proposition the strategy has designated. They make decisions about how to allocate promotional resource, but this is an operational decision, not really the marketing strategy.

So marketing strategy involves first deciding what to offer the customer – or, to put it more succinctly, the value proposition. However, this decision is mostly about allocating resources internally. That is, spending our money within the company to create superior product performance, for instance, or premium service or lower price or whatever is the basis of our value proposition. This is the decision that is equivalent to how to manufacture or where to do R&D.

Unlike those other functional strategies, however, marketing strategy also has an external resource allocation decision. In addition to what to offer the customer, the marketing strategy also involves the choice of allocating resources externally, across the market. Some companies skip this decision and sell to everyone who may buy their product or service, but most strategies involve some targeting within the market. This targeting is the second component of marketing strategy, the second half of the resource allocation decision made by strategic marketers.

Marketing strategy, therefore, has two sub-components: what to offer and who to offer it to. This isn't a new idea. Peter Drucker seems to have originated it, as he did so many of the underlying concepts of modern management (Drucker, 1974: 96):

> One has to decide in which segment of the market, with what product, what services, what values, one should be the leader.

The same idea is echoed by all the more thoughtful writers in the field. Henry Mintzberg summarized it as below, this time emphasizing that positive decisions about what to offer and who to offer it to imply concomitant negative choices (Mintzberg, 2000):

> Whom should I target as customers and who should I not? What should I offer these customers and what should I not? How can I do this in the most efficient way?

'What to offer and who to offer it to' has a certain ring to it, but it doesn't emphasize enough that these can be a complex set of management decisions. Even a simple company can have several propositions and several targets. In that case, the marketing strategy would consist of several statements of proposition/target pairs. Also, however pithy, 'what to offer and who to offer it to' wouldn't stand up to the four tests of a good definition discussed earlier in this chapter. We can, however, meet those tests quite easily by rephrasing the definition of a marketing strategy. For the remainder of this book, marketing strategy will be defined as follows:

> Marketing strategy is that set of management decisions which identify which customers will be targeted and what value propositions will be made to them.

Note that this is entirely consistent with Mintzberg's perspective on strategy as a sustained pattern of resource allocation, and with Porter's view as of it as a set of activities. Further, it fits with Drucker's position and passes the four tests of a definition. No marketing strategies would be excluded from this; and commonly mistaken entities such as marketing objectives and promotional plans are excluded from this definition. It successfully describes the content, not the process, of marketing strategy so that we know a marketing strategy when we see one. Finally, this definition doesn't depend on how the strategy was made or any other circular argument.

Application point: What is your marketing strategy?

The preceding section synthesizes the views of several leading authorities to create a workable definition of marketing strategy. Whilst the precise wording used is not critical, it is important that an organization's marketing strategy defines both target customers and the offer made to them. It is also important that these decisions are made explicit and are agreed by the management team.

- What is your marketing strategy?
- Who are your target customers and who are not?
- What value propositions do you make to them and what do you not?
- How explicit and widely understood is this strategy in your management team?

We've now defined what marketing strategy really is. Our next task is to learn to differentiate strong marketing strategies from weak ones.

What does a strong marketing strategy look like?

Clearly, a definitive picture of what a strong marketing strategy looks like, and how it differs from a weak one, would be helpful. Apart from anything else, it would act like a quality control check for our strategy making process. More to the point, it would allow us to test the strategy before it was implemented. Developing marketing strategy can be expensive, in terms of both research and management time, but it is cheap in comparison to the implementation phase, which includes both the direct and opportunity costs of the strategy. If there is a point in time at which it makes most sense to sanity-check our marketing strategy, it is at the point between making it and implementing it, before we bet the company and our careers on it. There are, however, two problems with defining good and bad strategies; rather, there are two ways of approaching the problem that would not be useful for marketing practitioners.

The first is a contingency approach, as the academics would call it. A contingency approach would involve describing a strong marketing strategy but with a conditional rider: X would be a strong strategy in situation A, Y would be good in situation B, Z in C and so on. For a practitioner, this would leave the problem of diagnosing which situation the company was in. Even if such diagnoses were straightforward and the contingency approach identified many situation/strategy matches, the likelihood is that most companies would straddle situations and the practitioner would need to hybridize the two or more optimal strategies for an appropriate mixture of situations. This wouldn't be a usable tool. What is needed is a set of quality criteria that are independent of context – that is, a set of characteristics that identify a marketing strategy as strong, independent of what industry or sector the strategy is for.

The second is an overly simplistic definition of what we mean by 'strong'. This is an issue that often confuses pragmatic and tightly focused practitioners. Intuitively, a strong strategy is one that creates good results, such as shareholder value. It follows that all we need do is look at the strategies of successful companies and benchmark ourselves against them. Hence the strategies of companies that are performing well become the standard by which we assess our strategy making process and our pre-implementation check. It's a nice idea, but it's fundamentally flawed in two respects: our definition of 'successful', and the role of marketing strategy in creating that success.

First, assessing companies' success by any one criterion or set of criteria ignores the fact that different companies have different objectives. One company may be acting as a cash cow, generating cash for its owners; another may be deliberately absorbing shareholder funds whilst it builds a long-term, competitive position. In truth, the only criterion that can be used to assess the success of a company is how it performs against its owners' goals. Externally imposed measurement criteria ignore this and make 'success' a poor marker for identifying strong strategies.

Secondly, strategy strength and success, by any measure, are not directly related. Between a company deciding to allocate resources in a certain way and the results that company achieves are innumerable other factors: the strategy may not be implemented; the competitive environment may change; the market may grow or shrink unexpectedly; luck may get in the way. Simply to correlate success with strategy strength is naïve. This point has already been discussed in more detail in Chapter 2.

What is needed, therefore, is a set of criteria and parameters for marketing strategy strength that passes two pragmatic tests:

1. They can be applied irrespective of context, so that a strategy that passes the tests is likely to succeed whatever market industry or sector the company is in.
2. They are derived not simply by copying the strategies of firms that are currently making great profits, but from long-term studies of many firms with a variety of objectives.

This need for a rigorous and context-independent way of assessing the strength of a marketing strategy was one of the core practical difficulties in implementing the research that this book is based upon. At the beginning of the work, there was no definitive, agreed way of telling if a strategy was strong or not.

Ironically, and as is often true in the academic literature, there were lots of useful part-answers, in which eminent researchers gave partial or incomplete views, based on extensive studies and using broad measures of success (for a more detailed review of these studies, see Smith, 2003). These part-answers were remarkable for the degree to which they overlapped. After allowing for semantic differences, there was little fundamental disagreement between the researchers involved in this field. Taken together, their views reflected the sort of consensus that typically emerges when a research field is stable and well understood. Part of the contribution of the research underlying this book was to draw that consensus together and develop it into a practical tool for objectively assessing the strength of a marketing strategy.

In short, the previous work, stretching back over twenty years and including the work of most of the leading authorities in marketing, identified ten characteristics of marketing strategy that could be used as diagnostics to differentiate strong strategies from weak ones.

These characteristics, which were labelled marketing strategy diagnostics because of their ability to test strategies, are summarized in Table 5.1 and detailed in the following paragraphs. Their breadth helps us to understand why it is so difficult to make strong marketing strategies and so easy to make weak ones. Success in marketing strategy means getting all or at least most of the characteristics right, whilst a weak strategy can by attributed to any one or two characteristics. When, as in this research, the criteria were used to examine the marketing strategies of real companies, the parallels with the Tolstoy quotation at the beginning of this chapter became clear. Strong

Table 5.1 Strategy diagnostics

Strategy diagnostic	*Description*
Target definition	Strong strategies target real segments (see section on HDAV segments in main text); weak strategies target descriptor groups.
Proposition specificity	Strong strategies make propositions that are specific to the segment; weak strategies 'tweak' a standardized offer for each segment.
SWOT alignment	Strong strategies leverage strengths and minimize or negate weaknesses; weak strategies fail to understand strengths and weaknesses.
Future anticipation	Strong strategies anticipate future changes in the market; weak strategies fail to do so.
Uniqueness	Strong strategies target different customers and make different propositions from the competition; weak strategies offer the same thing to the same people.
Synergy creation	Strong strategies enable either internal or external synergy or both; weak strategies do not take account of synergies.
Tactical guidance	Strong strategies make the corresponding tactics obvious; weak strategies give room for diffusion and dithering.
Objective proportionality	Strong strategies are proportional to the marketing objective in both target size and proposition strength; weak strategies are neither.
Risk management	Strong strategies reduce market risk and implementation risk to acceptable levels; weak strategies take no account of risk levels.
Resourcing	Strong strategies are resourced in relation to the target market and the nature of the proposition; weak strategies are not resourced adequately.

marketing strategies are all alike; every weak marketing strategy is weak in its own way.

Marketing strategy diagnostics: the differences between strong and weak marketing strategies

As introduced above, twenty years of work by previous researchers has revealed a set of ten common characteristics shared by marketing strategies that work. This work ranges across many industries and types of company. It looks at success in many ways, and does all it can to remove distorting effects of anomalous market conditions.

Chapter 12 considers how strategy diagnostics are used by marketing practitioners. It is this knowledge which is distilled in the following sections. As with any rules, they are, to use the proverb, meant for the guidance of wise men and the rigid obeisance of fools. That said, they provide us with the set of context-independent, process-independent and objective criteria we need if we are to improve our strategy making.

Readers may find their understanding of these improved if, before reading on, they write down the marketing strategy of their own business, or one they have knowledge of, in the form of 'target and proposition' defined above.

Strong strategies define real segments as targets

Almost any marketing strategy can be expressed in terms that define which customers are to be targeted. Perhaps the single most important differentiator between weak and strong marketing strategies, however, lies in the way those targets are defined. Simply put, strong strategies use real segments whilst weaker ones do not. Some explanation of that is necessary, of course. Real segments differ from false segments in that they pass four important tests, as laid down by Philip Kotler (1991). According to his seminal tome, real segments are groups of people that are homogeneous, distinct, accessible and viable (HDAV, if acronyms are useful to you).

Homogeneous means that every member of the group has similar needs and motivations as regards this product or service. They will therefore react similarly in response to any given proposition. Note that this does not mean that these people are all identical or similar in age, gender, company size, industry or whatever; it simply means that they want the same proposition as everyone else in the segment.

Distinct means that, as regards this product or service, members of the group have different needs and motivations from members of other segments. They will therefore react differently from those other segments in response to any given proposition. They may be identical or similar to members of other segments in terms of age, company size or other descriptors, but still differ in needs, wants and motivations. 'Distinct' simply means they want a different proposition from people in other segments.

Homogeneous and distinct are really the two fundamental tests for real segments. However, Kotler also applied two other tests (accessible and viable), which are less definitive but more pragmatically oriented and help to characterize real segments and effective strategies.

Accessible means that the segment can be identified and reached through whatever research and communication mechanisms are available. There is little point in a segment, however homogeneous and distinct, which can't be reached.

Viable means that the needs of the segment can be met at a profit, or in some other way that is practically feasible. There is little point in a segment, even a homogeneous, distinct, accessible one, which is so small or so transient as to not be worth the effort.

So, strong marketing strategies are those that define real segments (HDAV segments) as their target. These tests may seem to the practitioner either theoretical or obvious, depending on your perspective, but the importance of real segments as a strategy diagnostic really becomes clear when we consider what most companies call segmentation and what happens when false segments are used.

Most companies define their targets in terms of something they refer to as a segment. However, strategies that use real HDAV segments are very rare. Instead, it is common to refer to targets in terms of products or services (the package holiday market, for instance, or pensions, or immunoassay analysers) or in terms of channels (the retail banking market, or the out-of-town v. high street store segments). It takes little analysis so see that these targets are neither homogeneous nor distinct, even if they are accessible and viable.

When pushed, companies will often reveal an implicit level of segmentation within their explicit targeting. Hence financial services are often aimed at 'high net worth individuals', pharmaceuticals at 'opinion leaders' and information technology at MNCs (multinational corporations) or SMEs (small to medium enterprises). This is better, since these definitions might imply greater homogeneity and distinctiveness than the earlier labels.

However, these implicit targeting definitions are still sub-optimal; they are still not as good as the best strategies in two important respects. First, they are still a long way from homogeneity and distinctiveness. Not all high net worth individuals are driven by the same motivations; not all MNCs make their IT investment decisions on the same basis. Secondly, the implicit targeting is not company wide; it arises from fine tuning at the point of customer contact (for instance, by the sales team). This means, in effect, that only those resources that are at the discretion of the sales team (or other point of contact functions) are targeted at the implicit segment and other resources (product development say, or logistics or research) continue to work on the old, explicit targets which are not real and do not pass the HDAV tests. These poorly defined target segments can be thought of as false segments, since they are often mistaken for real segments.

What are the implications of using false segments as the 'target' part of the marketing strategy definition? What happens as a result of such targeting? The answer to those questions relates back to our definitions of homogeneous and distinct, as described earlier.

In real segments, every customer reacts the same way to a proposition (remember, by proposition we mean the whole package of product, service, image, price – everything). So, a proposition seen as valuable by one customer in a real segment will be seen as valuable to all customers in that segment. By contrast, false segments are not homogeneous and actually may consist of many real segments. Think, for instance, of the 'family car market' and how that splits up into real segments defined by the many varying needs of different families. As a result, a proposition aimed at a false segment will only ever appeal to (i.e. be valued by) some of the members of the false segment, those that happen to be in the real segment for which the proposition is valuable. By definition, all the other members of this heterogeneous false segment will be turned off, to some degree, by the proposition. Cars that appeal to status-conscious families may not appeal to those who see themselves as pragmatic and cost-conscious, for instance, even if the proposition is acceptable in all other respects.

This may seem academic, but is one of those aspects of academic research that is very useful in practice. It is evidenced in the Pareto effect seen in the sales figures of many companies with poor target definition. These companies wonder why, say, 80 per cent of sales come from 20 per cent of customers. The answer lies in true segmentation. The 20 per cent or so who are providing the sales (i.e. are accepting the proposition) are doing so because the proposition is right for them; they are a real segment within the poorly defined, false segment, target market. The other 80 per cent of customers represent various different real segments for which that proposition is not valuable and is not accepted. The small amount of product they buy is incidental, the marketing equivalent of collateral damage and, if costs could be allocated accurately, probably unprofitable.

In short, using false segments as targets leads to wasted resources and poorer results.

By contrast, companies with strong strategies use real, HDAV segments as company-wide, explicit targets. Almost invariably, these are defined not in terms of descriptors but in terms of the customers' psychology and motivations. Examples of this include *The Economist* magazine. Published by Pearson Group, this weekly newspaper competes in the fiercely aggressive market where the rare currency is less money and more executive reading time. As such, it could define its market as business people, or even senior managers with an interest in current affairs. However, it goes further in targeting business people with a certain mindset, one characterized by ambition, self-confidence and perhaps a smattering of paranoia. Its proposition includes its wide spread of reporting and the depth and integrity of its analysis. As is often the case, the proposition is nicely summarized in its advertising slogans, such as 'If you've got a point, sharpen it'.

In a similar vein, BMW's competitive position is based on a corresponding motivational segmentation. In a market where 'segments' are traditionally defined by product characteristics, BMW aims tightly not just at executive drivers, but at those who are motivated by the emotional pleasure of driving and the aspirational needs that are associated with that. Again, the simplicity of the advertising slogan belies the sophistication of the targeting: 'the ultimate driving machine'.

In both examples, the targeting is much closer to the ideal of HDAV tested, real segments than their closest competitors and, whilst the chosen examples are consumer (for ease of understanding), similar examples exist in less well-known business-to-business markets. Exel in logistics, Ethicon (a division of Johnson and Johnson) in medical devices and Zurich in corporate insurance all define their targets in this rigorous and effective way. By contrast, the relative weakness of UK retail chains like WH Smith, Boots and Sainsbury's can all be attributed in part to their inability to grasp and implement real segment targeting (*Marketing Week*, 21 October 2004).

In Chapter 12 we will consider how great companies apply segmentation, but for now it is important to grasp the key lesson of this point. Strong strategies define targets as real segments, not false ones.

Application point: Are your targets real segments?

The preceding section described how strong strategies define targets that are real segments and not simply descriptor groups.

Without well-defined targets, resources are poorly targeted and value propositions are weaker than they can be.

- Who are your target customers?
- To what extent are they real segments that meet the tests of a real segment?
- Do you instead target groups that are actually heterogeneous or indistinct?
- What are the implications of this for your resource allocation and your value proposition?
- How might you improve the situation?

Strong strategies make segment-specific propositions

Even in weak marketing strategies, the target (or targets) is usually explicitly stated, albeit in a way (as discussed above) that is sub-optimal and reduces effectiveness. By contrast, many marketing strategies are much less explicit about what constitutes their proposition or propositions. Often, the proposition is not espoused simply because it seems obvious – we sell pensions, or hydrophilic polyurethanes, or intranets. In other words, many companies see their proposition as synonymous with their product or service. However, strong strategies can be seen to contain propositions that are not only broader than the product or service but also have three characteristic properties in that they are:

1. *Consistent.* Strong strategies make propositions that are completely consistent with the needs, wants and motivational drivers that define the segment. Propositions aimed at convenience seekers are convenient; those aimed at technical buyers are technically sophisticated, and so on.
2. *Complete.* Strong strategies make propositions which consider all elements of the marketing mix, the famous four or seven Ps (see Chapter 1). They recognize that the customer, in both business and consumer markets, makes a holistic decision based on how the whole offering meets their needs in their entirety, not in the chunked-up way implied by the salesperson's detail aid.
3. *Coherent.* Strong strategies make propositions in which all elements of the marketing mix reinforce the proposition in a coherent

way, conveying a coherent message. They recognize that individual management decisions about elements of the proposition, such as pricing and promotion, can easily result in an overall proposition that contains internal contradictions, which the customer sees as inconsistent and unbelievable.

It can be seen from this that strong propositions are closely linked to using real segments as targets. It's practically impossible for a proposition to be consistent with all the varying needs of a heterogeneous, false segment, since those needs are, by definition, varied and often contradictory. A complete proposition usually requires the sort of customer insight associated with understanding real segments; false segmentation often leads to incoherency in the proposition and an internally incoherent mix. Some examples of when and how this occurs serve to make the point.

A lack of consistency with the needs of the customer is exemplified by some phone operators. A high value, non-price sensitive and relatively discerning customer is presented with a proposition, via advertising, customer service and product features, geared to an undemanding, price sensitive occasional user. The proposition does not match his or her needs and is not perceived as giving value. Readers can probably also supply their own examples of this situation. Although inertia and similarly weak competitors may mean the customer stays, these are not factors the phone company would wish to rely on. By contrast, a retail financial services provider such as the Royal Bank of Scotland's One Account conveys a proposition consistent with the needs of their target segment (complex, flexible needs, high degree of control, seeking overall value, not simply low price).

The source of proposition inconsistency with customer needs seems to lie in the internal conflict that most organizations face between efficiency and effectiveness. Almost all organizations are, to some degree, driven by the need to optimize efficiency and reduce operating costs. For most, this equates to standardizing the proposition as much as possible and reducing the number of variables that generate costs. Henry Ford and the Tin Lizzy are the archetype of this.

By contrast, most organizations attempt to target more than one segment, which implies variation in the proposition and concomitant inefficiency. Since internal drivers are usually more tangible than external, efficiency wins over effectiveness and a more or less standardized proposition is delivered to the marketplace, which is inconsistent with at least some of the segment's needs – perhaps all of them. The typical work-around is to tweak the proposition at the point of delivery, standardizing core elements of the proposition (the product or core service) and adapting the outer elements of the proposition (the pricing, the channel choice, the extended service) to be adapted. Whilst this is better than Henry Ford's approach, it is still sub-optimal and a long way from delivering a proposition that is specific to the needs, wants and motivations by which the segment is defined.

Incompleteness of the proposition is arguably the least common of the weaknesses found in propositions, especially in mature markets. However, its impact on strategy strength is sufficiently important to make it worth understanding. An incomplete proposition is one in which one or more important elements of the mix are absent, either wholly or completely.

Examples of this are found in retail outlets where the people component of the mix – staff to advise and support customers – is thin on the ground beyond even what is reasonable at busy times. By contrast, effective retailing operations such as the UK's John Lewis chain seem to recognize the availability of trained staff as integral to the proposition. This availability of people is quite distinct from cases where stores compete on price or product and the customer may expect lower levels of service. It seems representative of a collective forgetting of part of the proposition. Other examples might be significant industrial purchases where substantiating promotional material is absent, or where distribution density is so low as to make the product hard to access.

The origins of proposition incompleteness seem to lie in the natural tendency of an organization to become product focused. In such organizations, so much collective thought goes into ensuring that the product is right (in pricing, performance standard, range, or all three) that the other parts of the proposition are simply forgotten, or at least not given the amount of management attention required. This problem seems to be more prevalent in organizations that are culturally more product-oriented and less common in those in which the cultural orientation is around service. This latter group of companies, exemplified by John Lewis with their unusual partnership governance model, is more able to see the proposition as a multifaceted whole, not a product with things going on around it.

Lack of coherence in propositions is a remarkably common feature, and is an especially good differentiator between strong and weak strategies. Incoherent propositions are those in which different components of the proposition actually seem to contradict each other.

An example of this, current in the UK, is Stella Artois, a brand of lager beer that competes in a crowded market both in retail outlets and in bars and cafés. In trying to differentiate itself, the brand tries to leverage its heritage and 'foreign' brand values with the strap line 'reassuringly expensive'. In itself, this seems a sensible approach designed to create a premium position. Any visit to a retail outlet, however, will find huge piles of Stella Artois, crudely labelled with a card marked with a special low-price offer. Such is the vigour with which Stella Artois' regional merchandisers have implemented this point-of-sale tactic that this price-led approach is at least as visible as the extensive and expensive television advertising supporting the contradictory premium position. It may be possible to argue the strength of either the premium or cost-led approaches, but the net result leaves the customer believing neither the claim of quality nor that of low price.

Compare this with the Malmaison hotel chain, attempting a 'stylish' proposition aimed at those seeking something different from the anonymity of large chain hotels. Their proposition includes location, pricing, interior design and the millions of little details, from soap to menus, that define a hotel. Whether you personally like or dislike the Malmaison proposition, its coherence is nonetheless evident in everything from its name to its choice of décor.

Lack of coherence in a value proposition derives from the management structures of the organization. Coherent propositions arise from strong, directed leadership with a clear vision of what the proposition is and who it is aimed at.

There are many organizations which, for good reasons, choose more fragmented or incremental approaches to management. Whatever the advantages of those management approaches, they make it much harder to create proposition coherence and easier to create internal contradictions. Individual functions, with individual sub-objectives, rarely create value propositions that are internally coherent unless internal communication and control is exceptionally strong.

So the second defining characteristic of a strong strategy is that the propositions are truly segment-specific and not simply standardized then tweaked. Segment-specific propositions are consistent, complete and coherent – and quite rare.

Application point: How segment-specific are your value propositions?

The specificity of a value proposition to a target segment is the basis of its attractiveness to that segment and therefore your competitive strength. To the extent that the value proposition is made generally to a number of different segments, the degree of customer preference created is reduced.

- How specific to each target are your value propositions?
- Does each segment see a distinct marketing mix, or do you offer essentially the same thing to all target segments?
- Is the specificity built into the proposition, or do you rely on minor adjustment of the value proposition at the point of delivery?

Strong strategies are SWOT aligned

The first and fundamental characteristics of a strong marketing strategy are targets that are real segments and propositions specific to those segments. Strategies with these properties alone will be streets ahead of most competitors in most markets. However, the marketing-strategy making process is not simply a matter of addressing and understanding customer needs. It also involves doing so in a way that matches the organization to the market well. To caricature, it would be perfectly possible to choose a strategy with real segments and specific propositions, but that is the best strategy for another company and not ours.

In short, the marketing strategy is the way that an organization aligns itself to the market, leveraging its strengths and either negating or minimizing its weaknesses.

The established tool for ensuring that the company is optimally aligned to the market is the oft quoted but less understood SWOT analysis (Strengths, Weaknesses, Opportunities, Threats). Thanks to its memorable mnemonic and its superficial simplicity, this technique has become perhaps the most well recalled strategic management tool. Sadly, the level of recall seems to bear little relation to knowledge of its application, and use of SWOT analysis often degenerates into nothing more than a subjective listing of good and bad points about the market situation. So extensive is this misuse of what is a valuable tool that Terry Hill and Roy Westbrook thought it merited a product recall! (Hill and Westbrook, 1997). Notwithstanding abuse of the tool, however, SWOT alignment is so important a characteristic of strong strategy that it deserves better understanding.

Simply put, a SWOT-aligned marketing strategy is one in which the choice of targets and propositions allows the organization to do two things:

1. Make good use of its strengths by applying them to market opportunities.
2. Either negate or minimize its weaknesses so that they are less vulnerable to market threats.

It is notoriously difficult to achieve real self-knowledge, to see ourselves as we are seen by others. This is equally true of organizations. Management teams can identify external threats with relative ease and market opportunities with confusing frequency, perhaps because they are signalled by external stimuli. However, identifying and understanding internal strengths and weaknesses is a flaw in much marketing-strategy making.

Again, the issue of academically siloed knowledge has a bearing on this because the great body of work on strategy theory is often neglected by marketers, as marketing is often disparaged as atheoretical (i.e. lacking a sound theoretical base) by strategists. In fact, there is a currently topical area of strategy research that has a direct and useful bearing on how marketers make their strategies SWOT aligned. A body of research known as resource dependency has illuminated how strong strategies are those that understand and allow for the resources that organizations have at their disposal. This area is wide-ranging, and the interested reader is directed to the work of Jay Barney (2001b) for further background.

The most relevant aspect of resource-dependency theory for marketers is the criteria it provides for understanding what strength and weakness is with a degree of objectivity that is difficult for practitioners immersed in the necessary detail of their business. Indeed, the reader may find it useful, before reading further, to write down their current perceptions of their organization's strengths and weaknesses and to test them against these criteria.

The resource-dependency view sees strengths and weaknesses as either tangible or intangible assets, ranging from brand to relationships, technology to financial depth, processes to knowledge. Almost anything about the organization can be a strength or weakness, but relatively few things are. This makes it all the more important to identify them and align them to the market opportunities or threats.

The mistake made by many organizations is to use internal reference points. From this perspective, strengths are the things we are best at compared to everything else we do, and weaknesses are the things we are worst at compared to our other activities. If we make good products expensively, for instance, products are called a strength and our costs a weakness. This perspective is fundamentally flawed, of course, because the customer doesn't know or care about our internal comparisons. They compare us with our competitors. In fact, our strengths are what we are better at than our competitors and our weaknesses *vice versa*.

The tool from resource-dependency research that helps us to filter our internally perceived strengths and find the real ones goes by the mnemonic VRIO (Barney, 2001a) as described below. In this scheme, genuine strengths are:

1. *Valuable.* They matter in a positive way to the customer to an extent that they will change buying behaviour. Product performance, relationships, distribution density and price are all examples of things that customers may, but do not necessarily, perceive as valuable.
2. *Rare.* They are relatively uncommon or unique in the eyes of the customer. No matter how good the strength is in absolute terms, if all your competitors have it, it ceases to be a strength.
3. *Inimitable.* The strength is difficult, costly or impossible to copy or substitute for. Price, for instance, is notoriously easy to copy, whilst brands are protectable. Factors that are valuable and rare but are easily copied may provide a temporary strength, but not one on which sustainable competitive advantage can be built.
4. *Organizationally aligned.* The organization is capable of using those strengths. A novel technology may be valuable, rare and inimitable, but if the organization is constructed so as not to be able to deliver it (for instance, with inappropriate sales teams or distribution channels), it will remain a potential but unrealized strength.

These four points help us to understand the importance and difficulty of SWOT alignment for our marketing strategy. They are further illustrated by the equivalent characteristics of weaknesses (Smith, 1999). In this scheme, genuine weaknesses are:

1. *Meaningful.* The customer cares about them. An antiquated IT structure might be a huge irritation to the management team, but it is a matter of supreme indifference to customers unless it implies some meaningful difference in the proposition delivered – such as incorrect invoicing.

2. *Uncommon.* The weakness is not shared by major competitors. An advertising budget or sales team that is less than desired by the marketing director, or a lack in product features, is not a weakness if each is comparable to the competition.

3. *Difficult to correct.* The weakness is not easily corrected by the company. Short-term, occasional out-of-stock problems are an irritation but are not a weakness if they can be corrected by good customer service and using couriers.

4. *Uncompensated.* The weakness is not rendered irrelevant by other factors. High costs are not a weakness if they result in greatly superior utility; similarly, merely adequate service is not a weakness if it can be offset by low prices.

Using these criteria for what real strengths and weaknesses are helps us to differentiate between real strengths and weaknesses on the one hand and simple unevenness in our resources and competencies on the other. Simply put, strong marketing strategies identify real strengths and weaknesses and ensure that the choice of target segment and proposition use the strengths and negate or minimize the weaknesses.

For instance, BMW's 'ultimate driving machine' strategy, discussed earlier in this chapter, uses their brand, engineering and design strengths. It also minimizes their relatively high cost base by selecting a less price sensitive market. With a completely different strategy, easyJet uses its low-cost base model and negates its weaknesses of airport bases and customer service levels, which are unimportant to its chosen, price-sensitive customer segment.

By contrast, the frozen food chain Iceland completely ignored the concept of SWOT alignment when it attempted to reposition. Long established and successful at offering low-cost frozen food to a relatively price-sensitive target, Iceland attempted to respond to the competitive pressures resulting from the consolidation of the UK retail food market. It identified that, paradoxically, it had quite a strong record concerning the avoidance of food additives and genetically modified food. It attempted to leverage this by targeting a relatively upmarket 'green' segment of customers who sought to avoid additives etc. The attempt failed horribly and the company has now reverted to something close to its former strategy. Simply put, this 'strength' was not of interest to its existing customers, and the organizational alignment (especially its store design, location and brand) meant that it was unable to access those customers that might have wanted additive-free, more 'wholesome' food (Kleinman, 2004).

How good managers look for SWOT alignment of marketing strategy is discussed in Part 3 of this book. In the meantime, however, it is important to realize that aligning real strengths and weaknesses to the market is a fundamental characteristic of strong marketing strategies.

> **Application point: How SWOT aligned is your strategy?**
>
> The preceding section described the importance of objectively assessing your organization's strengths and weaknesses and effectively aligning them to external market opportunities and threats. Failure to do so wastes the organization's distinctive competencies and exposes its weaknesses.
>
> - How SWOT aligned is your strategy?
> - How well do you understand your strengths and weaknesses?
> - What key issues arise when you align these to the external market?
> - To what extent does your choice of target customers and value propositions leverage your strengths and minimize your weaknesses?

Strong marketing strategies anticipate the future

A picture of what we want to emerge from our marketing-strategy making process is now emerging. We need a marketing strategy that states who we are targeting and with what. We need real segments addressed by specific propositions, the combination of which uses the organization's real strengths and minimizes or negates its weaknesses.

There are, however, two contexts in which a marketing strategy can meet all three of the preceding criteria and still be flawed, as well as five other factors that contribute to the strength of marketing strategies in a less obvious way. The first of these is that the strategy may be perfect for today's conditions, but undermined by changes in the market. Strong strategies anticipate the market and choose targets and propositions accordingly. Weak strategies either ignore market changes or, foolishly, attempt to change the market to fit with the strategy.

To anticipate the future, strong strategies need to anticipate the separate or combined effects of changes in the three spheres of the market environment: customers, competitors and channels. Most companies spend considerable effort in monitoring these areas, but the indicators of change (customer demands, competitive offerings, channel capabilities) are all lag indicators as opposed to lead indicators. By the time we pick up on what is happening in the market, we are already behind and have to change quickly (perhaps more quickly than our organization is capable of) to catch up.

As described in Chapter 3, there is a lot of evidence that formal planning processes struggle to keep up with turbulent markets. The most current live example of this is Kodak. Despite (or perhaps because of) its dominant positioning in imaging technology, current indications are that it has been placed at a disadvantage by the rapid development of digital imaging (*The Economist*, 30 December 2004). Compare this to the relatively nimble way with which GKN has responded to the changes in the car components market, despite the consolidation in the industry and the way that their customers' habits changed (Owen, 2004).

To understand better how strong strategies anticipate market changes, we need to understand the sort of market changes that can undermine a marketing strategy. As indicated above, these fall into three categories:

1. *Customer changes.* These are changes in the nature of real segments in the market and the distribution of customers between them. An example of this is the large 'middle market' segment, upon which Marks and Spencer depended, and the fragmentation of it, to which the company subsequently failed to respond.
2. *Competitive changes.* These are changes in the targeting and propositions of competitors, but also in the indirect competitive forces implied by Porters' Five Forces (Porter, 1980). An example of this is the entry of major retailers into financial services, a market previously dominated by generalist retail banks (*Marketwatch: Financial Services*, 2004).
3. *Channel changes.* These are changes in the existence and capabilities of channels by which the proposition is communicated and/or delivered to the targets. The obvious example here is the impact of web-based channels on many markets, from books to housing to packaging, all of which have seen a degree of 'disintermediation' and 'reintermediation' (Smith and Manna, 2004).

Strong marketing strategies are characterized by the way in which they anticipate these market changes. The usual tool used for this in formal planning processes is SLEPT analysis, also variously named PEST, STEP or PESTLE, all of which are acronyms for the combination of macroenvironmental (social, legal, economic, political, technical and environmental) factors that impact on the market. As with SWOT analysis, these tools for anticipating market change have been more honoured in the breach than in the observance, and frequently result in mere listings of obvious factors. Such travesties of analysis provide little information for anticipating market change by choice of target or proposition. By contrast, strong marketing strategies are usually created by strategy making processes that have successfully done three things:

1. Identified the macroenvironment factors that are changing significantly from amongst the mass of insignificant changes that clutter the organization's 'radar screen'.
2. Understood the consequences of the macroenvironmental changes so as to interpolate the likely implications of those changes for the market.
3. Combined the multiple implications of macroenvironmental change into a manageable number of significant changes.

The obvious difficulty in doing these three things well helps us to understand why failure to anticipate market changes is one of the most common weaknesses in marketing strategies. The earlier examples illustrate this and contrast well with Xerox, which seems effectively to have anticipated the implications of the information revolution and repositioned itself from a copier company to a documentation management company. This required changes to both targeting and propositions, which is all the more admirable given the market-dominant position from which they began that journey (Mulcahy, 2004).

As with the other characteristic of a strong marketing strategy, the concepts of anticipating the future will be developed later in this book. For now, it is important to understand that failure to anticipate market changes may have no impact on the performance of a marketing strategy at all, if it operates in a static market. The increasing rarity of such stable market conditions, however, implies the increasing importance of this particular strategy diagnostic.

Application point: Does your marketing strategy anticipate the future?

The preceding section described how strong marketing strategies anticipate changes in the market and align the organization to future, rather than past, opportunities and threats. They do this by identifying effectively the implications of macroenvironmental factors (for instance, by SLEPT analysis) and how they will impact on customers, channels and competitors.

- How well does your marketing strategy anticipate the future?
- To what extent, if any, does it predict changes in market segmentation, competitive forces and channel structure?
- Does your process gather and interpret information about SLEPT factors and use them to estimate trends in the market?

Strong marketing strategies are unique

Failure to anticipate the future market is the first major way in which a SWOT-aligned marketing strategy with real segments and specific propositions can still fail. The second is the degree of uniqueness of the strategy. In other words, marketing strategies are more effective when the choice of targets and propositions is different from that made by the competition. Similarly, they are less effective when we offer the same thing to the same people as our competitors do. In our research, the concept of strategy uniqueness was notably difficult to grasp for those organizations with weaker strategies. Typically, two polarized responses were evoked; they either claimed 'our strategy is already unique' or that 'strategy uniqueness is impossible'.

In companies that claimed strategy uniqueness, this claim was supported by the evidence in only a few cases. Most often, the targeting was exactly the same as that of the competition, driven by traditional industry structures and sources of market data. In many markets, for instance, the market research supply is dominated by one or two companies, and the way those information suppliers choose to structure the market defines the segmentation used by the whole industry sector. Further, identical targeting was compounded by very similar propositions. Although all companies can detail the differences between their proposition and the competition in terms of product features, closer examination revealed very little substantive difference in the product or service offered. To paraphrase one respondent, 'On reflection, despite our claims of differentiation, we offer the same thing to the same people in the same way (as the competitor)'.

Those companies that saw strategy uniqueness as impossible were fewer, but similarly blinded by lack of perspective. With some justification, these companies would point out that the choice of customers is defined by the market, and to have a truly unique proposition was a rare and very fortunate circumstance, usually attributed to successful product development. With the market defining one half of the strategy and technical limitations defining the other, these companies saw strategy uniqueness as a hypothetical idea. Pragmatically, they saw competitive advantage as arising from better tactical implementation of the same strategy used by their competitors.

Although taking seemingly opposite views, companies that saw strategy uniqueness as either impossible or already in place actually shared a common view – namely that strategy differences arose from one source: differences in the core product. By contrast, those companies that had created relatively unique marketing strategies used some combination of three sources of strategy uniqueness:

1. *Core product uniqueness.* Whilst this could apply to either a product or service, in practice it was more common in technologically based product markets, especially those at an embryonic stage in which the intellectual property was more easily defendable. An example is Olympus' use of Osyris electronic tagging technology for patient management in hospitals.
2. *Extended product uniqueness.* This was found in more mature markets and in services where core product uniqueness was more difficult to sustain. It involved creating proposition uniqueness by the innovative development of the extended product, including service and related activities. An example of this is the way in which Jungheinrich is attempting to differentiate itself in the market for forklift trucks. With decreasing differences between the trucks themselves, the way in which the trucks are provided and maintained has become their point of strategy uniqueness, protected by organizational competencies rather than intellectual property rights.
3. *Target definition uniqueness.* This was found in the most mature of markets, where both core and extended product uniqueness had been eroded by competitors. It involved creating and using a better understanding of segmentation within the traditional market definition, and using that to devise unique targeting and propositions. An example of this is NatWest, a UK retail bank that seems to have identified a need for 'traditional' banking services. The corresponding real segment, emerging as a reaction to competitors' cost-cutting, has become their target, and they have changed their proposition to reflect that. In this case, strategy uniqueness in

both targeting and proposition is protected by proprietary market knowledge, management skills and the brand.

In the absence of strategy uniqueness, performance is more related to market inertia and organizational mass than strategy design. Market share changes little from the *status quo* and settles to levels proportional to how much advertising, or how many sales representatives or distribution partners, each competitor employs. Since all of these cost each company about the same, no real differential value is created. Ultimately, in the context of a publicly owned company, none of the competitors is creating superior shareholder value. Markets in which strategy uniqueness is low are liable to commoditization and a downward spiral of returns.

When a relatively unique strategy is developed, however, market share changes disproportionately to mass and spend. Companies win share in proportion to the value of their proposition to their target segment, and relative to the size of the target segment. Companies with relatively unique strategies often remark that they don't have any 'real' competition, in the sense that no one is offering the same thing, or going after the same customers. In such cases, the driver of growth is not winning overall market share, but migrating customers from one (non-target) segment into the target segment. Within the target segment, the unique strategy company will usually have a dominant, almost monopolistic, share. An example of this is Bravissimo, a 'clicks and bricks' retailer of lingerie for women who seek both femininity and fashion but in larger sizes.

Strategy uniqueness is the last of the five 'first-tier' differentiators of strong and weak marketing strategy. How practitioners use the concept of strategy uniqueness is considered in Chapter 12, but for now it is important to assimilate the logic of this research finding. Weak marketing strategies define the same targets and offer the same propositions as the competition. Strong strategies redefine the market segmentation, target within that, and offer substantially different propositions. As with all the strategy tests, strategy uniqueness is relatively unusual and it is this that makes it a source of competitive advantage.

The remaining five strategy diagnostics all emerged from our research in the same way as did the former five. They were not as strongly evidenced as the first-tier five, but this should not be equated to lack of importance. In fact, each of the following can be as important as any of the first-tier five. However, whilst the first-tier five strategy tests appeared to be important in all cases, the second-tier five appeared to be important only in some of the cases studied. They would appear to be significant only in certain organizational and market contexts, as described below. We should not, therefore, relegate them to minor factors, but selectively consider which of them are important in our organizational and market context.

Application point: How unique is your marketing strategy?

As described above, strong marketing strategies differ, either in their targeting or their proposition or both, from those of the competition. In so doing, they effectively side-step direct competition and reduce competitive intensity. Weak strategies compete head-on and depend on resource advantages.

- How unique is your marketing strategy?
- Is the basis on which you segment the market different from the competition?
- Do you target the same or different segments?
- Are your value propositions significantly different, or are they identical at all but a detailed level?

Strong marketing strategies create synergies

In some of the strongest marketing strategies, the targets and propositions chosen interacted in a positive manner. That is to say that two or more sets of targets and propositions chosen reinforced each other, so that the company was more effective than two separate companies attacking the same targets with the same propositions separately. Of course we call this phenomenon synergy, but as with other terms in strategy it is used more often than it is really understood. For a deeper understanding of synergy, the reader is directed to the work of Michael Goold and Andrew Campbell, two senior academics from Ashridge Management School (Goold and Campbell, 2000), but, in short, marketing strategy can enable or disable two types of synergy:

1. *Internal synergy.* The advantage arises from the fact that propositions can be made either better or cheaper together than they can apart. Typically, examples of this are companies that can effectively serve a segment by adaptation of a proposition originally aimed at another segment. The conversion of civilian airliners into military

transports is one simple illustration of this. Perhaps more impressive is the way in which Renault has attacked several disparate segments with propositions that are all based on the same basic design (the Megane). By sharing development, manufacturing, procurement and service assets, Renault gains economies of scale. This amounts to greater efficiency than if they had attacked segments that could not share these resources.

Of course, Renault is not alone in doing this and the car market is not unique in this approach. Nor is internal synergy always the domain of manufacturing firms. Spinning off knowledge and expertise into several segments is the business model of many service and retail companies, and is another example of internal synergy. Whichever internal asset is employed, internal synergy is the most common form of synergy attributable to choice of target and proposition. Arguably, it is the least valuable in that its benefits are limited to the finite cost savings possible.

2. *External synergy.* The advantage arises from the fact that targets interact positively in some way. This is often seen in technical markets and, superficially very different, fashion markets. Small segments that lead opinion can be difficult to penetrate and unprofitable, especially if they are 'promiscuous' and switch brand frequently. Despite this, companies target them because of the influence they have on other, more intrinsically valuable segments.

The influence of one segment on another is not always in this innovator-to-follower direction. Staying with the example of the car market, Mercedes seems to have unlocked a source of external synergy with the A Class. Small and inexpensive, by Mercedes standards, the A Class seems to be targeted at a 'second car segment' of those who currently drive a large Mercedes as a first car. The communication of the brand values from, for instance, spouse to spouse seems to have helped Mercedes penetrate this competitive segment when its costs and well-engineered reputation might otherwise have hindered it. The converse of external synergy is possible too, of course. Some have argued that the difficulty of Rover in maintaining a premium brand reputation was related to its 'stretching' the brand as far as the Metro – a small, cheap super-mini. In this case, the cheaper segment interacted negatively with the more upmarket segments targeted with larger Rovers.

Internal and external synergies are not mutually exclusive, and strong strategies try to realize both simultaneously. The lesson to learn from synergistic companies is that they seem to look for synergies, rather than stumble across them. For those companies, synergy plays a large part in the narrowing down of strategy options.

Synergy is not always an important denominator of strong strategy. In markets where segments do not interact significantly or where costs cannot easily be shared, synergy is a relatively unimportant factor. However, markets where synergy is not a significant feature of strong strategy are few and far between.

Application point: How synergistic is your marketing strategy?

Whilst not universally important, the synergy created by choice of target segments and choice of value propositions can significantly multiply the relative strength of your organization. Failure to realize internal or external synergies is effectively wasting resources.

- Does your marketing strategy create synergy?
- Is the choice of target market or the choice of value propositions made with synergism in mind?
- What is the mechanism of any synergy?
- Is it based on the interaction of customers or of your own assets and resources?

Strong marketing strategies make tactics obvious

Although many of the characteristics of a strong marketing strategy were theoretically based and then tested by observation, one test emerged inductively from the multiple observations of the researchers. In many organizations the critically limited resource is management time, and inefficient use of it is a significant threat to the company's goals. When comparing the usage patterns of this crucial asset between companies with strong and weak marketing strategies, two distinct groupings can be observed:

1. Those companies in which the strategy allows a very high degree of freedom in the low-level decisions that represent the implementation of strategy. In these cases, small but important decisions about all elements of the marketing mix (product, price, promotion, place (distribution), people, process and physical evidence) were open to wide interpretation by the junior managers responsible for them. This had two consequences: diffusion and dithering. Diffusion

resulted from multiple small decisions made inconsistently, each one blurring the original sharp focus of the strategy and weakening it. Dithering resulted from the multiple units of management time allocated to the small decisions, magnified by company bureaucracy and politics, and resulted in the wastage of important management time. In both cases, the latitude allowed by the strategy hindered rather than helped implementation.

2. Those companies in which the strategy allows relatively little freedom in the low-level decisions that represent the implementation of strategy. This is not to be confused with an autocratic culture. In these companies, the strategy simply precluded many of the options associated with the small but important decisions about all elements of the marketing mix. In effect, the clearly communicated and well-understood choice of targets and propositions meant that many decisions (about product design, pricing, channel or media, for instance) were, to quote one manager, 'no-brainers'. The dithering and diffusion created by high degrees of freedom were obviated by the choice of targets and propositions in this group. As a result, myriad small decisions were faster, more consistent and less consuming of management time. In this way, the marketing strategy definition, combined with the clarity of its communication, aided its implementation.

An important point to grasp here is that the two groups were not defined by level of control or autocracy. Autocratic companies were as vulnerable to dithering and diffusion as democratic ones. The latter situation of fewer, simpler, faster and less time-consuming decisions resulted from targeting real segments and defining complete, coherent and consistent propositions. Together, these effectively reduced many implementation decisions to a choice of one option. For instance, Apple's strategy in the PC market involved targeting segments characterized by individuality and a degree of iconoclasm. Accordingly, its broad marketing mix decisions included a high-specification but stylish product, premium pricing, some channel specialization and so on. At the detailed implementation level, invisible to outside observers, this greatly restricted many management choices, kept the strategy focused and made implementation faster and more efficient.

Making tactics obvious is a derivative strategy test, in that it arises when companies meet the real segment and specific proposition tests. However, the clarity with which dithering and diffusion can be observed makes this a useful test for strategy strength. It is especially important in situations where there would otherwise be lots of tactical options, such as in media choice, or pricing structures. It is less important when the situation naturally limits the tactical options in any case. However, a plethora of implementation choices for most marketers makes tactical guidance a very important feature of many strong marketing strategies.

Application point: Does your strategy make tactics obvious?

As described in the preceding section, strong marketing strategies improve marketing efficiency by reducing the time and indirect costs associated with designing tactical programmes. This happens when well-defined segments and segment specific value propositions make the required design of the marketing mix quite clear.

- To what extent does your marketing strategy direct your choice of tactics?
- Is the segment definition such that it guides decisions about pricing, product design, promotion and distribution?
- Equally, does the prioritization of segments make it clear which tactics would not be appropriate?

Strong marketing strategies are proportionate to their objectives

The intent of most marketing strategies is to change the buying behaviour of the target customers in some way, to get them to start buying or using us. In some cases the objective is to maintain purchasing, but that is simply an objective of change compared to what will happen if we don't act. Whatever the detail of the objective, strong and weak strategies can be differentiated by the extent to which they compare in scale to the objective. In other words, strong strategies are those that are in proportion to the scale of the objective, whilst weak strategies are out of proportion. Both the target and the proposition components of a marketing strategy can be examined for proportionality.

In strong strategies, the total size of the target segment or segments is at least a little larger than the revenue objective. This may seem obvious, but some marketing objectives, set on a 'last year plus' basis or driven by abstract financial goals, are way beyond the total size of the target. Whilst large, even dominant, share is a reasonable goal, a revenue objective that is larger than the target market size is clearly naïve. Closely related to this, profit-level objectives need to be proportionate to the pricing and costs attainable in the target segment. This may also seem obvious, but our research revealed numerous cases of strategies in which pricing was set for a premium segment and costs for an economy segment, seemingly ignorant of the internal contradictions in this approach.

In strong strategies, the relative strength of the proposition is proportionate to the degree of change sought. Where the objective requires a large growth in share, or maintenance against a well-resourced competitor, the proposition must be significantly more consistent, complete and coherent than that of the major competitors, or else compensated for by promotional and other resources. By contrast, weaker marketing strategies expect shifts in share or substantial price premiums even though the proposition is not significantly more consistent, coherent or complete than that of the competition. Again, this may seem obvious, but the habit of companies to focus on the minor advantages of their proposition often leads them to lose perspective and see their offer as much stronger than it really is.

Strategy proportionality is especially important in situations where the objectives are particularly challenging, such as when large share growth is planned or entry into a new market against established competitors is required. This test is less relevant when the objective is incremental growth in existing markets. A good example of strategy proportionality being considered is the UK supermarket giant Tesco. Recognizing the practical limitations on further differentiating its main, edge-of-town supermarket proposition, their leader Terry Leahy has scaled down their growth targets for this segment in recent years. Instead, he has shifted the burden of growth onto smaller 'convenience' segments and international growth.

Application point: Is your marketing strategy proportionate to your objectives?

Strong marketing strategies target segments that are large enough to satisfy the organization's objectives with value propositions that are sufficiently compelling to create the change in customer behaviour implied by those objectives. By contrast, weak strategies appear unconnected to the marketing objectives.

- What is the connectivity between your marketing strategy and the objectives it is trying to achieve?
- Are the target segments sufficiently large to allow your financial goals without resorting to unrealistic segment share hopes?
- Are the value propositions sufficiently strong and compelling to create the customer preference and segment share you require?

Strong marketing strategies manage risk levels

Marketers traditionally think in terms of sales and profit, not the underlying business objective of return on investment and its more fundamental corollary, risk-adjusted returns. As a result, risk is often neglected by marketers and left in the domain of the finance department. It is a complex subject, and for a more detailed understanding the reader is referred to the work of Professor Keith Ward at Cranfield School of Management (Ward, 2003). In simple terms, strong strategies differ from weak strategies in the way they seek to minimize the risk associated with the strategy. For any given level of return on investment, of course, the lower-risk strategy leading to that return is the more desirable. Two types of risk are attributable to marketing strategy:

1. *Market risk,* which is the risk that the target (or targets) may not exist or is not as large as anticipated. The level of market risk is proportional to the level of novelty in the target and proposition. As summarized in the famous Ansoff Matrix (Ansoff, 1965), the more novel the combination of target market and proposition, the riskier it is. This does not imply that only current markets and propositions are low risk. Target markets not yet served by the company, but clearly served by other companies, are still regarded as low risk. Propositions not previously delivered by this company or to this target, but successfully delivered by another company or to another target, are similarly low risk. Market risk is really a measure of how much the strategy has to assume about the market size, as opposed to how much we know. Strong strategies are those that are based on fewer assumptions and more knowledge. Weaker strategies are those based on the reverse situation. Market risk can be reduced by evidence of the size of the market and acceptability of the proposition, be that direct (actual sales) or as a result of market research.
2. *Implementation risk,* which is the risk that the revenue or profit levels anticipated may not be achieved due to competitive response.

Implementation risk arises when the competitor improves its proposition in some way, such as by lowering price, improving the product or increasing promotional effort. The level of implementation risk is proportional to the likelihood that the strategy will evoke a competitive response during implementation. Hence a strategy that involves strongly attacking a segment seen as important by the competitor, or one in which the proposition is easily responded to (for instance, a low-price based proposition), is one of high-implementation risk. Conversely, a strategy that involves taking a small share from a number of segments of peripheral interest to the competition, and which is hard to respond to (for instance, being based on 'soft' factors like relationships or brand values), is one of low-implementation risk.

Examples of risk management are seen in the proliferation of line extensions over true new product development and a preference for increased penetration of an existing market, rather than entering wholly new markets. Examples of truly new propositions, like the Apple iPod, are so rare as to prove the rule, and even what initially looks like a new market development, such as Dell's entry into consumer electronics, is on closer examination relatively low risk, given the activity of other players in that market.

Risk management is an important criterion of strategy strength in two situations. The first is when the business unit is part of a portfolio of businesses and is supposed to constitute the low-risk part of the organization's portfolio. The second is when the success of the strategy is especially important, either because it is the organization's only strategy or because the organization is depending on this business to fund other businesses. In either case, the degree to which the choice of target and proposition reduces risk to acceptable levels is an important characteristic of strong marketing strategies.

Application point: How risky is your strategy?

As described above, strong strategies allow for risk and try to minimize it. Low-risk strategies involve a choice of target and proposition that has both low-market risk and low-implementation risk.

- What level of risk is inherent in your marketing strategy?
- Are the target segments well proven and well researched?
- Is the implementation risk minimized by avoiding competitive reaction or by avoiding propositions that provoke competitive response?

Strong marketing strategies are appropriately resourced

As defined at the beginning of this chapter, strategy is about resource allocation. From this perspective, competitive advantage arises from allocating resources more effectively than the competitor. However, there is an important implicit assumption in this view that the resources available for allocation are capable of delivering the strategy when they are properly allocated. This is not always the case. As with proportionality to marketing objectives, marketing strategies are often resourced simplistically, using internal reference points such as last year's budgets. In some cases this leads to a situation in which the resource allocated to a strategy is inadequate to allow its implementation, no matter how intelligently it is allocated. There are two dimensions along which the overall allocation of resource to marketing strategy may be tested:

1. *Proportional to the target.* The resource required to implement a marketing strategy is related to the target segment or segments in two ways. First, larger volume segments require more resources to support promotion, distribution, service and other volume-related aspects of the proposition. Secondly, the nature of the segment may dictate larger resources if it is difficult to access or requires especially expensive contact, such as a technical sales team. Strong strategies are those that are resourced in relation to the volume of target customers and the costliness of accessing and communicating with them.
2. *Proportional to the proposition.* The resource required to implement a marketing strategy is related to the proposition or propositions in two ways. The first is the nature of its differentiation from the competition; simply differentiated propositions (such as price-based differentiation or differentiation based on clearly novel technology) generally require fewer resources to support them than propositions differentiated in a complex way, such as by many small product differences or intangible service differences. The second is the extent of the proposition's difference from the competition; closely related propositions requiring little change in customer habits, and with low 'switching' costs, require fewer resources to support them than propositions which require the customer to change behaviour significantly.

Appropriate resourcing is an important test for marketing strategy in two situations. The first is when the combined resources of the competition are very large compared to the resources available to the strategy, such as when attacking a dominant incumbent. The second is when the resources used to develop the proposition (for instance, R&D) or make the proposition (for instance, manufacturing) have been limited, such as for those companies which adopt a 'customer-intimate' business unit strategy or have failed to create significant value (in relative performance or price).

A strong example of appropriate resourcing is that of AstraZeneca's launch of Nexium™ into the market for ulcer drugs. Faced with many large competitors, a premium price and less than desired efficacy differentiation from competitors, AstraZeneca supported the product with huge resources, including 2000 sales representatives in the USA alone. Frustratingly for authors, examples of poorly resourced marketing strategies are hard to find, since they tend to sink without a trace.

Application point: Is your marketing strategy appropriately resourced?

The resourcing of marketing strategy often derives from accounting processes and 'last year plus' allocations. As a result, the resource allocation is sometimes inadequate to the scale of the strategy. This can be seen in the size of the resources when compared to the target markets or the nature of the proposition, or both.

- To what extent is your resource allocation derived from the nature of the marketing strategy, or is it simply an accounting mechanism?
- Are the resources allowed sufficient to address all the customers in the target segment?
- Are those resources proportionate to the nature and strength of the overall value proposition planned?

Using strategy diagnostics

The characteristics of a strong marketing strategy described in this chapter have a very strong pedigree. They are developed from many years of research by the most respected researchers in strategy and marketing strategy (Smith, 2003). Building on the academic research described in this chapter, they are expressed in the form used by practitioners in Chapter 12. However, the reader should remember that we are dealing with marketing strategy here, a complex, multidimensional pattern of resource allocation. We should not expect to be able to reduce it to a simple checklist in which boxes replace thought. At best, the strategy diagnostics are a guide to the thinking of reflective practitioners. At worst, they can be used selectively to 'snapshot' a marketing strategy from one angle to give a misleading view.

The reader is encouraged to avoid the latter approach!

Power points

- Strategy is a sustained pattern of resource allocation.
- Marketing strategy is that set of resource allocation decisions about which customers to target and what to offer them.
- Strong marketing strategies have five key characteristics: they target real segments, make segment-specific propositions, are SWOT aligned, anticipate the future and are unique.
- Five other characteristics can also be used to differentiate strong from weak marketing strategies: strong strategies create synergy, make tactics obvious, are proportionate to the objectives, are appropriately resourced and manage risk.
- Marketing strategy is a complex thing; use the strategy diagnostics as a guide and not a simplistic checklist.

Reflection points for marketing practitioners

- What is your marketing strategy, when expressed as target(s) and propositions?
- How well does your marketing strategy pass the first five strategy diagnostic tests?
- Which of the second five strategy diagnostic tests are most applicable to your situation, and how well does your marketing strategy pass them?
- Based on your answers to the questions above, what steps might you take to improve your marketing strategy?

Chapter 6

We know that real companies are not entirely rational

Rationality is the recognition of the fact that nothing can alter the truth and nothing can take precedence over that act of perceiving it.

(Ayn Rand)

Humankind cannot stand very much reality.

(T. S. Eliot)

Introduction

We are on a mission here. We are trying to make ourselves better at a difficult but crucial business process called strategic marketing planning. It is difficult because it involves aligning one complex entity (our organization) to another (the market). This is not a simple problem. A heart transplant is a better analogy than a jigsaw puzzle. It is crucial for two reasons. First, from our marketing strategy flow most of our other business decisions and hence our organizational effectiveness. Secondly, although we can get help in marketing strategy, we must do it ourselves and, unlike most other management processes, we can't outsource the process.

In the course of our mission we've established a number of important things, resulting from decades of research into what differentiates those companies that are good at making marketing strategy from those that are not. First, we blew away the hype and the froth and recognized that strategic marketing planning is an agreed and stable process consisting of three fundamental steps (see Chapter 1). Secondly, we waded through the practical difficulties of correlating organizational effectiveness to anything and found that, although not a panacea, strategic marketing planning works (see Chapter 2). Thirdly, we dug beneath the worthy claims of practising marketers and found that, for the most part, companies don't do strategic marketing planning, at least in the way the textbooks prescribe (see Chapter 3). Then, in Chapter 4, we tried to understand this conundrum of intelligent managers neglecting a proven and important process. We concluded that there was little wrong with the basic science and concept, but that strategic marketing planning is a failed technology in the sense that its intended users are not able to use it.

We have not yet bottomed out what is going wrong, but it seems to be due to market conditions and organizational culture, or both. To summarize what we have found and connect it to the two telling quotations at the head of this chapter: rationality is important, but real organizations have trouble coping with it. That finding is useful, but it does not yet make us better at strategic marketing planning.

If we have not yet accomplished our mission, we have at least begun to ask the right questions. What does a strong strategy look like? What do real companies do when they try to make one? What works in real life?

In Chapter 5 we found that, despite the huge variation between different organizations and markets, we could discern common trends in what differentiated strong and weak strategies. Armed with that knowledge, we can explore what real companies do. This chapter, therefore, describes what real companies do from two perspectives:

1. How strong are the marketing strategies that companies make in practice?
2. What do they actually do that leads to those strategies?

In Chapter 7 we look at what kind of strategy making works in real life.

Weak marketing strategies are more common than strong

In the last chapter, we looked in some detail at what a good strategy looks like. We looked at examples of strengths and weaknesses in extant marketing strategies, and made comparisons between strong and weak strategies. It turns out that the specific traits that characterize a strong strategy can be identified through noting the common qualities that crop up over and again in successful strategies. Of course, this is not the same as suggesting that all companies should go after the same targets with the same propositions. Apart from anything else, this would contradict the need to be unique. Further, identical target and proposition choices cannot always be SWOT aligned since not all companies have the same strengths and weaknesses.

The strategy diagnostic tests discussed in Chapter 5 point to a series of properties we should aim for when we make marketing strategy. These tests emerge from years, in fact decades, of research studying different strategies and looking for common trends. Even if those researchers did not have a solid research base, they would still be credible. The strategy diagnostic tests ring true with our own experience. It seems obvious that we have to use our strengths, avoid head-on competition, anticipate change and create synergy. None of the tests is counter-intuitive, even if it does look hard (indeed, it *is* very difficult) to score highly on all of them simultaneously. Even that last point resonates. We should expect making a strong strategy to be difficult and making a perfect one almost impossible – but at least the strategy diagnostics help us by pointing us in the right direction. And we don't need to be perfect – this is the real business world, after all – we just need to be significantly better than the competition.

Of course, a strong strategy does not guarantee success, and success does not always indicate a strong strategy. Aside from the relativity factor (we might succeed or fail because of the weakness or strength of the competition rather than because of our own strategy), there are innumerable factors that get between strategy and end result. We might implement poorly, or what we implement might actually be a stronger strategy than we planned. Only the naïve manager thinks that what is done is identical to what he or she instructs.

We might succeed despite a weak marketing strategy if we are saved by the outputs of, for instance, our research and development strategy. If our product development process delivers something that is both patentable and vastly more attractive to customers than the competition, we can succeed despite poor targeting and wasting resources. Those instances are few, however, and are becoming fewer as markets mature and differentiation of the core product becomes more difficult.

We might be saved by the genius of our operations colleagues, who work out how to make our product or service cheaper or of better quality than the competition. This, again, is becoming increasingly difficult in a world of benchmarking and shared production facilities and suppliers.

Then there is just dumb luck – good or bad! It is impossible to plan for one's CEO standing up in front of television cameras and telling the world your product is 'crap', as happened to the Ratner's jewellery store chain. Nor can, for instance, a company always respond sufficiently to change, as New World Pasta found recently when the Atkins Diet suddenly undermined its core market. Conversely, manufacturers of airport security equipment would need to try hard to fail in a post-9/11 marketplace. Similarly, SSL, the troubled healthcare company, was very lucky when press scares about deep vein thrombosis sent sales of their elastic surgical stockings through the roof. Notwithstanding luck or the competition, we have to act within our own sphere of control, which means that we must try to make the best strategy we can. The strategy diagnostic tests tell us how near to that destination we are.

The strategy diagnostic tests, when compared with what companies actually do, tell us more than simply what to aim for. When used to look at the strategies of a sample of companies, they also give us an idea of the typical levels of strategy strength that are found in real companies. This examination of real marketing strategies tells us that many (perhaps most) companies create, in absolute terms, relatively weak strategies.

In the original research underpinning this book, no companies scored excellently against all of the strategy diagnostics. Even the best scored well against only some of the criteria, and these factors varied from company to company. Many companies scored poorly in comparison to most of the determinants of a strong strategy – in other words they had a pretty weak strategy by any standards. Since what we are trying to create is a strategy that is strong relative to other companies, these findings are useful. They help us to see where on the weak-to-strong spectrum we are, and therefore how much improvement is needed. A summary of these findings is shown in Table 6.1, which develops Table 5.1 from Chapter 5 and compares the best, typical and worst characteristics of the marketing strategies examined. In Chapter 12, we will consider how exemplary managers use the same principles to test their marketing strategy during development and before and during execution.

As the saying goes, all generalizations are wrong – including this one. The research for this book examined lots of strategies that varied from the awful to the excellent. Further, their awfulness or excellence was not along a single dimension but along the ten aspects represented by the strategy diagnostics. It follows that it is potentially misleading to say what a typical marketing strategy looks like. It risks being as misleading as describing a human being in three 'vital statistics'.

Notwithstanding that, it is possible to draw from the research a sort of median marketing strategy description that is not too distant on any dimension from the majority of marketing strategies examined. In simple but practically useful terms, we can say that most marketing strategies look like the stereotypical one described in the third column of Table 6.1.

In this typical case, targets are described in terms of descriptor groups, not as true segments sharing common needs. The value proposition is only superficially differentiated between different segments, and is mostly defined by what the company can make. The company's understanding of its strengths and weaknesses is subjective and shallow, so that such SWOT alignment as exists is that which is imposed on the company by the customers and the competitors. The market situation addressed by the strategy is that described by subjective assessment or market research, and as such is yesterday's market not tomorrow's. The choice of target and the nature of the value proposition is the same as that of the competition, clouded by minor and inconsequential product differences. Synergy is poorly understood, and occurs more by accident than design. Whatever merits the strategy has are diluted by the tactics going 'off message', by the objectives being disproportionate, the resources inadequate and the risk level unconsidered.

For this stereotypical company, success (if it occurs) comes despite, rather than because of, the marketing strategy. The marketers can thank their colleagues in operations, or in research, or their competitors, or market conditions, for their salvation. Their marketing-strategy making process is a source of competitive disadvantage rather than the opposite.

Table 6.1 The range of marketing strategy characterization in relation to the strategy diagnostic tests

Strategy diagnostic test	*Best case*	*Typical case*	*Worst case*
1. Target definition	Target markets are defined as needs based groups within already well-defined product based sectors.	Target markets are defined by descriptor group (e.g. size, usage rate).	Target markets are defined solely by a product or channel definition.
	These needs based segments are homogeneous, communicated widely within the company and used as the basis for market research, proposition development and organizational structure.	These groups are homogeneous as regards basic needs but heterogeneous as regards higher, differentiating, needs.	These groups are heterogeneous in terms of customer needs.
2. Proposition specificity	A core product proposition is clearly subdivided by variations in product design and, especially, in the extended product offering, such as service and support. Alternatively, target customers are allowed to 'tailor' propositions individually from a 'menu' of options. Where the organization cannot tailor the proposition alone, there is clear evidence of alliances or other means of enabling the tailored proposition.	There is superficial 'tweaking' of a fairly standard service or price according to potential, usually carried out at point of delivery.	The proposition is largely standard across the customer base, with no significant tailoring.

3. SWOT alignment	Both tangible and intangible strengths and weaknesses are clearly understood and, where possible, tested or substantiated.	Strengths and weaknesses are understood in a limited, often implicit, manner.	There is a clear misunderstanding of the nature of the organization's relative strengths and weaknesses. Such alignment as there is occurs only at point of delivery and then is often imposed on the company by customers and competitors.
	The choice of target segments is strongly driven by strengths and weaknesses so that strengths are leveraged and weaknesses are negated or reduced.	'Accidental' alignment is caused by *de facto* selection by customers in the context of better differentiated competitors.	
4. Future anticipation	The macroenvironmental drivers of the market are understood and deliberately monitored.	The more important macroenvironmental drivers are recognized and monitored in an informal manner.	The most important macroenvironmental drivers are not recognized, understood or monitored.
	The combined implications of trends in those drivers are resolved into opportunities or threats that the strategy addresses.	The implications of trends in the drivers are drawn, but only in a haphazard manner, and their impact on strategy design is small.	The strategy is designed largely in ignorance of the future trends in the market.
5. Uniqueness	Initial targeting, at product-sector level, is similar to that of the competition, but with sub-targeting on different motivational criteria.	Very similar explicit targeting and propositions to the competition.	Target description is identical to that of the competition and there is little proposition differentiation. Such differentiation as occurs is driven by 'market follower' or benchmarking activity, and is unsustainable.
	There are similar core product propositions, but with distinctly different augmented products.	To a limited extent, this is improved by targeting and proposition refinement, within narrow limits, at point of delivery.	

Table 6.1 *(Continued)*

Strategy diagnostic test	*Best case*	*Typical case*	*Worst case*
6. Synergy creation	The mechanisms of synergy are well understood by the organization. These may arise from internal factors such as shared assets, or external factors such as segment interaction.	The existence of some synergy is recognized, but the mechanisms of synergy are poorly understood by the organization.	The existence and mechanisms of synergy are barely recognized and not understood to any significant degree.
	The choice of target segments is deliberately made to realize these synergies.	The choice of target segments may accidentally realize synergies, but this is not a deliberate act.	The choice of target segments is not influenced by possibilities of synergy realization, although it may occur accidentally in asset utilization.
7. Tactical guidance	The choice of targets and broad value propositions makes the design of the marketing mix self evident. Only the detailed points of execution remain to be decided.	The choice of targets and propositions allows the 'ruling out' of some tactical options, but still allows significant room for the strategy to be 'blurred' during implementation.	Target segment heterogeneity is such that conflicting ideas of customer needs inform the design of the marketing mix.
	The detailed execution of the marketing mix is supported by a widespread understanding, both tacit and explicit, of the marketing strategy.	Understanding of the marketing strategy is restricted to senior levels, and the degree to which it therefore supports execution is limited.	As a result, the marketing strategy has little influence on the design of the marketing mix.
			Consequently, design and execution decisions for the marketing mix are carried out at a low level, resulting in conflicting and incoherent programmes.

8. Objective proportionality	The accessible size of the target segments, when allowing for customer inertia and competitive environment, is such that the revenue and profit targets are realistically achievable.	The accessible size of the target segments and the degree of differentiation of the value proposition, taken together, are small in relation to the marketing objectives.	The marketing objectives are not significantly considered in the choice of target markets or value proposition.
	The degree of differentiation of the value proposition is sufficient (relative to the competition) realistically to enable the required shift in customer preference.	The achievement of the marketing objectives, therefore, requires a very fortunate set of circumstances, such as weak competition and favourable customer reaction.	As a result, the accessible target size and value proposition are grossly disproportionate to the objectives. Usually the objectives are too high; rarely, they are too low.
9. Risk management	The marketing strategy emphasizes targets and value propositions in which the level of risk is the minimum compatible with the marketing objectives.	The marketing strategy does not fully exploit low risk opportunities before attempting growth in new segments and with new propositions.	The marketing strategy does not consider the level of risk involved and relies heavily upon growth in new segments and from value propositions, typically employing unproven strengths.
	This usually entails targeting segments that are already well penetrated, with value propositions based on current, well-proven strengths.	This usually entails a mixture of target segments and value propositions based on current and new strengths.	This usually entails a pattern of limited penetration in many segments, without dominant share in any.
10. Resourcing	The level of resourcing of the strategy is derived quantitatively from the size of the target segments and the nature of the intended value proposition.	The level of resourcing of the strategy is derived qualitatively from the size of the target segments and the nature of the intended value proposition.	The level of resourcing of the strategy is not linked to the size of the target segments and the nature of the intended value proposition.
	Typically, this entails a high level of concentration of resources with concomitant 'starvation' of non-target segments.	Typically, this entails some level of concentration of resources but with that concentration compromised by reluctance to withdraw resources from non-target segments.	Instead it is derived from a combination of past history and internal negotiation and constrained by short term financial considerations.

This may seem a pessimistic appraisal. It is, let us remember, a generalization. Many companies are better than this, and some are excellent. However, the picture painted in Table 6.1 and in the above pen-portrait is a reasonably accurate picture of what happens in many companies. If you are sceptical, think of most of your experiences as a customer. How many of them left you feeling as though you had received fantastic value and a great experience? These findings beg a question. What are companies doing to create such inadequate marketing strategies? We know from Chapter 1 that it is unlikely to be that strategic marketing planning has not yet had time to be assimilated, because the technique is long established and stable. We know, in any case, that companies that use strategic marketing planning seem to succeed, relative to those that don't, as discussed in Chapter 2. However, the research examined in Chapter 3 tells us that strategies of any kind are rarely the result of rational, logical, textbook planning.

We need to understand what is going on inside real companies. In other words, we need to shift our thinking from the prescriptive to the descriptive. Prescriptive thinking, as recorded in strategic marketing planning textbooks, tells us how the author thinks we should do it. Descriptive research, by comparison, offers no judgements about what to do, but limits itself to understanding and describing what real companies actually do when they try to make marketing strategy. As we have seen in Chapter 3, prescription is a poor description of reality. As the next section shows, the difference between prescription and description is illuminating, and in that light we see the beginnings of the accomplishment of our mission. When we look at what real companies do and find out what works in which cases, we will begin to understand what we should do in our own specific organizational and market context.

Application point: What are the weaknesses in your marketing strategy?

Very few marketing strategies are strong in all of the dimensions described in this section and in Chapter 5; similarly, very few are universally weak. Most can be improved significantly. Understanding the causes of weak marketing strategy is aided by understanding which are the weakest parts of it. Both strengths and weaknesses of marketing strategy are, of course, relative to other companies and especially competitors.

- Consider Table 6.1 in the context of your own marketing strategy and the discussion in Chapter 5.
- What are the principal strengths and weaknesses of your marketing strategy?
- At this stage, have you any thoughts on what has caused these?

Real companies are rational, visionary and incremental

As a species, humankind likes to think of itself as rational. With some justification, we view rationality as one of the reasons we are superior to other species and as being something that differentiates the wise from the foolish. Nowhere is this affection for rationality more obvious than in the espoused behaviour of organizations like commercial companies. In public, companies like to point to their rationality and the evidence on which their decisions are made. Phrases like 'facts are friendly' and 'what gets measured gets done' become part of the argot of business life. If companies really are as rational as they say they are, there ought to be very little difference between the rational prescription of the textbooks and the reality described by researchers who look at the strategy making behaviour of real companies. As we will see, the reality of description is both more complex and more valuable than the prescription of rationality.

Before looking at this, we need to make another very brief aside into the world of management research. Earlier in the book we talked about how academics are like cattle, grazing one field of research until they have exhausted the 'contribution to knowledge' upon which they are judged. The metaphor usefully describes not only how research moves on, but also how it is a kind of herd mentality. This 'herding' phenomenon, which becomes quite clear when one reads the research literature over the years, has another side effect too – the single-perspective researcher. Academics work in clusters (often geographically spread) united not only by an interest in a discipline (like marketing) or sub-discipline (like marketing planning) but also by their 'perspective', such as 'the role of organizational culture in marketing planning'. Usually, management researchers look at a management problem from a single perspective and try to understand the problem from that point of view.

For a practitioner reading the literature, this approach has pros and cons. On the plus side, the practitioner benefits from the fact that the researcher understands this aspect of management behaviour extremely well. Good academics have read virtually everything in their field from their perspective and thought about it carefully. On the down side, the perspectives are narrow, they almost never explain a management problem on their own and, taken out of context, they can look silly, simplistic or obvious. One memorable PhD presentation (anonymous, to protect the guilty) described five years of research and concluded that organizations with happy staff were better at customer retention than those with miserable employees. A 'contribution to knowledge' perhaps, but something a practitioner might have been happy to assume without proof.

To understand how companies really make marketing strategy, we need to walk around the problem and look it at from several different angles. A good place to start, therefore, is by considering each of these different academic perspectives and what they tell us individually. Then we can move on to what they tell us when taken as a whole. There have been various attempts to categorize the different perspectives on strategy making. The two best-researched and most comprehensive are by Henry Mintzberg (Mintzberg *et al.*, 1998) and Andy Bailey and Gerry Johnson (Bailey and Johnson, 1995).

These writers suggested that there are, respectively, ten and six different approaches to making strategy. However, there is an element here of academic hair-splitting. Mintzberg and his co-authors, for instance, have two successive chapters describing strategy making as first a formal process and secondly an analytical process. To the eye of the manager, he is talking about pretty much the same thing.

For practical purposes, there appear to be six ways that marketing strategy is made – or, more accurately, six ways of looking at the process. Each of these perspectives sees the core process of making marketing strategy (understanding the market, choosing the strategy, deciding the actions, as discussed in Chapter 1) as happening in different ways. As we will discuss later, the reality of business life is that companies combine these approaches into a complex hybrid marketing-strategy making process. However, to understand the hybrid and, later, work out what is best for our organization, we need to have some understanding of these different perspectives. These, based on Bailey and Johnson's work, are summarized in Table 6.2 and discussed below.

Making marketing strategy by formal planning

The reference point for the descriptive research into strategy making is the prescriptive approach; non-planning approaches to making strategy compare themselves to what the textbook says. We've already described (in Chapters 1 and 3) what the formal, rational approaches to strategic marketing planning involve. The authors of prescriptive textbooks took their ideas from the best practice they observed and assembled their findings into an 'ideal' planning process. Formal planning is characterized by data, process, and deliberate, explicit actions. Evidence of formal planning is provided by the use of tools and techniques, and the existence of a written marketing plan. From a formal planning perspective, understanding the market is based on explicitly analysing market information and reducing it to a manageable number of key issues. Choosing the strategy also uses tools like portfolio management to rationalize the choices. Deciding the actions flows from the strategy in a very deliberate way, and is explicit about actions, objectives and responsibilities.

Making marketing strategy by trial and error

Probably the first 'revisionist' view of how strategy is made came in the understanding of incrementalism. The seminal text in this area is by Lindblom (1959, 1979). Although both 'trial and error' and Lindblom's term 'muddling through' sound slightly pejorative, Lindblom saw this approach as positive and in some cases superior to the formalized planning that was the latest fad in the 1950s. The approach was better labelled by Brian Quinn (1980) as logical incrementalism, and was seen as an answer to one of the constraints on planning: uncertainty. The incrementalists observe that in the real world our information is often inaccurate and always incomplete, thus weakening the basis of formal planning. As an alternative they note that many real companies practise incrementalism, which involves different approaches to the three stages of making strategy. Understanding the market is limited to looking at those areas we know something about (usually small extensions to current knowledge) and drawing limited conclusions about the key issues. This informs a choice of target and proposition that is not too distant from the current strategy. Implementation actions are usually

Table 6.2 Six perspectives on marketing-strategy making processes

Perspective	*Understanding the market*	*Choosing a strategy*	*Deciding on actions*
Making marketing strategy by formal planning	Characterized by collecting data and using formal tools, this approach describes an explicit process that translates market knowledge into key issues for the business.	Characterized by deliberate comparison of different choices of target markets and value propositions in the context of explicit key issues. Often involving the use of portfolio management tools.	Characterized by the explicit cascading of actions that flow from the chosen strategy and the translation of those actions into plans which are often quantified and specifically assigned within the organization.
Making marketing strategy by trial and error	Characterized by limited experimentation and incremental learning, this approach describes a process that is only partly explicit and identifies key issues when they cause an activity to fail or succeed.	Characterized by deliberate or accidental attempts at different strategies, often on a limited scale. Successful attempts are developed whilst the unsuccessful are abandoned or modified.	Characterized by multiple, small, sometimes conflicting actions that are assigned in a pragmatic rather than formal manner. The action plan is continually revised to reflect the outcomes of earlier initiatives.
Making marketing strategy by political negotiation	Characterized by synthesizing the market knowledge of different powerful groups within the company, this approach describes a largely implicit process, in which the key issues are partly weighted by the power of the group postulating them.	Characterized by the influence of different political groups inside the organization, the selection of targets and propositions is often biased towards the internal situation rather than key issues in the market.	Characterized by compromise and arbitration, actions flow from the strategy as agreed by the stronger groups but are moderated by lesser political forces during implementation.

Making marketing strategy by organizational culture	Characterized by the persistence of long-established and unquestioned ways of doing things, this approach describes a mostly implicit but pervasive process in which the key issues are rarely made explicit but expressed in terms of habitual responses.	Characterized by an implicit inertia and habit in target markets and propositions, strategy selection is usually implicit and rarely different from previous patterns of resource allocation.	Characterized by unquestioned and habitual acceptance of actions that are sometimes explicit but rarely deliberate. Actions are frequently seen as the natural extension of past activity.
Making marketing strategy by enforced choice	Characterized by the existence of strong external forces on the organization, this approach describes a process that either implicitly or explicitly identifies the key issues which constrain the organization's strategic freedom.	Characterized by very limited options, the strategy selection is a minimal process involving the explication of that which is determined by the outside forces.	Characterized by limited room for variation or choice, actions are largely dictated by the situation and sometimes explicitly constrained by laws or regulation.
Making marketing strategy by leadership	Characterized by the dynamism and influence of a single person or small group, this approach describes an explicit but informal process, in which the key issues arise from the market understanding of the leadership group.	Characterized by relatively intuitive and simple decision-making processes and communicated by hierarchies, strategy choice typically does not involve those outside the leadership group.	Characterized by communication of broad strategy and objectives rather than detailed plans, actions are often decided at middle and junior levels within the resources and instructions flowing from the leadership.

carried out in small steps and their outcome determines whether those actions are developed, modified or abandoned. In this way, incremental strategy makers gradually extend their knowledge and strategy without taking large risks. Clearly, incrementalism is a realistic and useful additional perspective on strategy making. It seems to complement the idea of planning without contradicting it.

Making marketing strategy by political negotiation

Not too distant from the incrementalists are the politicians: those who describe strategy making in terms of negotiation between powerful individuals or groups within an organization. This perspective has its roots in group psychology and the behavioural theory of the firm – ideas initiated by Cyert and March (1963). The basis of this perspective is that organizations are groups of human beings and, as such, they will be influenced by the political habits and instincts that are deeply embedded in our nature. This perspective has therefore been championed by organizational anthropologists like Andrew Pettigrew (Pettigrew, 1973). The political negotiation perspective sees managers as acting, at least to some degree, non-rationally, and driven by the interests either of the firm as they see it, or of their group or themselves as individuals. The usual lack of agreement between different power blocks in the company is reconciled by negotiation and arbitration, a process influenced by the relative power and interdependency of the players and by the structure of the organization (Pugh *et al.*, 1968; Hinings *et al.*, 1974; Hickson *et al.*, 1986). For marketing-strategy making in particular, this is well described by Paul Anderson (1982).

From a political perspective, understanding the market comes not from objective data but from information that is filtered and value-weighted by those who manage the data. The choice of strategy is not made purely against the criteria of the firm's objectives, but the criteria of those objectives as seen by powerful players and biased by their own objectives. Deciding the actions is not only a consequence of the strategy, but also of the current and hoped-for power of those implementing the actions.

As with incrementalism, political negotiation should not be taken as a critical term. In organizations where coordination of resources is vital (i.e. most organizations), politics is as necessary as it is inevitable. Once again, the perspective provides colour and shade to our understanding of strategic marketing planning without refuting the value of rationalism.

Making marketing strategy by organizational culture

Many authors have written about the way that organizational culture helps to form strategy. Shrivastava (1985), for example, sees culture acting as a kind of substitute for rationality and, as we discussed in Chapters 3 and 4, organizational culture is often seen as a barrier to planning processes. However, it cannot be assumed that strategies derived from the organizational culture are always weak. Barney (1986) reckoned that an organization's culture could be a source of advantage if it created value in the marketplace, if it was relatively rare or unique and was hard to imitate. Dunn *et al.* (1985) have identified certain cultural profiles, such as customer closeness, that correlate to organizational effectiveness.

While culture can, like other influences, help or hinder strategy making, it is fairly clear what happens in culturally based processes for making marketing strategy. Understanding the market comes less from analysis and more from the deeply held, often hidden assumptions about how the market works. The choice of strategy flows from these assumptions, and the target markets and value propositions are not deliberately chosen. Instead, they 'emerge' from the value, habits and traditions of the company. Similarly, the actions to implement the strategy develop almost unconsciously, directed by cultural artefacts like systems and structures. As with the other perspectives on how strategy is made in real companies, the cultural view does not contradict the others. Rather, it is one particular view of what is clearly a complex and multidimensional process. The cultural and other research perspectives help us to gain a deeper understanding of how strategy is made.

Making marketing strategy by enforced choice

The above perspectives on strategy making assume that the organization has freedom of choice. They take for granted that the company can choose to change its target markets and value propositions. However, some researchers (for instance, DiMaggio and Powell, 1983; Hannan and Freeman, 1984) have pointed out that this freedom is often constrained, often severely so. These constraints can be internal in origin, stemming from organizational inertia and lack of resources. Alternatively, they can come from outside the organization. This is the case when an industry and company are heavily regulated.

In between these two extremes are the constraints placed on subsidiary business units of larger organizations. In these cases, freedom of action is effectively reduced by the resource allocation choices of the higher body. In situations of enforced choice, the core process of making marketing strategy is simplified. Understanding the market is largely a case of recognizing the implications of the constraints. The choice of target market and value proposition is reduced to minor adjustment of that implied by the situation. Deciding the action plan is condensed into selecting from and ensuring coherence in a very limited set of alternatives implied by the implementation context. As with other ways of looking at strategic marketing planning, enforced choice is a facet of what really happens rather than a complete description, and the prominence of the facet is characteristic of the organization and market.

Making marketing strategy by leadership

The final, and perhaps overarching, perspective on how strategy is made in reality concerns leadership. The leadership of an organization can be seen to drive strategy formulation either directly or via its influence on the other approaches to making strategy, such as planning. Recently, some researchers have even pointed out that especially charismatic leaders can make a significant difference to the resources available to a firm by influencing investors (Flynn and Staw, 2004). When leaders directly contribute to strategic choice, it is often referred to as vision (Westley and Mintzberg, 1989). There is no clear pattern to this, as the leadership team is itself driven by its background and its structure (Jensen and Zajac, 2004).

However, we can see that visionary leadership differs from other ways of making marketing strategy in each of the three stages. Market understanding is carried out in the mind of the leader or core leadership team. This may be more or less rational, but it is usually implicit and informal. The choice of target markets and value propositions, at least at a broad level, also takes place in this small group. All that is left to subordinates is the choice of detailed action plans, and in some cases this is also closely directed by the senior team. Clearly, visionary leadership is at least a partial description of what happens in all companies. Hence this perspective provides another insight into reality whilst failing to provide a complete picture on its own.

Thus the descriptive research into how companies make strategy suggests that six approaches are involved. The approaches, however, are not mutually exclusive, and even overlap to some extent. They are most accurately seen not as different ways of making marketing strategy, but rather as different components of a complex process. Perhaps the best analogy for the different perspectives was that used by Mintzberg when he referred to *The Elephant and the Blind Men*, a nineteenth century poem in which the groping men variously decided the animal was a tree, a snake, a wall and other things, depending on which part of the beast they got hold of. Like the blind men, none of the perspectives on planning is better than the others, but they all add to our understanding of what goes on when real companies make marketing strategy.

Application point: Which perspective gives you most insight into your own strategic marketing planning?

All six of the given perspectives on strategic marketing planning are useful to some degree. They allow practitioners to step back and better understand what is going on in their own company. Usually, however, one or more perspectives provide special insight and illuminate something about a company's strategy making that has been implicit.

- What does each of these six perspectives tell you about your company?
- Do any of them provide a particularly accurate description of how your company makes strategy?
- If so, is there any connection between that and any strengths and weaknesses you may have identified in your marketing strategy?

A rainbow of strategic marketing planning

These six perspectives on how companies make strategy in real life are not alternatives. They merely represent different ways of looking at the same complex phenomenon. The key lesson here is that all of the researchers are partly right and none of them is totally correct. Firms make strategy in a variety of ways. Each of these ways of making strategy is a mixture of the different approaches to making strategy described above. Mintzberg (Mintzberg *et al.*, 1998: 372) summed up this hybrid nature of strategy making by saying:

> Strategy formation is judgmental designing, intuitive visioning and emergent learning.

Whilst Mintzberg was talking about strategy making generally, much the same view had been taken earlier by McDonald (1996) with respect to strategic marketing planning in particular:

> It can be hypothesized that in a manner similar to that in which the three primary colours can, in various proportions, combine to form all other colours, so might all shades and hues of planning approaches be possible according to proportions of the components (logical rational models, pragmatic incremental models, subjective visionary models).

As you can see, what both Mintzberg and McDonald did was to rationalize the six perspectives into three. Broadly speaking, enforced choice and leadership were condensed into visionary command. Cultural, political and incremental were subsumed into just incremental, and formal planning was classified as rational. Despite the slight variation in terms, we can see that these and other researchers formed a consensus about how marketing strategy is made. It is not made by planning alone; it is made by a mixture of visionary command, rational planning and incremental processes. Further, the precise blend or hybrid used seems to be specific to an organization. There is no single way of strategic marketing planning; there are perhaps as many ways to create strategies as there are companies trying to make them. This is what Figure 6.1 tries to sum up, using McDonald's colour metaphor.

This colour metaphor, which we will stay with for the rest of the book, is useful in three ways. First, it fits with the idea that there is an infinite number of combinations of colours, just as there is an infinite number of possible hybrid marketing-strategy making processes. Secondly, it fits with the idea that, despite the infinite number of possibilities, there are in practice only a few colours that we recognize and use as our reference points to other colours. In the same way, whilst there are innumerable hybrids of rational planning, incrementalism and visionary command that might be used by companies, we

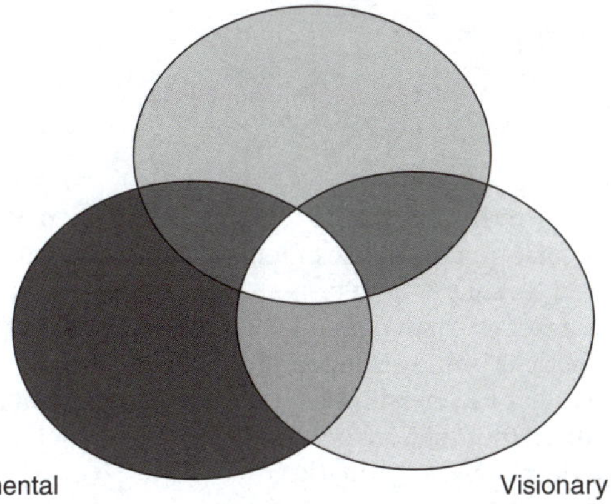

Figure 6.1 The three contributing processes of marketing-strategy making (after McDonald, 1996). See colour plate 6.1.

can understand them better as variations around seven stereotypical ways of making strategy. To help explain this, we will use a broad analogy to the seven colours of the rainbow. These seven stereotypes of strategic marketing planning are described below and are used to help improve our strategy making in subsequent chapters. They are summarized in Table 6.3.

Finally, just like the natural colours we observe in nature, these colours are not monochromatic. In other words, marketing-strategy making is never purely planning, incrementalism or vision. Even the most extreme cases have some of each of the other two.

The following paragraphs describe different colours or types of marketing-strategy making observed in the research, how common they are, and any observed correlation with type of company. Further, the descriptions of each colour describe the broad differences between them at each of the three stages of making strategy (understanding the market, choosing the strategy, deciding on the actions). These are stereotypes. They probably do not describe any single organization perfectly. However, they are close enough to a large number of organizations' strategic marketing behaviour to help us understand what is going on and, later in the book, to improve it.

(A note for physicists. This rainbow analogy is merely a learning device. The author, originally a chemist, is aware of the limitations of the analogy and the different ways that primary colours and the visible spectrum are expressed. Try not to let your specialist knowledge get in the way!)

Table 6.3 Examples of hybrid marketing-strategy making processes

Colour of marketing-strategy making process	*Description*	*Occurrence*
Blue – mostly rational planning	Characterized by explicit, formal processes, use of tools and techniques and of market research data.	Relatively rare, mostly found in larger companies and in those without a strongly technological culture.
Yellow – mostly visionary command	Characterized by dominant leader or leadership team (or, in multinationals, by a dominant home market) dictating strategy.	Very common, especially in smaller companies and those run by their founder.
Red – mostly incremental	Characterized by continual, incremental development of existing value propositions or target markets.	Relatively rare, incrementalism is much more common as a supporting element of strategy making.
Green – a mixture of rational planning and visionary command	Characterized by the overlay of rational planning onto either a visionary strategy, or one enforced by regulation or market conditions, or one dictated by headquarters.	Fairly common, especially when normally visionary companies need to execute complex strategies or when normally rational companies make radical new strategies.
Orange – a mixture of visionary command and incremental	Characterized by the overlay of incrementalism (usually the cultural, political variety rather than the logical kind) onto either a visionary strategy or one enforced by regulation or market conditions, or one dictated by headquarters.	Common, especially in the international subsidiaries of multinationals, where the application of financial processes gives the outward appearance of being rational planning but tools and techniques are not used.
Violet – a mixture of rational planning and incremental	Characterized by a rational planning process which decides broad strategy but uses incrementalism (especially of the logical type) to deal with uncertainty in the market.	Relatively rare. Seen mostly in companies with strategically aware managers who have recognized the limitations of pure rational planning and have overlaid logical incrementalism.

Table 6.3 *(Continued)*

Colour of marketing-strategy making process	*Description*	*Occurrence*
White – a mixture of rational planning, visionary command and incremental	Characterized by a relatively even balance of visionary command, rational planning and incrementalism. The different components are emphasized differently in different parts of the strategy making process.	Very rare, only observed in relatively sophisticated companies. Financial and other administrative processes may give orange (visionary command + incrementalism) processes the outward appearance of a rational planning process, but white processes use tools and techniques of strategic planning.

Blue strategy making – mostly rational planning

As described in Chapter 3, companies who make their marketing strategy mostly by rational planning, correctly using tools and techniques, are rare. Mostly they are larger, mature companies. In addition, they are more prevalent in markets in which the customer is the consumer (as opposed to another company) and in which the value proposition is built around a simple core product with an important branding component. In other words, rational planning is typically, but not exclusively, found in big FMCG companies.

As might be expected, all three parts of making marketing strategy are dominated by explicit, rational processes that are usually formalized and documented. Market understanding relies on formal analysis; the strategy is explicit and justified and the implementation actions are overt and often quantified. However, there are usually elements of visionary command and incrementalism in the process. The most obvious examples of this lie in the market definition and therefore the boundaries of the rational planning process. Either internally based enforced choice factors, such as fixed assets and limited resources, or a core of strategic vision, such as direction about the basis of competition (e.g. 'We are a research-based company') limit the scope of the rational process.

As well as this visionary command component, blue (mostly rational) hybrid marketing-strategy making processes also always have an incremental component. This may be 'rationally incremental', involving test marketing of new ideas in a deliberate way, or it may be 'culturally incremental', for instance when a culturally democratic organization allows functions a degree of freedom in the implementation of the strategy. Both visionary command and incremental components therefore play a minor part in even the purest form of strategic marketing planning.

Notwithstanding these additions, the process remains predominantly blue – that is, rational planning led.

Yellow strategy making – mostly visionary command

Companies who make their marketing strategy mostly by visionary command processes are surprisingly common. They are concentrated in smaller firms, especially those operating in specialist technical niches. Often they are firms that are still run by their founder or in which the founder's influence still runs deep. However, the visionary command process can also frequently be seen in larger organizations. Sometimes this is when the command process arises from enforced choice (such as regulation or resource constraints), but more often it is seen when a powerful centre controls the subsidiary business units via higher-level strategies and the concomitant structure. For instance, a European subsidiary of a US telecoms company is constrained by government regulation, technical and structural inertia, and the core research strategy, which is usually a head office function. In other words, the visionary process is typically seen in two contexts: owner-managed SMEs, and overseas subsidiaries of multinational corporations.

In visionary command organizations, understanding the market, choosing the strategy and deciding implementation actions are all dominated by the leader or the leadership team or the enforced choice factors, such as regulation or inertia. Market understanding derives from the perceptions and intuitions of the leaders. In the case of international subsidiaries, this understanding is often based upon conditions in the home market. Similarly, the choice of target markets and value propositions is made in that core group. In organizations which are very strongly visionary command, the direction of the core group extends down into the detail of the implementation. Even when leadership is less involved in implementation, the choice of strategy and control of resources indirectly provides little room for manoeuvre at a tactical level.

However, there are usually elements of rational planning and incrementalism in the most visionary-command of processes. Rationality is most usually represented by a strong financial planning system that forces some degree of formality and quantification. Sometimes rationalism is added by a limited rational planning process contained within the leadership team. In these cases, the leaders do some formal planning themselves or get the help of management consultants. Both financial budgeting and leadership planning are a long way from full-blown rational strategic marketing planning, but provide a rational tinge to an otherwise non-rational process.

Incrementalism is added to visionary command processes in implicit, sometimes accidental, ways. Sometimes, the practical limitations on the leadership's capacity to direct the detail of implementation allow space for cultural or political incrementalism. Alternatively, locally specific conditions may force the leaders to allow a degree of local tailoring of the strategy, for adjusting the detail of target priorities and value proposition composition. In spite of this, these hints of incrementalism are not usually of the deliberate, experiment-and-learn type. Hence the process remains yellow (i.e. visionary command), even allowing for the minor additions of blue rational planning and red incrementalism.

Red strategy making – mostly incremental

Companies who make their marketing strategy mostly through an incremental process are relatively rare. As we will see, incrementalism seems to play mostly a supporting role to rational planning and visionary command-led processes rather than a lead role in making strategy. This is due to the quite granular nature of strategic decision-making. That is, strategic decisions about resource allocation frequently have to be made in large lumps that cannot be broken down. Examples of this might be the development of a core technology or the targeting of a certain market.

Where incrementalism does play a larger role, therefore, is in businesses where the resource allocation can be dismantled into smaller decisions. Examples of this are in some financial service and consumer technology sectors where a core technology (for instance, equity investments or digital recording media) can, at relatively little cost, be re-engineered into new value propositions for new targets. Naturally, how the core process of strategy making is implemented differs from visionary command and rational planning situations.

In incremental companies understanding of the market is inferred from real data from adjacent markets, rather than technical analysis or the leaders' intuition. Consequently, the strategy flows from making small, low-investment steps from current activity. It tends not to involve a fundamentally new decision. Likewise, the action plan for implementation is most likely to be an extension of current actions.

There are usually significant elements of rational planning and visionary leadership in most incremental processes. Rationality is expressed as assessing the incremental movements in a logical manner, even though strategic management tools are not employed. Such assessment is often aimed at determining how close the new target or value proposition is to the current strategy.

Visionary leadership is added, as it is to rational planning processes, by prescribing the limits of the current activity and setting the resources available to the limited steps. In this way, tints of these two approaches to making strategy are added to what is mostly an incremental process, but it remains visibly red.

Green strategy making – a mixture of rational and visionary command

Companies who make their marketing strategy via a mixture of visionary command and rational planning are fairly common, but are made up of a number of sub-groups. They may be subsidiaries whose strategy is largely decided by headquarters but who plan their local variations rationally. In the same way, regulated or constrained organizations may use what freedom they have in the context of a plan. Alternatively, companies who are usually planning-oriented may leap into a new area, which is difficult to plan for, under the volition of a powerful leader's vision. In this case, the rational planning tends to be concentrated in the leadership team rather than endemic to the organization.

As might be expected, the three core stages of making strategy consist of both rational planning and visionary command elements. Understanding of the market is based on some analysis of a market whose basic shape comes from the intuition of the leaders or the constraints of the market. The choice of strategy, targets and propositions flows from that view of the market but is much refined by careful planning. The development of the action plan is an example of systematic planning, but within the boundaries laid down by the leaders' vision or the market constraints. Hence examples of this green hybrid of planning and vision are most often seen when large, normally planning-led companies move into new uncharted areas.

Within this green hybrid there are still minor traces of incrementalism. They may be evidenced as trial markets, or as the action planning being shaped by the culture of the company or by political negotiation by old and new resource bases. These important traces of red do not change the predominantly blue and yellow hybrid marketing-strategy making process, which remains noticeably green.

Orange strategy making – a mixture of visionary command and incremental

Companies who make their marketing strategy via a mixture of visionary command and incremental process are perhaps the most common category observed. They seem to fall into two groups, broadly correlating with SMEs and divisions of large companies. In SMEs, this orange blend of central leadership and step-wise followers flows from organizations that were once almost purely visionary command but have grown too big for the leaders to manage alone. To cope with the growth their leadership is augmented by incrementalism, especially the cultural and political kind.

These tend not to exhibit the sort of rational incrementalism demonstrated by test marketing and deliberate organizational learning. In divisions or strategic business units of larger companies, it is a similar story but writ large. The visionary command element comes from decisions made in headquarters about core technologies or broad business strategies (for instance, product excellence, operational excellence or customer intimacy, as described in Chapter 5 under *What is marketing strategy?* and in Treacy and Wiersema's (1995) work). The subsidiaries are left with local implementation within that fairly tight straitjacket. Unless something leads them to be planners (for instance, a planning devotee in the role of subsidiary leader), they tend to fulfil their role by incrementalism.

In companies whose marketing-strategy making process is orange, the three stages all contain elements of visionary command and incrementalism, but there is a gradation. Understanding the market is primarily a leadership function and, as in mostly yellow processes, this understanding is based largely on the leaders' intuition and perception. It is to some extent informed by the outcomes of each incremental change in strategy as these results are observed by the leaders, but market understanding is more yellow than red. The choice of strategy flows from that understanding and is therefore also largely determined by the leaders. The choice of targets and design of the value propositions may be blurred or adjusted by the culture or politics, but they start with the leaders' vision. In these cases, there is sometimes an observable difference between the espoused strategy (what the leaders say) and the enacted strategy (what happens 'on the ground'). The actions that flow from the strategy tend to be decided piecemeal and within the limits imposed by the leaders' vision of the strategy. Cultural artefacts (like structure and systems) determine actions, and political negotiation further blurs the intended into the actual.

Although the orange process is clearly dominated by visionary command and incrementalism, suggestions of rational planning can still be seen. Again, financial budgeting imposes a degree of formality. In technically based organizations, external protocols (such as industry standards or regulatory approval procedures) may force a level of prescribed behaviour. In some cases, human resource or manufacturing systems such as management by objectives or good manufacturing practice may be in evidence. However, these should not be mistaken for rational strategic marketing planning. Tools and techniques such as real segmentation and directional policy matrix are noticeable by their absence. Even the presence of other formal elements does not change the fact that the strategy making process is noticeably orange.

Violet strategy making – a mixture of rational planning and incremental

As with all cases where truly rational planning is involved, violet strategy making is relatively rare. As with orange and green approaches, violet companies seem to have evolved from two directions. They were either planning companies that added incrementalism, or, more commonly, incremental companies that added rational planning. Again, larger companies seem predisposed towards this approach and heavily technical companies against it. A third characteristic of companies who blend planning and incrementalism is a business-educated leader, or leadership team, who tends to be pro-planning.

Violet companies show a gradation of rational planning and incremental process across the three stages of strategy making, although it is a reversal of the pattern seen in orange companies. Rational planning seems more in evidence in the earlier stages of understanding the market and choosing the basic outline of the strategy. Incrementalism takes up the slack and refines the choice of target market and value proposition, and takes the lead in setting the action plan. Hence the use of tools, techniques and written plans is clearly observed at higher levels, sometimes aided by consultants. Similarly, the grain of the culture and political negotiation can be seen to fine tune the strategy. However, violet companies are more likely than others to attempt 'logical incrementalism', with deliberate experimentation and managed organizational learning.

As ever, there are traces of the third component, visionary command. The rational planning system picks up the implications of enforced choice and to some degree acts as a conduit to impose the leaders' view of the world. This does not detract, however, from the dominant influence of rational planning and incrementalism. To anyone looking at the company, it has a discernibly violet approach to making its marketing strategy.

White strategy making – a mixture of rational planning, visionary command and incremental

Whilst all of the colours of strategy making process are polychromatic (i.e. they have elements of all three colours and even variation within those colours), one approach is truly a blend, a relatively balanced combination of visionary command, rational planning and incrementalism. Staying with the analogy, this approach is white, since it combines all the colours. This seems to be especially difficult to manage and is commensurately rare.

Companies who manage to blend visionary command, rational planning and incrementalism into a white approach to strategic marketing planning are relatively homogeneous in their features. They tend to be large and have what has been called 'organizational slack' – that is, they are successful enough to not live hand-to-mouth and are able, therefore, to allocate a lot of resources to making their management processes work well. Although no link can be proven, white approaches to making strategy are often associated with advanced approaches to other 'soft' processes, such as recruitment and retention, knowledge management and change management. White processes are therefore rarely seen outside of big, blue-chip, multinational companies, and are not common even in those paragons of corporate effectiveness.

The rarity and complexity of white hybrid marketing-strategy making processes makes it hard to see a pattern similar to the two-way hybrids. Even on close inspection, it is hard to separate the influence of visionary command, rational planning and incrementalism at each of the three stages. Understanding the market does rely heavily on tools and techniques, but these tools often push the company towards minimizing risk and therefore taking incremental steps. This tendency to be violet is, however, counteracted by vision, which enables leaps in the strategy by intuition and perception. Deciding the strategy is based on a strong understanding of the market derived from formal analysis, but is polished and improved by incrementalism. Cultural, political and deliberate learning make up for limitations in the analysis by refining both the targeting and the value propositions. The risk of 'blurring' a strong strategy is kept in check by a well-communicated vision, which is transmitted through the culture. Rational planning, complemented by the other advanced 'soft' processes, provides a framework for the implementation actions. However, the implementation is lubricated by cultural and political incrementalism, whilst the visionary command ethos helps overcome unforeseen contingencies. Like an orchestra in full flow, it is not easy to see who is doing what, and rational planning, visionary command nor incrementalism seems to be taking either leading or supporting roles.

Using the rainbow analogy

As suggested above, these seven stereotypes of strategic marketing planning behaviour are not meant to describe perfectly the way that marketing strategies are made in every company. In reality an individual company is likely to be none of these colours, but instead may best be described as 'dawn cerise' or a 'sunset yellow' or any of the other exotic colour names we usually associate with the sales aids of paint companies. Extremes of blue, red or yellow are rare, and all companies use some of everything. The aim of the analogy is to help us understand the complexity of how strategies are made in the real world. As complex as this analogy suggests strategy making is, remember that it is based on a simplification of Mintzberg's ten and Bailey and Johnson's six approaches into just three components of strategy making: visionary command, rational planning and incrementalism. Absolute reality may be more complex still, but the colour analogy is a pragmatic compromise. It is simple enough to use, and complex enough to be useful.

Application point: What colour is your company?

There are probably real examples of every possible shade of marketing-strategy making process, but research suggests that companies are not evenly distributed in their strategy making habits. Instead, they appear to cluster into stereotypes. Identifying which stereotype is the closest description of your own company is useful in understanding and eventually improving your strategic marketing planning.

- Which of the seven colours of strategic marketing planning do you think most closely approximates to your company's behaviour?
- In what ways, and to what extent, does your company differ from the stereotype?
- What examples of strategy making behaviour cause you to hold those views?

Back to the mission

The aim of this chapter was to understand what real companies do in the real world when they try to make marketing strategy. We have moved from the prescriptive textbooks about how to do strategic marketing planning to the descriptive research about how it is done in practice. In the course of this chapter we uncovered that weak marketing strategies are much more common than strong ones, and explored some of the detailed differences between strong and weak marketing strategies. We then went into the different ways that companies behave when they do their planning. We saw that this can be understood from a number of perspectives, each of which is valuable but doesn't make complete sense on its own. The reality of strategic marketing planning is a complex hybrid. All the different approaches described by the academics are happening at once.

We rationalized this, using McDonald's colour analogy, to three contributing 'primary' colours and seven different modes of strategic marketing planning. These are descriptions, remember, not prescriptions. Even as descriptions, the seven colours are necessarily approximations. In fact, every company has a slightly different shade of strategic marketing planning process.

These conclusions help us in our mission to improve our strategic marketing planning in two ways. First, they help us to avoid asking the wrong question. Much of the work described in Chapter 2 was based on the question: 'Does rational planning work?' We can now see that measuring a company's strategy making process along one simple dimension (i.e. how much rational planning it does) is naïve. Secondly, two companies with the same amount of rational planning could have very different approaches to making marketing strategy (that is, they could be shades of green, violet or even white), so it is impossible simply to correlate 'degree of formal rational planning' with effectiveness (even if we could measure that).

What we really need to know is: 'What colour of strategic marketing planning works best?' This chapter has helped us form that question. Chapter 7 answers it for us.

Power points

- Weak marketing strategies are more commonly observed than strong ones.
- There is a variety of different perspectives on how companies actually go about making marketing strategy, and each of them offers some insight into our own process.
- The actual strategic marketing planning behaviour of companies can be described in terms of visionary command, rational planning and incrementalism. This lends itself to the rainbow analogy.
- Every company has its own particular colour of marketing-strategy making process, consisting of a blend of the three main types of behaviour.
- Companies cluster in their behaviour, and there are seven stereotypes of strategic marketing planning behaviour which are approximate but practically useful in understanding our own company.

- It is naïve to ask simply if rational planning works. We need to know which colour of strategic marketing planning works best.

Reflection points for marketing practitioners

- Compared to other companies, how strong or weak is your marketing strategy?
- What are the strengths and weaknesses of your marketing strategy?
- Have you any idea what is causing those strengths and weaknesses?
- Which of the various perspectives on strategic marketing planning provides most insight into how your company works?
- Which of the seven colours of strategic marketing planning is most like your company?

Chapter 7

We know that what works is what fits

For a successful technology, reality must take precedence over public relations, for Nature cannot be fooled.

(Richard Feynman)

Introduction

This book is a learning experience, as was the research that underpinned it. Those who study learning and education often refer to a stage in the learning process that is characterized by bewilderment and a feeling that what has been learnt so far has confused rather than informed. This stage, which we are all familiar with, follows the necessary deconstruction of old incorrect perceptions and precedes the construction of new and more useful understanding. We are at that stage of this book now. Hang in there; we are about to start creating new knowledge.

So far, we have established some important precepts by looking at the research into strategic marketing planning. We have established that we know what it is and that it is not an unstable, evolving embryonic management process. It is a stable process for aligning the company to the market by understanding the market, choosing a strategy and deciding what to do. The fads and fashions should not confuse us. We have also established that strategic marketing planning works, in that it contributes to organizational effectiveness.

In the process we learned that to view any single management process as a panacea would be naïve. We further uncovered that strategic marketing planning is not used much and that both the external market conditions and internal organizational culture seem to hinder its use. These three findings led us to the conclusion that strategic marketing planning is a failed technology. The science is sound, but we need to find a way of making it work better in the real world. As Richard Feynman, the Nobel Prize-winning physicist, said, technologies have to recognize reality.

In Part 2, we have been looking at what happens in the real world. We assembled the research to support the argument that a good marketing strategy can be characterized by ten factors, independent of the market it is for. Although this codification of strategy diagnostics is original work, it is also fits with our intuition. We are trying to fit with the market, so it follows that we have to fit with homogeneous bits of it (real segments) and make offers suited to them (segment-specific value propositions). The choice of target and proposition works best if it anticipates the future, is SWOT aligned and is different from the competition. Those and the five other diagnostic tests are common sense, even if they are research-supported common sense.

This codification of common sense helped us to evaluate the strategies of real companies. We found that no companies are perfect and, although some are very good, many are very weak indeed. If there is an average, it is the company that sells an undifferentiated proposition to a heterogeneous market, that fails to grasp both SWOT alignment and future trends, and that ends up going head-on with the competition.

In the final stages of deconstructing our knowledge, we learned that companies make strategies by a hybrid marketing-strategy making process. They blend visionary command, rational planning and incrementalism in as many different proportions as there are companies. The rainbow metaphor is useful because, although there are innumerable possible combinations, we can reference them against seven stereotypical planning behaviours. This better understanding of planning helps us in one way but not in another. We now know that it is not simply a question of how much planning to do, but rather which blend of all three colours is the most effective. This is a useful step forward from the 'Should we do formal planning or not?' question.

However, the research looking at the effectiveness of different colours of marketing-strategy making process does not seem to help us much. We see strong strategies emerging from almost every blend.

Similarly, we see weak strategies emerging from the same hybrid marketing-strategy making processes that in another company led to a strong strategy. At this stage, it is understandable if the reader feels confused and is hungry for an explanation. Hold on, we're almost there.

From a scientific perspective, this lack of correlation between which colour of strategic marketing planning is used and the quality of the resultant marketing strategy is surprisingly helpful. Both natural and social scientists see this phenomenon all the time. Educational achievement is not directly correlated to IQ. Crime rate is not closely matched to educational attainment. Cancer is not simply related to smoking. Global warming is not straightforwardly linked to carbon dioxide emissions. When scientists see that, it screams 'multifactorial' at them and they look around for other factors. Complex relationships are multifactorial relationships. The lack of a simple correlation between process used and output tells us that something else is involved. If we can figure out what else is involved in the association between colour of strategy making process and quality of marketing strategy, we begin to build a profound and useful understanding of what is happening in real life. Armed with that understanding, we can work out what we should do in practice. To figure out this complex relationship, however, requires a small but valuable digression into explanations of how organizations work.

How do organizations work?

This little question has more to it than meets the eye. To answer it well, we need to understand it well. Look at the noun and the verb: 'organization' and 'work'. What do we mean by each of these things? A pragmatic view is as follows.

By 'work' we mean achieve the objectives, whatever they might be. By 'organization' we mean a group of people with the same objective, such as a company. So our question is, how do groups of people reach an objective? Our comparison is the same number of individuals trying for the same goal. It sounds theoretical and impractical, but it is an important question. The most common entity in business is the company, not a loosely linked virtual network of individuals. That is only the case because the company usually outperforms the network; companies only exist because the whole is in some way greater than the sum of the parts. We need to understand why that is the case.

If we can gain insight into how organizations (and in particular businesses) work, we will be in a better position to understand how their processes, such as strategic marketing planning, work.

As one might expect, the question of how organizations work has been central to much of management research for many years. There is a whole body of work – organization theory – that attempts to understand and explain organizations. Within this vast and eclectic area of knowledge there is a spectrum of philosophical positions, comparable to that in organizational culture discussed in Chapter 3. At one end, sit those who believe that all organizations can be understood by generally applicable models. From the extremes of this perspective, one way of doing things is correct in all cases. This would include, for instance, those who believe that either hierarchal or flat structures are best, or those that believe in either autocratic or democratic management. The point is, this school of thought thinks that there is a single best way of running a business. Most practising managers would regard this as a naïve theory of how organizations work, at least in its most extreme form. It is, however, the basis of most textbooks that prescribe the best way to manage.

At the other extreme, sit those organizational theorists that believe in nothing. More accurately, they believe that every situation has a unique context and no generalizable lessons can be drawn from one context to another. From the extremes of this perspective, no lessons can be learned from other companies and managers have to understand their world from an *ab initio* position. Most practising managers would recognize the importance of context but would regard this perspective as practically unhelpful.

In the middle of these two extremes lies a perspective called contingency theory. Contingency theorists hold the view that there is more than one right way of doing things, that context is important but that generalizations can be drawn across similar cases. When asked 'How do organizations work?' or 'What's the best way to do this?', those with a contingency approach say 'It depends'. They neither offer a single panacea answer nor say that there are no answers. Instead they try to identify what it is about the situation that determines the best way to manage in this case. In this way, contingency theory reflects the often implicit philosophical position of the practising manager. It offers a useful approach to understanding how organizations work and, as we shall see, how strategic marketing planning can be made to work.

Contingency theory is usually said to have started with the work of Tom Burns, who, with George Stalker, wrote a seminal book in

1961 called *The Management of Innovation* (Burns and Stalker, 1961). In it, Burns and Stalker found that different management styles (they labelled them 'mechanical' and 'organic') worked more or less well to achieve innovation in different markets. Their thinking, and that of other contingency theorists, was that organizations work best when they adapt their behaviour to the environment around them. Now, this seems axiomatic and obvious, but in an age of unbridled 'scientific management' this was a novel idea. Then, as today, many business schools and consultants peddled a single solution to each problem. Textbook strategic marketing planning is just one example of this.

Later, in 1967, the whole idea of adaptation and contingency was developed by Jay Lorsch and Paul Lawrence (Lawrence and Lorsch, 1967a, 1967b). They saw the effectiveness of organizations as depending on two things: specialization and integration. As they saw it, a company of, say, 1000 people outperforms 1000 individuals because the company people can specialize. In this way, each is more effective and efficient at a particular task than someone who has to do many tasks. As a marketing specialist, for instance, you can concentrate on marketing and not have to learn accountancy or polymer chemistry. Your colleagues in other departments can do likewise. You are each more effective at what you do than an individual trying to do all of those things at once. However, the greater effectiveness and efficiency of the company can only be realized if the different specializations can be integrated. Further, the cost of integration must be less than the benefit of specialization. To the individual, the cost of integration is negligible; it is all in his or her head. The company people have to spend time communicating with the other specialists. To put it in prosaic terms, we work better as a team only if we save, by specializing, more time than we spend in meetings trying to integrate with other specialists. Again this seems obvious to a practising manager, but this work was really seminal in helping us to understand how organizations succeed or fail. Lawrence and Lorsch's work implied that organizations work when the benefits of specialization outweighed the costs of integration. Further, both costs and benefits were determined by how well each function or business process fitted into its external (e.g. the market) and internal (e.g. the company) environments. Since those environments differ between companies, different ways of doing this would work best in different situations. Lawrence and Lorsch had provided a mechanism for contingency theory.

As a result of the contingency theorists' work, management researchers began to think that there was not a single best way of doing things, but that the best way depended on adapting processes to the particular context of the business. This thinking was developed and crystallized by two organizational sociologists, Gibson Burrell and Gareth Morgan, in their 1979 book *Sociological Paradigms and Organizational Analysis* (Burrell and Morgan, 1979), a classic in its field. Burrell and Morgan saw organizations as a number of sub-systems which we practitioners would equate broadly to business processes. Research and development, marketing and manufacturing are all examples of such sub-systems. Further, they believed that how well or otherwise an organization worked depended on how well each sub-system or process fitted (that was adapted to) its particular context. Importantly, they saw the context of any sub-system as having both internal and external facets. Burrell and Morgan's congruency hypothesis, as it was called, explained organizational effectiveness in terms of two factors that are very important to the rest of this book:

1. *Macrocongruence*, which is defined as how well each part of the business fits the particular external context with which it has to interact.
2. *Microcongruence*, which is defined as how well each part of the business fits the particular internal context with which it has to interact.

According to the congruency hypothesis, therefore, companies work well not when they adopt any particular way of doing things, but when the way they do something achieves macrocongruence and microcongruence by fitting with their particular context. As we will see, this apparently esoteric concept, imported from a body of knowledge not usually considered by marketing managers, explains the lack of correlation between the strategic marketing planning process used and the quality of marketing strategy. Further, it suggests how our process might be adapted to get a better result, by considering the macrocongruence and microcongruence of the strategic marketing planning process used. In short, contingency theory and the congruency hypothesis provide an answer to the question, 'What colour of strategic marketing planning should we use?' – and the answer is, 'whatever fits your company and your market'.

Application point: What's your philosophy?

The different philosophical positions adopted by management theorists can seem impractical and indulgent to a practising manager. Most managers, however, actually adopt a philosophical position without even thinking about it. Although not an everyday tool, it is useful to consider the practical implications of your own philosophy. It can help expose some implicit flaws in your thinking.

- Consider the short section above and the idea of a 'philosophical spectrum' from 'there is a single answer to everything' to 'there are no answers', with contingency theory in the middle. Where do you think you sit on that spectrum?
- More importantly, when your company learns of a new idea, does it accept it as a panacea, think about how to adapt it to your situation, or reject it out of hand?
- How much has your company thought about adapting strategic marketing planning to make it work in your context?

The practical implications of the congruency hypothesis

The preceding section necessarily involved looking into an area of management research that seems only distantly relevant to strategic marketing planning. However, the implications of the contingency approach and the congruency hypothesis are actually very direct and important in improving how we make marketing strategy. It begins to explain why there is no simple correlation between what colour of hybrid marketing-strategy making process we use and what quality of marketing strategy we get.

The first implication of congruency hypothesis is that it is not the colour of strategy making process *per se* that matters, but its fit with its context. More specifically, the colour of hybrid marketing-strategy making process used is only important inasmuch as it determines the extent of macrocongruence and microcongruence. Any blend of rational planning, visionary command and incrementalism might lead to a strong strategy if it is congruent to the external environment (i.e. the market) and the internal environment (i.e. the organizational culture). This implication of the congruency hypothesis is summarized in Figure 7.1. It flows directly from the common-sense views of the contingency theorists. In addition, however, it is entirely consistent with what we know about barriers to strategic marketing planning described in Chapters 3 and 4. According to the

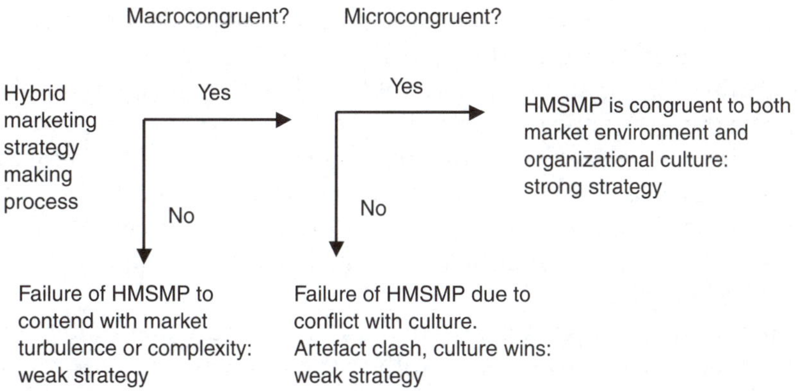

Figure 7.1 The bicongruence explanation of strategic marketing planning effectiveness

congruency hypothesis, the failure of strategic marketing planning to cope with certain market conditions (for instance, highly turbulent markets) is merely an example of macro-incongruence. Similarly, cultural hindrances to strategic marketing planning are examples of micro-incongruence.

The second important implication of the congruency hypothesis for strategic marketing planning is that one kind of congruence is not enough. It is necessary for a business process such as strategic marketing planning to fit with its market conditions (i.e. be macrocongruent), but this alone is insufficient for the process to work well. It is essential for strategic marketing planning to fit with the organizational culture (i.e. be microcongruent), but that situation alone is not enough to ensure the process works. For any marketing-strategy making process to work well, it must be bicongruent – that is, it must fit with *both* the market conditions *and* the organizational culture.

These two implications then combine to make a third. If it is the fit that matters and bicongruence is necessary, then the internal and organizational contexts are largely what determine the effectiveness of any particular colour of strategic marketing planning. Since every organization has a different organizational culture and operates in a particular market situation, then the optimal marketing-strategy making process is unique to each organization. Any single, prescribed process (such as the textbook approach to strategic marketing planning) is bound to fail in some, perhaps most, organizations. The only process that will work is one which has been crafted individually to be bicongruent to the particular circumstances of the organization in question. In short, strategic marketing planning must recognize the realities of our situation and not be led by the pedagogy of planning textbooks – hence the quotation at the head of this chapter. This view also supports and illuminates Malcolm McDonald's view that the strategic marketing planning process must be 'requisite' to the company, as discussed in Chapter 4. More usefully, it begins to help us see what requisite might mean. In this sense, requisite simply means bicongruent.

Having woven together explanations of strategic marketing planning effectiveness from many different management thinkers, we now have a generally applicable explanation of what works: bicongruence. But what does this mean to practitioners? What do we have to do? In short, the practical inference of the congruency hypothesis and its implications is that we need to understand bicongruence and work out how to achieve it. Those two things are what the rest of this book is about. The next part of this chapter explores the nature of macrocongruence, microcongruence and bicongruence. In Chapter 8, we look at how great companies achieve it through both conscious and unconscious means. In Part 3, we develop a process for creating a bicongruent strategic marketing planning process in your organization.

Application point: What are the implications of the congruency hypothesis for your company?

Despite its origins in academic sociological research, the congruency hypothesis is both beautifully simple and extremely practical. For practitioners, it implies a different way of approaching management problems. Rather than jump on a bandwagon of somebody else's solution, the need for bicongruence drives us to understand the internal and external context better then adapt our processes to them. This is a more difficult but much more valuable approach than looking to each new three-letter-acronym fad as our saviour.

- Can you identify examples of where the congruency hypothesis might change the way you and your company approach business processes?
- Are there any key processes, such as strategic marketing planning, that would benefit from tailoring more to the context of your business?

What does bicongruence look like?

The research for this book involved both surveys and in-depth interviews of marketing strategists in companies in many different market environments and organizational cultures. They employed a huge variety of different colours of strategic marketing planning and achieved very variable results in terms of the strength of their marketing strategy. Interconnecting all those variables, however, were complex patterns in the way their process fitted their situation. Their answers, usually very carefully observed and thought out, revealed a detailed picture of what bicongruence and bi-incongruence looked like. Obviously, this consisted of variances in both macrocongruence and microcongruence and, although both are equally important, they are perhaps best understood separately. To that end, this section describes what our research told us about first macrocongruence and secondly microcongruence. In each case, we will examine how the research revealed exactly what the strategy making process was congruent or incongruent to, what macrocongruence, microcongruence and their opposites looked like, and what that tells us about the mechanisms of bicongruence. Our aim of course is to understand enough to be able to create and manage bicongruence.

What does macrocongruence look like?

Macrocongruence, the degree to which the marketing-strategy making process fits the external market environment, was illuminated by the answers of the research respondents in two different ways. Positively, practitioners reported how what they did coped well with the demands of the market. Sometimes managers could describe this quite clearly, as when their rational analysis made sense of apparently complex market phenomena. In other cases it was intuitively sensed, as when incremental steps created the expected result and built into a successful outcome. Negative responses were also explicit at times and implicit at others. Some respondents could cite clear failings of visionary leadership to communicate strategy into actions plans. Others could see failings in the outputs of their rational analysis but not articulate the mechanism of failure. From the line-by-line content analysis of the interview transcripts, a functional description of macrocongruence and macro-incongruence emerged.

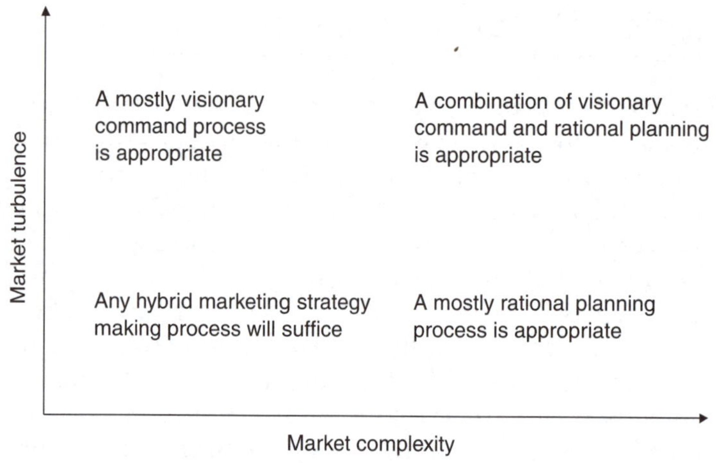

Figure 7.2 Macrocongruence of hybrid marketing-strategy making processes to differing market conditions

Understanding macrocongruence, of course, means understanding both the process and the market. The processes, characterized as stereotypical colours, have been described in detail in Chapter 6. A similarly detailed characterization of the market environment was also needed and was developed in the research. Surprisingly, the determinants of macrocongruence were not as might have been expected. Industry sector, size of company or other predicted market characteristics did not seem to be relevant to which process coped and which did not. Instead, the results echoed the separate findings of Eisenhardt and Frederickson, already discussed in Chapter 3, about market complexity and market turbulence. At the uppermost level of analysis, it is these two dimensions of the market that matter. By considering how these two factors affected the effectiveness of strategy making processes, a clear pattern of macrocongruence became visible.

In overview, this pattern is as described in Figure 7.2. Strategy making processes that are dominated by rational planning cope well with market complexity. Conversely, they struggle with turbulent or otherwise uncertain environments. Hybrid marketing-strategy making processes with high-visionary command content showed the obverse macrocongruence characteristics. They coped better with turbulent markets but were not well matched to complex markets. The third component, incrementalism, sat between the two. Processes that were largely incremental coped well with moderate amounts of both complexity and turbulence, but not with extremes of either. Finally, markets that were both stable and simple were well addressed by any colour of strategic marketing planning. These outline patterns, which combine to form the picture shown in Figure 7.2, give us the first, tentative indications of how to create macrocongruence. However, they are not enough to enable us to set about creating macrocongruence and avoiding macro-incongruence. We still need a deep understanding of macrocongruence. Our next step therefore is to look more carefully at what macrocongruence looks like and what that tells us about the mechanism of macrocongruence. Before we can do that, however, it is necessary to understand some of the more detailed lessons that emerged from the research about the nature of market turbulence and market complexity. In particular, we need to comprehend what different levels of market complexity and turbulence look like. That is the purpose of the next section.

The nature of market turbulence and complexity

Essential to understanding and creating macrocongruence is an appreciation of market turbulence and market complexity. We need to know where our market is in the continuum of Figure 7.2 so that we might predict which colour of strategic marketing planning is likely to be macrocongruent. This understanding of the market is hindered by our subjectivity, and many managers, close to the detail of their market, perceive themselves as operating in very complex and turbulent environments. By contrast, our research suggested that complexity and turbulence were rarer than suggested by managers' perceptions. In addition, by asking a lot of questions about the detail of market conditions, it provided a set of objective criteria by which the nature of the market environment might be more accurately assessed.

The first lesson to emerge was that the whole idea of 'the market' was an over-simplification. Detailed discussions about market conditions with the respondents revealed that complexity and turbulence have their roots in the macroenvironment (the SLEPT factors mentioned in Chapter 1) but manifested themselves in four independent aspects of the market. It was the aggregate of these four factors that led to different levels of market complexity and turbulence. These market factors were:

1. *Customers* – the number of different customer segments to be considered.
2. *Competitors* – the number of different competitor types to be allowed for.
3. *Channels* – the number and significance of channels to market involved.
4. *Value proposition* – the number of different components involved in the value proposition.

In other words, it is too simplistic to estimate market complexity or turbulence as single variables. Markets are a complex web of customers, competitors, channels and value propositions, and it is the aggregate of these that makes up market complexity. Similarly, it is the rate of change of these four market components that determines market turbulence.

Illustrations of complexity and turbulence from these four component elements of the market are shown in Tables 7.1 and 7.2. These tables, compiled from the observations of the case study companies, show the spread of market complexity, from simple to complex, and of market turbulence, from stable to turbulent. In Chapter 12 we will consider how excellent companies apply strategy diagnostics in practice. For the moment, it is useful simply to look at the tables and try to make a rough guess as to where your own market lies.

As Tables 7.1 and 7.2 reveal, neither market complexity nor market turbulence are simple measures. Market complexity is not simply a matter of how many competitors, customers, channels etc. there are, but of their significance. Multiple competitors following the same strategy (i.e. in the same strategic group) do not add significantly to market complexity, whereas even one novel competitor does. Multiple channels do create market complexity when they each add different amounts of value and in different ways. Many distributors operating in the same way and adding little value do not. Similarly, market turbulence is not simply a matter of the number of changes in the four factors, but more a measure of the significance of those changes. A myriad of frequent changes to the microscopic detail of the value proposition adds less to market turbulence than a single fundamental shift in core technology. Waves of market consolidation into fewer, larger competitors may be less important than the acquisition of one minor player by a well-resourced new entrant. For now, however, it is sufficient to have a broad appreciation of what market

Table 7.1 Features of market complexity

Market component	*Features of a complex market*	*Features of a moderately complex market*	*Features of a simple market*
Customers	There are several (e.g. more than three) true market segments of significance. The decision-making process is protracted, and involves a decision-making unit of several people.	There are one to three true market segments of significance. The decision-making process is neither instantaneous nor protracted and, although it involves others, is primarily in the hands of an individual.	There is only one significant market segment. The decision-making process is near instantaneous and involves only one significant decision-maker.
Competitors	There are several (e.g. three or more) strategic groups (i.e. competitors or groups of competitors with distinctly different strategies). There are, or is the threat of, more than one of the indirect competitive forces (i.e. buyer or supplier power, new entrants or substitutes).	There are two significant competitors, or several but forming only two strategic groups. There is, or is the threat of, only one of the indirect competitive forces (i.e. buyer or supplier power, new entrants or substitutes).	There is only one significant competitor or several, but they are all in the same strategic grouping (i.e. all competitors follow a similar strategy). There is little or no threat of indirect competitive forces.
Channels	There are several (e.g. more than three) different types of channels to market, and they add significant value to the proposition.	There is only one indirect channel to market, and it adds some value other than physical distribution.	The channel to market is direct or simply involves physical distribution with little value added to the proposition.
Value proposition	The value proposition is technologically complex; it consists of several components (for instance, product, service, support) and offers benefits at both functional and emotional levels.	The value proposition is technologically complex, or it consists of several components (for instance, product, service, support) or offers benefits at both functional and emotional levels but not all of these.	The value proposition is technologically simple; it consists only of the core product and offers benefits only at a functional level.

Table 7.2 Features of market turbulence

Market component	*Features of a turbulent market*	*Features of a moderately turbulent market*	*Features of a stable market*
Customers	The nature of market segmentation is changing fundamentally and unpredictably over the strategic timescale.	The nature of market segmentation is changing slowly and predictably over the strategic timescale.	The nature of market segmentation is essentially static over the strategic timescale.
Competitors	The number and types of strategic groups is changing rapidly over the strategic timescale.	The number or types of strategic groups is changing slowly over the strategic timescale.	The number and types of strategic groups is essentially static over the strategic timescale.
Channels	The available channels to market and their capacity to add value are changing rapidly over the strategic timescale.	The available channels to market or their capacity to add value are changing slowly and predictably over the strategic timescale.	The available channels to market and their capacity to add value are essentially static over the strategic timescale.
Value proposition	The underlying technology and the components of the value proposition (e.g. product, service, support) are changing rapidly over the strategic timescale.	The underlying technology and the components of the value proposition (e.g. product, service, support) are changing slowly and predictably over the strategic timescale.	The underlying technology and the components of the value proposition (e.g. product, service, support) are essentially static over the strategic timescale.

complexity and turbulence look like. Given that appreciation, we can now take a more informed look at what happens when the strategic marketing planning process either fails or succeeds in keeping up with those market conditions.

Application point: How turbulent and complex is your market?

The failure to make strategic marketing planning work in practice does not have a simple explanation, but failure to fit the process to the market is a large part of it. One of the reasons companies fail to adapt their process is a very subjective, and false, view of their market conditions. Forming an objective and balanced view of the market conditions requires a framework based on the aspects and dimensions described above.

- How complex and turbulent is your market?
- Based on the section above, how would you characterize your market conditions?
- What are the implications of those conditions for how you make marketing strategy?

Examples of macrocongruence

It's all very well to say that a certain colour of strategic marketing planning either copes or does not cope with market turbulence and/or market complexity. It also seems fairly obvious that a team of planners copes with complexity better than a visionary leader, but that it is less good at reacting quickly. To make progress, we need a better understanding of 'coping' or 'fitting' with the market conditions. This insight into the reality of planning success and failure was therefore a major goal of the research study. A selected list of examples of macrocongruence and macro-incongruence is shown in Table 7.3. These examples reveal a level of detail that turns macrocongruence from a theoretical concept into a 'Yes, that happens to us' thought. As the examples show, macrocongruence is manifested in failures of the strategic marketing planning process at all three stages of the core process (understanding the market, choosing the strategy and deciding the actions). Macrocongruence

Table 7.3 Examples of macrocongruence and macro-incongruence

	Complexity	*Turbulence*
Macrocongruence	Effective understanding of macroenvironmental factors (e.g. regulatory or demographic changes) and their implications for the marketing strategy.	Effective screening of new product opportunities at an international rather than local level, especially in the face of multiple 'line extension' opportunities.
	Effective understanding of market segmentation complexity, especially regarding intangible needs.	Rapid transfer of effective responses to market turbulence (e.g. competitor activity or new technological developments) across geographical and market sector boundaries.
	Clear understanding of the factors which determine the attractiveness of alternative segments, especially factors beyond segment size.	Early identification of the combined implications of macroenvironmental changes such as technology and globalization, especially when these changes are not obvious or dramatic.
	Clarification of competitive threats, especially the indirect kind, and 'stratification' according to timescale and nature of the threat (e.g. to sales or to profit margin).	Forewarning of competitive threats arising in other markets, both direct and indirect, especially as regards the spread of threats from leading to following markets.
	Coherence between local and international objectives, especially as regards either achieving rapid penetration or maintaining a premium position.	Efficient transfer of both explicit and tacit knowledge within market, either by formal methods or by the use of *ad hoc* teams.
	Coherence between geographical strategies, especially trans-national learning regarding the effectiveness of different components of the value proposition.	

Macro-incongruence	Failure to give due weight to local market factors when consolidating plans, especially as regards non-core elements of the product. Undue weight given to personal opinions of key individuals, especially when data are not available, or 'political' manipulation of data. Failure to use market data properly when data are consolidated across markets, especially failing to recognize subtleties or inconsistencies in data. Failure to evaluate properly some intangible data (e.g. relationship strength) and undue emphasis given to 'hard' data, even when these are based on weak implicit assumptions. Failure to understand significant differences between market sectors, especially regarding decision-making processes, non-core product components and emotional, intangible needs.	Reduction in speed of innovation created by centralized or bureaucratic processes, especially financial justification processes. Failure of fixed, often calendarized, planning schedules to allow for shortening lifecycles or unplanned contingencies. Weakness in learning the lessons from previous turbulence, especially when staff turnover or merger/acquisition occurs. Failure to contextualize temporary market anomalies and therefore mistaken estimation (either high or low) of the importance of new market features.

is demonstrated in understanding various different factors in the market, and their interplay, whilst there is still time to act on that knowledge. It enables good target definition and prioritization, and then supports the implementation of those strategic choices. By contrast, macro-incongruence tends to lead to oversimplification of the market and/or a delay in understanding the market until only reaction is possible. It results in simple and/or out-of-date target selection, and leads to incoherent implementation.

Application point: How macrocongruent is your strategic marketing planning process?

Macrocongruence and macro-incongruence are clearly observable in the everyday workings of your company. This is sometimes explicit but more often implicit. In either case, an ability to recognize when your strategic marketing planning fits well or is failing to cope with the market is necessary to improving the process. The examples in Table 7.3 are useful but not exhaustive.

- What examples of macrocongruence and macro-incongruence do you see in your company?
- Are they critical or merely interesting?
- What aspects of your market and your strategic marketing planning process do they spring from?

What is the mechanism of macrocongruence?

The examples in Table 7.3 can be thought of as the symptoms of macrocongruence and macro-incongruence, but they are not an explanation of the phenomenon. What is going on when good managers fail or succeed to cope with their market? Can we define the mechanism that is operating well enough to correct it or copy it? The examples in Table 7.3, and the many more that were observed with greater or lesser frequency in the research, do seem to imply a mechanism. More accurately, they imply that some combination of six different things is going on, the net result of which is the mechanism of macrocongruence. These six things (the product of three component processes with complexity and turbulence) are summarized in Table 7.4, and can be described as follows.

Table 7.4 Mechanisms of macrocongruence and macro-incongruence

	Visionary command	*Rational planning*	*Incrementalism*
Complexity	*Mechanism: comprehension overload and over-simplification.* Visionary command processes have limited ability to comprehend market complexity. In cases of low market complexity, this is sufficient. In cases of high-market complexity, the visionary command process over-simplifies the complexity of the market, leading to a compromised understanding of the market conditions.	*Mechanism: analytical comprehension.* Rational planning processes have a large capacity to comprehend market complexity. In cases of low market complexity, this is sufficient but not necessary. In cases of high-market complexity, the rational planning process enables both comprehension and communication of market conditions.	*Mechanism: resource limited comprehension.* Incremental processes have some ability to comprehend market complexity, but are resource intensive when doing so. In cases of low-market complexity, this is sufficient. In cases of high-market complexity, the incremental process is either profligate of resources or, more usually, insufficiently resourced, leading to a compromised understanding of the market conditions.
Turbulence	*Mechanism: intuitive comprehension and communication.* Visionary command processes have a large capacity to sense and act upon significant (but not small) market changes. In cases of market stability, this is rarely needed. In cases of market turbulence, this capacity enables both comprehension and communication of changes in market conditions and of local responses to those changes.	*Mechanism: analysis paralysis.* Rational planning processes have limited capacity to react quickly to market turbulence. In cases of low market turbulence, this is sufficient. In cases of high-market complexity, the rational planning process hinders timely reaction to changes in market conditions.	*Mechanism: bounded reactivity.* Incremental processes have some ability to react to market turbulence, but are resource intensive when doing so. In cases of low-market turbulence, this is sufficient. In cases of high-market turbulence, the incremental process is either profligate of resources or, more usually, insufficiently resourced, leading to a compromised understanding of the market conditions.

1. *Comprehension overload and over-simplification.* This occurs when a heavily visionary command process meets a complex market and leads to macro-incongruence. Simply put, the members of a small group, or the leader, can't, without the aid of planning techniques, get their heads around the implications of multiple channels, segments, competitive groups and a complex value proposition. In attempting to do so, they oversimplify and miss the key issues. The resulting strategies and implementation plans are built on flawed foundations.

2. *Analytical comprehension.* This occurs when rational-planning led processes meet complex markets, leading to macrocongruence. The complexity that arises from the different market components is simplified but is not simplistic. The choice of strategy is based on a good understanding of the market, and the analysis forms the basis of well-communicated implementation plans.

3. *Resource limited comprehension.* This occurs when incremental processes attempt to cope with complex markets, leading to partial macro-incongruence. To some extent the gradual process works, but in doing so it consumes a lot of resources through experimentation and failure. In most companies, resource availability means it is only possible to 'increment' enough to cope with limited amounts of complexity. Market understanding and the subsequent strategy and implementation are limited by the firm's capacity to use incrementalism.

4. *Intuitive comprehension and communication.* This occurs when market turbulence is addressed by visionary command processes, leading to macrocongruence. Leadership intuition and closeness to the market allows prescience of market changes and rapid action unhindered by due process. As long as the market is not complicated, this understanding and action results in strong strategy.

5. *Analysis paralysis.* This occurs when market turbulence is addressed by rational planning processes, leading to macro-incongruence. The time taken to gather and analyse data means that the process is overwhelmed by constant changes in the information. The planning process attempts to compensate by becoming still more sophisticated, and the resulting spiral leads to paralysis and no useful end result.

6. *Bounded reactivity.* This occurs when incremental processes attempt to manage market turbulence, leading to partial macrocongruence. To some extent the gradual process works, but each failed increment requires resource. In practice, it is only possible to 'increment' enough to cope with limited amounts of turbulence. Market understanding and the subsequent strategy

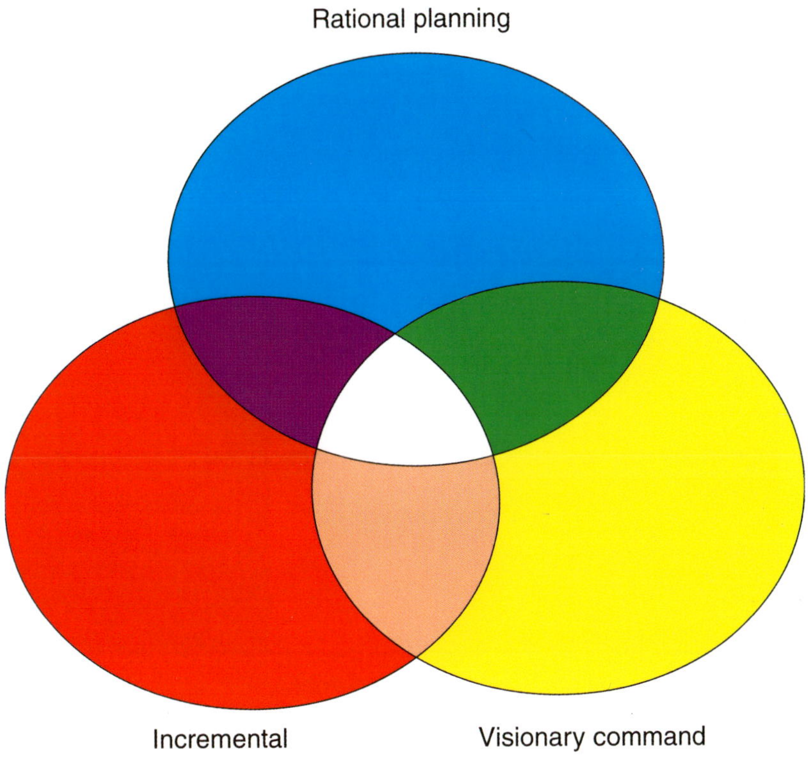

Plate 6.1

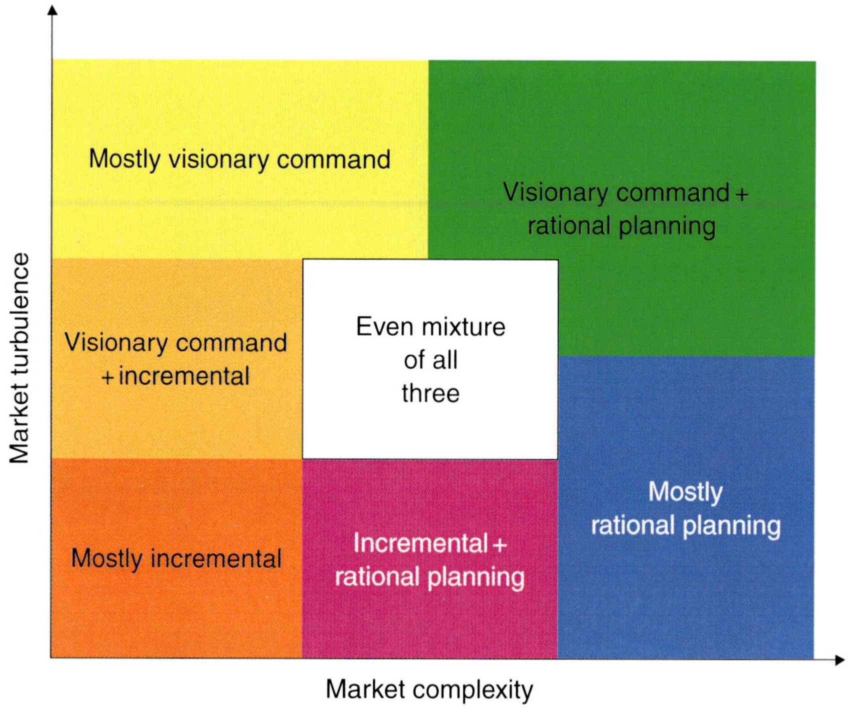
Mostly visionary command
Visionary command + rational planning
Visionary command + incremental
Even mixture of all three
Mostly incremental
Incremental + rational planning
Mostly rational planning
Market turbulence
Market complexity

Plate 10.1

and implementation are limited by the firm's capacity to use incrementalism.

In a typical situation, therefore, a hybrid marketing-strategy making process attempts to cope with a market that is, to some degree, either complex or turbulent, or occasionally both. Some or all of these six mechanisms come into play to create some level of macrocongruence. Since, in a typical situation, the hybrid process has not been designed to be macrocongruent, the more usual result is a significant degree of macro-incongruence and, as the congruency hypothesis suggests, a weak strategy is created. Already, having only considered the mechanisms of one-half of the bicongruence idea, we can begin to see why it is so hard to make good strategy. And now we need to look at the other half of bicongruence, microcongruence.

Application point: Which mechanisms of macrocongruence can you see in your company?

The mechanisms by which macrocongruence arises are not simple. In most companies, some of each of them contribute to an overall level of macrocongruence or macro-incongruence. However, there are usually one or two primary mechanisms, which vary between companies. Identifying these is useful for practitioners.

- Which of the six mechanisms of macrocongruence do you see as operating most strongly in your company?
- What are the causes of it, and what are the implications for your strategy making process?

What does microcongruence look like?

Macrocongruence arises from the way the hybrid marketing-strategy making process fits the market it has to cope with. It is an external fit issue. By contrast, microcongruence stems from the way that process is supported or hindered by the surrounding organizational culture. It is an internal fit issue. Microcongruence differs from macrocongruence in another important respect; it is more difficult to unravel.

This is due to the much greater complexity of organizational culture compared to the market.

When we try to understand macrocongruence, we first try to characterize the market environment with which we want our process to be macrocongruent. Although, as we have seen, it is not straightforward, we do have some tangible concepts to work with. We can identify and measure two dimensions (complexity and turbulence) and four aspects (customers, competition, channels and value proposition) of the market. Using these, we can attempt a match with the process. To revert to the heart transplant analogy, we might measure the height and width of the major blood vessels leading from the heart and compare these with those of the blood vessels in the body of the transplant patient. It's not easy, but we have things to measure and agreed dimensions. In the same way, the two dimensions and four aspects don't tell us everything about a market, but they give us a pretty good approximation.

Trying to understand microcongruence is more difficult. We have done part of the job, when we characterized the different colours of strategic marketing planning in Chapter 6. This is important, but we still need to measure or characterize the organizational culture in some way, just as we did for the market conditions. However, an organizational culture is a much more complex and intangible phenomenon than the market. It has three layers, only one of which is visible whilst two are implicit and hard to see. There is no useful or agreed set of dimensions of company culture comparable to turbulence and complexity that we might use to measure the market. Further, whilst there are tangible artefacts of culture, like systems, structure, procedures and so on, there are too many to measure easily. Imagine trying to measure everything, from the timekeeping of meetings to the décor of the CEO's office. Those are all examples of corporate culture artefacts and the sort of thing that would be necessary to characterize an organizational culture fully. It would be extremely difficult, perhaps practically impossible, to characterize our organizational culture in the same way as we have previously characterized the market. Lots of models and attempts have been made at it, but they tend to be insufficiently subtle to be of practical use to us in achieving microcongruence. Despite this difficulty, it is still possible to understand microcongruence by coming at the problem from another, deductive direction.

Because we lack a broad guideline for microcongruence, one that would be equivalent to Figure 7.2, we can't equate one type of culture to one colour of strategic marketing planning – at least not in that simple manner. However, it is possible to make sense of microcongruence by working backwards from observations of macrocongruence. By asking companies what aspects of their culture support or hinder their process, we can build a picture of the cultural artefacts that are significant to making marketing strategy. Then, by comparing which artefacts hinder and support each company to the processes employed by those companies, we can begin to say which aspects of culture hinder or support different colours of strategic marketing planning (see Table 7.5). This is not exactly the same as saying culture X is microcongruent to process Y, but it is a functional proxy – and a functional model is what we, as practitioners, need.

Application point: What does microcongruence look like in your company?

The match and mismatch of organizational culture to the strategic marketing planning process is a complex issue. The examples given in Table 7.5 are far from exhaustive, and merely indicate the sort of cultural artefacts that help and hinder strategic marketing planning.

- What artefacts of your company culture are important to the way you make marketing strategies?
- Which artefacts support, and which hinder?
- What component of your strategic marketing planning process do they relate to?

Examples of microcongruence and micro-incongruence are shown in Table 7.6. Even from this simplified list, we can see that many different cultural artefacts are important and interact to create microcongruence. Some cultural artefacts that are supportive of some processes hinder other processes and, while some are generally good or bad, there are few absolutely good or absolutely bad cultural artefacts. Organizational culture is horrendously complex, and its fit with a hybrid marketing-strategy making process even more so. However, looking at this complex matching process in enough detail does reveal a mechanism of microcongruence, a way in which it seems to work.

As with macrocongruence, microcongruence is the aggregate of several simultaneous mechanisms. These individual component mechanisms result from the interaction, both positive and negative,

Table 7.5 Supporting and hindering artefacts of organizational culture

Process component	*Supportive cultural artefacts*	*Hindering cultural artefacts*
Visionary command	Clear demarcation between the roles of central and local resource allocation.	Strong financial drivers combined with autocratic style, reducing mutual trust.
	Autonomy of SBUs within an agreed strategic framework.	Turnover or ideologically fragmented top management team, leading to confused or contradictory messages.
	Multiple, rather than annual, linkages between central and local processes.	Meddling of senior management on relatively small scale by politically high-profile business decisions.
	Small, ideologically coherent top management teams.	Locally strong culture at variance with command culture, leading to local resistance.
	Highly quantitative management information systems.	
	Stable top management teams and enculturation of newcomers.	
	Close monitoring of performance indicators by functional 'barons'.	
	Leadership of globally homogeneous market by most advanced market.	
	Product led cultures and technically complex products.	
	Leadership autocracy and venture capitalist pressure.	
	Rigorous and short-term financial measurement.	
Rational planning	Prevalence of formal planning knowledge and skills.	Belief in primacy of product or technical knowledge or skills.
	Top management team endorsement of rational approaches.	Belief in primacy of hard data over soft, intangible data.
	Rapid increases in business complexity (e.g. via acquisition) allowing a basis for challenging former non-planning processes.	Resistance to use of formal information and control systems.
	Acceptance of the need for market research and allocation of appropriate resources.	Reluctance to speak out openly, often a cultural 'lag' effect from former command processes.

	Market, rather than product, oriented IT systems.	*De facto* isolation of planners, either self imposed or imposed by other functions.
		Adherence to rigid planning processes.
	Dedication of resource to extensive internal communication processes.	
	Appointment of new, external, managers with planning orientation.	Weak habits of communication across functions.
	Allocation of time and resources to planning skills training or consultancy.	Fear of data costs, often a cultural lag of command cultures.
	Process driven approach within a command framework.	
	Cross functional working between departmental silos.	
Incrementalism	HR policies designed to provide staff with skills greatly superior to nominal role.	Bureaucracy of decision approval.
	Symbolism and example to reduce blame culture.	Flat structures, requiring multiple peer approval rather than approval by a limited number of superiors.
	Demarcation of large and small decisions between management levels.	Technical complexity of R&D projects, increasing lead times and costs.
	HR policies designed to reduce turnover.	Interference by senior management with relatively low level changes to resource allocation.
	Actively managed cultures, by identification and communication of core beliefs.	Belief in primacy of hard data, increasing the barriers to change.
	Reduction in level of quantification required for decisions, allowance for decision makers' 'instinct'.	Requirements to justify financially incremental change to a detailed level.
	Habits of small, incremental, proposition changes rather than discontinuous proposition changes.	Close management control (e.g. low-budget approval limits on managers).
	Development of clusters of expertise within functions.	Weak communication processes across functions.
	Habits of measurement and feedback on incremental changes.	

Table 7.6 Mechanisms of microcongruence and micro-incongruence

	Visionary command	*Rational planning*	*Incrementalism*
Microcongruent cultures	*Mechanism: cultural homogeneity and acceptance.* Visionary command processes are enabled by strong, homogeneous cultures that include widely held assumptions about the primacy of the top management team.	*Mechanism: cultural sophistication and openness.* Rational planning processes are enabled by cultures in which process sophistication is valued and cross functional working encouraged.	*Mechanism: cultural generosity.* Incremental processes are enabled by cultures in which resources are not strictly controlled and experimentation is condensed.
Micro-incongruent cultures	*Mechanism: cultural heterogeneity and rebellion.* Visionary command processes are hindered by weak, fragmented cultures in which assumptions about the primacy of the leadership are questioned.	*Mechanism: cultural rigidity and conflict.* Rational planning processes are hindered by cultures in which process sophistication is countered by process rigidity and cross functional working is hindered by control measures.	*Mechanis: cultural pettiness.* Incremental processes are hindered by cultures in which resources are bureaucratically controlled and experimentation failure is feared.

of planning, vision and incrementalism with the company culture. They are summarized in Table 7.6, and can be described as follows:

1. *Cultural homogeneity and acceptance.* This is the mechanism that supports visionary command processes. In such cultures, the culture is strong (i.e. the core assumptions are widely held in the company) and its values include an acceptance of leadership authority.
2. *Cultural sophistication and openness.* This is the mechanism that supports rational planning. In such cultures, the values include openness of communication and a respect for sophisticated processes.
3. *Cultural generosity.* This is the mechanism that supports incrementalism. In such cultures, a *laissez-faire* attitude allows experimentation and individual freedom is more highly valued than conformation to rules.
4. *Cultural heterogeneity and rebellion.* This is the mechanism that hinders visionary command processes. In such cultures, assumptions are not commonly shared and authority is either actively challenged or passively ignored.
5. *Cultural rigidity and conflict.* This is the mechanism that hinders rational planning. In such cultures, an adherence to process over task and an excessive value placed upon accountability hinder open communication and reduce processes to mere mechanics that add little value.
6. *Cultural pettiness.* This is the mechanism that hinders incrementalism. In such cultures, bureaucratic processes and blame habits hinder experimentation and restrict autonomy.

Application point: Which mechanisms of microcongruence can you see in your company?

The mechanisms by which microcongruence arises are not simple. As with macrocongruence, some of each of them contribute to an overall level of microcongruence or micro-incongruence. However, there are usually one or two primary mechanisms, which vary between companies. Identifying these is useful for practitioners.

- Which of the six mechanisms of microcongruence do you see as operating most strongly in your company?
- What are the causes of it, and what are the implications for your strategy making process?

As with macrocongruence, these multiple mechanisms not only unravel microcongruence; they show why microcongruence is hard to achieve, is often notable by its absence, and leads to weak strategies. If the difficulty of achieving either macrocongruence or microcongruence is great, then the challenges of achieving both (i.e. bicongruence) must be even greater. From what our research tells us, it seems miraculous that any company achieves bicongruence. This in itself begs a question: how do companies achieve bicongruence? Most companies have been successful. If not, they would not be here to worry about their strategy. Some of those successful companies, as we have seen, are in this happy position because of luck or the relative incompetence of their competition. It is too much to suppose, however, that all currently surviving and thriving companies were either lucky or merely just a bit better than their pathetic competitors. No. Lots of companies must have been bicongruent once and then lost it, or manage to remain bicongruent despite changes in market turbulence and complexity. It is those companies that we look at in Chapter 8.

Power points

- There is no simple correlation between what colour of strategic marketing planning is used and the quality of the resultant strategy. There is no 'best way' to make marketing strategies.
- Contingency theory, tacitly adhered to by most managers, explains the effectiveness of business processes in terms of its fit with the internal and external environments.
- The congruency hypothesis explains the effectiveness of strategic marketing planning in terms of its bicongruence, that is its fit with the market conditions and the organizational culture.
- Macrocongruence arises from a complicated mixture of mechanisms as the rational planning, visionary command and incremental processes attempt to cope with market complexity and market turbulence.
- Microcongruence arises from a complicated mixture of mechanisms as the cultural artefacts either support or hinder the hybrid marketing-strategy making processes.

Reflection points for marketing practitioners

- What is the philosophical position, tacit or explicit, of you and your colleagues?

- How might the congruency hypothesis change the way you accept, reject or adapt new ideas for business processes?
- How complex and turbulent is your market?
- To what extent is your strategic marketing planning process macro-congruent with your market?
- To what extent is your strategic marketing planning process micro-congruent with your company culture?
- Does the level of bicongruence you observe in your strategic marketing planning process correlate to the quality of your marketing strategy, as observed in Chapter 5?

Chapter 8

How great companies make strong marketing strategies

> It is the nature of all greatness not to be exact.
>
> (Edmund Burke)

Introduction

It is possible, probable even, that some readers have come straight to this chapter, skipping the previous seven in the hope of saving time and getting the answer in one quick and easy hit. Such a tactic is entirely understandable, given the time pressure we are all under. The pressured reader will gain something from reading this chapter alone, but not everything. Ultimately this book is about creating sustainable competitive advantage, and that phrase is a *non sequitur* with quick and easy. If the lessons in this book were quick and easy to apply, everyone would do so and it wouldn't lead to sustainable competitive advantage.

In addition to the inherent difficulty of achieving sustainable competitive advantage, however, there is another reason why this chapter will give useful but not instant benefit to the pressured reader. As captured in the quotation from Edmund Burke, there is no single, clear, way in which great companies make great marketing strategy. They each do it in a different way, and that way is often ill-defined, partly unconscious and variable. A virtuoso performance in strategic marketing planning, just as in any other field, cannot be reduced to a simple checklist. That doesn't mean, however, that there are no useful lessons for practitioners who want to improve their strategic marketing planning. Like watching virtuosi in any discipline, careful observation will help us to understand greatness. And like those who learn to be fluent in any skill, improvement is less by mimicking the experts' moves than by assimilating their knowledge into our own. This chapter therefore looks at why and how some companies fail in strategy making, considers carefully what we can learn from those who succeed, and culminates in identifying a process that enables us not simply to ape the actions of great companies, but also to learn their lessons so that we develop our own virtuosity in strategic marketing planning.

The story so far

Those who have read the previous chapters and are blessed with good memories can skip this section if they so wish. For the pressured and those who want to place this chapter in context, a refresher is hopefully worth a few minutes.

In Part 1, we found that strategic marketing planning is a failed technology. We looked beyond the fads and gimmicks to find that the core process is decades old, stable and well accepted. Further, it does, or rather can, work. We now know better than to link any management process directly to success, but forests-worth of learned papers conclude that those who plan generally perform better than those who don't. Despite this, the use of strategic marketing planning is the exception rather than the rule, although this is not obvious, hidden as it is beneath the charades of strategic marketing planning that many companies play. When we explore the reasons for this, we find that the science is sound, but company culture and market conditions make it hard to apply in practice. So hard, in fact, that most companies give up and make strategy another way. A technology is a tool based on a science and, in the sense that most of us can't use it, strategic marketing planning is a failed technology.

In Part 2, we explored what great companies do. We found that we can define what marketing strategy is (our choice of target customers and what we offer them) and what a strong marketing strategy looks like. Independent of context, strong strategies share the ten characteristics that are described in detail in Chapter 5. We also found that few companies achieve strong strategies. This fits well with our observation in Chapter 4, that our strategy making technology is flawed. In trying to understand and improve this unhappy situation, we moved from the prescriptive to the descriptive and looked at how companies make marketing strategy in the real world. We found that textbook planning was a poor description of reality. What real companies do is to blend rational planning, incrementalism and visionary command approaches in a manner that we described in a way broadly analogous to the primary colours. Each company has a different colour of strategic marketing planning and, from the myriad possibilities, they can be understood in terms of a rainbow of seven stereotypical planning behaviours. Frustratingly, none of these hybrid processes is good and none is bad; what works is what fits. Effective strategic marketing planning is macrocongruent to the market conditions and microcongruent to the organizational culture. In short, it is bicongruent. The best colour to use is therefore different for every company, because each company operates in a particular environment of market conditions and organizational culture. Companies that make strong marketing strategies do it via bicongruent strategic marketing planning, not by following a prescribed process that is bicongruent only for another company in another market.

To return to Edmund Burke's observation, how great companies find that bicongruence, and its consequences of strong strategy and success, is not an exact method. We can learn from them, but their art is too subtle simply to mimic. This chapter looks at what those companies do, but before considering those paragons of virtue it is worth considering why we are not all exemplars of marketing strategy.

Application point: Do you understand what is happening in your company?

The preceding chapters are aimed at helping the reader to understand what strong marketing strategy is and why most companies fail to create it. In this chapter, we will consider what goes on in companies that make strong marketing strategy. You will learn more if you have already paused to reflect on how our understanding of marketing-strategy making sheds light on the workings of your own company. Based on your reflections about the previous chapters in this book, try to formulate answers to the following.

- How strong is your marketing strategy?
- To what extent does it meet the criteria of a strong strategy laid out in Chapter 5?
- Which of the strategy diagnostic tests illuminate particular strengths and weaknesses of your strategy?
- What does the strength of your marketing strategy imply about the effectiveness of your marketing-strategy making process?

- How does your company make marketing strategy?
- What blend of rational planning, incrementalism and visionary command approaches to making strategy does your company employ?
- Which of the seven stereotypes of strategic marketing planning (as described in Chapter 6) is the closest description of how strategy is made in your company?

- How bicongruent is your marketing-strategy making process?
- Are the market conditions in which you operate stable or turbulent, complex or simple?
- To what extent is your marketing-strategy making process macrocongruent to those market conditions?
- What are the most salient artefacts of your organizational culture?
- What underlying values and assumptions do those artefacts reflect?
- To what extent are your organizational culture and marketing-strategy making process microcongruent?

What goes wrong?

The description of bicongruence in Chapter 7 shows just how difficult it is to achieve. There is so much more to consider than simply: 'Should I do formal planning or not?' We must not only craft a three-way hybrid process, but also one that matches the particular complexity and turbulence of our market. And, if that were not enough, we have to provide a supporting and non-hindering organizational culture. We could be forgiven for thinking that making good strategy is an impossible task, too difficult for mere mortals. If, on the other hand, you think that I have 'over-egged' the problem for the sake of book royalties, then look again at Chapter 5. If we want to be sure of succeeding by dint of our own efforts and not because we are lucky, we need to score highly on those tests. As both the research and the high-failure rate of businesses show, precious few companies have strong marketing strategies. So, making strong strategy is both difficult and desirable. The complexity of bicongruence is not an overstatement; it is a good explanation for why so many of us make weak strategies.

However, some companies do make strong strategy. More than that, many companies must have made strong strategy at one time. The logic flows like this: assuming your company is more than a few years old, it has had some success; assuming that you were neither very lucky nor blessed with weak competition, that success implies a strategy that, if not perfect, was good enough. That logic raises an interesting question: if many companies had, at one time, strong strategies but most now seem to have weak ones, what went wrong? The congruency hypothesis predicts that weak strategy flows from lack of bicongruence. So our question becomes: 'How do companies move from being bicongruent to bi-incongruent?' It is an important question, because we want our own companies either to stay bicongruent or to become bicongruent in order to be able to make strong strategy and thereby succeed. It is a question that our research, as it evolved, set out to answer.

As well as assessing the current effectiveness of strategic marketing planning in the firms we interviewed, we were also interested in what had happened historically. In this, we were aided by an almost universal habit that managers have when asked to describe their business. When managers talk about their business, they tend to talk in terms of stories and histories. It is in human nature to weave observations into a time-based narrative. Many hours of tape were filled with war stories, anecdotes and reflective observations. As a result, longitudinal patterns did emerge and an explanation for the rise and fall of bicongruence over time was apparent. It is a complicated story, nuanced and differentiated for every company. Notwithstanding this, a theme emerges. It is possible to explain the loss of bicongruence in the simplified story of a typical firm, as follows.

When firms are born, they don't come out of nowhere. They are groups of people, and those people have histories, experiences and, as a result, a set of beliefs and attitudes. In short, when a company is founded it is founded with a culture, a set of beliefs about what works (and doesn't work) in the marketplace. That culture, usually based on the personal beliefs of the founders, quickly forms its own set of values and cultural artefacts. One of those artefacts of the company culture is the way the company makes its marketing strategy. In start-ups, it is often very heavily visionary command. Whatever colour the strategy making process is, it springs from the culture. Inevitably, therefore, the process is initially microcongruent and is supported rather than hindered by the other artefacts of the organizational culture. The cultural assumptions about what works in the market may or may not be correct, but in the latter case the company dies quickly. The strategy making process may or may not be macrocongruent, but in the latter case the company again dies quickly. In any event, a company that survives start-up must, almost by definition, have a bicongruent strategy making process. If it did not, it would not survive. Exceptionally, benign market environments might allow bi-incongruent companies to survive, but these exceptions prove the rule. As in any competitive ecology, survival usually implies fitness – which in this case means a bicongruent and successful strategic marketing planning process. As a successful start-up grows, its culture becomes embedded.

Initially, the growth of a new company is usually within the market it was founded in. Typically it is a niche market, with few segments, competitors and channels. It is relatively simple, although it can be either turbulent or stable. The market niche is in the simple half of the macrocongruence diagram (see Figure 7.2) The usual case, then, is an early growth phase company with a largely visionary command strategic marketing planning process (albeit supported by incrementalism and perhaps a small amount of planning). This colour of strategic marketing planning is microcongruent to the culture from which it sprang, and macrocongruent to the relatively simple market with which it needs to work. The process is bicongruent, so it creates strong strategy. The result is growth and, coincidentally, the further embedding of the culture.

Then something happens. Growth often outstrips the niche or, more often, success tempts firms to move out of the niche. In a version of 'the other man's grass is always greener', firms often think it is easier to win share in new markets than in their current one. Even within the niche, growth might require new product categories, entering new segments, facing new competitors or using new channels to market. Whatever the reason, this growth results in the market environment becoming more complex. Our market, which may be turbulent or stable, starts to drift from the simple to the complex half of Figure 7.2. The strategic marketing planning process that used to have to deal with only a simple situation now needs to cope with some degree of market complexity. The market may also become more or less turbulent, but the usual change pattern is for an increase in complexity. Rarely does the market context become simpler over time. As a result, the existing process is no longer macrocongruent. Bicongruence is lost, and the strategy making process begins to create a weak strategy. As always, luck may sometimes uncouple the link between strategy quality and results, but more usually the formerly successful company starts to flounder or at least slow in its growth.

In well-run companies this loss of macrocongruence is identified, even if only at an intuitive level and not in the terms we are using. Most frequently it is expressed in terms of 'needing to get more organized about our strategy', and results in the attempt to increase the extent of formal, rational planning. This may be done by training, consultancy or recruitment, but, whatever the method, it is an attempt to cope with increased complexity by adding more rational planning to the hybrid marketing-strategy making process. Sometimes the attempt fails, if the training, consultancy or recruitment is ineffective. In that case, the company becomes another failure statistic, albeit one in which we now understand its failure more. Let's assume, though, that the company succeeds in turning its mostly visionary command process into one that is partly or even mostly rational planning. In other words, the company manages to restore macrocongruence between its strategic marketing planning and its now more complex market conditions. Surely they have now restored bicongruence and will start making good strategy again?

No, because culture, as we have already described, is pervasive and persistent. It changes gradually, but is strongly resistant to deliberate management and change. The newly rational strategic marketing planning process is macrocongruent with the more complex market, but it has now lost its microcongruence to its organizational culture. Cultural artefacts like autocracy, which supported the old visionary command process, now start to hinder the newly rational process. Similarly, lack of cross-functional working and a distrust of tools and techniques make the newly rational planning ineffective. The company continues to make weak strategy, but now it is for reasons of micro-incongruence instead of macro-incongruence. The original state of bicongruence has deteriorated because the market conditions changed and although the process did change to maintain macrocongruence, in doing so it lost microcongruence with the unchanged company culture.

Of course the loss of bicongruence can also occur because a market becomes more turbulent, but the principle remains the same. Culture, market and process which started out 'in sync.' get out of step because the market, culture and process change at different rates. This phenomenon of 'congruence drift', as we shall call it, was described, explicitly and otherwise, in many of our case studies. It is a strong explanation of how companies that were successful start to make weak strategies and then fail. It also explains why newly recruited MBAs and professionally trained marketers fail when imported into a company with no tradition of marketing. Although it is not the only explanation, it is closely linked to the concept of 'strategic drift', as described by Johnson and Scholes (2001), in which companies with previously strong strategies lose touch with their marketplace.

Congruence drift affected most of the companies in our study. Those companies that succumbed to it rarely understood what was going on. Even when they could clearly see the symptoms of poor macrocongruence and microcongruence, they failed to grasp the underlying cause of those symptoms. Even those relatively few companies that managed to maintain bicongruence did not do so in an entirely deliberate and explicit manner. It would be more true to say that they did so by a process that was 'unconsciously competent', in that their skilled management took steps to fix what they saw as going wrong without considering the concept of bicongruence. How they did that is the subject of the following sections. Turning their unconscious competence into your conscious competence is the subject of Part 3 of this book.

Application point: Has congruence drift occurred in your company?

Congruence drift, the idea that companies lose their initial bicongruence because the market, culture and strategy making process change at different rates and therefore get out of sync., is a powerful explanation of why companies make weak marketing strategy. It is worth considering whether it has occurred in your company.

- Have your market conditions changed since the formation of the company?
- Has either market complexity or market turbulence increased since the organizational culture was formed?

- Has the strategy making process developed to maintain macrocongruence?
- Has the process become more rational to cope with complexity, or more visionary to cope with turbulence, or both?
- Has the organizational culture changed to maintain microcongruence?
- Have underlying assumptions, values and cultural artefacts changed to maintain a supportive and non-hindering environment for the strategy making process?

What goes right?

Management researchers enjoy a luxury and a privilege not afforded to many practitioners. They get to talk, at length, to a large number of companies about their strategy and their market. Even if time allowed, the typical executive would not be given access to such detail, if only for reasons of commercial confidentiality. The researcher, therefore, has the opportunity to compare and contrast a much larger sample of companies than a typical manager, and at a greater depth. From these comparisons emerge striking differences and similarities between companies. Such comparisons go to inform books like this. Our work revealed five key differences between situations in which strategic marketing planning went right and when it went wrong, and these are discussed below.

Great companies judge their market conditions well

In our research, one of the most striking differences between companies was their ability to judge and appreciate their own market conditions. By this is meant the accuracy of their judgements about market complexity and market turbulence. All of the case studies were asked the same questions about the numbers of segments, channels, competitors and other aspects of market complexity. Similarly, they were all asked the same questions about the rate of change of those factors (i.e. the level of market turbulence). Using these data, and a huge amount taken from published sources, an objective assessment of their relative market complexity and market turbulence was made. The interviews also included direct questions to the executives about both complexity and turbulence, with the aim of uncovering their personal perceptions of market conditions. The two sets of data, concerning objective and perceived market conditions, were very enlightening, because they revealed a great divide in the companies we studied.

The research concerning objective measures revealed a wide spread of different market conditions, from the complex to the simple and from the stable to the turbulent. In the same way, the questions about perceptions indicated that managers viewed their markets in various parts of the complexity/turbulence box. Strikingly, however, the correlation between perception and reality was polarized into two groups: those whose perceptions fitted well with the objective assessment and those whose did not. In other words, some managers seem to be good at assessing the complexity and turbulence of their market and some do not. This conclusion about individual managers, however, can also be extended to companies as a whole, since there was a high level of agreement between different managers in the same company. As will become clear, this difference in market-judging competency is fundamental. It begins to explain why some companies achieve bicongruence, and its consequences of strong strategy and success, whilst others don't.

Whilst the fact that some companies are better at judging the dynamics of their market is interesting, the underlying mechanism of that variance is what interests us. How and why some companies are better than others at assessing the relative complexity and turbulence of their market was an important question and outcome of the research. The answer, as befits the theme of this chapter, is that greatness is inexact. Companies who properly judged their market conditions did so via a messy and often unconscious mixture of two complementary mechanisms: external cognition and internal sensitivity.

External cognition is the ability that companies have to translate their data about the market into valuable information. It is part of what Karl Weick called 'sensemaking' (Weick, 1995), and what Sparrow and Hodgkinson called 'strategic competence' (Hodgkinson, 2002). Whilst those authors talked about the whole process of assembling a view of the external environment, our research found that a particular subset of it was important to making strategic marketing planning work. We found that companies with good external cognition skills were able to assess accurately the complexity and turbulence of their market. Armed with an appreciation that the market is, say, complex, this naturally predisposes a company to make strategy via a process that involves a high degree of rational planning. Similarly, companies that perceive their market as turbulent are more inclined to rely on visionary command processes. Note that external cognition is not synonymous with gathering more or better data; it is the capability to process those data effectively. Differences in external cognition skills can dramatically influence the way the company makes strategy, and consequently its bicongruence, strategy strength and performance.

A good current example of this lies in the market for mobile phone handsets. Historically, Nokia has been the market leader and has consequently gained the advantages of scale, channels and brand name. Until recently, Nokia seemed unassailable. The principal market followers, Samsung, Sony Ericsson and Motorola, seemed ill placed to erode Nokia's lead. Yet in April 2004 Nokia announced a profit warning and a 5 per cent drop in share over the preceding year. The market for telephone handsets had been turbulent (driven by technology and rapid market development) but relatively simple. As with many embryonic markets, market segmentation was limited. As the market matured, however, new segments emerged based not on technical product needs as such, but on lifestyle and emotional needs. Design and multifunctionality became more important to customers than technically defined performance. In product terms, this was reflected by a rapid increase in the range of handsets available. A narrow range of traditional and undifferentiated 'candy bar' phones exploded into a dense catalogue of PDA phones, camera phones, clamshell designs and so on. This change in product design, however, merely reflected the fragmentation of a relatively homogeneous market into one containing multiple needs-based segments. Nokia's inability to see the significance of this change in the market was understandable but damaging for them. It appears they lost sight of the relative importance of market segments in the mass of information about new technology, geographic expansion and market penetration. By contrast, their competitors saw segmentation as critical and acted on it. Although not an example taken from our primary research, the handset phone market is a good example of the external cognition mechanism. From this perspective, Nokia did not translate the market signals it received into indications that its market was becoming more complex with respect to market segmentation. It therefore stuck to its relatively visionary command process, and the resulting macro-incongruence led to a weak strategy. In terms of the strategy diagnostic tests, they failed in defining segments correctly and therefore in creating segment-specific value propositions. They tried to sell candy bars to everyone.

A further example of the external cognition mechanism has already been touched on in Chapter 5. Kodak was not slow to pick up the early signs of digital photography. Although well placed, in theory, to pick up on the emergence of this technology, Kodak failed, in practice, to react quickly enough. Its CEO, George Fisher, announced in 1996 that it would 'drive digital imaging to new markets'. Yet it took until September 2003 for his successor, George Carp, to announce that they would make no more big investments in traditional film, and still longer for the company to stop selling the old technology in developed markets – this despite the fact that digital cameras had already overtaken film cameras in terms of US sales. In 2004, Kodak announced a 20 per cent reduction in its labour force. By contrast, companies that Kodak did not traditionally count as competitors, such as Hewlett Packard, acted upon the strategic implications of digital technology earlier. We can now see that Kodak failed to see that digital technology meant a rapid increase in the level of turbulence of their market. They therefore carried on with their heavily planning-led process for making marketing strategy. The resultant micro-incongruence (this time incongruent to the turbulence, whereas Nokia's was incongruent to complexity) led to a weak strategy. In terms of strategy diagnostics, they failed to anticipate the future and as a result did not achieve SWOT alignment.

Good external cognition skills therefore help companies accurately to sense the complexity and turbulence of the market. That then predisposes them to create an appropriate colour of strategic marketing planning. However, we found that external cognition was only half of the mechanism that companies used to help decide the best way to make strategy in their particular market. The other half was internal sensitivity. This can perhaps best be described as the corporate equivalent of self-knowledge, in that it is the recognition of strengths and weaknesses. Our observations were that some companies were sensitive to both the strengths and weaknesses of their own way of making strategy. Others, however, were relatively complacent in that they gave little thought to their strategic marketing planning process, and when they did were arrogantly confident of its strength. Sensitivity to the strengths and weaknesses of the marketing strategy seemed to alert firms to macro-incongruence and thereby predispose them to consider and adapt their strategy process.

Examples of internal sensitivity come directly from our research, and therefore have to be anonymous and slightly disguised. Three companies illustrate a range of sensitivity to macrocongruence.

The first (and worst) was a company that operated in a horribly complex market. Although relatively focused in its product range, it operated in both consumer and industrial markets. Both markets involved several different types of channel to market and featured entirely different competitors, as well as a range of indirect competitive forces. Both markets were segmented, and in the industrial market the decision making process was convoluted. In both markets, the value proposition was moderately complex. By any measure, this company faced a complex market. Its strategy making process was heavily visionary command supported with an element of cultural incrementalism. Little evidence of rational planning, beyond financial controls, was evident. This process was strongly microcongruent, being well supported by hierarchical structures and a very tight culture in a small leadership team. As might be expected from a visionary command process in a complex situation, the process showed lots of signs of macro-incongruence. Although the managers interviewed clearly had great knowledge of the facts of the market, they completely failed to synthesize those into key issues to be addressed by the strategy. They saw their market as simple, and the key issues as being related to manufacturing. Although detailed questioning led them to comment on several areas where their strategy making process failed to understand the market, choose the strategy or decide the action, they were unconcerned and saw strategy making as something that 'just happens'. They were a clear example of internal insensitivity to macro-incongruence.

The second example was a very large multinational. It operated in a complex and moderately turbulent market. Complexity arose from a complex value proposition along with channel complexity. There was also a significant degree of segmentation and decision making complexity. The competitive scenario was only moderately complex, consisting of several competitors but in only two strategic groups. Market turbulence arose from some steady but important changes in SLEPT factors that resulted in changes in the customer aspect of the market. It was then amplified by competitor reaction. The company operated a strongly rational planning process, albeit with a sub-component of visionary command. The process was largely bicongruent. The relatively flat structure and process-driven culture supported the process quite well, and the market complexity was moderately well accommodated by the planning process. More interesting, however, was the fact that the company was sensitive to what macro-incongruence did occur. This showed when the relatively slow planning process failed to react quickly enough to market changes. The natural slowness of planning was, in this case, exacerbated by a cultural habit of consensus seeking. Managers were aware of this, and were trying to fix it, but the cultural issues were baffling them. Notwithstanding that, this company is an example of moderately good internal sensitivity to macrocongruence.

The third, and best, example of internal sensitivity was an unusual case. Although a very large company, it was split into quite autonomous divisions, each dedicated to a market niche. As a result, each division operated in relatively simple market conditions. Its market was moderately turbulent, the aggregate effect of technological development and regulatory inertia. This company operated a strongly visionary command approach, originating in its US headquarters and strongly driven by its research function. This colour of strategic marketing planning was well supported by its culture, with clear demarcation and acceptance of roles. By any standards, this company was strongly bicongruent, a fact further evidenced by its strong strategy and market-leading position. However, the company had astutely recognized the first signs of emerging macro-incongruence. The market was going through a technologically driven transition phase, resulting in even higher than usual turbulence. Even with a quite visionary command process, it was failing to keep up in some small but important ways. To counter this, the company set up a number of small, well-resourced and quite independent think tanks of scientists, marketers and customers. The role of these think tanks was to sense the implications of new technology and feed them into the centre. These small-scale units were an example of incrementalism. This company is therefore an example of being exquisitely sensitive to early signs of macro-incongruence and modifying the strategy making process to restore macrocongruence.

So, in trying to understand how great companies make strong marketing strategies, we have identified their first step. Compared to their lesser rivals, they have a much better understanding of where their market sits in the complexity/turbulence spectra. They use external cognition skills to judge where their market sits in these spectra, and internal sensitivity to pick up early signs of macro-incongruence. This knowledge forms the basis for creating a colour of strategic marketing planning that works for them. Of course they rarely, if ever, see it in those terms, but that is clearly what is going on. It was not clear, from our research, why some companies are good at external cognition and internal sensitivity. To refer to our earlier analogy, we have explained how a virtuoso performer differs from an amateur, but not explained the gene expression that gives him or her that ability. We observed that great companies emphasize recruiting and retaining good people, but that doesn't help us much in our quest to imitate them. It is indeed beyond the scope of this book to prescribe how to create a company of virtuosi. What we can do, however, is provide a set of tools that allow us lesser mortals to imitate the skill of great companies at judging market complexity and market turbulence. Such tools for judging market conditions are described in Chapter 9.

Application point: How well does your company judge its market conditions?

The first characteristic of companies that make strong strategy is that they judge the complexity and turbulence of their market well. They do this by a combination of external cognition of market forces and internal sensitivity to strengths and weaknesses in their strategy making. It is useful to reflect upon how well these processes operate in your company.

- How much attention does your company pay to the complexity and turbulence of the marketplace?
- Does it manage to put the myriad of different inputs into perspective to form an objective judgement of market conditions, or does it lose perspective and judge the market subjectively?

- How much attention does your company pay to the strengths and weaknesses of your marketing strategy?
- Does it attempt to assess the performance of its strategy making process, or does it just apply the process and not think too much about what it is doing?

Great companies evolve the right colour of strategic marketing planning

As described in the previous section, there were a number of observable differences in behaviour between those companies that achieved bicongruence, and hence strong strategy and good results, and those that did not. The first was the ability to judge the market conditions and their implications for the colour of strategic marketing planning to use. This ability to judge market complexity and market turbulence well was usually unconscious, and it did not automatically lead companies to adapt their strategy making process. However, it did make them predisposed to the necessary adjustment of the ratios of rational planning, visionary command and incrementalism.

The second competence difference between the companies studied was the manner in which they adapted their strategy making to respond to current or anticipated macro-incongruence – in other words, how they changed the colour of their strategic marketing planning. As implied by the generally poor standard of strategy noted in Chapter 5, not all companies attempted actively to manage their strategic marketing planning process. Many, even those who actively manage other management processes, seem to be either unconscious of strategy making as a process or else complacent about their current process. Of those that did attempt to change the way they made strategy, however, it could be observed that some approaches worked and others did not. Since such process tailoring inevitably involves adding one or more of the three component processes, failure and success is best described in those terms.

The addition of rational planning to the hybrid strategy making process

The addition of rational planning to an otherwise visionary command or visionary command plus incrementalism process was the most commonly observed attempt at managing the strategy making process. Two contrasting examples from the research illustrate the point well.

In the first (and worst) case, the company had been driven to increase rational planning less by macrocongruence needs and more by fashion. Undoubtedly the moderately complex, stable market did require an element of rational planning, but the company had not sensed this through either external cognition or internal sensitivity. Instead, a happenstance of several managers, each with business school training, led the company to invest a lot of effort in a formal rational planning process. In addition to their externally learned ideas, they employed a well-known firm of management consultants who imposed more externally derived prescriptions. Hence an elaborate strategic marketing planning process, a good example of the textbook approach, came into being in quick order. It was a source of pride to the managers who had initiated it, who felt the consultants' fees well justified. However, the process failed to create strong strategies. This was partly due to a lack of microcongruence, caused by the cultural lag, as the process changed faster than the culture did. However, the process also failed because it was never fully implemented. Instead, it became a charade of going through the motions – a triumph of process over task.

Compare this to another company in a similar market. It, too, had decided to invest much resource into a more 'textbook' approach. However, the idea for this seems to have originated from a new CEO who, in our terms, clearly judged the complexity of the market and sensed the macro-incongruence of the current visionary command plus incremental process. In some ways, the approaches of the two companies looked similar. Both, for instance, made it a high management priority and used consultants. However, there were three remarkable differences and many smaller contrasts in style. The first difference was that, in the stronger example, new individuals were recruited to some key posts. These differed from the weaker example, in that they had both formal training and experience of implementing textbook planning. Secondly, they made less and different use of the consultants. In this case the consultants' time was used judiciously to execute only those parts of the task that the in-house managers, for want of time or knowledge, could not. Even then, it was done so that the managers could learn from it and do it themselves next time. Finally, in the stronger example, much effort was expounded on an internal selling exercise to enculture all involved in the discipline of rational planning. Rather than being imposed, formality was sold as a necessary virtue. This attempt to add rational planning to the hybrid marketing-strategy making process was a success, especially in its outcomes of market understanding and strategy choice.

The contrast between the two companies' approaches can be summarized as injection versus infusion. To add rational planning effectively to the strategic marketing planning process, it has to be infused; injection will not work. Along with other examples in the research and published data, these examples show that the imposition of rational planning, even when done from within, does not work. If it is not rejected, it is twisted into a travesty of formal planning that is as ineffective as it is wasteful. By contrast, infusing the practices of textbook planning does work, so long as it is supported by well thought out recruitment, consultancy and internal selling. As one of our respondents put it:

> Making our people plan has a cost to them. They have to give up old and pleasurable habits like reacting to events and abdicating responsibility upwards. We should not expect people to do it on command.

The addition of visionary command to hybrid strategy making processes

The second most commonly observed attempt at managing the strategy making process was the addition of visionary command to an otherwise rational planning, or rational planning plus incrementalism, process. It was seen in cases where a previously stable market had become turbulent and that change had been recognized, either by external cognition or internal sensitivity, or a combination of both. Such cases are less common than the addition of rational planning to hybrid strategy making processes discussed previously. This is because whereas increasing complexity is a result of normal business growth, increased turbulence usually only results from external changes such as demographics, globalization, regulation or, sometimes, macroeconomic cycles. Two recent examples illustrate the point.

The media industry has, in recent years, moved from the stable to the turbulent. Although complicated, the causes of this can be summarized as globalization and technology. Those forces have caused the collapse of national and sector boundaries in a remarkably short timescale. Press, television and other media have coalesced, and a previously localized industry has become pan-national. Vivendi, Time Warner and Bertelsmann, Europe's biggest media company, are examples of this. Although a family-based firm, Bertelsmann has long been run by professional managers. This changed with the departure of its CEO, Thomas Middelhoff, and the assertion of the Möhn family direction. This seems to have been driven by the board's perception that the rational planning approach of the professional management was not coping well with the market turbulence arising from market forces, an example of their internal sensitivity. This sudden shift to a more visionary command strategic marketing planning process seems not to be going well. The recent pattern of business restructuring at Bertelsmann shows none of the understanding of the market that is supposed to flow from visionary command processes. The acrimonious departure of the Chairman of the supervisory board seems to confirm the difficulties faced by the firm. Critics of Liz Möhn, the family representative on the board, talk of a 'matriarchal dynasty' and meddling in managers' roles at a detailed level.

Compare Bertelsmann to Janus Capital Group, one of the leaders in the US mutual fund industry. That sector, too, has undergone times of turbulent change after a decade or more of steady, benevolent market environments. The turbulence has arisen from both internal sources, such as ownership changes, and external forces, especially the macroeconomic environment and industry regulation. In response to this turbulence, Janus has moved its strategy making away from a planning and incremental approach, adding a large element of visionary command. This comes not from a single leader but from a duo, Steven Schied and Gary Black. Importantly, both men are outsiders. In contrast to Liz Möhn, this duo seem focused on setting strategic direction and ensuring its communication flowed out from the centre. This approach assumes that professional management will fill in the detail in the spaces defined by the strategic direction. The approach has resulted in a better grasp of the key issues in the mutual fund market, such as attitudes to ethics and risk, and the renewed importance of cost control. At the time of writing, Janus' results show it to be emerging from the trough it entered when both market factors and macro-incongruence led it astray.

The contrast between Janus and Bertelsmann illustrates two very different approaches to coping with turbulence by asserting visionary command. The Janus duo concentrated on understanding the market and communicating their strategic choice. Their involvement in operational matters is limited to a small number of symbolic actions that support the strategic direction, such as changing compensation structures. This approach seems to recognize the time limitations on any leader or leadership group, and the implication that they can only direct and frame action but not manage it closely. The Bertelsmann situation demonstrates the opposite – that visionary command fails when it is applied from the bottom. In this sense, rational planning and visionary command processes are opposites, in that the first must be infused throughout the company and not injected from the top, whilst the latter has to impose frameworks but not attempt to involve itself in the detail.

The addition of incrementalism to hybrid strategy making processes

The addition of incrementalism to the hybrid marketing-strategy making process is the least commonly observed, since incrementalism is present to a significant extent in almost all companies. This existing incrementalism often takes the form of political or cultural incrementalism, driven by implicit processes, but in its rational form it can usefully ameliorate the limitations of unalloyed rational planning or visionary command processes. It follows, therefore, that successful examples of adding incrementalism to the hybrid marketing-strategy making process are those that take the form of rational, rather than political or cultural, incrementalism. Two very different examples illustrate this.

IBM's recent history is often held up as an example of a visionary command strategy making process coping with the turbulence of the IT market. In their case, this involved shifting from a product-led company to a predominantly services company. However, the IBM case is more interesting as an example of rational incrementalism because, although CEO Sam Palmisano and his predecessors have clearly driven the strategic vision, IBM's market is too complex for visionary command alone. Faced with competition from both product and service companies and an incredibly fragmented market, IBM used incrementalism to aid their understanding of the market and choice of strategy. Long before IBM took the huge step of buying PwC it took many small incremental steps, from selling mainframes with basic support, to helping companies design systems, to managing clients' IT systems for them. PwC was a huge step, but part of a journey. That journey is now continuing as IBM moves to on-demand computing and changing the IT services market into something akin to utilities. The key to IBM's success at incrementalism has been the scientific principle of controlled experiments. Leveraging its strength and diversity, they were able to try out different approaches to services in different sectors and different countries. Each time, the number of strategy variables (the different components of the value proposition, the types of target customers) that were changed was limited. When incremental steps failed or succeeded, the change that led to those results was identifiable. In that way, the results of each experiment were understood and generalized across the rest of the company. Since this transfer of knowledge happened largely through the centre of the organization, IBM provides a good example of visionary command plus rational incrementalism coping well with a turbulent and complex market.

The comparison to IBM is Marks and Spencer, the retailer that is also something of a British institution. Faced with increased market turbulence and complexity arising from sociological change and radically changing competitive forces, Marks and Spencer tried innumerable tweaks to their proposition in an attempt to develop, or perhaps uncover, a stronger strategy. Their failure to do so, until recently, lay in their inability to draw conclusions from the results of their activity. For instance, they greatly increased the number of sub-brands used in their clothing section, at the same time as trying to reach new segments. They tried to develop several areas of their business at once, with new food-only stores, outlet discount centres and massive new out-of-town stores. The results were mixed and, more importantly, unclear. The interconnectivity of different parts of the Marks and Spencer strategy, through the umbrella brand and segment interaction, meant that neither successes nor failures could be used to provide generalizable lessons. Marks and Spencer's strategy at that time was a good example of the limitations of incrementalism. To their credit, the appointment of Stuart Rose, and subsequent changes in Marks and Spencer's strategy, suggest a recognition of these limitations as discussed below.

Characteristically, then, companies that add incrementalism effectively to their hybrid marketing-strategy making process do so in a controlled manner, allowing lessons to be learned. Ineffective addition of incrementalism is usually reactive, frenetic and uninformative.

The experience of both our case studies and those companies in the public domain does show that there is a best way, and a worst way, to add each of the three approaches to making strategy to a hybrid marketing-strategy making process. Combined with an objective appreciation of market complexity and market turbulence, this knowledge (which, remember, is usually tacit) allows a firm to achieve macrocongruence. How the firm achieves the microcongruence required to make them bicongruent is described in the next section.

Application point: To what extent does your company manage its strategic marketing planning process?

The second distinctive competency that is associated with making strong marketing strategy is the deliberate adaptation of the process to suit the market conditions of turbulence and complexity. This inevitably involves the addition of rational planning, incrementalism or visionary command, and there appear to be good and bad ways to do each.

- To what extent has your company attempted to add rational planning, and did it attempt to impose it from the centre or infuse it into the organization?
- To what extent has your company attempted to add visionary command processes, and did it attempt to create frameworks or to micro-manage the strategy process?
- To what extent has your company attempted to add incrementalism, and did it do so in a controlled or haphazard manner?

Great companies adapt their cultural artefacts to fit their planning process

As we consider what great companies do, we must remind ourselves that we are now looking at a small minority of companies. Most companies pay remarkably little attention to the effectiveness of their strategy making process. Ironically, this is true even in companies that pay a lot of attention to other processes that flow from their strategy, such as operations or supply chain management. However, some companies do work hard at getting their strategy making process to work. In this book we have named the way they do this as 'achieving bicongruence', although that is not a term that would be recognized by these companies.

As implied by the order of the previous two sections, bicongruence seems to start with macrocongruence and then requires microcongruence, not the other way around. Although it is not always easy to discern an order of events, this market-led approach is a better description of the way companies do it than the reverse. We did not, generally speaking, observe companies trying to change their markets to suit their culture and strategy making process. It was more often a case of judging the market, adapting the process to minimize macrocongruence, and then changing the culture to become microcongruent with the already macrocongruent strategic marketing planning process. This order of events is not surprising, of course. It is just being market led and reflects the reality that managers generally have more control over their internal processes than they do over their marketplace.

There are some notable and informative exceptions to this generalization of macrocongruence then microcongruence. These are when companies appear to change their market in order to suit their strategy making process. Of course, companies cannot usually change their market turbulence or complexity, and it is not strictly true to say that these exceptions do. What they do, in fact, is to choose to address markets in such a way as results in a *de facto* change in the market conditions. The unusual example of Johnson and Johnson illustrates the point. This massive global healthcare and consumer company operates in a very large number of professional medical sectors, such as pharmaceuticals, medical devices and *in vitro* diagnostics. In addition, it is a major consumer goods company. Some of its markets, like medical devices, are fragmented. Its market is at the extreme ends of the complexity scale. If it wishes to achieve macrocongruence, a heavily rational planning approach seems appropriate. However, this would be at variance with its strongly visionary command culture. Johnson and Johnson is famous for its 'credo' and strong corporate culture. In this case, changing the culture seems more difficult, and probably less desirable, than changing the market. This has led the company to adopt an approach that is the reverse of most bicongruent companies. What Johnson and Johnson do, in effect, is to reduce the complexity of its market by an extreme form of divisionalization. In the medical sector, for instance, it operates five relatively autonomous companies in addition to its pharmaceutical division. Each of these 'franchises', as they are called, operates solely in one sub-sector, such as orthopaedic implants, wound closure and so on. This structure has some costs in loss of economies of scale and internal transaction costs, but these are outweighed by its benefits. These benefits stem from the fact that each company is operating in a relatively simple sub-sector with few competitors, segments, channels etc. Each simple market is macrocongruent to Johnson and Johnson's visionary command strategy making process. That visionary command process itself flows from, and is microcongruent to, the strong company culture. The company has simply achieved the same result in a reverse order of events from most bicongruent companies, and this approach is vindicated by its market-leading position in most of its business areas. Few examples of this approach exist. However, Stuart Rose's strategy to fix Marks and Spencer's problems (as discussed above) may be an example of market simplification. He has reportedly questioned the need to stock 'twenty-three kinds of tomato', and has promised to reduce the complexity of its business by reducing store types, simplifying the value proposition, and focusing the segmentation and targeting of the core business. Such examples of market simplification are rare, however, and go to prove the rule that most companies adapt their culture to the process and hence to the market, rather than *vice versa*.

If macrocongruence then microcongruence is one observed 'rule' of achieving bicongruence, then avoiding wholesale culture change is another. As was described in Chapter 3, culture is persistent and pervasive. Attempts to change a company culture wholesale rarely succeed, and the cases in which they do are extreme – such as Jack Welch's dismissal of 15 000 middle managers at GE. This difficulty is due to the structure of organizational culture, as described by Edgar Schein's model of artefacts, values and assumptions (see Chapter 3), and the hidden, embedded nature of every organization's cultural assumptions. The companies that we observed to change their culture were notable in the small scale of their ambitions. They sought not to revolutionize their culture, but to tweak it with small, deliberate changes to parts, not all, of the culture. In general, the way these companies approached cultural change was to identify or anticipate cases where the culture hindered the strategy making process, and then adjust the offending cultural artefact. In some cases this involved not only changing the artefact (such as the structure) but also challenging and realigning the values and assumptions that underpinned it. By contrast, what these companies did not do was attempt to introduce a whole new set of assumptions and rebuild the culture from scratch.

So, companies that successfully achieve microcongruence do so by tweaking their cultures to make them less hindering and more supportive of their by now macrocongruent colour of strategic marketing planning process. As might be inferred from how companies achieve macrocongruence, this in effect means changing the culture to better support an increased proportion of rational planning, visionary command, incrementalism or all three. In each case, there are potentially hundreds of cultural artefacts that might ideally be changed. However, it is simpler in practice. Pragmatically, the huge number of individual artefacts can be consolidated into a manageable number of cultural themes which, when enacted, create the bulk of microcongruence. If we are to emulate the great companies, it is an understanding of those key themes of microcongruence that is critical. Equally, we need to understand the reverse of those themes which lead to microincongruence. Both sides of cultural adaptation are considered in the following sections.

Achieving microcongruence with rational planning

As discussed earlier in this chapter, adding rational planning to make a different colour of strategic marketing planning process is the most commonly observed phenomenon we noted. This is usually a response to increasing market complexity and a perception that the organization needs to become 'more formal and organized'. As those practitioners who have tried and failed to apply textbook planning will recognize, it is easy for this attempt to fail in the face of unsupportive cultures. Our research identified three major cultural themes that determined microcongruence to rational planning:

1. A deep understanding of rational planning tools and techniques
2. Senior management endorsement of rational planning
3. Minimal-disruption implementation.

A deep understanding of rational planning tools and techniques

Companies which successfully added rational planning to their strategy making exhibit an entirely different level of understanding of strategic management tools when compared to their less successful rivals. Both good and weak examples of rational planning microcongruence show superficial 'window dressing' and much use of jargon and acronyms, but the strong companies actually understand how the tools work. As a result, cultural artefacts like planning protocols and language are remarkably different. This is achieved by different means in different cases. Recruitment of outsiders, training, and use of consultants are all used to create a fundamental and deep understanding of how the various tools (as described briefly in Chapter 1) work and fit together. In particular, segmentation, targeting and positioning is understood as a coherent process and the tools are seen as aids to that process.

This is perhaps better illustrated by the less microcongruent companies. In these cases, recruitment favours industry insiders over planning experts with no industry knowledge. Training and 'academic' qualifications are superficial and consultancy is used blindly to provide answers, not to imbue skills. The best example of this was exhibited by a large multinational that had invested large resources on an in-house 'marketing academy' to ensure that all its marketing executives gained a formal qualification. However, because the training defined its objectives in terms of exam passes and did not measure applicable understanding, the result was failure. The marketing executives boasted of their qualifications while demonstrating their lack of understanding of segmentation, targeting and positioning. Arguably, the complacency bred by the training made them even less competent than they were prior to the training.

In short, cultures that are supportive of rational planning require marketers to be as competent at their functional skills as their counterparts in finance or research and development or any other function. Untrained marketers are an artefact of an unsupportive culture, and poorly skilled marketers are perhaps worse, in that they pretend to skills they don't have.

Senior management endorsement of rational planning

A key theme in company cultures that are microcongruent with rational planning is the active endorsement of rational planning and all that flows from that endorsement. Rational planning microcongruent cultures are characterized by senior management talking in the language of target segments and specific value propositions. Just as importantly, they ask for reports in that language. They also make resources available for the antecedents of rational planning, such as adequate market research. They also emphasize symbols that communicate a culture supportive of planning. For example, one of our respondent executives changed the content of his annual sales and marketing conference presentation. He de-emphasized the merits of working long hours and reacting to crises. He replaced those passages with encouragement to 'work smarter, not harder', and singled out as many business analysts for praise as the traditionally lauded sales representatives.

As with an understanding of rational planning tools, the antithesis of senior management endorsement is not that leaders refute the value of planning. Superficially, companies who failed to achieve microcongruence to rational planning did have senior management endorsement. However, their actions belied their public statements. They failed to provide resources, and still used the language of selling products rather than true marketing. One frustrated respondent in our study pointed to the symbolism in her company culture:

> The managing director talks about us being a market-led company, but he uses the marketing department budget as a contingency fund to make profit targets if we are below revenue goals at quarter end.

Another respondent pointed out that his annual sales and marketing conference had an hour-long after dinner session at which no less than twenty awards were given to sales representatives for sales results. Yet nowhere in the organization was there recognition given for understanding market structure or designing the value proposition.

For rational planning to work, senior management endorsement is a key cultural theme. This endorsement must be more than lip service. It must result in both tangible actions, like resourcing market research, and visible cultural symbols, such as praising market understanding. Arguably however, clearly unsupportive leadership is the second worst option, and leadership teams who fake support for rational planning are more harmful.

Minimal-disruption implementation

The final, but by no means unimportant, key cultural theme in rational planning microcongruent firms is that of planning implementation. Microcongruent firms are characterized by a relatively seamless transition from thinking to doing. Their cultural artefacts include allowing implementers time to plan, rather than creating isolated think tanks. Further, their cultures include organized processes for implementation and an appropriate level of cross-functional discipline to make the plans work. As one marketing manager described:

> Once the strategy is decided, we try not to make it look new. We're a process-driven company and we love it if there are protocols and manuals. So we just write the marketing action plan as if it were, say, a plan to install new plumbing in head office. That way the troops, who don't like new ideas and initiatives, just get on with it without really realizing it is a change. We call it stealth marketing!

By contrast, firms that are micro-incongruent to rational planning have cultures which magnify the changes that flow from the marketing strategy. Think tanks, created to provide time for planning, yield fewer 'reality checks' than do implementers who are given time to plan alongside their routine tasks. The resultant strategy looks more radical than it is – a fact exacerbated by the think tank's need to justify itself. The cultural habits of the organization then promote implementation by setting up new teams, new structures and new processes, rather than using or adapting existing ones. The point was well illustrated by one experienced marketer:

> It's as if we have to give everything a new name every year. We all have the sense to realize that actually it's pretty much the same as last year but we have to play the game. Eventually, you become a bit cynical about the plan.

Creating minimal disruption to existing, culturally embedded habits is a visible theme in companies that achieve microcongruence with rational planning. That is not to recommend the acceptance of practices and procedures that contradict rational planning (for instance, ignoring market segmentation). It is to suggest that good companies resist the temptation to do their rational planning in ivory towers and then announce it with a fanfare. Instead, they try to use existing practices and modify them as necessary.

Hence there are three keys to achieving microcongruence with strategy making processes that have a significant rational planning content: a deep understanding of the tools and techniques, senior management endorsement of rational planning, and minimal disruption to existing cultural habits. Conversely, lip-service to those tools, faked commitment of senior managers and causing more cultural change than is necessary will all lead to micro-incongruence and the failure of the rational planning component of strategy making.

Achieving microcongruence with visionary command

Adjusting the organizational culture to make it microcongruent with visionary command processes is less common than its rational planning counterpart, but by no means unusual. It is necessary in cases where the market is turbulent and the strategy making process has been adapted, by the addition of more visionary command, to cope with that. It is characterized by a feeling of being left behind by the market and outpaced by competitor responsiveness. As with the preceding section on rational planning, it is possible pragmatically to condense the innumerable cultural changes necessary to achieve visionary command microcongruence into three broad themes:

1. The strategic competence of the senior management team
2. Role demarcation and acceptance of authority
3. Multiple linkages between strategic and tactical processes.

The achievement of these creates the majority of the necessary microcongruence.

The strategic competence of the senior management team

The fundamental cultural characteristic necessary to make visionary command processes work is strategic competence. By that, we mean the ability of the senior management team to understand the market, choose a strategy, and decide the necessary actions. Despite the obvious nature of this observation, such competences are far from common. Frequently, senior managers exhibit an operational rather than a strategic focus, with a marked preoccupation with measures of efficiency rather than effectiveness. In many cases, they exemplify the 'Peter Principle' by their great competence at their previous role but not at their current one. When senior teams do exhibit strategic competence, it can come from a variety of sources. Experience, training and appropriate consultancy all combine to help allow senior management to be competent in their strategic role. Further, it is enabled by good team management (e.g. delegating well to free up time to think strategically) and support systems (e.g. useful management information systems). As one marketing director explained it:

> Our biggest challenge is to ask and answer the big questions. What makes it hard is the 'comfort zone' of concentrating on numbers and ratios and details.

Compare this to the revelatory comment of another senior manager:

> Until you asked, I've not really tried to articulate our strategy in those terms [target market and propositions]. Frankly, it is all I can do to keep on top of the day-to-day fire fighting.

For visionary command to work, the senior team must be strategically competent. This requires them to be close, in a knowledge sense, to the market, and to have the skills and attributes to make strategy. Further, it requires them to make the time to make strategy, rather than the more pleasurable task of doing their subordinates' work.

Role demarcation and acceptance of authority

Connected to, but distinct from, senior management strategic competence is a cultural theme that is, apparently, essential to making visionary command processes microcongruent. In microcongruent companies, visionary command processes are supported by the clear demarcation of senior strategic roles, and tactical managerial roles. Further, this demarcation is accompanied and complemented by an acceptance of authority that is not present in macro-incongruent visionary command firms. In simple terms, exemplars of this form of microcongruence show the following behaviour: leaders dictate strategy and managers implement it. Each group exhibits a high degree of trust and confidence in the other, and does not concern itself greatly with the detail of their activity. As one marketing manager expressed it:

> We have to assume two things; that they know what they are doing and that we're wasting time questioning the strategy. We have enough on our plate doing our job without attempting to do theirs.

This situation forms an interesting contrast to those firms where microcongruence appears to have broken down in this respect. In those cases, leaders preoccupy themselves with the minutiae of their subordinates' roles at the cost of their own strategic role. Similarly, managers persistently critique and question the strategy at the expense of their own tactical implementation role. In other words, strategic leaders and tactical managers spend their time doing each other's jobs. This is graphically illustrated by the case of one UK subsidiary of a multinational trying to enact an initial public offering. A previously clear cultural artefact about demarcation of roles and acceptance of authority fractured under the pressure of the acquisition. The UK commercial director described it vividly:

> Since the start [of the IPO attempt], we've noticed a marked deterioration of the working relationship. They [the main board] are so paranoid about the acquisition that they are terrified we won't make our targets. All of a sudden, they are going over our plans with a fine toothcomb. Under that sort of pressure, we end up questioning their decisions too.

For visionary command processes to be supported by the culture, therefore, it requires the culture to include artefacts that lead to role demarcation and acceptance of authority. Where these do not exist, or are damaged by external pressure, the culture hinders visionary command processes and micro-incongruence develops.

Multiple linkages between strategic and tactical processes

The third but by no means tertiary cultural theme necessary to support visionary command processes concerns the connections between the leadership and the management. It is also an interesting corollary of the capacity of these processes to cope with market turbulence. Firms that exhibit microcongruence exhibit a cultural habit that is best described as frequent synchronization checks between the strategy and its implementation steps. These involve meetings or other communication between the leaders who make the strategy and the managers who implement it. In this communication, it is not the detail of the implementation that is approved (which would contradict the demarcation habit described above) but only its consistency with the strategy. That is, the leaders ask and the managers answer questions such as 'Do these actions target the target segments we said we would aim at, or are we drifting off target?' and 'Do these actions reinforce or contradict the value proposition we said we were going to make to this target segment?'. Such synchronization checks are therefore not exhaustive, but they are incisive. Further, they happen at a relatively high frequency that is consistent with the level of turbulence of the market. One manager in a market intelligence function of a very large multinational described it thus:

> We used to have a sort of annualized ritual through which the strategy was cascaded down and then monitored. We found that it turned into a not very useful ritual in which we [the managers] felt like schoolboys and they [the leaders] felt like schoolteachers. It wasn't very productive and, insofar as it was, the input was too late. Now we have fewer formal meetings but more quick reviews. In those, there is a tacit agreement that we don't do detail, just report against milestones.

This frequent synchronization of tactics to strategy should be contrasted with the behaviour seen in micro-incongruent cases. These often appear to be cultures that are very process driven and, to some extent, better suited to rational planning. In these cases, frequent incisive testing of the coherence between strategy and tactics is replaced with rarer, usually annual, detailed examination of past failures and future plans. Notably, the time limitations faced by all firms mean that useful insight is displaced by wasteful focus on detail. This was described by a manager, rather than a leader, as follows.

> It [the strategy review process] is widely regarded as a waste of time. We have perhaps two meetings a year but spend ten times that preparing for them. The management team feels like it is on trial and we have to second guess their line of attack. They ask questions like 'what would you do with half the promotional budget?' and 'where is the proof that this campaign will work?' We inflate spend and reduce targets, they do the opposite and we end up in the middle somewhere. Then we forget about it until next year's round. It's just a game really.

Enabling frequent and constructive synchronization between strategy making and strategy implementation is therefore the third cultural theme which emerges from companies in which a visionary command process is microcongruent with the culture. It involves a frequency of contact that is much more than annual, and a type of contact that avoids detail and aims to ensure only that the tactics are consistent with the choice of target and value proposition.

As with rational planning, therefore, there are three keys to achieving microcongruence with strategy making processes that have significant visionary command content: the strategic competence of the senior management team, role demarcation and acceptance of authority and multiple linkages between strategic and tactical processes. On the other hand, Peter Principle leaders, meddling and authority resentment, and annualized planning rituals will all lead to microincongruence and failure of the visionary command component of strategy making.

Achieving microcongruence with incrementalism

Deliberately adding incrementalism to make a different colour of strategic marketing planning process is the least commonly observed phenomenon noted in our research. Almost always, the existing process contains a significant element of political and cultural incrementalism. Where incrementalism was added intentionally, it was of the rational kind. This was usually in response to uncertainty and in an effort to reduce risk, expressed along the lines of 'We're not sure, let's just try it a little bit and see what we get'. Hence incrementalism was a deliberate response to an amount of market complexity or turbulence that was just beyond the capabilities of the current strategic marketing planning process. It was, in a sense, an intermediate step before adding either visionary command (to cope with turbulence) or rational planning (to cope with complexity). As with microcongruence to both visionary command and rational planning, our research identified three major cultural themes that determined microcongruence to incrementalism:

1. Organizational slack
2. Experimentation competence and permission
3. Learning mechanisms.

Organizational slack

The first and apparently prerequisite cultural theme that is notable in companies with cultures supportive of incrementalism is organizational slack. It is most accurately described as having some spare resources, although that description may well seem a little alien to many practising managers. More realistically, organizational slack describes a culture in which a 'state of emergency' does not exist and therefore one in which not all resources are fully allocated to survival. Companies with organizational slack are still under pressure, but they have some freedom to move resources around and are not in fear of their organizational lives.

The deliberate creation of some organizational slack seems common in most non-crisis situation companies. It is achieved by not fully committing all resources, or by delaying or cancelling non-critical spending. This was described by one respondent as follows:

> I wouldn't describe our market as turbulent. It's technically complex and that, together with regulatory requirements, means that it only changes slowly, or at least predictably. However, things always crop up, so I have a rule of thumb to commit only 80 per cent of my [spending] budget. On paper it's 110 per cent allocated, of course, but in reality I keep some room to manoeuvre.

Compare this situation to a firm in which organizational slack usually existed but at the time of the research interviews was in a time of crisis. This crisis had absorbed all organizational slack, as described by a business unit manager:

> This [severe and unexpected delay in product launch for technical reasons] is a very unusual situation in that it occurred very late in the pipeline, after we had committed to our business plans. In such a situation, there is little room to move the goalposts and the board say to us: 'So what are YOU going to do about it?' Not only do we have to revisit spending plans, but it also creates, temporarily at least, a new corporate mindset. Everything is questioned and more tightly controlled. For this year, we've just had to become a lot more autocratic.

Hence organizational slack, which arises from previous success but is tacitly engineered by line managers, is a cultural prerequisite for incrementalism. It is destroyed by business crises both tangibly, as budgets are cut, and intangibly, as mindsets harden.

Experimentation competence and permission

Built on top of a degree of organizational slack is the second cultural theme that is notable in companies whose culture is microcongruent to incrementalism: permission and competence to experiment.

This is a complex aspect of culture that supports incrementalism in two ways. First, the culture allows experimentation. It does this by both granting permission and reducing the fear of failure. Secondly, the cultural artefacts include the knowledge and skills to experiment effectively. The first part of this mechanism of cultural support was humorously described by the marketing manager of a medium-sized UK subsidiary of a technically based firm:

> You see that stone slab in front of the building [a piece of sculpture]? That's the whipping stone! If any one [makes a well-intentioned mistake] then we say 'that's fifty lashes, outside now!'. It's just our way of saying if you don't make mistakes then you don't make anything.

The same cultural trait was articulated by Liam Mahoney, CEO of CRH, one of the world's biggest materials companies, in a recent *Financial Times* interview in which he not only summarized his cultural values but also gave his people permission to fail:

> We don't encourage people to screw up, but you are more likely to get fired for covering up than for screwing up.

The second component of experimentation is competence. One of the important but hard to discern cultural artefacts of incremental microcongruent companies is what might be described as empiricist managers. When they attempt some new component of strategy, whether it be a new element of the value proposition or, more rarely, a new target, they know what results and indications of results they are looking for. Often, such experimentation takes what scientists call an inductive, rather than a deductive, approach. This means that they look at what is happening in their business and try to draw out an explanation, rather than think of an explanation and try an experiment to test it. This approach was typified by the comments of one sales and marketing director:

> I find the variance between different bits of the business tells me a lot. If you compare performance between countries or regions that are selling the same product, you see differences. Look and listen carefully and you can often attribute differences in performance to either what we are doing [different distributors, pricing, whatever] or the market [different type of customer profile, different competition]. We're lucky in that we are big enough to be our own benchmark.

The opposite of this experimental competence can be either incompetence or constraint. Managers who are not empirically minded tend, under pressure, to react by changing lots of things at once. Not only does this prevent them from drawing conclusions, but the positive and negative effects of the changes also cancel out, producing no discernible result. In some companies, however, the challenge is not so much incompetence as cultural constraint. If, as in very small companies, the cultural artefacts do not provide adequate management information or the opportunity to experiment, then incrementalism is hindered.

The permission and capability to try incremental experiments, even when they are inductive 'thought experiments', is therefore a necessary cultural theme in cultures which must support incrementalism. Company cultures that involve habits of blame, or do not include the competences and capacity to experiment, are micro-incongruent to incrementalism.

Learning mechanisms

A third but very important cultural theme that is clearly observed to support incrementalism is that of learning mechanisms. Libraries of important research have been written on the subject of organizational learning, but two cultural artefacts are dominant in the learning mechanism that is part of achieving microcongruence to incrementalism. These can be summarized as memory and teaching. Incrementalism requires that companies not only learn lessons from their incremental steps or experiments, but also remember those lessons and transfer them within the company. Despite the promise of IT-enabled knowledge management, the cases studied effected this mainly through tacit human systems. In particular, the lessons were stored in the memories of long-serving individuals who, in addition to their normal tasks, acted as repositories of the company memory and informal teachers, as described by a strategic business unit manager:

> If it's not too arrogant, I think that I, and people like me, are very important to how we make strategy. I'm a lifer, been with the company a long time, and we're unusual in having a fair number of long-servers spread around the SBUs. When a keen young product manager wants to try something new, it is sometimes genuinely innovative but it is sometimes re-inventing the wheel. I see myself a bit as the wise old head [said with irony, as the respondent was in his 40s] helping us avoid repeating mistakes of the past.

A similar sentiment was voiced by a long-serving manager in a medium-sized company that had recently been absorbed into a much larger group:

> The takeover resulted in a lot of senior management change as [the founder and his immediate team] were gradually replaced. The new guys have little knowledge of our market and [my colleague] and I, as the last of the old team, have to keep reminding everyone of the lessons we have already learned.

This memory and teaching role might be supported by written records, but these are usually secondary to the memories of team members. When such organizational memory is not present, the company seems to get stuck in a permanent but inconclusive learning loop. As one relatively new-in-post respondent put it:

> We're aware of a sort of folk memory. Some of the older customer service people and reps say 'we did something like that before, not sure why we stopped', but we can't find out exactly what was tried, why and what happened. It's frustrating.

This capacity to learn, via memory and teaching, is the primary mechanism of successful incrementalism. If organizational cultures lead to high staff turnover or prevent access to the corporate memory (for instance, by de-layering the organization and firing older managers), then the culture is micro-incongruent to incrementalism and that component of the hybrid marketing-strategy making process fails.

Microcongruence to incrementalism therefore requires organizational slack, permission and competence to experiment, and a learning mechanism of memory and teaching. Without these cultural themes, incrementalism is either paralysed or reduced to an infinite loop which does not add positively to the strategy making process.

Summary

So far, then, we have identified three things that great companies do in order to make strong strategy. They judge their market well and then adapt the colour of their strategic marketing planning process to be macrocongruent. Then they tweak their culture, but don't change it wholesale, to make it microcongruent to the newly adapted process. Once again, it is worth remembering that companies do not do this consciously. The observations in this chapter come from a close and rigorous examination of their tacit behaviour. Nor is the process linear. The apparent linearity of the process is the result of describing it in a book, and should not be taken as an accurate description of what happens in reality. However, the preceding sections are an accurate and useful explication of what is a tacit and unconscious pattern in bicongruent companies.

Once this behaviour is enacted within a company, then a bicongruent strategic marketing planning process exists which both copes with the complexity and turbulence of the market and is supported, rather than hindered by, the company culture. All that remains, it seems, is to carry out the process and then implement the resulting strategy. We might now expect the company to go on to make strong strategy and meet success. We have indeed now uncovered the core of the process by which companies make strong marketing strategies. However, our research uncovered two further aspects of behaviour that differentiated great companies from those that made weak marketing strategy. These are, in effect, steps that companies take to ensure that the right process does in fact produce the right result. To make a comparison with manufacturing processes, these two further stages can be loosely equated to a quality assurance process and a quality control process. The first assures quality by ensuring that the appropriate process is adhered to. The second controls quality by testing the output of the process. These steps are described in the following two sections.

Application point: How, if at all, does your company achieve microcongruence?

Creating a supportive and non-hindering culture for whichever colour of strategy making process is used (i.e. achieving microcongruence) is the third notable characteristic of companies which make strong strategy. It usually, but not always, follows from achieving macrocongruence. It is important to understand how a company does or does not achieve microcongruence.

- To what extent does your company attempt to manage the culture?
- Does your company deliberately manage the cultural artefacts that impact on strategy making, or does it ignore them?
- If your company has attempted to modify its culture, did it attempt wholesale change or did it carefully select those parts of the culture it needed to change?

- Which cultural artefacts do you think may need to be changed in your company – those that support rational planning, incrementalism or visionary command processes?

Great companies use their process

Having crafted, by dint of great skill and effort, a strategic marketing planning process that works (i.e. it's bicongruent), the challenge is then to make sure that it is that process which makes the strategy, and not some other. This isn't as straightforward as might be expected. The crafting of a tool is not the same as using one. Deliberately designing a bicongruent marketing-strategy making process is not the same as executing it to create a strong marketing strategy. Whilst each colour of hybrid process involves different approaches to understanding the market, choosing the strategy and deciding the actions, our work exposed a phenomenon that we might call 'process drift', in which the intended strategy making process was subverted into a rather different colour. This phenomenon of process drift was driven by managerial autonomy and enabled by lack of codified processes.

Managerial autonomy exists naturally in all but the smallest and most autocratic companies. Even when little or no managerial autonomy is intended, the natural limits of senior management control lead to some level of executive freedom. In simpler terms, it just isn't possible to be a total autocrat in the real world because the would-be autocrats don't have the time, ability or knowledge, even if they have the inclination. Similarly, even the most rigidly bureaucratic companies do not codify every process, or even completely prescribe the most important ones. Even if the intention to do so exists, most complex management processes are simply too intricate and subtle to be captured in their entirety in a standard operating process or manual. Hence the strategic marketing planning process in all companies is incompletely (sometimes barely) codified, and is to some extent at the discretion of managers with a degree of autonomy. Like a huge game of Chinese whispers, the designed marketing-strategy making process is at risk of adulteration into something slightly, or even significantly, different.

In practice, we observed that every colour of marketing-strategy making process comes under pressure during execution to drift into another colour. Rational processes drift towards visionary command

and incrementalism. Visionary command processes slide towards incrementalism and rational planning. Incremental processes gradually migrate towards rational planning and visionary command. The phenomenon of process drift is reminiscent of a child's paint palette, in which every bright and pristine colour eventually becomes a muddy, indeterminate mixture of all colours.

Practitioners will have no difficulty recognizing the real-world mechanism by which this process drift occurs. Autonomous managers, without the restrictions of absolute codification, seem naturally inclined to change what they are given. To whatever process they are given, they add and subtract, deliberately or accidentally, like a medieval monk transcribing a manuscript. They add elements of rational planning (driven by a liking for order), visionary command (driven by a tad of megalomania) and incrementalism (driven by a desire to experiment). The opposite drivers lead them to subtract the same elements. Maintaining the bicongruent colour of the hybrid process intended requires as much care as not muddying the colours of the child's paint palette.

The ways in which companies effectively protect their process, and avoid the unintentional loss of bicongruence, are many, varied and rarely explicit. In effect, they are sensitive to the risks of process drift and act to stop it, but rarely in a deliberate manner. More often, managerial behaviour which is instinctive and culturally embedded prevents drift. Hence attempts to add rationality are countered by an instinct to 'kiss' (keep it simple, stupid), and attempts to lessen rationality are countered by the demand for proof and analysis. Attempts to add visionary command are countered by an instinctive leaning towards democracy and consensus, whilst attempts to lessen the visionary command element are countered by a respect for or fear of authority. Drift towards incrementalism is reduced by cultural limitations on the resources needed to experiment, but reduction of incrementalism is hindered by the dispersed and hard to control nature of this approach. The key difference between those companies that maintain a hard-won bicongruent process and those that allow it to be subverted is cultural control. Companies with strong cultures (widely held assumptions and common values) are less likely to let their process drift from one bicongruent colour to another bi-incongruent one. However, neither drifting nor culturally controlled companies are aware of this phenomenon. It seems to be a by-product of a strong culture, which is largely tacit. This tacit property is, however, not the same as being invisible and therefore inimitable. By identifying how good companies adhere to their bicongruent process, we put ourselves in a position to imitate their tacit processes with explicit ones, as described in Chapter 12. In effect, the cultural reduction of process drift is analogous to quality assurance for the bicongruent marketing-strategy making process. It ensures that the process, designed to create strong strategy, is actually applied.

Application point: How might your marketing strategy making process drift?

Process drift is the phenomenon by which a bicongruent strategic marketing planning processes gradually becomes incongruent with either the external market or the internal organizational culture. Driven by universals of managerial autonomy and incomplete codification, all companies are at risk of this happening.

- To what extent might your strategic marketing planning drift?
- In what direction do you think it is inclined to drift?
- How might you prevent this drift?
- How might you be alert to such drift and what corrective steps might be needed?

Great companies test their strategy

If the quality assurance process for marketing-strategy making comes in the form of cultural control of process drift, what is the analogue of quality control? How do companies ensure that the end product of marketing-strategy making meets requirements?

We have already come across the foundations for the quality control of marketing strategy in Chapter 5, when we discussed what a strong marketing strategy looks like and coined the phrase 'strategy diagnostics'. From decades of research, it is clear that strong marketing strategies can be distinguished from weak ones by the examination of ten properties. These properties are context-independent, and so can be used as a quality control check irrespective of the market or the company. Essentially, the fifth and final stage of strategy making employed by the best companies in our study was to apply these strategy diagnostics to what had emerged from their bicongruent and quality assured strategic marketing planning process. This final stage immediately preceded the implementation of the marketing strategy.

However, as with other stages of the process, it would not be a good description of reality to say that companies deliberately and explicitly tested their strategy prior to implementation – at least not in a formal sense. As with the earlier stages, the reality is an intuitive and largely tacit process. It is only years of research that have made it explicit and, as described in Chapters 5 and 12, useful to practitioners.

In our research, we asked the question: 'How do you know the marketing strategy you have made is any good?' Those companies of which the marketing strategy exhibited weak properties almost invariably answered something to the effect: 'We'll know if it works' – a response barely more reassuring than if it were proffered by a pilot or a brain surgeon. By contrast, those companies who exhibited strong strategies described a process of intuitive, judgemental assessment of the marketing strategy prior to the commitment of resources to actually implement the strategy. Deeper probing revealed that they were looking for the same properties as those identified by previous researchers and described in Chapter 5 as the strategy diagnostics. In segment definition, for instance, companies described a good strategy as one which 'went after our sort of customer', a phrase which also neatly captures SWOT alignment. Similarly, a sense of good strategy was associated with 'not running the same race as [the major competitor]', which is clearly a rephrasing of the need for strategy uniqueness. In other words, then, close observation of companies that create strong strategies reveals that the final stage in their process for making strategy is one of quality control by the use of what we have called strategy diagnostics.

It is useful to compare this with what those companies with weak marketing strategies do. In addition to the 'we'll know if it works' answer, they also often exhibit a behaviour which we labelled tactical seduction. This is best described as being led astray from the objective use of strategy diagnostics by the glitter of superficially clever tactics. In companies that were technically oriented (and thus often staffed with scientists-turned-marketers), tactical seduction took the form of becoming enchanted by clever creative advertising or witty copy. In less technically oriented companies (often staffed by non-scientists), tactical seduction sometimes took the form of being disproportionately obsessed by technical wizardry. In short, marketers were easily impressed by tactics that were novel to them, and this led them to judge the tactics at the expense of the strategy. Tactical seduction was not witnessed in all cases, but was observed frequently enough to suggest that it was a mechanism behind the failure to test marketing strategy. It is therefore a detailed example of a difference between makers of strong and weak strategy.

Application point: To what extent does your company test its strategy prior to execution?

The final characteristic of companies that make strong strategy is that they are neither complacent about their strategy nor seduced by the tactics. Instead, they test the strategy that comes out of their strategic marketing planning process before they take the risk of implementing it. This is a useful lesson to apply in your own company.

- How do you know if your marketing strategy is any good?
- Do you belong to the 'we'll know if it works' school, or do you assess the strategy before you execute?
- Is your management team prone to tactical seduction, or do you manage to keep a perspective on what is important in a strategy?

This chapter has considered what can be learned from the small minority of companies that make great strategies. These are difficult lessons to learn, because what they do is both complex and unconscious. If it were simple and obvious, of course, then all companies would make great strategy. From the examination of good companies, we can draw out five key characteristics – ingrained habits that differentiate them from their lesser competitors. Although useful, this leaves us with the problem of emulating their ingrained, unconscious behaviour in a conscious, explicit manner. Fortunately, analogues of this best practice behaviour can be made, and these are the subject of Part 3 of this book.

Power points

- We know from earlier chapters that what works is what fits. In other words, the way that great companies make strategic marketing planning work is to make it bicongruent.
- Good companies achieve bicongruence by a process that is usually unconscious, but five key stages listed are discernible.
- Good companies judge the complexity and turbulence of their market by a combination of external cognition and internal sensitivity.

- Good companies design their strategic marketing planning process to suit the complexity and turbulence of the market.
- Good companies adjust those cultural artefacts needed to support the appropriate strategic marketing planning process. They don't attempt wholesale cultural change.
- Good companies use the designed bicongruent process to create their strategy and avoid process drift.
- Good companies test their marketing strategy before they implement. They avoid complacency and tactical seduction.

Reflection points for marketing practitioners

- How good do you think your company is at making marketing strategy?
- To what extent do you think your company has achieved bicongruence between its strategic marketing planning process and the market and your culture?
- How complex and turbulent is your market?
- How might you need to change your strategic marketing planning to make it macrocongruent?
- What cultural artefacts might you need to modify to achieve microcongruence?
- What might you need to do to prevent process drift?
- How might you test your marketing strategy before implementation?

Part 3

How your company can make a strong marketing strategy

Part 3 of *Making Marketing Happen* moves from analysis to action as it develops the ideas of Parts 1 and 2 into actionable processes for marketing practitioners. Based on the idea that strategic marketing planning is weak technology (as described in Part 1) and an understanding that great companies make strong strategies by using bicongruent processes (explored in Part 2), Part 3 develops a systematic process for creating and using a marketing-strategy process that is bicongruent and hence leads to a strong marketing strategy. This begins with assessing the market environment and designing a strategy making process that fits those conditions. Next, the organizational culture is adapted to remove hindrances and to support the new process. The strategy making process, now bicongruent to the external and internal context in which it operates, is applied to create a clearly defined strategy. Finally, the resultant strategy is tested, prior to implementation, against the standards of a strong strategy. Throughout Part 3, the emphasis is on translating the often unconscious competence of exemplar companies into a deliberate process that can be taught and learned.

Chapter 9 deals with understanding the impact of the external environment. In particular, this chapter considers how market complexity and market turbulence impact on the strategy making process, making it necessary to adapt the process to suit the uncontrollable environment. It provides practical tools for making objective assessments of the level of complexity and turbulence in your marketplace and combining those factors to characterize the strategy making environment. In doing so, Chapter 9 not only helps you to understand your market, but also provides the basis for designing the optimal strategy making process for your organization.

Chapter 10 builds on the outputs of Chapter 9. It designs a process to make marketing strategy which will fit the external environment, as characterized in Chapter 9. This design involves considering which hybrid of planning, visionary leadership and incrementalism is the best fit to the external market. This environment-fitting, hybrid process is then translated into specific management actions for creating a well-defined marketing strategy. Chapter 10 therefore creates an actionable process for making marketing strategy which fits with, and will not be overwhelmed by, the complexity and turbulence of the external environment. Further, it provides the basis for anticipating and managing the interaction between your organizational culture and the strategy making process. This deliberate management of the culture/strategy making interface is the subject of Chapter 11.

Chapter 11 sets out to create an organizational culture that supports rather than hinders the marketing-strategy making process created in Chapter 10. To do so, it enables the identification of the specific aspects of your organizational culture that are important to the making of marketing strategy. It goes on to compare these to cultures that support or hinder different hybrid marketing-strategy making processes. Practical fixes for any cultural mismatches uncovered are then explained. Hence, Chapter 11 enables the organizational culture to be adapted to support the process. Taken together with Chapter 10, the result is a marketing-strategy making process that fits both the external and internal contexts in which it must work.

Taken together, Chapters 9, 10 and 11 enable the reader to create strategic marketing planning process that is bicongruent and therefore effective. Chapter 12 aims to enable the reader to execute that process well. It therefore describes the lessons and experiences of companies studied in this research. This includes positive and negative lessons about understanding the market, choosing strategies and deciding actions in all seven of the colours of strategic marketing planning. Finally, Chapter 12 considers how practitioners apply strategy diagnostics in a tiered manner which allows them first to test the strength of the strategy, then tests its appropriateness to their company so they can ensure it is as low risk as possible.

Chapter 9

Understanding the market

Furious activity is no substitute for understanding.

(H. H. Williams)

Introduction

The quotation from H. H. Williams that heads this chapter has a double relevance. First, it is by way of a justification. We have spent two-thirds of this book explaining the whole concept of strategic marketing planning and the idea that it only works if it is bicongruent. Only now do we get on to how to apply this knowledge. As the quotation suggests, this is deliberate. As a recent *Economist* article pointed out, many books on management are awful. Part of the reason for this is that they try to satisfy managers' appetite for quick and easy solutions to long-term and difficult problems. The purchasers of such books expect to get a lot for a little, and often get what such naïvety deserves. To gain real and lasting competitive advantage, it is not enough to go through the motions of what is recommended by academics; you really have to understand it. My hope is that the first two parts of this book give that understanding, preventing this book from being one of the awful ones.

The second relevance of the quotation is that this chapter is all about understanding, because the first distinctive difference between those companies that make strong marketing strategy and those that don't is that they understand the complexity and turbulence of their market. Before we go further, however, it is worth a short reprise of what we have covered so far. I know from experience that business books are often read in fits and starts as time allows, and the reader may not have total recall of the preceding eight chapters. If you are lucky enough to have such a memory, or to have read the whole book in a short time, please feel free to skip the next section.

What we know so far

We know, from almost half a century of research and writing, what strategic marketing planning is. It is a process for aligning the organization to the market. Like *Homo sapiens* and early hominids, strategic marketing planning is not to be confused with its ancestor, the discipline of distributing and selling what we make. Further, we know that this process works. Firms that do it perform better, overall, than those that do not. However, most of us do not do strategic marketing planning as it is prescribed in the textbooks. This is because most of us have problems making the prescribed process work in the context of our market and our organizational culture. Instead of following the textbook, companies create marketing strategies by a complex hybrid of rational planning, incrementalism and visionary command processes.

We know what a strong marketing strategy looks like and how to differentiate it from a weak one. It is the targeting of real segments with segment-specific propositions. This targeting uses our strengths, minimizes our weaknesses, anticipates the future and is relatively unique. There are other important characteristics of a strong strategy too, as discussed in Chapter 5. However, most companies make relatively weak marketing strategies and survive by being lucky enough to have even weaker competitors. Those companies that make strong strategies are distinguished from their more numerous weaker rivals not by the way they make strategy, but by the fact that their approach is bicongruent. They use a mixture of the three approaches to making marketing strategy that copes with their market complexity and turbulence, and is supported, not hindered, by their organizational culture. The difficulty of achieving bicongruence, and the fact that companies can easily drift into bi-incongruence, explains why so few companies make strong marketing strategy.

Companies that achieve and maintain bicongruence do so in a way that is mostly unconscious and tacit. They are 'unconsciously competent' at making marketing strategy. However, by close study of what goes on in these companies, it is possible to discern a five-stage process by which they make their strategic marketing planning processes bicongruent and thereby make strong strategies. That process begins with understanding the complexity and turbulence of their market. A deliberate, explicit, conscious approach to mimicking this market understanding is the subject of this chapter.

Market understanding should not be confused with market audit

There is a subtlety in the language of this book that potentially leads to an important misunderstanding. This chapter is going to address understanding the market. Note, however, that by this term we do not mean the same thing as 'understanding the market' normally associated with the 'market audit' or 'situational analysis' part of rational, textbook strategic marketing planning. Those formal processes, as referred to in Chapter 1, have a different function and a different output. Textbook market audits look at the market and attempt to draw out the implications, positive and negative, for the company. We label these positive and negative implications 'opportunities' and 'threats' respectively, and they form half the input into a SWOT analysis. The other half, of course, is strengths and weaknesses, which are internal factors. The process of market audit involves looking at macroenvironmental factors (for instance, by SLEPT analysis), customers (by segmentation analysis among other methods), channels (by market mapping, perhaps) and competitors (by Five Forces analysis, for example).

In our present context, 'market understanding' means something rather different, although it looks at similar factors. The market-understanding process comes before the market audit or any less rational method of identifying opportunities and threats. By market understanding, we mean an objective and realistic evaluation of the complexity and turbulence of the market – in other words, an understanding of where we sit within Figure 7.2. We need this in order to make a judgement about what colour of strategic marketing planning is most appropriate to our situation. That is, a good understanding of the complexity and turbulence of our market allows us to judge the right blend of rational, incremental and visionary command processes to use in making our marketing strategy. This is an entirely different process from the market audit or situational analysis described in the textbooks. It involves not just observing the different facets of the market, but also judging their complexity and turbulence, and placing them in the context of other markets. The axes of Figure 7.2 are, of course, relative rather than absolute. This relativity is what makes it hard for practitioners, immersed in one market and (usually) with little experience of different markets, to make an objective assessment. In short, it is both easy and very forgivable for a marketer to believe honestly that his or her market is at one place in Figure 7.2 when it is really at another. We need tools to help our objectivity.

Application point: Where in the market complexity/turbulence diagram is your market?

Fundamental to making strong marketing strategy is creating a bicongruent strategic marketing planning process. Fundamental to achieving bicongruence is an objective assessment of how complex and turbulent your market is. The rest of this chapter provides tools for this assessment, but it will aid your learning if you give a few minutes thought to the following questions.

- How complex, on a scale of 0–100, do you think your market is?
- What factors lead you to make this assessment?
- How turbulent, again on a scale of 0–100, do you think you market is?
- What factors lead you to this assessment?

Understanding market complexity

When we say market complexity, we mean the intricacy and convolution of that external environment with which we are trying to align our company. It is important to us, because leaders and leadership teams cope well with market turbulence but less well with market complexity. The complexity of our market therefore determines the balance we need to make between responsive but simplistic visionary processes for making strategy, and comprehensive but slow rational planning processes.

The first step in understanding market complexity is to grasp that 'the market' is what academics call a 'complex construct'. By this, we mean that it is not made up of one factor that can be measured by one dimension. A simple construct would be something like purchase price or market volume. These can be characterized by one or two simple and agreed dimensions, such as currency units or units of sale. By contrast, we can't accurately measure market complexity by one or two simple units, because it has many dimensions. If it helps your understanding, think of a simple construct as a cube of wood (which can be characterized by width, height and length) whilst a complex construct is more like a tree. The three dimensions begin to describe the tree, but only in a simplistic way.

So, if we have established that both market complexity and market turbulence are complex constructs and need to be assessed in a non-simplistic way, how do we go about it in practical terms? As ever, the comments and practices of the managers in our study will help us to decide this. They pointed out specific ways in which their process either coped or didn't cope with the complexity of the market, and these comments fell into the five categories of customers, channels, competitors, the value proposition and the macroenvironment. Every time they identified a success or failure of their planning in grasping complexity, it was in terms of one of those five things. There were many different types of success or failure, and they are used later in this chapter to help us recognize the detail of market complexity, but these five groups summed them up. In practice, therefore, we found that market complexity was in fact the sum of five different sub-components:

1. Customer complexity
2. Channel complexity
3. Competitor complexity
4. Macroenvironment complexity
5. Value proposition complexity.

These five sub-components have still further levels of detail, as summarized in Table 9.1 and Figure 9.1. It is worth spending a moment considering the table and figure before reading the next section, which describes market complexity in more detail.

Customer complexity

Customer complexity is that component of market complexity that exists in any market in which the customers are not identical to each other or do not make simple decisions on their own. Hence, all real markets have at least some degree of customer complexity, made up

Table 9.1 The nature and implications of market complexity

Sub-component of market complexity	*Complexity factors*	*Typically observed implications of failing to cope with this aspect of market complexity*
Customer complexity	Segment complexity: the number of substantially different market segments.	Failure to allocate resources effectively between segments or to create appropriately segment-specific value propositions.
	Decision-making unit complexity: the number of significant contributors to the decision-making unit.	Failure to address adequately all the significant contributors to the decision-making process or to allow for their needs in the value proposition.
	Buying process complexity: the length and number of distinct stages in the buying process.	Failure to address adequately all the stages of the decision-making process with subsequent failure of selling process.
Channel complexity	Channel type complexity: the number of different types of channel to market.	Failure to address adequately the needs of the channels to market, leading either to poor availability or to a weakened value proposition.
	Channel length complexity: the number of different tiers in the channel to market.	Failure to address adequately one or more levels within the channel to market, leading either to poor availability or a weakened value proposition.
	Channel value complexity: the extent to which the channel to market adds to the value proposition.	Failure to address adequately results in weakness in the value proposition with respect to those parts of it created or delivered by the channel to market.
Competitor complexity	Competitive force complexity: the number of different competitive forces significant in the market.	Failure to address adequately results in insufficient response to indirect threats, especially new or emergent competitive forces.
	Industry rivalry complexity: the number of different strategic sets into which direct competitors may be classified.	Failure to address adequately results in simplistic and inadequate response to direct competition which addresses only one strategic set.

Table 9.1 *(Continued)*

Sub-component of market complexity	*Complexity factors*	*Typically observed implications of failing to cope with this aspect of market complexity*
Macroenvironment complexity	Social complexity: the extent to which sociological factors have significant impact on the market.	Failure to address adequately results in poor anticipation of the implications of social factors and hence inadequate and/or belated response.
	Legal complexity: the extent to which legal factors have significant impact on the market.	Failure to address adequately results in poor anticipation of the implications of legal factors and hence inadequate and/or belated response.
	Economic complexity: the extent to which macroeconomic factors have significant impact on the market.	Failure to address adequately results in poor anticipation of the implications of macroeconomic factors and hence inadequate and/or belated response.
	Political complexity: the extent to which political factors have significant impact on the market.	Failure to address adequately results in poor anticipation of the implications of political factors and hence inadequate and/or belated response.
	Technological complexity: the extent to which technological factors have significant impact on the market.	Failure to address adequately results in poor anticipation of the implications of technological factors and hence inadequate and/or belated response.
Value proposition complexity	Range complexity: the number of different product components offered to the market.	Failure to address adequately results in incoherence of the value proposition across the product range.
	Technical complexity: the technological complexity inherent in developing, supplying and selling the value proposition.	Failure to address adequately results in failure to address technically based key issues, especially by new entrants.
	Extended product complexity: the extent to which the value proposition extends beyond the core product into higher benefits.	Failure to address adequately results in incomplete value propositions, especially with respect to higher, intangible benefits.

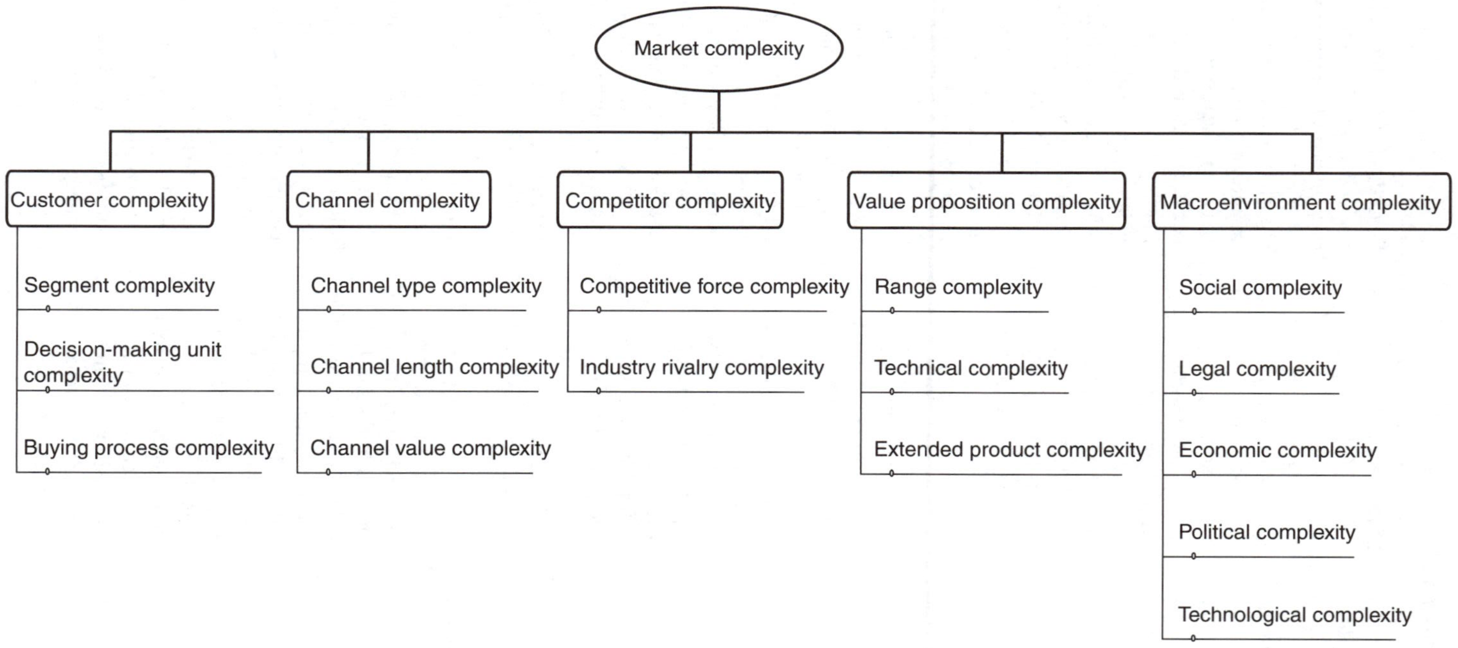

Figure 9.1 Components of market complexity

of three contributing factors: segment complexity, decision-making unit complexity and buying process complexity.

Segment complexity

Segment complexity arises when customers are not all identical – that is, the market is heterogeneous. In some markets, especially niches for luxury goods or in some highly specialized technical products or services, the differences between customers are small and insignificant. In most markets, however, customers fall into a small number of segments, and this represents a moderate level of market complexity. In some large markets, especially mature ones such as food retailing, for example, there are many distinct segments (as a rule of thumb, more than ten is many), contributing to a high level of market complexity. It is important to note here that we are referring to real segments (as described in Chapter 5) and therefore differences in customers' needs, motivation and behaviour. There is not necessarily a correlation between market complexity and a wide variety of customer descriptors (size, age, industry category etc.). Some 'commodity' products, such as paper towels in washrooms, go to lots of different types of customers but with very little segmentation in the market. The implications of failing to understand segment complexity can be fundamental. A strategy making process that does not cope with it (i.e. understand it) is unlikely to create value propositions that are sufficiently segment-specific. Even if it does, appropriate targeting of effort is very difficult without understanding the complexity of segmentation.

Decision-making unit complexity

Decision-making unit complexity is that component of market complexity that exists in any market in which individual customers do not make the buying decision alone. In industrial, technical and business-to-business markets, the decision is almost always made by a group rather than an individual. Even in consumer markets though, the complex interplay of friends and family influence apparently solo choices. Those readers with children will be familiar with 'pester power' and the parent–child decision-making unit. Between the extremes of the spectrum, there are many levels of decision-making unit complexity. A strategy making process that does not cope with decision-making unit complexity is unlikely to address all the needs of the market. In this case, the complexity of customers' needs increases in proportion to the complexity of the decision-making unit and contributes to overall market complexity.

Buying process complexity

Buying process complexity is that component of market complexity that exists in any market where the purchase decision is not instant and stand-alone. Hence anything but the most impulsive of impulse buys has some level of buying process complexity, and most markets have some. It is important to remember, of course, that the buying process does not always end with purchase. In many markets, the buying process continues in the form of affirmation of decision and continuing contact between supplier and customer. At the extreme of buying process complexity are major capital purchase decisions, such as cars and houses for consumers, and plant, equipment and service outsourcing for businesses. Again, there are innumerable levels between the extremes of a chocolate bar and a power station. A strategy making process that does not cope with buying process complexity may get the value proposition right but fail to manage it through a convoluted decision-making procedure. Like a strong chain with one weak link, the selling process may fail.

Channel complexity

Channel complexity is that component of market complexity that exists in any market in which the product or service does not go directly from the supplier to the customer via one single route, with little or no addition of value. Some markets are very simple in this respect, whilst others are hideously complex. Channel complexity is the aggregate of three aspects of channel intricacy: channel type complexity, channel length complexity and channel value complexity.

Channel type complexity

Channel type complexity arises when the market is addressed by more than one channel. At the simplest extreme, for instance, a management consultancy delivers its value directly to its customers and through only that direct channel. Its near-competitor, a business school, by comparison, might deliver its value directly, via overseas partners or distance learning. Each different channel adds a level of complexity through its different requirements. Failure to address those needs adequately may result in failure to deliver value because of absent or sub-optimal use of channels.

Channel length complexity

Channel length complexity arises when multiple levels exist in the channel to market. A manufacturer of agricultural chemicals might use a logistics firm to move products physically from the factory to localized specialized distributors. This distributor may then deliver the herbicide to the farmer. The wholesale chain in FMCG markets is another example. Levels of channel complexity, which can exist in several different channels at once, contribute to overall market complexity through the different demands of each tier. Failure to grasp channel length complexity is again evidenced by failure to deliver the value proposition when one link in the chain fails, even when the rest of the chain works.

Channel value complexity

Channel value complexity arises when the value proposition is partly created by the chain, as opposed to entirely by the manufacturer (or equivalent). In practice almost all channels add some value, but the extent of this varies greatly. In simple commodity markets, the value-adding role of the channel is limited to little more than physical logistics and perhaps breaking down or bundling product. More valuable channels add support, service and other forms of knowledge. The most valuable chains – for example, some value-adding resellers (VARs) of IT systems – design and manage the business process into which the product or service fits. As channels add value the difficulty of making this happen creates channel value complexity, which aggregates with the channel type and channel level complexities into overall channel complexity and thence market complexity. A strategy making process that does not cope with channel value complexity will fail to deliver the value proposition to a greater or lesser extent. Readers seeking an example of this need do no more than telephone a customer support helpline for a typical software or utility company. When eventually past the automated 'customer-irritation system', the reader will often find that huge opportunities to add value are being missed.

Competitor complexity

Competitor complexity is that component of market complexity that exists in any market in which more than one competitive force or direct competitor exists. As with the other components of market complexity, a broad spectrum of competitor complexity exists across different markets. Competitor complexity is the aggregate of two parts: competitive force complexity and industry rivalry complexity.

Competitive force complexity

Competitive force complexity arises when competitive pressure comes from more than one direction (e.g. from suppliers, new entrants, substitutes etc.). Rarely does the only significant competitive pressure come from the industry rivalry of direct competition. More usually, competitive pressures come from two or more of: industry rivalry, substitutes, new entrants, buyer pressure and supplier pressure. Rarely, the entire gamut of competitive forces impacts significantly on the market. Again, small or embryonic niches tend to be at the simpler end of the spectrum whilst larger and more mature markets are usually more competitively complex. Failure to comprehend the significance of competitive force complexity naturally leads to competitive disadvantage, normally as the result of being 'blindsided' to new threats.

Industry rivalry complexity

Industry rivalry complexity arises when direct competitors exist in more than one strategic set – that is, they compete via more than one strategy. In the simplest case, all of the direct competitors differ in detail but compete on the same basis, for instance on product performance. The most common scenario is of moderate levels of industry rivalry complexity, in which there are two strategic sets. An example of this is prescription pharmaceuticals, where the only two significant strategic sets are research-based ethicals and cost-based generics. Rarely, there are three or four strategic sets, each consisting of competitors focusing on one of: price, performance, service, distribution density or other forms of competitive advantage. The market for lifestyle magazines is an example of industry rivalry complexity, with multiple different strategic sets each based around a different basis of competition. In these cases, the more strategic sets there are, the greater the industry rivalry complexity. This contributes to channel complexity and thence to overall market complexity. Failure to appreciate the complexity of industry rivalry is manifested by overly simple responses to competitive activities, which address only one but not all of the strategic sets.

Macroenvironment complexity

Macroenvironment complexity is that component of market complexity that arises from what some call the 'remote business environment' – that is, the factors in the marketplace that impact less directly on the market than competitors and customers, such as social trends and technological development. That is not to say that this less direct impact is less important. Like global warming or demographic change, the imperceptibility of macroenvironmental changes can mask the importance of the bearing on the market. All markets are to some degree complicated by macroenvironmental forces, but again, markets range from the simple to the complex in this respect. Macroenvironmental complexity can be thought of as the aggregate of five sub-components: social, legal, economic, political and technological complexity.

Social complexity

Social complexity arises when social factors influence the market. Examples of this might be tangible, such as changes in demographics, or harder to discern, such as the decline in deference to authority commonly observed in westernized societies. An interesting current example of social complexity is the housing market in many countries, influenced as it is by demographics, the growing number of single-adult households and changing expectations about independence, and even personal wealth management.

Legal complexity

Legal complexity arises when legal factors influence the market. Examples of this might be direct, such as industry regulation in financial services, or indirect, such as the harmonization of duty on alcoholic drinks which has recently affected the cross-channel ferry market between the UK and France. This latter example has had an indirect but powerful effect on, for instance, P&O's reliance on the 'booze-cruise' segment.

Economic complexity

Economic complexity arises when macroeconomic factors influence the market. Again these influences can be direct, such as when recession impacts on the purchase of package holidays, or indirect, as when oil prices make alternative energy more or less competitive.

In the latter case, this impacts indirectly but strongly on, for instance, the makers of composite materials for wind turbines.

Political complexity

Political complexity arises when political forces influence the market. Direct examples of this are relatively rare but important. The UK government's strategic initiative in the early 2000s to drive up the percentage of GDP spent on health to EU average levels is a powerful illustration of this, and has impacted on many medical markets. More common, but less obvious, is the impact of political attitudes on trading agreements and procurement policies. For instance, the market for water-treatment infrastructure projects is heavily influenced by political factors, not so much in its size, but in its attractiveness and accessibility.

Technological complexity

Technological complexity arises when the development and application of new technologies has an impact on the market. Although nowadays 'technology' is used as a loose synonym for information and communications technology (ICT), technological complexity actually has broader origins. It can arise from ICT-enabled factors, such as the emergence of e-tendering in some commoditized markets like packaging, or the ability of customers to compare propositions on the web. More widespread, though, is the complicating impact of new technologies that relate to the market directly. One single technological development by Du Pont, namely Lycra, impacted hugely on the clothing market, especially in casual clothing sectors. Similarly, the development of genetics-based technologies is currently changing the face of some sectors of the medical diagnostics market.

Value proposition complexity

Value proposition complexity is that component of market complexity that exists in any market when the value proposition is more than a simple and unelaborated commodity. Almost all markets, even those superficially commoditized, have some level of value proposition complexity. As with the other components of market complexity, a broad spectrum of value proposition complexity exists across different markets. It is, in this case, the aggregate of three parts: range complexity, technical complexity and extended product complexity.

Range complexity

Range complexity arises when the value proposition requires the provision of multiple component products or services. It can exist in both product markets (for instance, companies which supply the car-parts market) and in the service sector (for instance, in contract research organizations which must offer a wide range of technical services). Range complexity is, therefore, simplistically correlated to the thickness of the catalogue, but the relation is more sophisticated than this, as multiple products are grouped into fewer basic types. Holding a thousand types of screw does not contribute to range complexity to the same degree as holding even a few different types of mass spectrometer. Product range adds to value proposition complexity by making it necessary to achieve proposition coherence across the range – always a difficult thing in practice.

Technical complexity

Technical complexity arises from the technology inherent in developing, supplying and selling the value proposition. Even the simplest markets (breakfast cornflakes, for example) are rarely as technically simple as they seem, but there is clearly a wide gap in technology between those and, say, some IT, financial services or other technically complex markets. It is important to note here that technical is not synonymous with scientific technology. Many legal, financial and other service markets are technically complex even without much of what we traditionally think of as technology. The application of advanced mathematics by actuaries is as much a technology as the application of advanced electronics by engineers. Technical complexity increases the number of factors that need to be considered in strategy making, and therefore contributes to the complexity of the value proposition and the market overall. It is often proportional to decision-making unit complexity, as 'technical' propositions are generally bought by units, not individuals. Failure to grasp the technical complexity of the market, often seen when new entrants enter a technically complex market, hinders the formulation of a compelling value proposition.

Extended product complexity

Extended product complexity arises when the value proposition extends beyond the core product or service. The least complex value propositions (again, usually commodities) offer benefits derived only from the functionality of the product. More common, and more complex, are the value propositions that offer additional benefits associated with service. The convenience of a local store is an example of this moderately extended value proposition. The highest levels of extended product complexity arise when the value proposition appeals to functional, service and emotional needs. Examples of this are those service or product/service combinations that rely heavily on relationships either with individuals (for instance, an agency account handler) or with a brand. Failure to understand extended product complexity leads to simplistic and incomplete value propositions. In everyday experience, the restaurant that excels in every way but for its surly staff is an example of an incomplete value proposition.

Summary

Market complexity is therefore a very complex construct indeed. To form an objective judgement of our own position on the simple-to-complex market spectrum, we need to understand that it is multifactorial. As outlined above, our research identified five components and sixteen sub-components that aggregate to form overall market complexity. Often, but not always, we can make some generalizations. Market complexity is associated with market maturity, business-to-business, technical and large markets. Simpler conditions are more likely to apply in embryonic and growth markets, smaller niches, impulsive consumer markets and those that do not depend on technology. However, these generalizations are not strong enough for us to make good guesses. In practice, each market must be assessed for complexity in a systematic manner. That is the goal of the following section.

Application point: What makes your market complex?

The mis-estimation of market complexity that many marketers make is often the result of not considering all of the factors that contribute to market complexity. It is difficult to assess market complexity systematically without some sort of aid to thinking. Before we progress, it will be useful to gather your thoughts about what it is that makes your market complex by answering the following question.

- Which of the five components of market complexity do you think contribute most strongly to your overall market complexity?

A process for evaluating market complexity

In simple terms, evaluating market complexity is no more than the aggregation of the complexity implied by the five contributing factors of customers, channel, competition, macroenvironment, and value proposition. However, we need to be cautious about simplistic approaches. The consequences of over- or underestimating the complexities of the market are serious. Our research observations were that it is more common to underestimate market complexity than to overstate it. In such cases, companies stick with their visionary-command and incremental hybrids, which are not up to the three tasks involved in making strategy in such markets: understanding complex markets, making difficult strategy choices, and implementing intricate action plans. Overestimating market complexity is less common, but still catastrophic to strategy making. It leads companies to over-engineer their strategic marketing planning and to get bogged down in bureaucracy. In both cases, the resultant marketing strategy is weak.

To evaluate market complexity in a more sophisticated way requires the incorporation of two further findings from our research. First, almost all markets exhibit tangible characteristics, such as the number of competitors or channels, which can be used to create a graduated complexity scale for each of the five sub-components. Secondly, these five sub-components do not all contribute equally to market complexity, so that simply adding up the complexity due to each doesn't give a true picture. These two findings imply that the accurate, objective assessment of market complexity involves two stages: quantifying the components of market complexity and then calculating a weighted aggregate, as opposed to a simple average, of those values.

Quantifying the components of market complexity

In short, quantifying the components of market complexity involves estimating where our market sits along each of five scales. Each scale represents one of the five market complexity factors described above, and runs from simple to complex. To do this, however, means assessing the level of market complexity arising from each sub-component. Table 9.1 summarizes these components and sub-components, whilst Table 9.2 uses our research findings to create an assessment scale for them. In Table 9.2, each level of complexity is described in general terms not restricted to any market. Hence by looking along the description one can estimate a level of market complexity for each sub-component. The average of these sub-component estimates forms the basis of estimating the complexity due to each of the five factors. This may seem a disproportionately long-winded way of assessing market complexity, but it has two significant merits when compared to less comprehensive approaches. First, it ensures that all factors are considered. The sheer number of factors contributing to market complexity can easily overwhelm a simpler approach, which leads to the relative neglect of key factors and hence a false judgement of market complexity. Secondly, breaking down the estimate into, effectively, sixteen smaller estimates that are then aggregated has the effect of reducing errors. This is because errors in each of the sixteen judgements tend to be made in both directions, and therefore combine to cancel each other out.

So the first stage of the process to evaluate market complexity is to use Table 9.2. Look along each line and make an estimate of which situation best describes your market. Clearly this is best done with reference to any data you have, and is also enhanced by doing it as a group exercise. However, even if done alone and using only tacit market knowledge, these multiple judgements are a better assessment of a complex construct than a simple estimate along one dimension.

Having made the sixteen estimates, combine the sub-component estimates into the five factors to make an estimate of the market complexity due to customers, channels, competitions, the macro-environment and the value proposition. At this level, weighted averages seem an unnecessary complication. It is enough simply to look at your judgements for the sub-components and make an assessment as to the combined complexity of each of the five factors. The output of this first step, therefore, is five numbers, one for each factor. Although the scale is in five steps, you will find it useful to make the assessment on a scale of one to ten, enabling you to 'shade' your answer to reflect your assessments of the sub-components. For instance, if your assessment of the five sub-components of macroenvironment complexity is a combination of 2s (moderately simple) and 3s (median complexity), then your judgement of macroenvironment complexity might be 2.5. The end result of this first part of the process for assessing market complexity is five numbers between one and ten. The next step is to combine them into a way that is straightforward without being simplistic.

Application point: What are the market complexity factor scores for your market?

The first stage in objectively assessing the complexity of your market is to make a good judgement of the scores for each of the five factors. This means considering each of the sub-components and then making a reasoned judgement.

Use Tables 9.1 and 9.2 to assess your five component scores before you proceed further.

Aggregating market complexity

As alluded to earlier, each of the five factors (customers, channels, competitors, microenvironment and value proposition) contributes to market complexity, but they do not do so equally. The origins of this unequal contribution lie in the observation that the visionary command component of any hybrid marketing-strategy making process is differentially sensitive to the five different types of market complexity. In other words, visionary command processes can cope better with some types of market complexity and less well with others. In our research, we noted that the leaders or groups that drive visionary processes coped well with some aspects of market complexity and less well with others. This is directly connected to how well the leader or group can 'see' that aspect of the market. How well they can 'see' each aspect of the market is determined by two factors.

First, the leader or group almost never has an unobstructed view of the market. Instead, they 'see' the market through the lenses of their subordinates or through information collected by others. The quality of their vision and their ability to cope with each aspect of

Table 9.2 Graduated scales of market complexity

Sub-component of market complexity	*Complexity factors*	*Simple (1)*	*Moderately simple (2)*	*Median complexity (3)*	*Moderately complex (4)*	*Complex (5)*
Customer complexity	Segment complexity: the number of substantially different market segments.	There is only one significant, real segment in the market.	There are two or three substantially different segments in the market.	There are four to six substantially different segments in the market.	There are six to ten substantially different segments in the market.	There are more than ten substantially different segments in the market.
	Decision-making unit complexity: the number of significant contributors to the decision-making unit.	The decision-making unit consists of only one person with little external influence.	The decision-making unit is one person but with significant influence from one or two other people.	The decision-making unit consists of two or three people, each with direct influence on the decision.	The decision-making unit consists of three to five persons each with direct influence on the decision.	The decision-making unit consists of more than five persons each with direct influence on the decision.
	Buying process complexity: the length and number of distinct stages in the buying process.	The buying process is near instantaneous with no discernible stages.	The buying process is of significant duration but in only one discernible stage.	The buying process is protracted but not formalized and has one or two discernible stages.	The buying process is protracted but not formalized and has three or more discernible stages.	The buying process is both formalized and protracted with three or more discernible stages.
Channel complexity	Channel type complexity: the number of different types of channel to market.	There is only one significant channel to market.	There are two or three significant channels to market but one is much more dominant than the others.	There are two or three significant channels to market. They are all of significant importance but differ from each other in only minor ways.	There are two or three significant channels to market. They are all of significant importance and differ from each other in significant respects.	There are four or more channels to market, each of which differs significantly from the others and carries significant volume.

	Channel length complexity: the number of different tiers in the channel to market.	There are no tiers in the channel to market; it is entirely direct.	There is only one tier in the channel to market and that channel only accounts for a small proportion of the business.	There is only one tier in the channel to market and that channel accounts for a large proportion of business.	There are two or three tiers in the channels to market but one channel is dominant.	There are two or more tiers in the channels to market and those channels are all significant to the business.
	Channel value complexity: the extent to which the channel to market adds to the value proposition.	The channels to market add no value other than physical distribution.	The channels to market provide physical distribution and some minor value such as stockholding and order processing.	The channels to market provide selection and use advice as well as stockholding and order processing.	The channels to market tailor the product significantly as well as providing other value.	The channels to market incorporate your value proposition into a broader offer.
Competitor complexity	Competitive force complexity: the number of different competitive forces significant in the market.	Only one competitive force (usually industry rivalry) is significant in the market.	There are two or three competitive forces acting on the market but one is much more significant than the others.	There are two significant competitive forces acting on the market.	There are three or more competitive forces acting on the market but two are dominant.	Four or five competitive forces impact significantly on the market.
	Industry rivalry complexity: the number of different strategic sets into which direct competitors may be classified.	There is only one significant competitor and it occupies the same strategic set as ourselves.	There is only one significant competitor and it occupies a different strategic set to ourselves.	There are two strategic sets each containing two or more competitors.	There are three or more strategic sets but each containing only one competitor.	There are three or more strategic sets each containing two or more competitors.

Table 9.2 *(Continued)*

Sub-component of market complexity	*Complexity factors*	*Simple (1)*	*Moderately simple (2)*	*Median complexity (3)*	*Moderately complex (4)*	*Complex (5)*
Macroenvironment complexity	Social complexity: the number of different social factors which impact significantly on the market.	The market is largely immune to social factors.	The market is only susceptible to one or two tangible social factors such as population size and structure.	The market is susceptible to a number of tangible social factors.	The market is susceptible to a number of either tangible or intangible social factors, such as fashion and attitudes, but not both.	The market is susceptible to multiple social forces both tangible and intangible.
	Legal complexity: the number of different legal factors which impact significantly on the market.	The market is largely immune to legal and regulatory factors other than the basic legal structure.	The market is influenced to a small extent by legal and regulatory factors from a single authority.	The market is influenced to a significant extent by legal and regulatory factors from a single authority.	The market is influenced to a significant extent by legal and regulatory factors from a single authority and to a minor extent by other authorities.	The market is heavily influenced by the legal and regulatory frameworks of multiple authorities.
	Economic complexity: the number of different macroeconomic factors which impact significantly on the market.	The market is largely immune to macroeconomic factors	The market is influenced to a small extent by macroeconomic factors but only in a single economic entity, such as a nation state or trading bloc.	The market is influenced to a significant extent by macroeconomic factors from a single economic entity.	The market is influenced to a significant extent by macroeconomic factors from a single authority and to a minor extent by other economic entities.	The market is heavily influenced by the macroeconomic factors of multiple economic entities.

	Political complexity: the number of different political factors which impact significantly on the market.	The market is largely immune to political factors.	The market is influenced to a small extent by political factors but only in a single political entity, such as a nation state or trading bloc.	The market is influenced to a significant extent by political factors from a single political entity.	The market is influenced to a significant extent by political factors from a political entity and to a minor extent by other political entities.	The market is heavily influenced by the political factors of multiple political entities.
	Technological complexity: the number of different technological factors which impact significantly on the market.	The market is largely immune to both ICT related and industry specific technological developments.	The market is influenced to a small extent by either ICT related or industry specific technological developments.	The market is influenced to a significant extent by either ICT related or industry specific technological developments, but not both.	The market is influenced to a significant extent by either ICT related or industry specific technological developments and to a lesser extent by the other.	The market is influenced to a significant extent by both ICT related and industry specific technological developments.
Value proposition complexity	Range complexity: the number of different product components offered to the market.	The product or service range consists of a single product or service or has only minor variants.	The product or service range consists of a small number of products or services with similar or complementary applications.	The product or service range consists of a large number of products or services with similar or complementary applications.	The product or service range consists of a small number of products or services with dissimilar or unrelated applications.	The product or service range consists of a large number of products or services with dissimilar or unrelated applications.

Table 9.2 *(Continued)*

Sub-component of market complexity	*Complexity factors*	*Simple (1)*	*Moderately simple (2)*	*Median complexity (3)*	*Moderately complex (4)*	*Complex (5)*
	Technical complexity: the technological complexity inherent in developing, supplying and selling the value proposition.	The value proposition is not technologically complex at any stage of the value chain.	The value proposition has some elements of technological complexity in some, but not all, stages of the value chain.	The value proposition has some elements of technological complexity in all stages of the value chain.	The value proposition has significant technological complexity in some stages of the value chain and some in other stages.	The value proposition has significant technological complexity in all or most stages of the value chain.
	Extended product complexity: the extent to which the value proposition extends beyond the core product into higher benefits.	The value proposition is entirely or mostly built around the core product or service.	The value proposition is entirely or mostly built around the core product or service, but with minor contributions from the extended product or service.	The value proposition is mostly built around the core product or service, but with significant contributions from the extended product or service.	The value proposition is partly built around the core product or service, but mostly from the extended product or service.	The value proposition is derived entirely or mostly from the extended and augmented product

market complexity is determined by the fidelity of that intermediary information process. In other words, if the factor can be objectively measured and reported (for instance, the structure of the channels to market), visionary command processes can cope well with that aspect of market complexity. If it is intangible and subjective (for instance, customer motivations), the leaders have poorer sight of it and visionary command processes work less well.

The second factor that determines how well visionary command processes can cope with different aspects of market complexity is the position of the leader or group in the company. The position of the leader or group that drives visionary command processes differs between organizations, and this position influences their view of the market. For instance, some leaders or groups have a very close view of the customers, or of the channels. This is common in some high-involvement business-to-business markets. In some cases, the leadership group is closely positioned relative to product development and has a good view of the value proposition. The ability of the visionary command process to cope with the different aspects of market complexity is determined by the extent to which the leaders can 'see' that aspect. The better they can see it, the better they can cope and the less significant that aspect is. Conversely, if they are distant from some aspects of the market they find it harder to 'see' it. Such is the case when non-scientist leaders head scientifically complex companies or accountants run sales-oriented companies. In those cases, the ability of the company to cope with the different aspects of market complexity may be hindered.

This explanation of how tangibility and position influence the contribution of the five factors to market complexity is important. It means that two companies in the same market may not have exactly the same level of market complexity because it is determined partly by internal factors. When carried through to the rest of the process for creating bicongruent planning, it is another example of tailoring strategic marketing planning to the company.

The second stage in assessing market complexity, therefore, is to estimate the relative contribution each of the five factors makes. If each of the five factors contributes equally, then market complexity would be a simple average of our five assessments. In practice, they impact differently on the strategy making process because of the internal factors mentioned in the preceding section. Because of this, a simple average is inadequate and a weighted average is needed. This is not much of a complication. It merely involves starting with the assumption of equal contribution (i.e. 20 per cent or two out of ten)

Table 9.3 Weightings for market complexity factors

Market complexity factor	*Increase weighting from 2 when . . .*	*Decrease weighting from 2 when . . .*
Customer complexity	The leadership team is separated from the customers by the internal structure and/or when the market structure is created by intangible, hard to measure factors.	The leadership has a direct and clear view of the customers and/or when the market structure is created by tangible, easy to communicate factors.
Competitor complexity	The leadership team is separated from the competitive forces by the internal structure and/or when the bases of competition are intangible, hard to measure factors.	The leadership has a direct and clear view of the competitive forces and/or when the bases of competition are tangible and easy to communicate.
Channel complexity	The leadership team is separated from the channels to market by the internal structure and/or when the channels to market are overlapping and unclear.	The leadership has a direct and clear view of the channels to market and/or when the channels to market are distinct and easy to discern.
Macroenvironment complexity	The leadership team is separated from the macroenvironment by the internal structure and/or the macroenvironment is confusing and hard to measure.	The leadership has a direct and clear view of the macroenvironment and/or when the macroenvironment is clear and well defined.
Value proposition complexity	The leadership team is separated from the value proposition by the internal structure and/or the value proposition is based on multiple intangible factors.	The leadership has a direct and clear view of the value proposition and/or the value proposition is based on a small number of tangible factors.

Table 9.4 Example of a completed market complexity assessment

Market complexity factor	*Weighting (assessed using Table 9.3)*	*Marketing complexity factor score (assessed using Table 9.2)*
Customer complexity	4	8
Competitor complexity	1	2
Channel complexity	1	3
Macroenvironment complexity	2	4
Value proposition complexity	2	7
Total	10	59 i.e. (4 × 8) + (1 × 2) + (1 × 3)+ (2 × 4) + (2 × 7)

and then shading up and down, as indicated by Table 9.3. The important point, of course, is that the weightings must add up to ten out of ten.

Table 9.4 gives an example of a completed market complexity assessment. The weightings for each factor are assessed using Table 9.3. In this case customer complexity is shown as especially important, as is often the case where the subtleties of segmentation are hard for leaders to see. The scores for each are assessed using Table 9.2. In this example, customer complexity and value proposition complexity are the most complex elements of the market, as is often the case in technical and business-to-business markets. The overall market complexity score is calculated by simply multiplying each factor score by its weighting and adding them up. In this example we have a market that is a little more than median complexity, suggesting that visionary command processes will struggle to cope and that a significant degree of rational planning is needed.

We have now completed the process of assessing the complexity of our market. At first it may appear a laborious process, but in reality it takes a management team no more than an hour or so. Even given the value of management team time, this is a small price to pay for the reward. We now understand the complexity of our market and what it is about the market that leads to its complexity. As with all management tools, there is at least as much value in the discussion needed to use the tool as there is in the end result. The end result, however, allows us to place our market on the horizontal axis of Figure 7.2. In the next section, we will perform a rather simpler exercise to find the vertical coordinate in that figure and hence inform our choice of strategy making process.

Application point: What is your assessment of the complexity of your market?

An accurate and objective assessment of the complexity of your market is the first step in achieving bicongruence and a strong strategy. It is a simple calculation using the weighting assessments and component scores.

- What are the market complexity component weightings for your situation, based on Table 9.3?
- Following the example in Table 9.4, what is your judgement of the complexity of your market, on a scale of 0–100, where 0 is simple and 100 is complex?
- How does that assessment differ from the one you made without these tools earlier in this chapter?

Understanding and evaluating market turbulence

The way companies understand and assess market turbulence is very similar to the way they understand and assess market complexity, so this section builds on the last and is correspondingly simpler. When we say market turbulence, we mean change and instability in the external environment with which we are trying to align our company. It is important to us because rational planning seems to cope well with market complexity but less well with market turbulence. The turbulence of our market therefore determines the balance we need to make between comprehensive but slow rational planning processes and responsive but simplistic visionary processes for making strategy.

As described above in our discussion of market complexity, the market is a complex construct. When we talk about market turbulence, therefore, we mean change and instability in the same five factors and sub-components we discussed when assessing market complexity. That is:

1. Customer turbulence
2. Channel turbulence

3. Competitor turbulence
4. Macroenvironment turbulence
5. Value proposition turbulence.

These five factors and their sub-components are summarized in Figure 9.2 and in Table 9.5. Two things will be immediately obvious to the reader. First, we are talking about the same aspects of the market and the same implications of failing to grasp them as we did in the preceding section on market complexity. Market turbulence is simply change and instability in the same factors, and failing to cope with change in market complexity leads to the same problems as failing to grasp it in the first place. Secondly, we can generalize (and generalizations are dangerous things) that there is less variation between the turbulence of different markets than between the complexity of markets. Markets are spread over a range from simple to complex, with a bias to the complex that is associated with market maturity. By contrast, there seems to be rather less spread of markets from stable to turbulent, and a marked bias towards the stable, again associated with market maturity. It is a useful starting point to think of markets as starting simple and turbulent and gradually becoming complex and stable, but the generalization is not strong enough to depend upon. We need to make the same assessment of the five components of market turbulence as we did for market complexity, along a graduated scale derived from our observations of real companies. We then need to aggregate the scores in a weighted manner, as we did for market complexity.

The gradations in market turbulence are shown in Table 9.6. As before, assessment involves looking along each line and judging which description best fits your market. The assessments for each sub-component are aggregated simply to create a 'marks out of ten' score for each of the five components of market turbulence. Again, the assessment is best made by a team and informed, where possible, by reference to known data or facts. Inevitably, the discussion is as valuable as the score, and any errors tend to cancel out, making the net scores more reliable. At the end of the process, the five component scores are used to calculate the overall market turbulence by means of a weighted average calculation.

There is a small but important difference in assessing the weighting factors, however. In the case of market complexity, we were concerned about the differential capacities that visionary command processes have, to cope with different components of market complexity. The differences, we determined, were due to the ability of the

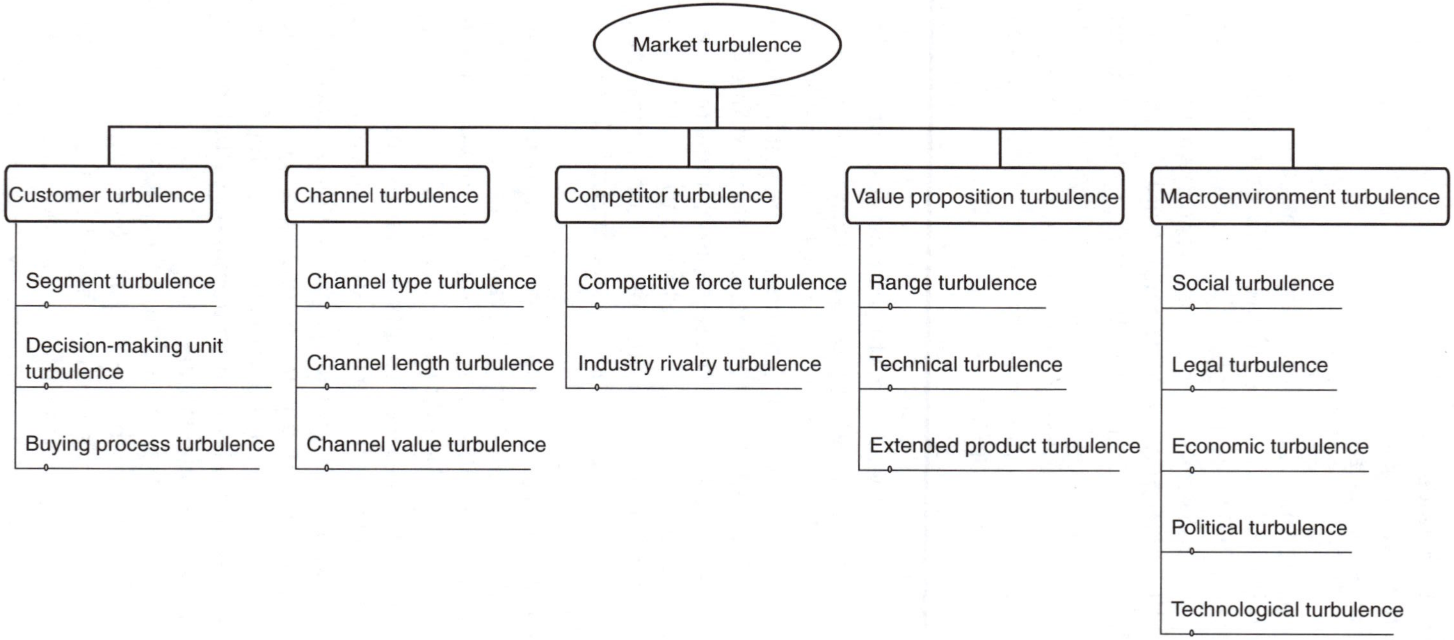

Figure 9.2 Components of market turbulence

leadership team to 'see' the complexity, and how tangible the factors were that determined complexity. In the case of market turbulence, we are concerned with the differential capacities that rational planning processes have, to cope with different components of market turbulence. These differences are also determined by the ability of the leadership team to 'see' the turbulence but also, by contrast, by the 'lead or lag' properties of the turbulence factor. In other words, turbulence factors which flag up their coming impact (such as legal changes, or emerging geographical markets) are easier for rational planning processes to cope with than those that are only noticeable as lag effects (such as gradual sociological changes in customer attitudes, or the unexpected interactions of socio-economic effects). Table 9.7 provides a guide for the weighting of the turbulence factors, again all based on assuming an equal weighting of two out of ten, then adjusting for the factors described.

Again consistent with the assessment of market complexity, the calculation of market turbulence is quite straightforward. A completed example is shown in Table 9.7. In this example, macroenvironment turbulence was judged to be the most important factor and the overall level of market turbulence assessed as quite low. This would imply that a rational planning process could cope well and that a large element of visionary command process was inappropriate.

Application point: What is your assessment of the turbulence of your market?

An accurate and objective assessment of the turbulence of your market is the second step in achieving bicongruence and a strong strategy. It is a simple calculation using the weighting assessments and component scores.

- What are the market turbulence component scores for your market, based on Table 9.6?
- What are the market turbulence component weightings for your situation, based on Table 9.7?
- Adapting the example in Table 9.4, what is your judgement of the turbulence of your market, on a scale from 0 to 100, where 0 is simple and 100 is complex?
- How does that assessment differ from the one you made, without these tools, earlier in this chapter?

Table 9.5 The nature and implications of market turbulence

Sub-component of market turbulence	*Turbulence factors*	*Typically observed implications of failing to cope with this aspect of market turbulence*
Customer turbulence	Segment turbulence: change and instability in the number of substantially different market segments.	Failure to allocate resources effectively between segments or to create appropriately segment specific value propositions.
	Decision-making unit turbulence: change and instability in the number of significant contributors to the decision-making unit.	Failure to address adequately all the significant contributors to the decision-making process or to allow for their needs in the value proposition.
	Buying process turbulence: change and instability in the length and number of distinct stages in the buying process.	Failure to address adequately all the stages of the decision-making process, with subsequent failure of selling process.
Channel turbulence	Channel type turbulence: change and instability in the number of different types of channel to market.	Failure to address adequately the needs of the channels to market, leading either to poor availability or a weakened value proposition.
	Channel length turbulence: change and instability in the number of different tiers in the channel to market.	Failure to address adequately one or more levels within the channel to market, leading either to poor availability or a weakened value proposition.
	Channel value turbulence: change and instability in the extent to which the channel to market adds to the value proposition.	Failure to address adequately results in weakness in the value proposition with respect to those parts of it created or delivered by the channel to market.
Competitor turbulence	Competitive force turbulence: change and instability in the number of different competitive forces significant in the market.	Failure to address adequately results in insufficient response to indirect threats, especially new or emergent competitive forces.
	Industry rivalry turbulence: change and instability in the number of different strategic sets into which direct competitors may be classified.	Failure to address adequately results in simplistic and inadequate response to direct competition which addresses only one strategic set.

Macroenvironment turbulence	Social turbulence: change and instability in the extent to which sociological factors have significant impact on the market.	Failure to address adequately results in poor anticipation of the implications of social factors and, hence, inadequate and/or belated response.
	Legal turbulence: change and instability in the extent to which legal factors have significant impact on the market.	Failure to address adequately results in poor anticipation of the implications of legal factors and, hence, inadequate and/or belated response.
	Economic turbulence: change and instability in the extent to which macroeconomic factors have significant impact on the market.	Failure to address adequately results in poor anticipation of the implications of macroeconomic factors and, hence, inadequate and/or belated response.
	Political turbulence: change and instability in the extent to which political factors will have significant impact on the market.	Failure to address adequately results in poor anticipation of the implications of political factors and, hence, inadequate and/or belated response.
	Technological turbulence: change and instability in the extent to which technological factors have significant impact on the market.	Failure to address adequately results in poor anticipation of the implications of technological factors and, hence, inadequate and/or belated response.
Value proposition turbulence	Range turbulence: change and instability in the number of different product components offered to the market.	Failure to address adequately results in incoherence of the value proposition across the product range.
	Technical turbulence: change and instability in the technological turbulence inherent in developing, supplying and selling the value proposition.	Failure to address adequately results in failure to address technically based key issues, especially by new entrants.
	Extended product turbulence: change and instability in the extent to which the value proposition extends beyond the core product into higher benefits.	Failure to address adequately results in incomplete value propositions, especially with respect to higher, intangible benefits.

Table 9.6 Graduated scales of market turbulence

Sub-component of market turbulence	*Turbulence factors*	*Stable (1)*	*Moderately stable (2)*	*Median turbulence (3)*	*Moderately turbulent (4)*	*Turbulent (5)*
Customer turbulence	Segment turbulence: the change and instability in the number of substantially different market segments.	There is no noticeable change or instability in the number and relative size of substantially different market segments.	There is no noticeable change or instability in the number of substantially different market segments but some slow change or mild instability in their relative size.	There is slow change in the number of different market segments and some slow change and mild instability in their relative size.	There is slow change in the number of different market segments and quite rapid change and instability in their relative size.	There is rapid change or significant instability in the number and relative size of substantially different market segments.
	Decision-making unit turbulence: the change and instability in the number of significant contributors to the decision-making unit.	There is no noticeable change in the number of significant contributors to the decision-making unit.	There is only small and slow change in the number of significant contributors to the decision-making unit.	There is significant but slow change in the number of significant contributors to the decision-making unit.	There is significant and constant change in the number of significant contributors to the decision-making unit.	There is rapid and sudden change in the number and relative size of substantially different market segments.
	Buying process turbulence: the change and instability in the length and number of distinct stages in the buying process.	There is no noticeable change in the length and number of distinct stages in the buying process.	There is only small and slow change in the length and number of distinct stages in the buying process.	There is significant but slow change in the length and number of distinct stages in the buying process.	There is significant and constant change in the length and number of distinct stages in the buying process.	There is rapid and sudden change in the length and number of distinct stages in the buying process.

Channel turbulence	Channel type turbulence: the change and instability in the number of different types of channel to market.	There is no noticeable change in the number of different types of channel to market.	There is only small and slow change in the number of different types of channel to market.	There is significant but slow change in the number of different types of channel to market.	There is significant and constant change in the number of different types of channel to market.	There is rapid and sudden change in the number of different types of channel to market.
	Channel length turbulence: the change and instability in the number of different tiers in the channel to market.	There is no noticeable change in the number of different tiers in the channel to market.	There is only small and slow change in the number of different tiers in the channel to market.	There is significant but slow change in the number of different tiers in the channel to market.	There is significant and constant change in the number of different tiers in the channel to market.	There is rapid and sudden change in the number of different tiers in the channel to market.
	Channel value turbulence: the change and instability in the extent to which the channel to market adds to the value proposition.	There is no noticeable change in the extent to which the channel to market adds to the value proposition.	There is only small and slow change in the extent to which the channel to market adds to the value proposition.	There is significant but slow change in the extent to which the channel to market adds to the value proposition.	There is significant and constant change in the extent to which the channel to market adds to the value proposition.	There is rapid and sudden change in the extent to which the channel to market adds to the value proposition.
Competitor turbulence	Competitive force turbulence: the change and instability in the number of different competitive forces significant in the market.	There is no noticeable change in the number of different competitive forces significant in the market.	There is only small and slow change in the number of different competitive forces significant in the market.	There is significant but slow change in the number of different competitive forces significant in the market.	There is significant and constant change in the number of different competitive forces significant in the market.	There is rapid and sudden change in the number of different competitive forces significant in the market.

Table 9.6 *(Continued)*

Sub-component of market turbulence	*Turbulence factors*	*Stable (1)*	*Moderately stable (2)*	*Median turbulence (3)*	*Moderately turbulent (4)*	*Turbulent (5)*
	Industry rivalry turbulence: the change and instability in the number of different strategic sets into which direct competitors may be classified.	There is no noticeable change in the number of different strategic sets into which direct competitors may be classified.	There is only small and slow change in the number of different strategic sets into which direct competitors may be classified.	There is significant but slow change in the number of different strategic sets into which direct competitors may be classified.	There is significant and constant change in the number of different strategic sets into which direct competitors may be classified.	There is rapid and sudden change in the number of different strategic sets into which direct competitors may be classified.
Macroenvironment turbulence	Social turbulence: the change and instability in the number of different social factors which impact significantly on the market.	There is no noticeable change in the number of different social factors which impact significantly on the market.	There is only small and slow change in the number of different social factors which impact significantly on the market.	There is significant but slow change in the number of different social factors which impact significantly on the market.	There is significant and constant change in the number of different social factors which impact significantly on the market.	There is rapid and sudden change in the number of different social factors which impact significantly on the market.
	Legal turbulence: the change and instability in the number of different legal factors which impact significantly on the market.	There is no noticeable change in the number of different legal factors which impact significantly on the market.	There is only small and slow change in the number of different legal factors which impact significantly on the market.	There is significant but slow change in the number of different legal factors which impact significantly on the market.	There is significant and constant change in the number of different legal factors which impact significantly on the market.	There is rapid and sudden change in the number of different legal factors which impact significantly on the market.

Economic turbulence: the change and instability in the number of different macroeconomic factors which impact significantly on the market.	There is no noticeable change in the number of different macroeconomic factors which impact significantly on the market.	There is only small and slow change in the number of different macroeconomic factors which impact significantly on the market.	There is significant but slow change in the number of different macroeconomic factors which impact significantly on the market.	There is significant and constant change in the number of different macroeconomic factors which impact significantly on the market.	There is rapid and sudden change in the number of different macroeconomic factors which impact significantly on the market.
Political turbulence: the change and instability in the number of different political factors which impact significantly on the market.	There is no noticeable change in the number of different political factors which impact significantly on the market.	There is only small and slow change in the number of different political factors which impact significantly on the market.	There is significant but slow change in the number of different political factors which impact significantly on the market.	There is significant and constant change in the number of different political factors which impact significantly on the market.	There is rapid and sudden change in the number of different political factors which impact significantly on the market.
Technological turbulence: the change and instability in the number of different technological factors which impact significantly on the market.	There is no noticeable change in the number of different technological factors which impact significantly on the market.	There is only small and slow change in the number of different technological factors which impact significantly on the market.	There is significant but slow change in the number of different technological factors which impact significantly on the market.	There is significant and constant change in the number of different technological factors which impact significantly on the market.	There is rapid and sudden change in the number of different technological factors which impact significantly on the market.

Table 9.6 *(Continued)*

Sub-component of market turbulence	*Turbulence factors*	*Stable (1)*	*Moderately stable (2)*	*Median turbulence (3)*	*Moderately turbulent (4)*	*Turbulent (5)*
Value proposition turbulence	Range turbulence: the change and instability in the number of different product components offered to the market.	There is no noticeable change in the number of different product components offered to the market.	There is only small and slow change in the number of different product components offered to the market.	There is significant but slow change in the number of different product components offered to the market.	There is significant and constant change in the number of different product components offered to the market.	There is rapid and sudden change in the number of different product components offered to the market.
	Technical turbulence: the change and instability in the technology inherent in developing, supplying and selling the value proposition.	There is no noticeable change in the technology inherent in developing, supplying and selling the value proposition.	There is only small and slow change in the technology inherent in developing, supplying and selling the value proposition.	There is significant but slow change in the technology inherent in developing, supplying and selling the value proposition.	There is significant and constant change in the technology inherent in developing, supplying and selling the value proposition.	There is rapid and sudden change in the technology inherent in developing, supplying and selling the value proposition.
	Extended product turbulence: the change and instability in the extent to which the value proposition extends beyond the core product into higher benefits.	There is no noticeable change in the extent to which the value proposition extends beyond the core product into higher benefits.	There is only small and slow change in the extent to which the value proposition extends beyond the core product into higher benefits.	There is significant but slow change in the extent to which the value proposition extends beyond the core product into higher benefits.	There is significant and constant change in the extent to which the value proposition extends beyond the core product into higher benefits.	There is rapid and sudden change in the extent to which the value proposition extends beyond the core product into higher benefits.

Table 9.7 Weightings for market turbulence factors

Market turbulence factor	*Increase weighting from 2 when . . .*	*Decrease weighting from 2 when . . .*
Customer turbulence	The leadership team is separated from the customers by the internal structure and/or when the market changes are hard to foresee and are evidenced mostly in lag effects.	The leadership has a direct and clear view of the customers and/or when the market changes are easy to foresee and 'flagged up'.
Competitor turbulence	The leadership team is separated from competitive forces by the internal structure and/or when the changes in bases of competition are hard to foresee and are evidenced mostly in lag effects.	The leadership has a direct and clear view of competitive forces and/or when the changes in bases of competition are easy to foresee and 'flagged up'.
Channel turbulence	The leadership team is separated from the channels to market by the internal structure and/or when changes in the channels to market are hard to foresee and are evidenced mostly in lag effects.	The leadership has a direct and clear view of the channels to market and/or when changes in the channels to market are easy to foresee and 'flagged up'.
Macroenvironment turbulence	The leadership team is separated from the macroenvironment by the internal structure and/or changes in the macroenvironment are hard to foresee and are evidenced mostly in lag effects.	The leadership has a direct and clear view of the macroenvironment and/or when changes in the macroenvironment are easy to foresee and 'flagged up'.
Value proposition turbulence	The leadership team is separated from the value proposition by the internal structure and/or changes in the value proposition are tracked by management information systems.	The leadership has a direct and clear view of the value proposition and/or changes in the value proposition are subtle and not well measured.

Combining the assessments of market complexity and market turbulence

By following the methods described in the preceding sections of this chapter, the reader should now have calculated two numbers – one an estimate of market complexity and one an estimate of market turbulence. Each estimate should have a value of between 0 and 100 and, taken together, they give a well-considered judgement of the market conditions. Remember that what we have done here is not a market audit. That analyses the market and draws out opportunities and threats. What this chapter has described is an assessment of the nature of the market, in much the same way as a sculptor might look at a piece of stone or an engineer might consider a machine. By understanding the nature of the market, we put ourselves in a better position to choose the right tools to address it. So just as sculptors or engineers might select tools to match their situation, marketers can select rational, incremental and visionary tools for the making of marketing strategy so as to fit the market (i.e. macrocongruent). Exactly how those two numbers lead to macrocongruence is the subject of Chapter 10.

Power points

- Strong marketing strategies are the result of bicongruent strategic marketing planning.
- The first step in achieving bicongruence is to make an objective, realistic assessment of the complexity and turbulence of your market.
- Both market complexity and market turbulence are complex constructs; simplistic approaches are misleading.
- The different components of market complexity and market turbulence can contribute differentially, depending on the market and the company.
- The tools in this chapter allow us to assess both market complexity and market turbulence for our market.

Reflection points for marketing practitioners

- How bicongruent do you think your strategic marketing planning process is?
- Do you think incongruence arises from market complexity or market turbulence, or both?

- What components of each do you think contribute most to an incongruence you observe?
- What are the implications of this incongruence for your marketing strategy?
- What do you think this chapter might imply for how you adapt your strategic marketing planning?

Chapter 10

Choosing the best way to make marketing strategy in your market

An apprentice carpenter may want only a hammer and saw, but a master craftsman employs many precision tools. Computer programming likewise requires sophisticated tools to cope with the complexity of real applications, and only practice with these tools will build skill in their use.
(Robert L. Kruse, *Data Structures and Program Design*)

Introduction

If there is a single word to remember from the 100 000 or so words in the preceding nine chapters, that word is *bicongruence*. Companies that make strong marketing strategies do not all use the same method, but they do all use a strategy making process that is bicongruent to their situation. They blend rational planning, visionary command and incrementalism in such a way that it copes with the complexity and turbulence of their market; then they adjust key parts of their culture to ensure that the culture supports, rather than hinders, the process. They take a sophisticated approach to a difficult problem, in stark contrast to more naïve marketers who think that unskilled use of simple tools will give the result they want. It's interesting to see, from the above quotation, that the same 'sophisticated tools for complex problems' lesson also applies in the completely unrelated discipline of computer programming. If this is true in, say, creating that annoying paperclip help assistant in Microsoft, we would be foolish to forget it when we try to match companies to markets.

In Chapter 9, we considered how to step back from our market and make an objective assessment of market complexity and turbulence. The result is two coordinates that define where our market sits in Figure 7.2. We already know from Chapter 6 that every company uses its own particular colour of strategic marketing planning, its own blend of the three approaches, to make strategy. We also know from Chapter 5 that only a small minority of companies make strong strategies. Whilst some of the reason for this is lack of microcongruence, part of the reason is lack of macrocongruence. In short, for every part of Figure 7.2, some colour of strategic marketing planning works better than any other colour. If we knew what colour of strategic marketing planning worked best in each part of Figure 7.2, then we could make the practical and desired leap from what kind of market we are in to and what we should actually do. So the question this chapter tries to answer is just that: What colour goes where?

Application point: How macrocongruent are you?

The work described in earlier chapters makes clear that macrocongruence arises when the colour of strategic marketing planning used is appropriate to the market conditions of turbulence and complexity. Before going on to explore the detailed mechanisms of macrocongruence, it is valuable to give some thought to the macrocongruence, or lack of it, of your current strategic marketing planning process.

- What colour do you think best describes your current strategic marketing planning process?
- How strong do you think your current marketing strategy is?

- To what extent, if any, do you think macrocongruence or macro-incongruence plays a part in any weaknesses in your marketing strategy?
- What do you imagine might be the optimal colour of strategic marketing planning for your situation?

Mechanisms of macrocongruence

We could be prescriptive about this. Our research data do allow us to generalize, quite strongly, along the lines of, 'in this sort of market, do this sort of strategic marketing planning'. Indeed, later in this chapter we do just that, complete with a diagram. However, in this case prescription is a poor pedagogy for two reasons. First, it makes for poor retention. The sort of reflective practitioner that this book is aimed at learns better when involved in the reasoning behind an assertion. Secondly, macrocongruence is an imperfect art. There are likely to be many cases where any prescription is only approximately correct and the reader will need to adapt the prescription to fit. For both reasons, therefore, it is useful to understand the mechanisms that underlie macrocongruence so as to be able to apply, rather than just recite, the findings of our research.

In Chapter 6, we recounted the observed successes and failures of the different approaches (rational, incremental and visionary command) to cope with market complexity and turbulence. From those observations, we can see that none of the approaches is ever either completely useless or absolutely omnipotent. There is no cut-off point at which, say, visionary command can no longer cope with market complexity, or rational planning cannot cope with turbulence. Instead, the capacity of each approach to cope with its nemesis declines gradually. Rational planning copes well with a limited amount of turbulence, but its efficacy deteriorates as the market changes faster and less predictably. Visionary command processes cope well with small amounts of market complexity, but are soon overwhelmed by increasing market intricacy. Incremental planning copes well with small degrees of both complexity and turbulence, but rapidly loses its power as either (or both) increases. The data are not sufficient to substantiate a mathematical relationship, but we can speculate that the efficacy of each 'pure' approach declines in an exponential manner as market conditions change against it. We can see and understand this gradual failure even better if we consider not strategic marketing planning as a whole, but rather the three fundamental subcomponents of it: understanding the market, choosing a strategy and deciding on actions.

Macrocongruence and market understanding

The three approaches to marketing-strategy making go about understanding the market in very different ways. Visionary command processes sense and intuit to discern the key issues to be addressed. Rational planning gathers data, and analyses and synthesizes to get to the same key issues. Incrementalism negotiates between key internal players, implements the resultant strategy in low-risk steps and draws conclusions about the key issues from the results of repeated incremental steps.

Each approach has its merits and demerits. Visionary command can detect and discern key issues long before the data are good enough to analyse and much faster than incremental, negotiated experimentation. However, the price visionary command pays, is to simplify at the risk of over-simplification. As more factors influence the market, and as they interact in a more convoluted and intricate manner, processes that are undiluted visionary command make mistakes and miss or misinterpret critical factors.

Rational planning copes with a myriad of interacting factors well. Planning-heavy processes simplify with much less risk of subjectivity, or errors of omission or commission, than do visionary command processes. They are also much more efficient at this than incremental processes, which use time and resources in proportion to the number of variables they are trying to understand. In complex markets, experimenting is just too resource-intensive to be practical. However, rational planning requires time and information of reasonable quality, which, in practice, means historical information. In a sense, rational planners are always analysing yesterday's market. Hence, when market turbulence means that tomorrow's market is fundamentally different from that of yesterday, rational planning churns out an incorrect assessment of the key issues.

Incrementalism has the advantages and disadvantages of both the other approaches. It uses negotiation to synthesize the subjective visions of many managers. This allows incremental approaches to sense and intuit key issues at a level of complexity beyond the capabilities of purely visionary command processes. Similarly, experimenting with micro-strategies, as it were, allows incremental approaches to understand markets at a level of turbulence higher than that amenable to very rational processes. However, incrementalism copes with complexity and turbulence at the cost of time and resources. As either complexity or turbulence increases, this consumption of resources becomes too onerous even for companies with a lot of 'organizational slack'. Even when resources allow, the capacity for multiple micro-strategies to be monitored and synthesized into key issues is limited, as the outcomes of experiments overwhelm the capacity of the strategy making group to make sense of them.

In short, then, we can describe a pattern that fits with both our intuition as managers and the empirical observations of our research. The pattern is one in which each pure approach gradually declines in effectiveness as the market becomes more complex or turbulent, or both. This pattern explains how macrocongruence and macro-incongruence develop in the first, important stage of making marketing strategy. Consistent with this, the same pattern is observed in the second stage of strategy choice.

Application point: How macrocongruent is your understanding of the market?

The degree to which a strategic marketing planning process enables understanding of the market is fundamental to its effectiveness. It is determined by the differential capabilities of different approaches to cope with market complexity and market turbulence. It is useful to reflect on what goes on in your organization.

- To what extent is your strategic marketing planning process able to understand the market?
- To what extent, if any, is that ability hindered by market complexity?
- To what extent, if any, is that ability hindered by market turbulence?
- What is it about your current strategic marketing planning process that leads to the limitations or ability to understand your market?

Macrocongruence and strategy choice

As we might expect, each of the three approaches selects strategy very differently from the others. Visionary command processes irrationally envision a strategy and proclaim it with little explicit process. Rational planning deliberately compares and contrasts explicit strategy options before selecting one to implement. Incrementalism also compares and contrasts strategy options but, significantly, this is done tacitly and based on negotiation and limited implementation trials.

As with understanding the market, each of the three approaches has its merits and demerits as a means of selecting a strategy. Visionary command makes the choice quickly and, in terms of resources, more cheaply than either planning or incremental approaches. However, visionary command again risks over-simplification and, in particular, the sort of cognitive biases described in Chapter 1. These risks increase in proportion to market complexity until they eventually outweigh the benefits of speed and efficiency.

Rational planning is very effective at judging the relative merits of different strategic options. The tools and techniques of planning do this with much less of the bias and over-simplification of visionary command and without such heavy resource demands of incrementalism. However, rational planning demands a reasonable quality of data, even if not as much as some data-driven managers think. When market turbulence means that data quality is poor, it overshadows the value of objectivity and rigour and leads to poorer strategic choices.

Incrementalism addresses the strategy choice problem in a manner intermediate between planning and vision. The negotiation and trial approach makes a better job of complex strategy comparisons than pure visionary command, by involving more people. It also copes with turbulence better than by pure rational planning, by providing its own, current data from experiments in the market. Both wider involvement and experimentation are costly of time and resources, however, and in practice can only be used to a limited degree. In reality, those resource limitations mean that incrementalism-heavy approaches can only handle limited amounts of market complexity and turbulence.

We therefore see a similar pattern in choosing the strategy part of strategic marketing planning as we did in the understanding the market phase. Each of the three approaches gradually declines in effectiveness as the strategic choice decision becomes less amenable to it. This picture reinforces our ideas about a mechanism for macrocongruence and extends them to this second stage in making strategy.

Application point: How macrocongruent is your strategy choice?

The degree to which a strategic marketing planning process enables choice of the best strategy is fundamental to its effectiveness. It is determined by the differential capabilities of different approaches to cope with market complexity and market turbulence. It is useful to reflect on what goes on in your organization.

- To what extent is your strategic marketing planning process able to choose well between strategy options?
- To what extent, if any, is that ability hindered by market complexity?
- To what extent, if any, is that ability hindered by market turbulence?
- What is it about your current strategic marketing planning process that leads to the limitations or ability to choose strategies well?

Macrocongruence and deciding actions

The three approaches translate strategy into action differently. Visionary command processes tend to explicitly direct and tacitly monitor. Rational planning deliberately cascades actions downwards via documents and public processes. Incrementalism blurs implementation into market understanding and strategy choice.

Again, there are strengths and weaknesses to each approach. A visionary command approach is fast and efficient, unencumbered as it is by either the formality of planning or experimentation of incrementalism. However, visionary command only works within the sphere of control of the leadership group. It breaks down when the tasks involved or the scale of the organization get beyond this limit of personal control. As the market or organization becomes more complex, the costs of poor control become higher than the benefits of responsiveness to change.

Rational planning is ideal for identifying, communicating and monitoring the multifarious tasks that flow from any strategy that is not simple. The processes and tools of planning make sure fewer things fall between the cracks and ensure coherence between what actions do take place. Omissions and incoherence are both failings of visionary command processes in complex markets. Planning processes also cope with a level of complexity greater than that achievable by incremental processes, and at less resource cost. However, market turbulence interferes with the information these rational processes need for implementation until, at higher levels of turbulence, planning cannot cope in its unalloyed form.

Incrementalism again blends the pros and cons of planning and vision. By its spread of involvement, it exceeds visionary command's capacity to manage complexity of action. It surpasses rational planning's tolerance for turbulence by making only small, step-wise decisions about actions and constantly reviewing them in the light of experience. All this, of course, at the cost in resources that effectively limit the range of incrementalism to the lower reaches of complexity and turbulence. Beyond those parameters, incrementalism needs the support of planning or visionary command, or both.

Application point: How macrocongruent is your deciding of actions?

The degree to which a strategic marketing planning process enables deciding of actions is fundamental to its effectiveness. It is determined by the differential capabilities of different approaches to cope with market complexity and market turbulence. It is useful to reflect on what goes on in your organization.

- To what extent is your strategic marketing planning process able to decide appropriate actions?
- To what extent, if any, is that ability hindered by market complexity?
- To what extent, if any, is that ability hindered by market turbulence?
- What is it about your current strategic marketing planning process that leads to the limitations or ability to decide appropriate actions?

Macrocongruence in deciding actions reinforces the patterns seen in both understanding the market and choosing the strategy. Together, these observations point to a mechanism of macrocongruence. Incrementalism works well in markets that are simple and stable, and even when small amounts of either complexity or turbulence develop. Beyond that, incrementalism begins to fail unless it is supplemented with rational planning (to cope with complexity) or visionary command (to cope with turbulence), or both (to cope with both). Rational planning works well in stable markets, whether complex or simple, but is probably overkill for the latter. As turbulence increases, it begins to lose its efficacy without the bolstering addition of some visionary command process. Visionary command processes work well in simple markets, whether stable or turbulent, but come into their own in simple, turbulent markets. When markets become more complex, visionary command processes begin to fail unless they are augmented by some degree of rational planning.

These observations about how the efficacies of the three approaches vary with market conditions add up to a complex equation. It is not a simple linear equation in which one variable on one side of the equation relates to one variable on the other. Instead, variation of complexity and turbulence on one side of the equation is related to three variables on the other. When these findings first emerged from our research, it seemed inordinately complicated. However, it seems to reflect reality better than simpler descriptions.

It is, of course, a version of contingency theory as we discussed in Chapter 7. If we know that what works is what fits, and half the fit is to be macrocongruent, then Figure 10.1 is a guide to what macrocongruence is, and what is not. The operative word here is 'guide'. It is relatively easy to say that simple, stable markets are best addressed with heavily incremental approaches, for instance, or that turbulent, simple markets need a visionary command-driven process, and stable complex ones need heavily planned approaches. Prescription becomes less valuable when markets lie at borderline

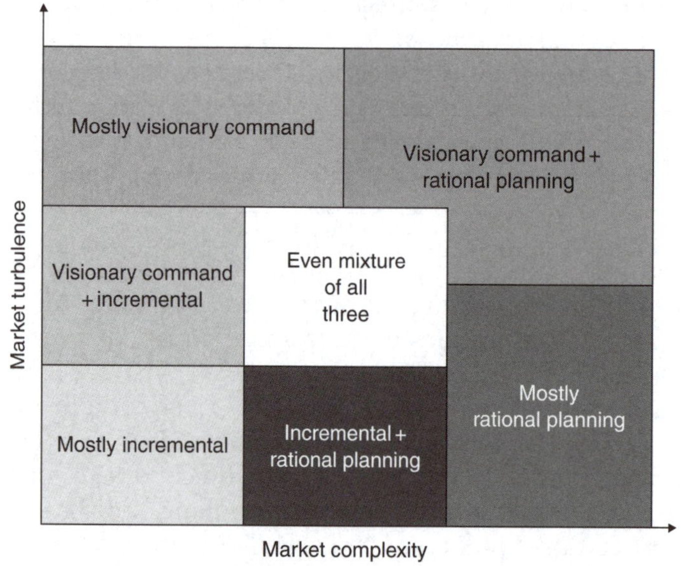

Figure 10.1 A guide to macrocongruence. See colour plate 10.1.

levels of complexity or turbulence, or both. In such cases we still need to use judgement to blend the three approaches, using Figure 10.1 as a guide. However, this is still a huge advance on the textbook model (do rational planning in all cases) or any other simple prescriptive model. The macrocongruence figure prescribes the best colour of strategic marketing planning to use in clear-cut situations, and still leaves room for guided managerial judgement in less well-defined instances. Such a balance between prescription and guidance is the inevitable output of a sophisticated, non-simplistic consideration of any complex business problem, and seems appropriate to the needs of the reflective practitioner. Note also that Figure 10.1 is significantly different from Figure 7.1. The two figures don't contradict each other; rather, Figure 10.1 is a development of Figure 7.2.

So, a careful consideration of the mechanism of macrocongruence takes us part way towards answering our question about what to do in any particular market situation. We know that, as summarized in Figure 10.1, certain colours of strategic marketing planning fit with certain market conditions. A quick reminder of reality, however – we must not forget that even this complicated diagram is still an approximation. In reality, the sharp lines between areas shade into each other. However, Figure 10.1 still provides a good enough approximation to be useful.

Application point: Which colour of strategic marketing planning is macrocongruent to your market conditions?

The mechanisms of macrocongruence allow us to understand why different colours of marketing strategy are macrocongruent to certain conditions of market complexity and turbulence and others are not, as summarized in Figure 10.1. Before considering what this implies for action, it is useful to consider your own situation.

- What does Figure 10.1 suggest is the macrocongruent colour of strategic marketing planning for your situation?
- How different, if at all, is this from your current activity?
- Is macro-incongruence, if any, of your current strategic marketing planning process consistent with your perceptions of your marketing strategy quality?

The gap in our knowledge now is not what to use when, but exactly what we mean when we say white or blue or yellow (or any other colour) strategic marketing planning. If we apply the tools in Chapter 9 and get an objective assessment of our market conditions, it places us somewhere in Figure 10.1, which then recommends that we adopt a certain hybrid marketing-strategy making process, a certain 'colour' of strategic marketing planning. We need to know what that prescription implies for practical action. That detail, what actions make up each colour of strategic marketing planning, is the subject of the next section.

The seven colours of strategic marketing planning as management activity

In Chapter 7 we described in outline seven 'colours', or typical styles, of strategic marketing planning. At that stage in the book, an outline was sufficient to differentiate between the different ways in which companies do their strategic marketing planning. We are now faced with the next stage of our problem: that of actually selecting one colour of strategic marketing planning to use in our own organization. Figure 10.1 and the preceding section gave us a guide, but to make an informed choice and to help us in the borderline cases we need a rather deeper understanding of the activities and processes that we have abbreviated with each colour metaphor. In short, we need to know what we actually have to do if Figure 10.1 suggests 'orange' or 'blue'. To get that deeper understanding, we need to consider the activities and processes that each colour involves at each of the three stages of strategic marketing planning: understanding the market, choosing the strategy and deciding the actions. Such an understanding will allow us to understand, compare and contrast each colour – a necessary step before we choose a colour to implement, or make the decision to create our own particular shade of planning.

Table 10.1 attempts to demonstrate the differences between each colour. It is laid out in tabular form to allow comparison between the activity at different stages for different colours. Note that the three 'purest' colours – blue, yellow and red – are quite different from each other, whilst orange, violet, white and green are essentially hybrids of the three primary colours. In reality, the strategic marketing planning process of any one company is likely to be a reddish-orange, or a yellowy-green, or some other intermediate colour. The implementation of each colour of strategic marketing planning is described later in this book, but for now it is necessary and valuable to note and appreciate the differences between them.

Application point: What activity does macrocongruence suggest for you?

To the extent that your current strategic marketing planning is not macrocongruent, the adoption of a macrocongruent process will require changes in activity patterns. Before proceeding, it is useful to consider what this might mean.

- What activity does a strategic marketing planning process that is macrocongruent to your situation require you to undertake?
- To what extent, if any, is that activity different from your current strategic marketing planning?
- What problems and opportunities do those changes in activity suggest to you?

Selecting a colour of strategic marketing planning that is macrocongruent to your market

In the preceding sections of this chapter, we moved our thinking on from understanding our market conditions to understanding what those market conditions imply for action. This involves two steps. The first is understanding that the limitations of visionary command, rational planning and incrementalism imply a 'contingency approach'. In other words, certain colours of strategic marketing planning are optimal for certain market conditions of turbulence and complexity. The second is understanding what each colour actually means in terms of activity to understand the market, choose a strategy and decide actions. Having taken these two significant steps in our understanding, we are now able to start the practical work of adapting our organizational culture to support, and not hinder, our particular colour of strategic marketing planning. That is, Chapters 9 and 10 allow us to achieve macrocongruence and prepare us to work

Table 10.1 Activities in each of the seven colours of strategic marketing planning

Colour of strategic marketing planning	*Activity in understanding the market phase*	*Activity in choosing the strategy phase*	*Activity in the deciding actions phase*
Blue – mostly rational planning	Deliberate division of the market environment into categories for analysis.	Identification and explication of strategic choices, normally in the form of market areas, by deliberate generation of options.	Exposition and communication of selected strategy and concomitant objectives to relevant functional leaders.
	Systematized use of strategic management tools to analyse each division of the market environment.	Development of the strategy sufficient to provide a reasonable estimate of the costs, risks and benefits involved.	Development and reiteration of middle and lower level resource allocation and objectives
	Collation of the outputs of market analysis, with quantification where possible.	Assessment of the strategy options against specific criteria (e.g. ROI, risk, synergy, cyclicity), often derived from higher corporate objectives.	Development, reiteration and cascading downwards of specific action plans.
	Alignment of internal and external factors, typically by SWOT analysis, to reveal key issues to be addressed by the strategy.	Selection of specific strategy option or options.	Measurement of results against performance indicators and feedback into short term, tactical revisions and longer term market understanding.
Yellow – mostly visionary command	Continuous scanning of the market environment in a relatively holistic manner.	Induction of core strategy from leaders' beliefs and values.	Communication of strategy and goals by informal, often charismatic, communication.
	Intuitive, non-deliberate analysis of the market environment by leader or leadership group, resulting in clear, simple view of key opportunities and threats.	Consideration, informal testing and revision of core strategy against the key issues derived from market understanding.	Setting of quantified objectives at higher, middle and lower levels in a directed, rather than cascaded, manner.

	Explicit, but usually instinctive, synthesis of market threats and opportunities into key implications for strategy choice.	Semi-structured testing of the revised strategy against organizational goals.	Continual direct monitoring of both quantitative and qualitative feedback, forming the basis for tactical revisions and refinement of market understanding.
Red – mostly incremental	Continuous scanning of the market environment by multiple members of leadership team, generally focused according to individual functional perspectives.	Identification of possible strategies, usually in the form of possible markets and propositions to address.	Development of action plans from trial strategies, but within limits or resource allocation and risk deferment.
	Synthesis of different market environment perspectives, via a process of political negotiation, into a limited-consensus view of the market.	Narrowing down of possible strategies by a process of political negotiation and consideration of practical constraints.	Incremental and limited-risk implementation of action plans, often multiple plans, often limited to specific channels or geographies.
	Agreement of implications of the view of the market for possible allocation of resources.	Agreement of limited trial strategies to attempt, with relatively limited commitment and with risk deferred as much as possible.	Monitoring of results, forming the basis to reinforce, modify or abandon trial strategies.
			Gradual interpolation of results into market understanding, usually politically interpreted and filtered.
Green – mixture of rational planning and visionary command	High level of leadership involvement in understanding the market.	Deliberate generation of options, but rapidly narrowed down to leave only those consistent with leadership vision.	Dictation of core strategy and goals to functional leaders.

Table 10.1 *(Continued)*

Colour of strategic marketing planning	*Activity in understanding the market phase*	*Activity in choosing the strategy phase*	*Activity in the deciding actions phase*
	Combination of intuitive visioning and rational analysis to identify key internal and external factors.	Rational assessment of remaining strategy options. by criteria explicitly skewed by leadership vision.	Development and reiteration of middle and lower level resource allocation and objectives using deliberate processes. but only within the leadership vision.
	Key issues identified by intuitive insight, but tested and substantiated by rational analysis.	Relatively autocratic selection of a specific strategy option.	Development, reiteration and cascading downwards of specific action plans but tightly constrained by the leadership vision.
			Rational, usually quantified, measurement of results against performance indicators; these results used both for short-term tactical revisions and longer-term market understanding by leadership group.
Orange – mixture of visionary command and incremental	Continuous scanning of the market environment in a relatively holistic manner by extended leadership team.	Identification of possible strategies within constraints of leadership vision.	Development of action plans from trial strategies, but limited within leadership vision and resource allocation.
	Intuitive, non-deliberate analysis of the market environment by extended leadership group, resulting in loose consensus about key internal and external factors.	Narrowing down of possible strategies by a process of political negotiation amongst extended leadership team.	Incremental and limited risk implementation of action plans, often multiple plans, often limited to specific channels or geographies.

	Explicit but informal synthesis of market threats and opportunities, influenced heavily by political negotiation amongst extended leadership team.	Agreement of limited trial strategies to attempt, with relatively limited commitment and with risk deferred as much as possible.	Monitoring of results, forming the basis to reinforce, modify or abandon trial strategies.
			Gradual interpolation of results into market understanding, usually politically interpreted and filtered.
Violet – mixture of rational planning and incremental	Deliberate division of the market environment into categories for analysis.	Identification and explication of strategic choices, normally in the form of market areas, by deliberate generation of options.	Development of explicit action plans from trial strategies but within limits of resource allocation and risk deferment.
	Systematized use of strategic management tools to analyse each division of the market environment, but only within the limits of available data and resources.	Screening of strategy options by rational assessment, but only so far as to reduce options to a manageable number.	Incremental and limited risk implementation of action plans, often multiple plans, often limited to specific channels or geographies.
	Collation of the outputs of market analysis, with quantification where possible, but coloured by political negotiation and results of trial activity.	Agreement of limited trial strategies to attempt, with relatively limited commitment and with risk deferred as much as possible.	Deliberate and usually quantified monitoring of results, forming the basis to reinforce, modify or abandon trial strategies.
	Agreement of implications of the view of the market for possible allocation of resources.		Formal and deliberate interpolation of results into market understanding.

Table 10.1 *(Continued)*

Colour of strategic marketing planning	*Activity in understanding the market phase*	*Activity in choosing the strategy phase*	*Activity in the deciding actions phase*
White – mixture of rational planning, visionary command and incremental	High level of extended leadership team involvement in understanding the market.	Broad range of strategic options, emerging from political negotiation around a loosely defined leadership vision.	Development of explicit action plans from narrow range of trial strategies.
	Combination of intuitive visioning and rational analysis to identify key internal and external factors, but moderated by political negotiation.	Range of strategic options narrowed by political negotiation in which rational analysis is used to support argument.	Planned and incremental implementation of action plans, often limited to specific channels or geographies.
	Key issues identified by intuitive insight but tested and substantiated by rational analysis.	Narrow range of (usually closely related) strategic options, emerging from extended leadership team.	Deliberate and usually quantified monitoring of results, forming the basis to reinforce, modify or abandon trial strategies.
	Significant degree of acceptance of ambiguity in interpretation of market environment.		Formal and deliberate interpolation of results into market understanding of extended leadership team.

on microcongruence in Chapter 11. However, macrocongruence is a necessary foundation for microcongruence, so it is worth closing this chapter with a step-wise exposition of what must be done to achieve macrocongruence.

Companies that make strong strategies do so via a process that is macrocongruent to their market conditions. They usually achieve macrocongruence in a way that is 'unconsciously competent'; however, we can learn from this and mimic their success, using an explicit, conscious process. To identify a strategic marketing planning process that fits the market conditions (i.e. is macrocongruent), we must follow five steps:

1. Carry out the assessment of market complexity and turbulence described in Chapter 9. This should result in two numbers, each between 0 and 100, which characterize the complexity and turbulence of your market. Be careful to carry out the assessment as rigorously as possible, using whatever qualitative and quantitative evidence is available.

2. Consider the numbers and pause for thought. It is easy for process to triumph over task and to follow methods unthinkingly. If the complexity and turbulence assessments do not 'feel' right, re-examine the assessment judgements and look for values that contradict your instincts. For those contradictory values, seek out more information and evidence. Use that to either substantiate or improve the assessment. Continue this iteration until you are comfortable with the assessment. This stage is important for two reasons: first, it improves the accuracy of the market conditions assessment; and secondly, it improves the commitment of the assessing individual or group to the judgement. Both are important to the success of strategic marketing planning.

3. Consider Figure 10.1 and what it implies in the light of your assessment of market conditions. It will imply that a certain colour of strategic marketing planning is appropriate to your situation. Pay particular attention to market conditions that are within about five assessment points of any border between approaches. These imply that the optimal process may be a blend of the indicated colour with some elements of the adjacent colour.

4. Based on this consideration, use Table 10.1 to create a list of activities that constitute a macrocongruent strategic marketing planning process for your situation. In borderline cases, it will be necessary to decide which part of the three stages of the strategic marketing planning process requires adaptation and blending with

the adjacent colour. This is a matter of managerial judgement, but there are two guiding principles. First, market complexity and turbulence arising to a significant degree from the value proposition usually requires addition of adjacent activity into the deciding actions or, sometimes, the strategy choice processes. By contrast, when a borderline assessment is heavily influenced by customer, channel competitor or macroenvironment factors, then it is the process for understanding the market that requires additional activity from adjacent colours of strategic marketing planning. The second (but still significant) factor to consider is the difficulty of change. Where 'shading' of the strategic marketing planning process to be macrocongruent requires a lot of change from current practice, the cost–benefit ratio is an important consideration. A difficult change in the current process may not be worth a small increase in macrocongruence.

5. Finally, the strategic marketing planning process developed in steps 1–4 provides the basis for the next steps in developing macrocongruence. Anticipate the changes to current practice that will be needed to implement the macrocongruent process, and the possible conflict with cultural artefacts that might be expected.

These five stages result in a design of strategic marketing planning process that is macrocongruent to our market – one that combines the rational planning, incrementalism and visionary command approaches in such a way as to cope with the complexity and turbulence of this particular market. The challenge now is to ensure that the organization can implement that process by providing supportive rather than hindering cultural artefacts. That is the subject of Chapter 11.

Power points

- Macrocongruence is the result of using a colour of strategic marketing planning that fits the complexity and turbulence of the market.
- Rational planning, incrementalism and visionary command approaches all have merits and demerits in their ability to cope with market conditions.
- These limitations lead to a mechanism of macrocongruence which, in turn, leads to the pattern of macrocongruence seen in Figure 10.1.
- The different colours of strategic marketing planning each involve different activities to understand the market, choose the strategy and decide the actions.

- Following a five-step process allows us to mimic the unconscious competence of companies that achieve macrocongruence.

Reflection points for marketing practitioners

- How macrocongruent do you think your current strategic marketing planning process is?
- What colour of strategic marketing planning is macrocongruent to your market conditions?
- What activities does this colour of strategic marketing planning suggest?
- How different from your current activity is this?
- What problems and opportunities does the required change suggest?

Chapter 11

Adapting your organizational culture to support your strategy making

> It will be easy to make changes that are congruent with present assumptions and very difficult to make changes that are not. In sum, the understanding of organizational culture would then become integral to the process of management itself.
>
> (Edgar Schein)

Introduction

Our goal is a strong marketing strategy – one that creates strong customer preference towards us rather than our competition. As we learned in the first two sections of this book, only relatively few companies manage to do this. The common factor they share is not so much the way that they make marketing strategy, but that the way they plan is bicongruent. Our approach, therefore, to achieving our goal of strong strategy is to make our strategic marketing planning process bicongruent – in other words, to ensure that the way we choose which customers to go after and what to offer them fits both the marketplace and our organizational culture.

Achieving bicongruence is not easy. Those few companies that attain it do so in a mostly unconscious way, and none of them knows the term bicongruence. That unconsciousness means that we cannot simply ask them what they do and repeat it. Instead, we need to turn their unconscious competencies into our conscious competencies. This third section is all about that – a conscious, deliberate process by which we can mimic or emulate that success. It starts with assessing the complexity and turbulence of the market, as we did in Chapter 9. An accurate assessment of our market conditions allows us, as in Chapter 10, to select the colour of strategic marketing planning that is macrocongruent to the market. By now, we are halfway to creating a bicongruent strategic marketing planning process. The other half of the journey is to achieve microcongruence, ensuring that the way we make marketing strategy is supported and not hindered by our organizational culture. That second half of our journey is what this chapter is about.

The challenge of culture change

Before getting into the detail of how organizational culture might be adapted to achieve microcongruence, it is worth briefly reiterating the nature of organizational culture and the limitations that it places upon culture change.

The culture of a company or any organization is rooted in its assumptions about what works in the market. These assumptions are usually implicit, and often stretch way back into the company's history. Although the assumptions can and do change over time, such change is usually gradual to the point of being undetectable. These stable core assumptions about the right way to do things lead to the values of the organization. For example, beliefs that product excellence is what matters lead to the valuing of research and development and quality control above, say, excellence in customer service or attractive design. In another case, a belief that relationships are the basis of business success leads the organization to value a certain attitude and approach in its sales people, and perhaps to devalue hard-nosed selling skills. There are countless possibilities for such assumption – value linkages; and each assumption is linked to many values and *vice versa*. Whatever the underlying assumptions, they lead to and are masked by a set of consequent and complementary values. Organizational values are usually much more pervasive, less visible and more complicated than implied by any explicit statement of company values. Whilst partly discernible to close examination, such cultural values are often invisible to those who hold and work with them. These values lead us to behave as we do – from the way that we structure the organization, to the way that we lay out our offices, to the procedures and protocols we have for getting things done. More insidiously, values permeate and influence the way we work together, how much we cooperate and challenge, what gets praised and what gets you fired. Anything that fits values is encouraged, and actions that transgress are discouraged and sometimes punishable, leading to a discernible and all encompassing pattern in the way a company does things. Taken together, these collections of 'the way we do things around here' are called cultural artefacts. It is our cultural artefacts that visibly interact with our strategic marketing planning process, but the roots of those interactions lie in our much less visible cultural values and assumptions.

The three-layer structure of organizational culture is of much more than academic interest. It has two important practical implications for those trying to make a strong marketing strategy, as eloquently captured by Edgar Schein in the quotation at the head of this chapter. The first is that culture is pervasive. Every activity that is involved in any colour of strategic marketing planning will either clash with, or be consistent with, an activity that flows out of the culture. If we decide we need to analyse the market carefully, it will be much more difficult in a 'let's just make it happen' culture than in one which values planning. If we decide to seize opportunities, it will happen faster in an entrepreneurial culture than in one where the accountants demand that all decisions be justified by a discounted cash flow analysis.

The second implication of the structure of organizational culture is that it is persistent and hard to change. There are two reasons for this. First, organizational culture is resilient, with lots of redundancy. Each artefact is informed and created by many values and assumptions. If you change anything, there is a strong chance it will change back. Like trying to shape a liquid, even the most forceful impacts are absorbed and, after a while, leave no apparent result. That is not to say that cultural change is impossible, but it is naïve to think of it as an easy first resort. The second reason that culture is hard to change stems from the unintended consequences of change. Any significant cultural change is likely to have inadvertent side effects, and not always desirable ones. Increasing freedom may reduce discipline, or improving customer orientation may reduce commercial 'horse sense'. In other words, the culture is what got you where you are today, bad and good, so changing it risks throwing the good out with the bad. A sort of corollary exists to the adage 'buyer beware', so that 'changer beware' is a practical mantra for managers attempting to manipulate organizational culture. Again, this does not mean that culture should never be changed – just never in a casual or simplistic manner. It also means that cultural change should only be attempted to the minimum degree necessary to achieve organizational goals. Cultural change done in an overzealous manner will almost always fail and often result in severely negative unintended consequences. If the achievement of bicongruence does require cultural change, then it should only be attempted in a limited manner and with much thought. The following sections are intended to guide the reader through this difficult stage, first by fathoming out the mechanism of interaction between organizational culture and strategic marketing planning; secondly by using our knowledge of that mechanism to allow us to identify and anticipate microcongruence and microincongruence; and finally by providing guidance about the careful adaptation of organizational culture to achieve microcongruence with particular colours of strategic marketing planning.

Application point: Has your company culture changed?

Amongst action-oriented managers, myths persist that company culture can be changed and moulded simply by issuing orders and redrawing the organization chart. Before getting into the mechanics of adapting culture to achieve microcongruence, spend a moment reflecting on previous cultural change in your organization.

- What attempts at cultural change have been made in your organization?
- What did those attempts involve?
- What was the net outcome?

Try to look beneath superficial changes in labels and terms, and political 'role playing', to identify any real changes in the way your company behaves. Try to put into perspective the efforts at cultural change, the time and energy consumed, and the real results.

- Has real and deliberate cultural change occurred, or simply natural and gradual change?

The mechanism of interaction between organizational culture and strategic marketing planning

As touched upon in Chapter 3, organizational culture is a huge domain of research and academic thought. It is not the purpose of this chapter to review that vast area of knowledge, but to extend and apply that knowledge in one particular area – that of its interaction with strategic marketing planning. What follows then is by way of development from the general to the specific. In particular, the following section arises from developing the work of Edgar Schein by incorporating the observations and findings of the field research upon which this book is based. It is worth remembering, however, that organizational culture is very complicated, and its study is led by several great minds with strongly contrasting perspectives. Each of these points of view has something to offer the practitioner, so the work of Joanne Martin, Linda Smirchich, Mary Jo Hatch, Dan Denison, Peter Drucker and many others has informed this section. Readers interested in knowing more about organizational culture are directed to the admirable works of those writers, as well as those of Edgar Schein.

The nature of core cultural assumptions

Edgar Schein's three-level model starts with core cultural assumptions (see Chapter 3, Figures 3.1 and 3.2). Schein believed that these assumptions began with the founders of the company and were only slowly amended or endorsed by experience. The origins of the assumptions mean that, in Schein's words, they were usually taken for granted, invisible and preconscious. The research work for this book also indicated that they were often very different from the explicit, espoused statements which were framed and hung in the company's reception area and highlighted in the annual report. The core assumptions of an organization are about what works. When questioned, managers do not see these as assumptions but as 'facts of life' and 'realities of the marketplace'. An organization's view of the world, its cultural paradigm, is made up of very many of these core assumptions, and their quantity as well as their invisibility makes them hard to understand. However, Schein created a useful way of categorizing the different types of assumption that make up a cultural paradigm. Translating his work loosely, organizations make assumptions about five different things:

1. *How the organization relates to the environment.* For our purposes, the environment translates to the market. Organizations make assumptions about what their market is, whether they are leaders or followers, whether their market is benign or hostile, and so on. Importantly, these assumptions also extend to how complex or turbulent the market is, and to the best way to compete in this market.
2. *The nature of truth and reality.* Although this sounds rather metaphysical, it is in fact practically important. Organizations make assumptions such as: only things that can be measured are real, or that the market is subtle, arcane, and susceptible only to management instinct.
3. *The nature of human nature.* Buried deep within an organization's cultural paradigm is a set of beliefs about human nature. These beliefs may be that human beings are honest, noble and perfectible, or that they are essentially untrustworthy and flawed. Of course these assumptions have multiple implications, in that they relate not only to employees but also to customers and other stakeholders.
4. *The nature of human activity.* The beliefs mentioned above, about the market, reality and human nature, are linked by beliefs about the right way for people to behave. Is it to be passive or active? High-minded or expedient? Intellectual or practical? These implications relate not only to the management team but also to subordinates, and the same assumptions do not always apply equally to both.
5. *The nature of human relationships.* Perhaps the most critical of organizational assumptions are those about the best way for people to interact with each other – competitively or cooperatively, independently or within clear rules, based on trust or measured transactions. Assumptions in this category apply to all relationships between

all stakeholders, but the same assumptions do not always apply universally to all groups.

Clearly, each of these five categories might contain hundreds or thousands of overlapping, sometimes contradictory assumptions. At a simple level, each one might lead in a straightforward manner to an organizational value. For example, an assumption that intellectual endeavour is valuable might imply that a high value is based on pure research and intellectual rigour. In practice, however, these straightforward linkages are diluted and coloured by input from other assumptions, making the relationship between assumptions and values obscure and hard to decipher. That is not to say the connection is entirely opaque, but simply to warn against drawing overly simplistic associations from one level of organizational culture to another.

Table 11.1 lists twenty-five of the most visible and influential cultural assumptions noted during the research for this book, grouped under Schein's five categories. The list is compiled from many companies, and is neither complete nor representative of any single company. Not only is the list incomplete, it is also selective, focusing on those assumptions that surfaced during in-depth discussions about strategic marketing planning. These are, of course, only the tip of the iceberg. The reality of any organizational culture, if it could be fully understood, is a confusing and sometimes contradictory mass of such assumptions. However, a complete and non-selective list of cultural assumptions, even if discernible, would be so large that it would hinder rather than help our cause. We are trying to make strong marketing strategy rather than bottom out organizational culture. This list has the virtue of illustrating the issue clearly and enabling readers, eventually, to build a similar list for the organization in which they work.

Application point: What are the cultural assumptions of your organization?

Although 'taken for granted, invisible and preconscious', the core cultural assumptions of an organization are fundamentally important to allowing any colour of strategic marketing planning to work. Adapting the organizational culture will eventually require some understanding of these assumptions, even if that understanding is imperfect and incomplete. It is useful, therefore, to consider the following questions.

- Using Schein's five headings and Table 11.1 as a guide, what core cultural assumptions do you perceive in your organization?
- To what extent, if any, do you agree with these assumptions?
- How might you expect these assumptions and their consequent values and artefacts to impact on your strategic marketing planning?

From assumptions to values

In Schein's model, core cultural assumptions lead to the culturally embedded values of the organization in an inexorable but non-straightforward manner. The word 'values' has been corrupted by overuse in modern management parlance, so it is worth taking a moment to be clear about the sense in which it is used here. In this sense, 'values' refers to how much we value things, rather than ethics or morals. Cultural values are a set of scales by which organizations assess the worth, correctness and appropriateness of some thing or activity. Of the innumerable decisions and choices made by managers every day, only the tiniest fraction is amenable to external, validated, objective assessment. The remainder require some other decision aid. Although many of these decisions are as small as signing a stationery order or changing a word in a subordinate's proposed email, they add up to a mass of decisions that are cumulatively important. In the absence of objective measures, we make these decisions against a set of internalized criteria which we call organizational values. If our organization values frugality, our decision about the stationery order may be different from the same decision in an organization that values strategic thinking and eschews micro-management. If we value individuality, we may let go an imperfectly worded email for the sake of not curtailing initiative. If we value discipline, we may take the time to correct and advise the subordinate's choice of words. Like the decisions of individual drivers in a city, these add up to a bigger picture of organizational activity. Note that, at this stage, we are making no judgements about which values are right and wrong, simply observing them to be the poorly understood means by which most of our organizational activity is controlled. The poorly understood but pervasive nature of organizational values has important implications for strategic marketing planning – we need a better understanding of where organizational values come from

Table 11.1 Examples of cultural assumptions relevant to strategic marketing planning

Underlying cultural assumptions about ...	*Typical cultural assumptions described during field research which were relevant to the effectiveness of strategic marketing planning processes*
How the organization relates to the market	What matters in this market is being technologically more advanced than the competition. What matters in this market is being more efficient than the competition. What matters in this market is being better at customer relationships than the competition. What matters in this market is the quality of our management thinking. What matters in this market is making things happen in the real world. Our market is best described in terms of the product we sell. Our market is best described in terms of the channels we sell through. Our market is best described in terms of the types of customer we sell to.
The nature of truth and reality	Truth is simple, absolute and amenable to quantitative measurement. Truth is absolute but complex and is best clarified by quantification. Truth is simple but relative and not entirely accessible to measurement. Truth is relative and complex and only really accessible to judgement.
The nature of human nature	All people are essentially good and capable of great things. Only a few people like me are good and capable of great things. Most people are essentially flawed and limited in their capabilities.
The nature of human activity	All of us should behave to the highest ethical standards. We should be guided by ethics but act pragmatically. We should take responsibility for our own actions. We have limited autonomy in the face of events.
The nature of human relationships	The coherence of the team is critical to our success. Individuality lies at the root of our success. Discipline is necessary to avoid disaster. Democracy, rather than autocracy, is most likely to succeed in the modern world. Organizations can mould human nature. Organizations must work with the grain of human nature.

and where they lead. In academic parlance, we need to understand the antecedents and consequences of our organization's cultural values.

The origins of an organization's values lie in its core assumptions, but via a frustratingly complex route. As alluded to earlier, some connections seem obvious, such as a belief that 'technical superiority is necessary to success' translating through to valuing intellectual rigour and scientific skills. However, organizational culture is more like a brain than a computer. Each value is informed by multiple assumptions, with each input varying with different contexts. Rather than having simple yes/no results, organizational values operate by a kind of fuzzy logic in which the same assumption may not always add up to the same value. For example, the assumption about technological superiority will influence the value placed upon research, but the value system may be shaded by other assumptions about the need for financial discipline and the importance of practical, market-oriented solutions. Overall, organizational values are not easily amenable to simplistic analysis. However, we can, with careful thought, discern a pattern of connectivity between assumptions and values that is pragmatically useful. In the same way that neuroscientists have not yet fathomed all the workings of the brain but know enough to improve treatment of depression, we can gain enough insight into the workings of our company culture to improve the way we make strategy – so long as we don't let hubris mislead us into thinking culture can be managed like the stationery budget.

In Table 11.2, the cultural assumptions noted in our field research are developed into typical cultural values. There are three things to note about this exposition of the research findings. First, these contradictory assumptions and values don't all come from one company; they are a composite of the findings from many companies. Secondly, the connection between each assumption and value is probabilistic, rather than certain, and indicates only one of the possible values arising from each assumption. In another organization, the influence of differently weighted, competing assumptions might lead to a different set of values. Finally, the values are illustrated as dyads – competing pairs of values – merely to illustrate the point better.

Table 11.2, like Table 11.1, is an incomplete simplification. It is incomplete in the sense that it lists only a small sample of the possible cultural assumptions and values that might impact on strategic marketing planning. It is a simplification in that it lists only the

Table 11.2 Examples of cultural values relevant to strategic marketing planning

Underlying cultural assumptions about . . .	*Typical cultural assumptions described during field research which were relevant to the effectiveness of strategic marketing planning processes*	*Typical cultural values relevant to strategic marketing planning and arising from this cultural assumption*
How the organization relates to the market	What matters in this market is being technologically more advanced than the competition.	Leading edge research and good scientists are more valuable than cost control and sales and marketing competencies.
	What matters in this market is being more efficient than the competition.	Operational efficiency and cost control are more valuable than leading edge research and sales and marketing competencies.
	What matters in this market is being better at customer relationships than the competition.	Sales and marketing competencies are more valuable than leading edge research or operational efficiency and cost control.
	What matters in this market is the quality of our management thinking.	Providing time and resources for considered management reflection is more valuable than allocating management time to implementation.
	What matters in this market is making things happen in the real world.	Allocating management time to implementation is more valuable than providing time and resources for considered management reflection.
	Our market is best described in terms of the product or services we sell.	Understanding the functionality and benefits of our products or services is more valuable than understanding our customer motivations or the needs of our channels to market.

	Our market is best described in terms of the channels we sell through.	Understanding the needs of our channels to market is more valuable than understanding of our customer motivations or the functionality and benefits of our products or services.
	Our market is best described in terms of the types of customer we sell to.	Understanding of our customer motivations is more valuable than understanding the needs of our channels to market or the functionality and benefits of our products or services.
The nature of truth and reality	Truth is simple, absolute and amenable to quantitative measurement.	We value quantified analyses of the market that simplify the picture rather than complicated syntheses of hard and soft data.
	Truth is absolute but complex and is best clarified by quantification.	We value sophisticated, quantified analyses of the market that give a sophisticated synthesis of everything we can measure rather than simple or judgemental views.
	Truth is simple but relative and not entirely accessible to measurement.	We value simplified assessments of the market, based on management judgement rather than purely quantitative analysis.
	Truth is relative and complex and only really accessible to judgement	We value sophisticated assessments of the market, based on management judgement rather than purely quantitative or simplistic judgements.
The nature of human nature	All people are essentially good and capable of great things.	Recruitment, development and retention of good people is more valuable than close management of subordinates.

Table 11.2 *(Continued)*

Underlying cultural assumptions about ...	*Typical cultural assumptions described during field research which were relevant to the effectiveness of strategic marketing planning processes*	*Typical cultural values relevant to strategic marketing planning and arising from this cultural assumption*
	Only a few people like me are good and capable of great things.	Leadership by a well-chosen management team is more valuable than involvement and democracy.
	Most people are essentially flawed and limited in their capabilities.	Close management by the leadership is more valuable than attempts to recruit, retain and develop subordinates.
The nature of human activity	All of us should behave to the highest ethical standards.	Time spent assessing the ethical implications of our decisions is more valuable than that spent discussing the detail of implementation and tactics.
	We should be guided by ethics but act pragmatically.	Time spent examining the practical outcomes of our actions is more valuable than that spent assessing the ethical implications of our decisions.
	We should take responsibility for our own actions.	Initiative and pro-activity is more valuable than pragmatism and ability to react to events.

	We have limited autonomy in the face of events.	Pragmatism and ability to react to events is more valuable than initiative and pro-activity.
The nature of human relationships	The coherence of the team is critical to our success.	Achieving a strong consensus is more valuable than achieving the strictly optimal decision.
	Individuality lies at the root of our success	Heterogeneity of views and allowing managed dissent is more valuable than achieving a strong consensus.
	Discipline is necessary to avoid disaster.	Close management is more valuable than any benefits arising from wider involvement in decision making.
	Democracy, rather than autocracy, is most likely to succeed in the modern world.	The benefits arising from wider involvement in decision making are more valuable than the benefits arising from close management.
	Organizations can mould human nature	Employing leadership and control to direct the way our people work is more valuable than trying to find people who fit in with our organization.
	Organizations must work with the grain of human nature.	Finding the right people is more valuable than trying to make people change the way they work.

extremes of the dyads and neglects the innumerable middle positions possible in a company's values. Both these deliberate compromises are made to reduce confusion and improve understanding. The resultant values in Table 11.2 are therefore mere illustrations of a very important point – that there is a practically useful, if convoluted, connectivity between assumptions and values. As described in the next section, these values, derived from assumptions, then lead to cultural artefacts. The artefacts interact with the strategic marketing planning process, and that series of linkages is the mechanism by which organizational culture interacts with strategic marketing planning. When that interaction is positive and supportive of the strategic marketing planning process, we call it microcongruence. When the opposite occurs, we call it micro-incongruence – a phenomenon which leads to the failure of much strategic marketing planning.

Application point: What are the cultural values of your organization?

The cultural values of an organization inform the decisions and choices of managers and others far more often than do explicit objective considerations. They therefore impact, via cultural artefacts, on strategic marketing planning.

- Using Table 11.2 as a guide, what cultural values do you perceive in your organization?
- To what extent, if any, do you agree with these values?
- How might you expect these values and their consequent artefacts to impact on your strategic marketing planning?

From values to artefacts

Unlike assumptions and values, artefacts, the top layer of Schein's model, are relatively easy to see. The difficulty is in understanding and clarifying the huge mass of them. Cultural artefacts include systems, structures and processes, but they also include our habits and style. Just as values derive in a convoluted way from the influence of many assumptions, so cultural artefacts reflect the combined influence of a web of organizational values. That said, the linkages are not entirely opaque, and with careful thought we can track back, with practical accuracy, from cultural artefacts to values and thence to assumptions.

Table 11.3, when considered with Tables 11.1 and 11.2, gives an illustration of the link between values and artefacts. As with the previous tables, these examples are incomplete, selective, and compiled from many companies. The aim of Table 11.3 is merely to illustrate the sort of artefacts that are important to strategic marketing planning and how they derive from values and ultimately assumptions. Close consideration of Table 11.3 reveals the interrelatedness of assumptions, values and artefacts as different assumptions and values overlap to reinforce or contradict each other, so that the same cultural artefacts can be traced back to more than one source assumption. Exactly how cultural artefacts manifest themselves is very company-specific. The artefact of an autocratic management style may reveal itself in things like sign-off limits on expenditure, or the devaluing of external, objective data. The artefact of limited resource allocated to understanding the market may reveal itself in limited market research budgets or the structure of the board, with manufacturing and research directors but no marketing director. It is such manifestations of corporate culture that clearly hinder or support different colours of strategic marketing planning and hence form the mechanism of microcongruence.

Application point: What are the cultural artefacts of your organization?

The cultural artefacts of an organization form the pervasive and powerfully influential context of every activity the organization undertakes. They therefore impact strongly on strategic marketing planning.

- Using Table 11.3 as a guide, what cultural artefacts do you observe in your organization?
- How do those artefacts reinforce and contradict each other?
- How might these cultural artefacts impact on your strategic marketing planning?

There is a balance to reach here between realism and pragmatism. Altogether, organizational culture is a horribly complex web that is only imperfectly comprehensible to us. However, the importance

Table 11.3 Examples of cultural artefacts relevant to strategic marketing planning

Typical cultural assumptions relevant to strategic marketing planning	*Typical cultural values relevant to strategic marketing planning and arising from this cultural assumption*	*Typical cultural artefacts relevant to strategic marketing planning and arising from this cultural value*
What matters in this market is being technologically more advanced than the competition.	Leading edge research and good scientists are more valuable than cost control and sales and marketing competencies.	Relatively generous allocation of resources to technical research and development at the cost of resources allocated to understanding the customer and market.
What matters in this market is being more efficient than the competition.	Operational efficiency and cost control are more valuable than leading edge research and sales and marketing competencies.	Compromise in the design of the value proposition (e.g. reduction in product functionality or service levels) in order to optimize manufacturing or operational processes.
What matters in this market is being better at customer relationships than the competition.	Sales and marketing competencies are more valuable than leading edge research or operational efficiency and cost control.	Relatively large allocation of resources to sales and marketing function at the cost of resources allocated to product development, operations or support.
What matters in this market is the quality of our management thinking.	Providing time and resources for considered management reflection is more valuable than allocating management time to implementation.	Relatively large allocation of time and top management support for strategic marketing planning at the cost of poorly managed implementation.
What matters in this market is making things happen in the real world.	Allocating management time to implementation is more valuable than providing time and resources for considered management reflection.	Relatively large allocation of time and top management support for implementation at the cost of poorly resourced strategic marketing planning.

Our market is best described in terms of the product or services we sell.	Understanding the functionality and benefits of our products or services is more valuable than understanding our customer motivations or the needs of our channels to market.	Time and other resources allocated disproportionately to improving product or service functionality as a basis of competition but on the basis of poor understanding of customer or channel needs.
Our market is best described in terms of the channels we sell through.	Understanding the needs of our channels to market is more valuable than understanding our customer motivations or the functionality and benefits of our products or services.	Time and other resources allocated disproportionately to supporting channels as a basis of competition but on the basis of poor understanding of customer needs or product/service functionality.
Our market is best described in terms of the types of customer we sell to.	Understanding our customer motivations is more valuable than understanding the needs of our channels to market or the functionality and benefits of our products or services.	Time and other resources allocated disproportionately to meeting the needs of the customer as a basis of competition but on the basis of poor understanding of channels to market or product/service functionality.
Truth is simple, absolute and amenable to quantitative measurement.	We value quantified analyses of the market that simplify the picture rather than complicated syntheses of hard and soft data.	Emphasis on quantitative, but relatively simple, analyses of hard data, potentially failing to understand aspects of the market that would be revealed by more complex analyses of market data.

Table 11.3 *(Continued)*

Typical cultural assumptions relevant to strategic marketing planning	*Typical cultural values relevant to strategic marketing planning and arising from this cultural assumption*	*Typical cultural artefacts relevant to strategic marketing planning and arising from this cultural value*
Truth is absolute but complex and is best clarified by quantification.	We value sophisticated, quantified analyses of the market that give a sophisticated synthesis of everything we can measure rather than simple or judgemental views.	Emphasis on complex quantitative data, but neglecting 'soft' data, potentially failing to understand aspects of the market that are inaccessible to quantitative measurement.
Truth is simple but relative and not entirely accessible to measurement.	We value simplified assessments of the market, based on management judgement rather than purely quantitative analysis.	Emphasis on instinctive and intuitive judgements, prone to cognitive biases that would be challenged by more objective quantitative analyses.
Truth is relative and complex and only really accessible to judgement.	We value sophisticated assessments of the market, based on management judgement rather than purely quantitative or simplistic judgements.	Emphasis on a mixture of rational and non-rational processes that may contradict or be poorly co-ordinated.
All people are essentially good and capable of great things.	Recruitment, development and retention of good people is more valuable than close management of subordinates.	Loose, democratic management style with implications for how planning is executed and plans are implemented.
Only a few people like me are good and capable of great things.	Leadership by a well-chosen management team is more valuable than involvement and democracy.	Relatively autocratic control systems with implications for how information flows up the organization and how plans are implemented.

Most people are essentially flawed and limited in their capabilities	Close management by the leadership is more valuable than attempts to recruit, retain and develop subordinates.	Relatively autocratic management style with implications for the company's abilities to be flexible and incremental.
All of us should behave to the highest ethical standards.	Time spent assessing the ethical implications of our decisions is more valuable than that spent discussing the detail of implementation and tactics.	Strong moral, ethical steer to strategic planning decisions, perhaps at the cost of not considering the practical implications of those decisions.
We should be guided by ethics but act pragmatically.	Time spent examining the practical outcomes of our actions is more valuable than that spent assessing the ethical implications of our decisions.	Strong pragmatic steer to strategic planning decisions, perhaps at the cost of not considering the ethical implications of those decisions.
We should take responsibility for our own actions.	Initiative and pro-activity is more valuable than pragmatism and ability to react to events.	Emphasis on freedom of action with implications for disciplined implementation and the capacity to react or act incrementally.
We have limited autonomy in the face of events.	Pragmatism and ability to react to events is more valuable than initiative and pro-activity.	Emphasis on reactivity and responsiveness to events with implications for ability to act incrementally and to plan rationally.
The coherence of the team is critical to our success.	Achieving a strong consensus is more valuable than achieving the strictly optimal decision.	Emphasis on consensus rather than on optimal decision may lead to decisions driven by consensus or political power rather than rational analysis.

Table 11.3 *(Continued)*

Typical cultural assumptions relevant to strategic marketing planning	*Typical cultural values relevant to strategic marketing planning and arising from this cultural assumption*	*Typical cultural artefacts relevant to strategic marketing planning and arising from this cultural value*
Individuality lies at the root of our success.	Heterogeneity of views and allowing managed dissent is more valuable than achieving a strong consensus.	Emphasis on individual expertise at the cost of consensus, leading to implications for 'buy-in' to plans and sharing of cross-functional expertise in complex markets.
Discipline is necessary to avoid disaster.	Close management is more valuable than any benefits arising from wider involvement in decision making.	Relatively autocratic management style with implications for the company's abilities to be flexible and incremental.
Democracy, rather than autocracy, is most likely to succeed in the modern world.	The benefits arising from wider involvement in decision making are more valuable than the benefits arising from close management.	Loose, democratic management style with implications for how planning is executed and plans are implemented.
Organizations can mould human nature.	Employing leadership and control to direct the way our people work is more valuable than trying to find people who fit in with our organization.	Relatively autocratic control systems with implications for how information flows up the organization and how plans are implemented.
Organizations must work with the grain of human nature.	Finding the right people is more valuable than trying to make people change the way they work.	Loose, democratic management style with implications for how planning is executed and plans are implemented.

of achieving microcongruence is such that we have no choice but to try, and that is the subject of the rest of this chapter. The reader should be encouraged by the observation that even limited understanding and microcongruence is enough to create sustainable competitive advantage over firms that have shied away from this task.

Adapting culture to achieve microcongruence

The complex, imperfectly comprehensible mechanism of microcongruence described in the preceding sections has important implications for practising marketers – microcongruence is important to manage, but it is difficult. Good managers know that something which is both important and difficult must be managed proactively. We can't just wait until our strategic marketing planning process, carefully honed to be macrocongruent, is sabotaged by our culture; we have to anticipate the problem and mount a pre-emptive strike, as it were. Further, our new understanding of the mechanism of microcongruence tells us that we must strike at the root assumptions in the culture, not merely at the artefacts. Attempting to manage only the superficial artefacts will be useless, because the unchanged assumptions and values will make them grow back, like the heads of Hydra in ancient Greek mythology.

Emulating those great and rare companies that achieve microcongruence and thence bicongruence, therefore, involves four essential steps:

1. Being clear about what colour of strategic marketing planning process is macrocongruent to the market conditions.
2. Anticipating the cultural artefacts that will be needed to support, and those that might hinder, the chosen colour of strategic marketing planning.
3. Tracing back to the likely assumptions and values that lead to those artefacts that are to be created, destroyed or adapted.
4. Modifying those assumptions, and creating new values and artefacts that are microcongruent to the new colour of strategic marketing planning.

The first of these steps was the outcome of Chapters 9 and 10. The subsequent three are described in the following sections.

Anticipating a microcongruent culture

Creating a microcongruent organizational culture is difficult in any case, and impossible without a clear idea of what is the necessary end-point. To steal a phrase from the personal development guru Stephen Covey, we must 'begin with the end in mind'. We need to know what cultural artefacts will support or hinder our chosen colour of strategic marketing planning before we set about creating such a cultural environment for our planning.

So what culture is microcongruent to each colour of strategic marketing planning? Well, at the risk of repetition, we are not trying to create or completely re-engineer our organizational culture; we are simply trying to do the minimal amount of adjustment needed to create microcongruence. We are anxious to avoid the costs, failures and unintended consequences of wholesale cultural revolution. Our question, therefore, becomes: 'What are the minimum cultural artefacts needed to achieve microcongruence with each colour of strategic marketing planning?' We have already touched on this in Chapter 7. The research results summarized in that chapter indicate what sort of things the subject companies found to support or hinder each of the three primary approaches to strategic marketing planning: visionary command, rational planning and incrementalism. These three primary approaches correspond, of course, to the three primary colours of strategic marketing planning: blue (mostly rational), yellow (mostly visionary command) and red (mostly incremental). As might be expected, the cultural artefacts that are micro-incongruent to the other four hybrid colours are a blend of those needed by the three primary colours.

For practical application, however, we need to simplify our description of the most important cultural artefacts needed by each of the seven colours of strategic marketing planning. Only then can we think about creating microcongruence by tracing back to assumptions and values and then modifying the existing culture. Table 11.4 is just such a simplification. It captures the most important aspects of culture with respect to supporting or hindering each colour of strategic marketing planning. These can be categorized into three kinds of cultural artefact:

1. Power artefacts – the structuring of power and influence in the organization.
2. Information artefacts – those systems set up to provide the information used to support decision making.

3. Attitudinal artefacts – the mindset of those most heavily involved in making strategic decisions.

Although obviously a pragmatic simplification, Table 11.4 allows us to create a microcongruence task list. Starting with the colour of strategic marketing planning we need to use in order to be macrocongruent, Table 11.4 describes the nature of both the cultural artefacts that are desirable and, equally importantly, those that need to be avoided. The observable variance between these artefacts and the current organizational culture indicates what we need to trace back and modify. It is worth restating that this is not a comprehensive list of all possible cultural adaptations; no list ever could be. Table 11.4 is intended to give the practitioner a task list that will create enough microcongruence to create bicongruence and therefore competitive advantage. At the same time, it is intended to limit cultural change to that which is practically possible and minimizes unintended consequences.

Application point: What is your organization's microcongruence task list?

Modification of the existing culture is usually a necessary corollary to changing the colour of strategic marketing planning. The extent to which culture must be modified is usually proportional to the degree to which the strategy making process is to be changed from its existing process.

- To what extent, if any, do you envisage having to change the colour of your strategic marketing planning, and in what way?
- What supporting cultural artefacts will you need to modify to create microcongruence?
- What supporting cultural artefacts will you need to modify to avoid micro-incongruence?
- What difficulties do you anticipate in making these cultural modifications?

Tracing back to relevant assumptions and values

The preceding section enables the creation of a task list of cultural artefacts to modify in order to achieve microcongruence. We know,

Table 11.4 Artefacts of microcongruent and micro-incongruent cultures for each colour of strategic marketing planning

Colour of strategic marketing planning	*Artefacts of a supportive, microcongruent culture*	*Artefacts of hindering, micro-incongruent culture*
Blue – mostly rational planning	*Power:* Cultures microcongruent to blue strategic marketing planning are characterized by power structures which are usually explicit and well-ordered. In particular, those charged with making strategy have significant authority in their own right and are integrated into, not isolated from, the line management structure.	*Power:* Cultures micro-incongruent to blue strategic marketing planning are characterized by power structures which, while superficially explicit, are more accurately described as implicit, political and opaque.
	Information: Blue strategic marketing planning processes are supported by adequately resourced information infrastructures, designed to manage both hard and soft information about the market, such as market size, structure and needs, and the activity of competitors and channels, rather than internal information.	*Information:* Blue strategic marketing planning processes are hindered by information infrastructures designed to manage only hard internal information required for financial control and operational purposes, such as sales, profit and costs by product, rather than market information.
	Attitude: In cultures that are microcongruent to blue strategic marketing planning, management attitudes towards tools and techniques are very positive. These are seen as essential tools with real value.	*Attitude:* In cultures that are micro-incongruent to blue strategic marketing planning, management attitudes towards tools and techniques are negative and cynical. These are seen as 'unproven theory' with little or no relevance to the organization.

Yellow – mostly visionary command	*Power:* Cultures microcongruent to yellow strategic marketing planning are characterized by power structures which are well demarcated. The leadership body makes strategy and avoids meddling in implementation tasks. The implementation level accepts this authority and concentrates on operational matters.	*Power:* Cultures micro-incongruent to yellow strategic marketing planning are characterized by power structures which, while superficially explicit, are actually divided and politically fractured between functional or regional 'barons'.
	Information: Yellow strategic marketing planning processes are supported by two kinds of information infrastructure. The first supplies accurate, timely, but often high level information to the leadership body concerning the marketplace. This system is often informal. The second supplies detailed, but simplified and regular, rather than constant information to the leadership body about operational matters.	*Information:* Yellow strategic marketing planning processes are hindered by information infrastructures that isolate the leadership body from the market. This is often the combined effect of 'filtering' by lower level managers and 'overload' with unnecessary operational information at the cost of market information.
	Attitude: In cultures that are microcongruent to yellow strategic marketing planning, management attitudes reflect respect for the leadership body's authority whilst that body demonstrates trust and recognition of the competencies of the implementation group.	*Attitude:* In cultures that are micro-incongruent to yellow strategic marketing planning, management attitudes embody a 'them and us' attitude with low levels of mutual professional respect and trust.

Table 11.4 *(Continued)*

Colour of strategic marketing planning	*Artefacts of a supportive, microcongruent culture*	*Artefacts of hindering, micro-incongruent culture*
Red – mostly incremental	*Power:* Cultures microcongruent to red strategic marketing planning processes are characterized by power structures which are unusually evenly distributed. Through over-skilling, organizational slack and 'loose' management, the power and authority to act is spread relatively evenly throughout the organization. *Information:* Red strategic marketing planning systems are supported by well-resourced information infrastructures designed to provide meaningful feedback on incremental activity. These are less concerned with market data and more with isolating the effect of localized activity in particular geographies, product sectors or channels. *Attitude:* In cultures that are microcongruent to red strategic marketing planning, management attitudes are characterized by a flexible learning attitude and a tolerance to well-intentioned failure.	*Power:* Cultures micro-incongruent to red strategic marketing planning processes are characterized by structures in which power is concentrated and tightly controlled. Through human resource and management control practices, the authority to act is consolidated and confined to limited areas. *Information:* Red strategic marketing planning processes are hindered by information infrastructures that consolidate information for simplicity and ease of understanding. Such infrastructures hinder incrementalism, either by masking the effects of localized activity or by building in a time lag that renders information useless. *Attitude:* In cultures that are micro-incongruent to red strategic marketing planning, management attitudes are characterized by a resistance to experimentation and a noticeable culture of blame, often disguised as 'accountability'.

Green – mixture of rational planning and visionary command	*Power:* Cultures microcongruent to green strategic marketing planning are characterized by power structures in which strategy is made by an entity close to and often involving the leadership, but not integrated into line management. Implementation is again left to operational managers who are guided by formal plans. *Information:* Green strategic marketing planning processes are supported by two information infrastructures. The first is designed to analyse and synthesize market (rather than internal) information for the leadership body, often via a strategy group. The second supplies regular and simplified internal data about operational matters to the leadership body. *Attitude:* In cultures that are microcongruent to green strategic marketing planning, management attitudes combine a very positive attitude to tools and techniques with respect for the demarcated roles of the leadership, strategy and implementation groups.	*Power:* Cultures micro-incongruent to green strategic marketing planning are characterized by power structures in which responsibility for strategy and implementation is implicitly disputed even when explicitly agreed. If a strategy making group is present, it is isolated and unrespected. *Information:* Green strategic marketing planning processes are hindered by two types of information infrastructures. First, those that isolate the leadership and/or strategy making body from the market, by filtering or information overload. Secondly, those which manage only internal product and financial data rather than market data. *Attitude:* In cultures that are micro-incongruent to green strategic marketing planning, management attitudes combine a 'them and us' attitude towards other groups with cynicism about relevance of strategic management tools and techniques.

Table 11.4 *(Continued)*

Colour of strategic marketing planning	*Artefacts of a supportive, microcongruent culture*	*Artefacts of hindering, micro-incongruent culture*
Orange – mixture of visionary command and incremental	*Power:* Cultures microcongruent to orange strategic marketing planning are characterized by power structures which combine clear demarcation between strategy and operational roles with an unusual degree of power allocation to operational levels. *Information:* Orange strategic marketing planning processes are supported by two kinds of information infrastructure. The first supplies accurate, timely, but often high-level information concerning the marketplace to the leadership body. This system is often informal. The second supplies meaningful feedback on incremental activity. This is less concerned with market data and more with isolating the effect of localized activity in particular geographies, product sectors or channels.	*Power:* Cultures micro-incongruent to orange strategic marketing planning are characterized by power structures which combine tight control of authority and resources with implicit political power structures that often contradict explicit, espoused structures. *Information:* Orange strategic marketing planning processes are hindered by two types of information infrastructure. First, those which isolate the leadership and/or strategy making body form the market, by filtering or information overload. Secondly, those which consolidate information for simplicity and ease of understanding. Such infrastructures hinder incrementalism, either by masking the effects of localized activity, or by building in a time lag that renders information useless.

	Attitude: In cultures that are microcongruent to orange strategic marketing planning, management attitudes combine respect for the leadership/operational demarcation with a flexible learning attitude and a tolerance to well-intentioned failure.	*Attitude:* In cultures that are micro-incongruent to orange strategic marketing planning, management attitudes combine a 'them and us' attitude towards other groups with a resistance to experimentation and a noticeable culture of blame, often disguised as 'accountability'.
Violet – mixture of rational planning and incremental	*Power:* Cultures microcongruent to violet strategic marketing planning are characterized by power structures which are usually explicit but distribute authority quite low down the organization. Within the rational and explicit structure, an unusual amount of latitude is given at operational level.	*Power:* Cultures micro-incongruent to violet strategic marketing planning are characterized by power structures which combine concentrated power with political, implicit, power structures dominated by functional or geographical 'barons'.
	Information: Violet strategic marketing planning processes are supported by information infrastructures designed to do two things. First, manage both hard and soft information about the market, such as market size, structure and needs, and the activity of competitors and channels, rather than internal information. Secondly, supply meaningful feedback on incremental activity. This is less concerned with market data and more with isolating the effect of localized activity in particular geographies, product sectors or channels.	*Information:* Violet strategic marketing planning processes are hindered by information infrastructures designed to manage only hard internal information required for financial control and operational purposes, such as sales, profit and costs by product, rather than market information. They are further hindered by information infrastructures that consolidate information for simplicity and ease of understanding, thereby masking the effects of localized activity or by building in a time lag that renders information useless.

Table 11.4 *(Continued)*

Colour of strategic marketing planning	*Artefacts of a supportive, microcongruent culture*	*Artefacts of hindering, micro-incongruent culture*
	Attitude: In cultures that are microcongruent to violet strategic marketing planning, management attitudes combine a very positive attitude to tools and techniques with a flexible learning attitude and a tolerance to well-intentioned failure.	*Attitude:* In cultures that are micro-incongruent to violet strategic marketing planning, management attitudes towards tools and techniques are negative and cynical. These are seen as 'unproven theory' with little or no relevance to the organization. In addition, experimentation is discouraged by a blame culture.
White – mixture of rational planning, visionary command and incremental	*Power:* Cultures microcongruent to white strategic marketing planning are characterized by power structures which are simultaneously explicit and transparent, demarcated between strategy and operational roles and have unusual amounts of delegation of authority.	*Power:* Cultures micro-incongruent to white strategic marketing planning are characterized by power structures which are opaque and political, concentrate authority and hinder demarcation by means of functional or regional 'barons'.

Information: White strategic marketing planning processes are supported by information infrastructures designed to do three things equally well. First, manage both hard and soft information about the market, rather than internal information. Secondly, supply meaningful feedback on incremental activity. This is less concerned with market data and more with isolating the effect of localized activity. Finally, supply accurate and timely, high-level information to the leadership body concerning the marketplace.	*Information:* White strategic marketing planning processes are hindered by information infrastructures that do three things. First, those which isolate the leadership and/or strategy body from the market, by filtering or information overload. Secondly, those which consolidate information for simplicity and ease of understanding, thus hindering incrementalism. Finally, they manage only hard, internal data and fail to integrate market and internal, and hard and soft, information.
Attitude: In cultures that are microcongruent to white strategic marketing planning, management attitudes combine a positive attitude towards tools and techniques, a flexible learning attitude and a tolerance to well-intentioned failure and respect for the leadership/operational demarcation.	*Attitude:* Cultures that are micro-incongruent to white strategic marketing planning combine management attitudes towards tools and techniques that are negative and cynical, a resistance to experimentation, a blame culture and a 'them and us' attitude, with low levels of mutual professional respect and trust.

from the discussion of the mechanism of microcongruence above, that such modification requires us to understand and address the cultural assumptions and values that give rise to those artefacts. In effect, we have to trace the steps back through Schein's three-layer model and modify the assumptions so that values change. Unless we do that, when we attempt to change the artefacts we will usually fail. Even if we initially succeed, they will change back like the re-grown head of Hydra. We need to work on the foundations of our culture, not simply the artefact superstructure. However, our understanding of the mechanism of microcongruence also alerts us to the difficulty of tracing backwards through our culture. We know that our organizational culture is more like a brain than a computer, and that there are the equivalent of thousands of neurones connecting assumptions to values and then to artefacts. In such a context, our retracing can only be approximate. We can trace back to the principal assumptions that mould the artefacts in which we are interested, but not all of the secondary, tertiary, quaternary assumptions and so on. Notwithstanding that caveat, we can, informed by the research, say something about the assumptions we need to change to achieve microcongruence for each colour of strategic marketing planning.

Assumptions and values relevant to blue, mostly rational planning

As can be seen from Table 11.4, rational planning is supported by an organizational structure in which power is distributed in a relatively even and explicit manner. That is not to say that a completely democratic structure is needed, but simply that each function is in control of its actions and is not 'subservient' to others. By contrast, rational planning is hindered by autocratic structures and ones in which some functions act as service functions to others. By way of illustration, consider highly technical companies, in which marketing is sometimes a mere service function to sales or R&D. Similarly, in a strongly consumer goods culture, marketing is often seen as dominant and 'calls the shots' to product development. Even when the espoused structure is democratic, an unspoken politic can dictate a different reality. In such cases, the artefact of subservience is dictated by a clear value system that values one function and set of activities over another. This value system is based on a set of assumptions about what works best and deserves the whip hand. Remember, we are not making a value judgement about these assumptions, simply uncovering them.

Rational planning is also supported by externally oriented information infrastructures that manage both soft and hard information well. They are hindered by internally facing infrastructures that handle mostly product and financial data. Again, these artefacts derive from values about what sort of information is most useful. In cultures that are microcongruent to rational planning, market data are valued equally to financial data and *vice versa*. Beneath those values lies the assumption that understanding the market, rather than controlling internal activity, is critical to business success. There is also another assumption that is important to the success of rational planning; this is the belief that the world is imperfectly quantifiable and measurable and that, to some extent, hard and soft data must be combined for a true picture of the market. Hence rational planning microcongruent cultures eschew hard proof in some cases and look for qualitative insight. By contrast, companies that have a purely positivist set of assumptions believe that 'what gets measured gets done', devalue soft data, and have information infrastructures that are unsupportive to rational planning.

Rational planning is also supported by cultures in which the tools and techniques of strategic marketing planning are regarded positively and used systematically. By contrast, rational planning fails when managers are cynical about the tools and pay only lip service to what they pejoratively term 'theory'. These artefacts result from value assessments about tools and techniques which arise from assumptions about what works. Cultural assumptions that such tools work lead to cultures microcongruent to rational planning and *vice versa*.

Hence cultures that are microcongruent to rational planning are built on at least three sets of assumptions: all functions are approximately equal in importance, market understanding is as important as internal control, and the tools work. There are other relevant assumptions, of course, but these three seem critical.

Assumptions and values relevant to yellow, mostly visionary command processes

Visionary command processes are microcongruent to cultures built on a set of assumptions that are markedly different from those which support rational planning. They require cultural artefacts in which power is clearly demarcated and authority accepted without much quibbling. Such cultures value discipline over creative ferment and assume, to put it simply, that the boss knows best. More accurately, they believe the leadership knows best about strategy and the troops know best about implementation. By contrast, cultures in which democracy is highly valued and some degree of autonomy is assumed critical to success are micro-incongruent to visionary command processes. The challenging and internal resistance simply causes autocratic approaches to grind to a halt.

In the same way, visionary command processes require different information infrastructures from rational planning. In particular, they need to connect the leadership closely to the market and allow the leaders to have an uncluttered perspective on implementation. Such infrastructures arise when the insight and perspicacity of the leadership is valued above all else. Interestingly, these values seem rooted in the same assumptions as those that lead to visionary command microcongruent power structures. That is, the boss knows best.

Similar assumptions seem to lie at the root of attitude artefacts that support visionary command. These include respect for the skills of both leadership and implementers. This respect flows from the distinct but equal valuation of each group's competencies. This valuation in turn flows from assumptions that leaders can lead but not implement, and implementers can put things into practice better than they can strategize.

So cultures that are microcongruent to visionary command are built on one closely related set of assumptions about relative competencies. In short, we are best doing our own jobs and not trying to do someone else's. This is an interesting contrast to those that underpin cultures supportive of rational planning.

Assumptions and values relevant to red, mostly incremental processes

Incremental processes are supported by cultures in which power is spread in an unusually even manner, through cultural artefacts such as over-skilling and organizational slack. Such artefacts have their roots in value systems that prize the ability and initiative of the individual or small unit and view bureaucracy as a wasteful cost. Beneath those values lie assumptions that committed people can make the difference, even without pooling their resources, and that the market is amenable to small-scale action.

Information infrastructures that support incrementalism tend to be internally focused, but at a small scale, given quick and often informal feedback on incremental activity. This is often difficult to reconcile with large-scale management accounting systems. These microscopic information infrastructures flow from similar values to distributed power structures; that individual initiative is better than the big plan. They also share assumptions about the difference enthusiastic small-scale action can make when repeated over and over.

The attitudes that support incrementalism are all to do with willingness to experiment, fail and learn. These attitudes come from the value placed upon individualism and courage, rather than concerted teamwork or orderly discipline. Underneath such cultures lie risk-accepting assumptions that it is better to try and fail than never to try at all.

Hence cultures that are microcongruent to incrementalism are built on a set of assumptions that free-thinking individuals will usually win out over disciplined organizations, so long as they are allowed to do so.

Assumptions and values relevant to hybrid marketing-strategy making process

In the majority of situations, in which some hybrid marketing-strategy making process is necessary for macrocongruence, it becomes even harder to trace back to the necessary supporting assumptions. The microcongruent artefacts can be identified, but they arise from values that are combinations of those for the component red, yellow or blue processes. The assumptions, buried deeper still, are also hybridized, and both values and assumptions may hold internal contradictions. At this point prescription loses its power, and management judgement, guided by what we have learned so far, comes into play.

We can judge that, for instance, green strategic marketing planning requires a blend of the culture needed to support both blue and yellow. Similar arguments apply to orange and to violet. White strategic marketing planning is most difficult of all, requiring that assumptions, values and hence artefacts from all three primary colours be blended. In this latter case, the possibilities for internal contradiction in cultures increase further and the difficulty of achieving microcongruence becomes still greater. However, the core assumptions needed by each colour of strategic marketing planning are now visible, even if they overlap in some cases. These assumptions provide a basis for understanding what we will need to challenge in order to achieve microcongruence and thence bicongruence, as described in the next section.

Application point: Do your current cultural assumptions need to change?

At the root of micro-incongruence, and therefore the failure of much strategic marketing planning, lies a set of assumptions about the world that need to be challenged and modified. Before proceeding, it is worth considering what these might be for your company.

- What are the principal changes to cultural artefacts you need to make to achieve microcongruence?
- What values and assumptions underpin the necessary cultural artefacts?
- How do these compare with your current values and assumptions?
- Which of your current values and assumptions need to change in order to allow microcongruence and thence bicongruence?

Modifying the culture to be microcongruent

In essence, what we know about organizational culture makes it easy to see what we have to do to modify the culture so as to be microcongruent to the strategic marketing planning process. The cultural artefacts needed by each colour are described in Table 11.4. By comparing those to our current culture we can develop a microcongruence task list, a list of cultural artefacts we need to modify if we are to achieve microcongruence. To change those artefacts, we need to identify and then change the cultural assumptions that underpin them. The preceding section describes the assumptions and values that underlie each set of artefacts, so that we can translate, with a little thought, our task list into assumptions we need to underpin our culture with. The boxed application point above was intended to help this process of identifying assumptions to be changed.

Knowing the assumptions that must be modified is not, however, the same as modifying them. By their very nature, these assumptions are likely to be fundamental, deeply held, and to have been ingrained in the company's belief system for some time. It would be naïve to expect them to change at the say-so of one person. Indeed, the study of cultural change in organizations shows that these core assumptions are almost impermeable to 'directed' change. Even if the CEO repeatedly screams the beliefs that he or she wishes to replace the existing cultural assumptions, the culture does not change much. The densely interlinked mass of assumptions, values and artefacts is analogous to a piece of rubber, which absorbs impacts and reverts to its original form.

So, what can be done? Is culture immutable? Are we cursed to live within the constraints of our culture? No. Cultural assumptions, and hence values and artefacts, can be changed, but this must be done in a parsimonious manner (i.e. change no more than necessary) and following a number of principles that emerge from research into cultural change. Studies of those attempts at cultural change show that it is only likely to show permanent results if the following guidelines are adhered to.

1. Change the right people
2. Use external facilitation
3. Expose the underlying belief
4. Allow evidence-based challenge
5. Communicate through symbolism
6. Follow through to artefacts.

Change the right people

The assumptions that underpin organizational cultures are not usually written down and explicit. They are, in reality, judgemental opinions formed on the basis of real experience, albeit in a subconscious manner. As such, they are located in the minds of those who run the company. Whilst cultural assumptions permeate the minds of almost everyone who has been in the company for any length of time, they are particularly significant, in both prominence and effect, in the minds of those that researchers have called 'culture carriers'. By and large these are at the senior levels of the company, but, importantly, culture carriers inhabit parts of the boardroom. These include departmental and functional 'barons', and sometimes long-serving people who have become 'part of the furniture'. Sooner or later the assumptions of all culture carriers will need to be changed, although it is usually pragmatic to start at the top and centre and work out and down. The important point revealed by other companies' experience is that it is insufficient to address only those parts of the company that are accessible. The selection of who is to be involved must be on the basis of how much they carry and communicate the culture of the company. Without such targeting, efforts at cultural change are wasted.

Use external facilitation

At a practical level, cultural change is much enabled by external facilitation. It is important to distinguish facilitation from imposition, in which an external consultant tells the culture carriers what to do and believe. External facilitation, in which the external consultant enables the work of the internal group, seems to have four important advantages over self-remediation. First, cultural change usually requires an amount of time and effort not freely available to someone doing another 'day job'. Secondly, it requires a level of specialist understanding of how organizational culture works that is usually beyond someone skilled in another area. Thirdly, understanding culture is helped by a degree of detachment and perspective that is impossible for an employee. Finally, the politics inherent in any company mean that internal facilitators are hindered by perceptions and constraints that do not impact on an external facilitator. Of course, external consultants may have the disadvantage of not knowing the details of the company or the market, but that is usually compensated for by the knowledge of the internal culture carriers.

Expose the underlying belief

The buried, deep nature of cultural assumptions makes them impossible to challenge until they have been raised (or surfaced), made explicit and recognized. Most companies have, in any case, a strong bias to action and a concomitant aversion to discussing more profound beliefs, especially if it leads to conflict of opinions. Most company cultures are inclined towards reducing interpersonal conflict. Even when underlying beliefs are discussed, semantics – the precise meaning of the words used – gets in the way. As a result, any effective challenge of the underlying cultural assumptions begins with making them explicit. Simply stating what they seem to be is not sufficient. Instead, the group of cultural carriers involved must be led from the cultural artefacts (which are visible, recognized and usually undisputed) to the values, and finally to assumptions. It is not so much that the group needs to agree that these are their assumptions; more that they need to agree that these are the assumptions on which the company seems to be operating. Table 11.1 and the section accompanying it provide examples of those assumptions most relevant to strategic marketing planning, but this is far from a comprehensive list. Effective surfacing of cultural assumptions is likely to work only when done in the context of the company, and not at a generic level.

Allow evidence-based challenge

Having surfaced the assumptions that underpin the company culture, it is then necessary to challenge and modify them. The fundamental issue here is the appropriateness of the assumptions. If the culture is built on the assumption that R&D is the dominant source of competitive advantage and other functions are secondary, what matters is the appropriateness of that assumption to the current and future markets. This example is chosen deliberately, as it surfaced frequently in the research. Often, companies that held this assumption could trace it back to their history in an embryonic market niche where product performance was what made a difference. Many of those companies had grown into mature markets in which product performance was necessary but not sufficient. The old assumption was now inappropriate, and was leading to a culture that hindered rational planning. Corresponding examples were seen in markets that had been relationship based but now were not, or had been dependent on the vision of a leader but now were staffed with teams of valuable subordinates.

Whatever the assumption that seems to be the cause of micro-incongruence, it will only change by the same method that formed it in the first place – real experience. Assumptions only change when the culture carriers holding them are allowed to assess and judge new evidence in which they have some faith. Examples of such evidence might be, for instance, if the market leader has me-too products but still wins, if the accounts that make most money are transactional and not relationship based, or if the notable current success of the company is coming from initiatives and actions of subordinates, not the leadership team. As with exposing the underlying assumptions, modifying them is not a simple prescriptive process. The detail of how assumptions change is extremely context-specific, and cultural change is most effective when done in a way that uses specifically relevant examples and information.

Communicate through symbolism

If, by this stage, the group of culture carriers has, with the help of an external facilitator, been facilitated to surface their cultural assumptions and has modified them with reference to external evidence, the challenge remains to communicate the new assumptions and values that flow from them. In short, those outside the culture carrying group have to be given the modified culture in a way that is understandable and acceptable. In addition, this must be done in a way that is economical of resources as well as effective.

Cultural assumptions and values are rarely communicated explicitly; nor are they communicated via the obvious channels of verbal and written communication. Communicating culture is a striking example of the maxim that action speaks louder than words. In particular, actions that are out of the ordinary and are highly symbolic are crucial in communicating new assumptions and values. For instance, cultural values microcongruent to rational planning may be communicated by public praise of some piece of strategic analysis. Incrementalism may be supported by deliberate and trumpeted changes in budget allocations and control mechanisms. Visionary command may be supported by the tactful but unmistakable reining in of local barons.

The point about communication of culture is similar to that about changing cultural assumptions. Assumptions can only be modified by the same process that forms them, reference to observable facts. Similarly, cultural modification is best communicated in the same way that the existing culture transmits itself, through symbolic actions rather than words.

Follow through to artefacts

Given the explicit and widespread communication of modified cultural values through deliberate symbolism, the ground is now prepared for the creation of cultural artefacts that are needed to support the new colour of strategic marketing planning. The artefact superstructure of the culture contains innumerable items of structure, systems and processes, as well as implicit rules and patterns of behaviour. As we have already discussed, it is both difficult and counterproductive to change the whole culture. A relatively limited set of artefacts has the most impact on strategic marketing planning, as described earlier in this chapter and in Table 11.3. The challenge at this stage is to select those artefacts that are worth changing and do it in an effective and efficient manner.

As with modifying and communicating cultural assumptions, good practice in modifying cultural artefacts seems to advocate going with the grain of the existing culture. That is not to suggest leaving things unchanged, but to recommend using as much of the existing cultural structure as is possible whilst still achieving microcongruence. If, as is usually the case, there already exist cultural artefacts that perform similar functions to those that are needed by the modified culture, then adapt rather than replace them. For example, modifying the agenda of board meetings is more effective than a complete rewrite. Re-tasking existing roles, committees or functions works better than scrapping and replacing them. Doing new things under old labels is more successful than giving things names that suggest something more original than it is. The compass for changing the cultural artefacts is what is needed to achieve microcongruence, not the need to make things visible. There appear to be two underlying reasons why this 'culture change by stealth' approach works in practice. First, it is less likely to provoke unintended change. Renaming a function seems to make it prone to empire building and meddling, for instance. Secondly, it is less likely to raise expectations that feed cynicism. Making things seems more new than they are gives rise to calls of 'the more things change, the more things stay the same' and the negativity that follows.

Hence changing the culture is at once difficult and possible, intangible but manageable. The points in this section distil the experience of other companies who have succeeded or failed in achieving microcongruence. Those experiences provide guidance and insight for companies attempting to emulate them, but should always be taken as guides and never as rules.

Application point: How will you change your culture to achieve microcongruence?

Changing an organizational culture to achieve microcongruence is often necessary, always difficult, and only partly amenable to systematic process. This chapter has provided guidance to cultural change whilst reserving the position that it must be done in a context-sensitive manner. Before proceeding it is useful to consider the following:

- Who are the culture carriers in your company, and which ones are the most important?
- What might you look for in an external facilitator?
- What cultural assumptions do you think might need to be modified?
- How might you surface them?
- What verifiable facts might you draw on to modify the cultural assumptions?
- What changes to cultural values do these modified cultural assumptions imply?
- What symbols might you use to communicate the newly modified cultural assumptions and values?

- What are the most important artefacts to change?
- How might you use the grain of the existing culture to make that easier?

Power points

- Microcongruence is the result of having a culture that is supportive of the colour of strategic marketing planning you have chosen to use.
- Organizational culture is difficult to change and this should only be attempted in a careful and parsimonious manner.
- The mechanism of how organizational culture interacts with strategic marketing planning involves cultural assumptions, values and artefacts.
- Cultural change involves tracking back from artefacts through values to assumptions, and modifying those assumptions so as to achieve microcongruence.
- Cultural change is achieved through culture carriers, and is helped by external facilitation and by working with the grain of the existing culture.

Reflection points for marketing practitioners

- How microcongruent do you think your newly chosen strategic marketing planning process is to your existing organizational culture?
- What artefacts of your organizational culture, if any, do you think need to be modified in order to achieve microcongruence?
- What cultural assumptions and values do you think need to be challenged and modified?
- Who are the culture carriers in your company?
- How might you use your existing culture to make cultural change easier?

Chapter 12

Making marketing happen

> Take time to deliberate, but when the time for action has arrived, stop thinking and go in.
>
> (Napoleon Bonaparte)

Introduction

This book has tried to avoid quick answers. This choice stems from two truths that are self-evident. First, the world is full of 'airport books' that are long on enthusiastic ideas but short on thoughtful analysis. This book seeks to counter that imbalance. Secondly, we face a difficult problem. We are trying to align one complex entity (our company) to another (the market) in the context of imperfect knowledge, changing conditions and intelligent, well-resourced competitors. The naïvety of tackling such a problem in a simplistic way seems obvious. This work that underpins this book has, therefore, attempted to understand and explain, rather than abridge and preach.

That said, there is a time for action, as captured by Napoleon in the quotation above. This final chapter aims to arm the reflective practitioner with some of the lessons learned from the companies that took part in this research or in the later application of it. The previous eleven chapters arose from painstaking, methodical analyses of questionnaires and interview transcripts; this chapter has its roots in the periods when interviewees asked for the tape recorder to be turned off, or as they talked over a drink afterwards. It begins with a brief résumé of what we have learned so far. Again, readers with good memories or who have read the book in one sitting may choose to skip the next section. The more human reader, squeezing in each few pages when the chance arises, may find it a useful reminder.

The answer is bicongruence

In Part 1, we considered the origins, nature and effectiveness of strategic marketing planning. The marketing concept arose in the 1950s, when thinkers like Levitt realized that companies that made what the customer wanted were more successful than those that simply sold what the company made. In the 1960s, this concept conflated with strategic planning to create a model of strategic marketing planning that is, despite the hype, much the same today. Many august researchers have sought to prove the linkage between strategic marketing planning and business success. The first lesson to emerge from that research was not to ask naïve questions. No business process is a panacea, and both success and the causes of it are too complex for simple correlations. However, the second lesson to emerge from effectiveness research was that, yes, strategic marketing planning does work, albeit as a contribution to and not the sole cause of success. Studies of strategic marketing planning also revealed a more disturbing truth: most companies cannot make it work. The problem lies not in the theory but in the practice. Both market conditions and organizational culture make it so difficult to execute strategic marketing planning that it is more honoured in the breach than the observance. In the sense that it is the practical application of the sciences of economics, sociology and psychology, strategic marketing planning is a technology. Sadly it is a failed technology, in that its proven benefits are left unrealized because of the difficulty of its use in practice. That disheartening deduction was the conclusion of Part 1.

Part 2 considered what we might learn from those few companies that do make strong marketing strategies. The first lesson was that strong marketing strategy can be distinguished from weak, despite the obscuring effects of context. Simply put, there is a set of properties that a strong marketing strategy should have. The more of them it has the stronger it is, and *vice versa*. The second lesson from exemplars was that rational planning is a poor description of real practice. In practice, great companies hybridize different approaches to making marketing strategy into their own, unique colour of strategic marketing planning. The effectiveness of these colours, in terms of how good a strategy they make, is a matter of fit. Strong marketing strategies arise not from any particular colour of strategic marketing planning, but from whichever is bicongruent to its context. Effective strategy process must be both macrocongruent to the market and microcongruent to the culture. Either one alone will not do. The final chapter in Part 2 considered how great companies achieve bicongruence. We learned that it is an unconscious competence that can be mimicked by a deliberate process.

Part 3 has considered that deliberate process in detail. The process begins with gaining a realistic and objective assessment of just how complex and turbulent the market really is. That enables a broadly guided choice as to which colour of strategic marketing planning is macrocongruent to that market. In turn, that choice guides the understanding of the necessary organizational culture. That understanding allows parsimonious modification of the current culture. This parsimony makes difficult cultural change practically achievable and yet sufficient to create microcongruence and hence bicongruence.

The research-based findings and recommendations made above take us to the position of having a strategic marketing planning process that is bicongruent to the organization's context. All that remains is to execute the process, test the resultant strategy and, if it is strong, implement it. The practical lessons in how to do that, observed at the front line of marketing practice, are described in the following sections.

Implementation wisdom: How practitioners execute the different colours of strategic marketing planning

The descriptions of the different colours of strategic marketing planning given in Table 10.1 give the explicit picture of how the different colours work, but they do not tell the whole story. To ease the implementation of any of the colours, it helps to understand the implicit lessons learned by managers who have tried, successfully and otherwise, to implement each colour. As with any process carried out by humans, there is a difference between the spoken and the enacted that appears small but leads to big differences in outcome. To ease our understanding of those hard-earned lessons, it is useful to consider the lessons in terms of the three major divisions of strategizing: understanding the market, choosing the strategy and deciding the actions.

Feeling not fumbling – red, mostly incremental planners experiment and learn to avoid confusion

Incrementalism, a combination of 'making it up as you go along' and political negotiation, sounds quite amateurish but can be very effective in the right circumstances. It is macrocongruent, however, to only those situations in which the market is both stable and simple. In practice, this tends to be smallish, niche sort of companies, often at early stages of their development. There is a sort of circular good fortune about this limited application of incrementalism. First, such companies are often not very capable of anything but incrementalism, since they usually lack the skills of rational planning and the gift of a visionary leader. Secondly, incrementalism does not work well in any context other than a niche, due to its incapacity to cope with much complexity or turbulence. In short, this is the only situation in which incrementalism works, and incrementalism is all they can do.

Red planners' manner of understanding the market is often hard to discern, as all three stages of strategizing conflate. However, two habits of successful reds did emerge from our work. The first was their ability to 'meta-analyse' existing data. In other words, they were good at making sense of the causes and effects of current success and failure without the need to experiment. The results of such meta-analysis (an often subconscious skill) meant that the many possible market experimentations could be honed down to a few likely successes, simply by a good understanding of current results. This ability to make economical use of 'free' experimental data was enabled by reds' willingness and ability to accept information that was 'good enough' and not to eschew information that was imperfectly supported.

The experiences of reds in choosing from strategic options are also informative. When done well, it is hard to separate from understanding the market or deciding actions. Reds start small experiments in the market and scale them up gradually, if successful. Equally, they retreat from failing or inconclusive experiments both easily and inexpensively. Compare this with reds that are less effective at strategic choice. They are characterized by failure to recognize what is working and what isn't. As a result, retreat is left too late and is expensive, and both these things prevent sufficient funding of successful experiments in the market. The underlying problem is not having the right sort of information. Traditional management information systems are built around the needs of finance and operations; as such, they are often too slow and too coarse-grained to meet the needs of incremental planners.

As with understanding the market and choosing strategies, deciding actions is hard to distinguish as a separate activity by incremental planners. Instead, all three activities tend to merge. Some noticeable features of action planning are cited, however, by successful reds. The first is the way they prioritize from a large list of possible actions, carefully trading off costs and benefits. When it works well, politics helps this trade-off analysis by providing a more rounded picture of the pros and cons than would, say, analysis or a single person's intuition. The second is the way that synergies between actions are noted, as when an existing product in one market is slightly (and cheaply) modified to be tried in another. The third noticeable habit is the tendency of reds to defer major costs or irreversible choices for as long as possible. All three of these tricks of the trade contribute to the way reds make incrementalism work at the deciding actions stage. In comparison, ineffective reds make their choices of decision on the basis of unclear strategic choices. The result is actions that at best fail to synergize, and at worst conflict directly. As one practitioner noted, incrementalism in these cases is spelled 'anarchy'.

Although red is arguably the hardest of the colours of strategic marketing planning to describe clearly, effective incrementalism seems to be best summed up in the word 'deliberate'. Although reds may appear to have no process, there lies beneath that façade a carefully thought-out approach to 'making it up as we go along'.

Demarcation rather than diktat – yellow, mostly visionary command planners split tasks respectfully to reduce meddling and conflict

Visionary command processes work best in markets that are relatively simple but turbulent. Two contrasting examples support this point. The visionary founder leader is especially important in the tightly focused but large companies that dominate some sectors of the ICT (information and communications technology) market. For instance, those great rivals Intel and AMD fit this description well. Similarly, the failure of just such visionary commanders to cope when the market gets more complex is equally well-known. Often this failure is at its worst when the market becomes turbulent not through a single obvious event but through gradual change. In those cases, their leaders are like frogs in a slowly heated saucepan. Failing to register gradual change, they boil alive.

The anecdotes surrounding successful visionary command processes indicate that, when yellows succeed in understanding the market, it is because they demonstrate two quite unusual features. First, the leader or leadership group is closely connected to the market. Leaders are the opposite of ivory tower managers, and are linked to the market by a web of formal and informal contacts. More than that, the leaders who drive strategy are connected to the right parts of the market, the leading-edge parts that are demonstrating the first signs of what tomorrow's market will be. Secondly, the leaders show an unusually strong ability to synthesize, often without the visible aid of any analysis. They just seem to be able to see the wood for the trees. The contrast with unsuccessful yellows is telling. In these cases, the leaders have either isolated themselves from the market (a habit usually associated with the trappings of self-importance) or they are 'plugged into' the wrong part of the market. This latter fault seems to arise from emotional inertia, in which the leader retains an attachment to some sector, product or geography in which the company's roots lie. That part of the market then has a disproportionate input into the leader's market understanding and, if it is a lagging or unrepresentative sector, leads to poor market understanding. By contrast to synthesis-capable leaders, ineffective yellows sometimes show signs of being rooted in technical expertise. When some aspect of operations or technology lies within the leaders' 'comfort zone' it can prevent them from taking a more broadly informed perspective. Leaders that are either not plugged into the right market or are looking through a strongly filtering lens seem prone to misunderstand the market.

The way yellows successfully chose from various strategy options was characterized by decisiveness. Enabled by personal confidence, leaders or leadership groups made a decision and stuck to it. They then communicated it clearly in word and deed. When yellows failed, it seemed to have its roots in personal insecurity, leading to 'flip-flopping' between strategic options. The confusion this created in subordinates was amplified by the 'Chinese whispers' inherent in any organization.

Deciding which actions should flow from the chosen strategy depended greatly on how well market understanding and strategy choice worked, because yellow companies usually have little capacity or capability to strategizc outside of the leadership group. When it worked well, actions were decided by those that would implement them – albeit within a clear framework set by the leaders. Further, the strategic framework and the tactical actions were connected by reporting systems that were simultaneously loose (concerned with key performance indicators rather than detail) and tight (frequent, timely and given high regard).

Although yellow may sound a simplistically autocratic approach to strategic marketing planning, the key word is not autocracy but demarcation. As much as strategy is powerfully led, such an approach only works when both strategists and implementers respect each other and resist the temptation to do each other's jobs.

Analysis not paralysis – blue, mostly rational planners uses tools and teamwork to ensure action

Rational planners, blues, are macrocongruent to complex but stable markets. Typically, but not definitively, these markets are in the late-growth or mature phases of the product form life cycle. This helps to explain why rationally taught MBAs sometimes struggle in start-ups, and why sudden increases in turbulence (for instance, when deregulation occurs) catch out previously successful blues.

When blues are good at understanding their market, they report two cornerstones to their success. The first is a genuinely high standard of effectiveness at using the tools and techniques of strategic marketing planning. This seems to require not just textbook knowledge of things like segmentation and SLEPT analysis, but also the sort of proficiency that comes from repeated practice. As a result, such skill is rare. Much more common is the superficial use of the tools. Paying lip service to the jargon and making half-hearted attempts at using the tools is a charade of rational planning frequently cited by managers who fail to grasp the fundamentals of their market. The second skill is real teamwork in which individual and functional expertise is recognized and respected. In those cases, the working patterns replace committee working with frequent updating. The key difference is that the latter allows little input into 'expert' tasks by non-experts. For instance, marketing tell finance what they are doing but do not seek much approval, and the same goes for finance decisions that marketing is apprised of. Importantly, it is this habit that reduces the risk of analysis paralysis that is the nemesis of blue strategic marketing planning. An illustrative contrast is provided by the research respondent who gently mocked his company's approach to teamwork.

> It's teamwork like an under-sevens' football team. Twenty people within two yards of the ball and no-one in their own position.

Blues' choice of strategic options needs to cope with the confusion of choices that complex markets usually imply. When done well, strategic choice involves a subtlety of resource allocation at a level higher than 'let's do this but let's not do that'. Good rational planners describe a range of resource allocation choices that is more sophisticated than yes/no, but better defined than trying everything but the obviously silly. In short, blues tend to say 'let's do lots of that, a little of that, some of that and none of that'. Often this range of strategic choices flows from some kind of portfolio analysis technique and manages the full range of strategy options as an integrated whole. Concomitant with that, effective blues are characterized by the way they make clear the implications for action that flow from the strategic choices. By contrast, ineffective blues try to prioritize everything, with the result that subsequent actions are poorly directed. Such a poor result can arise even when the tools are used well, if they are based upon poor market understanding. More commonly, however, poor blue planning results in strategy choice being made backwards, starting with the current tactical plans and retro-justifying them. This is, of course, a travesty of strategic marketing planning.

Effective blue companies are perhaps most noticeable not at the market understanding and strategy choice stages, but when they start to decide on actions. The clarity gained when complex markets are subjected to good rational planning makes much tactical decision-making a 'no-brainer', to quote one marketing manager, who went on to say:

> I used to spend most of my time struggling with tactical little decisions about where to advertise and what to price at. The (rationally planned) strategy now obviates most of that. We have fewer choices to make and those we have are easier.

In addition to this tactical simplification, blue planners anecdotally reported on the way their process illuminated 'gaps in our thinking', implying that the simplicity of yellows and the incrementalism of reds both led to missing important links in the action chain that were more often than not revealed by rational planning. In the same way that the deciding action phase highlighted the benefits of good blue planning, the faults of weak blue planning were more visible at implementation, too. Respondents cited 'a triumph of process over task' as planning became the end of management activity rather than the means. Given the pressures to act, this often led weak blues to have two parallel plans: the paper one in the desk and the real one enacted in the market.

The key word that captures the essence of what good blues do is 'reality'; reality in the use of tools and in the use of the term 'teamwork'. It seems that rational planning is especially susceptible to being pretended to, with results that are not only weak but also undeservedly endorsed by the stamp of an ersatz planning process.

Combining not competing – orange planners fuse visionary command and incrementalism to gain synergy rather than inconsistency

Orange strategic marketing planning is macrocongruent to relatively simple markets that are noticeably, but not extremely, turbulent. They do so by creating strategies in much the same way as red, incremental planners, but within the sort of strategy framework typical of yellow, visionary command planners. An orange approach to making marketing strategy therefore requires an unusual combination of closely involved leaders who are able to allow their subordinates to experiment. Just such an approach is most often needed when markets are in transition from simple and stable niches to still simple but turbulent markets, a phenomenon often seen in technologically advanced niches or in regulated service sectors.

When orange planners understand the market well, their comprehension usually has its roots in the visionary command process. As with yellow planners, effective orange leaders are not too isolated from the market and have some ability to synthesize and see the wood for the trees. Orange companies do less experimenting to understand the market than red companies, as they only experiment within their leaders' vision of the company. Similarly, they depend less on the leaders' intuitive grasp of the market and rather more on meta-analysis and directed trial and error to understand the market. When orange planners fail, it is from a combination of red and yellow failures. Leaders either fail to connect with the market, or trial and error is hindered by systems, or both. The same idiosyncrasies of poor information systems and a CEO's obsession with the market he or she grew up in are reported by both yellow and orange planners who fail to understand the market.

Unsurprisingly, choosing the strategy by orange strategic marketing planning is a blend of what yellow and red planners do, again with vision prescribing the scope of step-wise, deliberate experimentation. When it works well, it combines iterative, low-risk emergence of strategies with the clarity of direction. Practitioners report that:

> We know, broadly, where we are heading, but we tend to get there one step at a time, not in big leaps.

When it fails, it looks like a muddled anarchy of local tactics happening with little or no reference to any strategic vision. Practitioners reported that:

> Strategy is really just a word we use for whatever we're doing at the moment. There might be a grand vision but, if there is, we don't get to hear about it.

The effectiveness of orange planning in deciding the actions is, of course, dependent on the clarity of strategy developed. Practitioners who developed strong strategies reported starting with very limited actions and developing, as success was rewarded with more resources. This seemed to happen faster than in red planning, as the scope of experimentation was narrower, focused by a clearly directed strategic vision. In this sense, orange strategic marketing planning was faster and less wasteful of effort than red, but not as fast or efficient as yellow. However, the better information provided by the trial and error means that orange planning was less prone to catastrophic error than yellow strategy making. One interviewee used a quotation from Louis Pasteur, 'Chance favours only the prepared mind', to illustrate how his company's guided experimentation worked, thus eloquently describing how a well-communicated but incompletely formed strategic vision helped his action plan to emerge from observations of what worked and what did not.

In short, then, effective orange planning seems to pull off the difficult trick of combining clarity of strategic vision with the freedom to experiment within limited parameters. The key phrase seems to be guided incrementalism. Those companies that failed to accomplish this fell into a muddled anarchy from which neither strategy nor tactics emerged with any robustness.

Planning for today – violet planners use rational planning to structure incrementalism and reduce errors

Violet strategic marketing planning is macrocongruent to those markets that are stable but are at intermediate levels of complexity. A great many companies fit into this category, typically when they have grown out of their original niche to operate in several segments against several competitors. Making strategy by this hybrid process involves using incrementalism guided by planning in the same way that orange processes use incrementalism guided by vision. As such, it requires the ability to add some rational planning to the process in order to put limits on experimentation, making it more efficient than red processes but less able to handle complexity than blue processes.

Violet strategic marketing planning begins to understand the market by using a limited amount of rational planning tools and techniques. The limitations are usually more imposed than chosen, in that the companies observed to be 'violets' were limited in their planning skills and resources, especially information. Hence, good market understanding emerges from professional but semi-quantified use of the tools and techniques. The tools are fed with information that comes from the sort of meta-analysis of current activity typical of red companies. Trial and error in the market, such as pricing trials, are limited and directed by knowledge that comes out of the abbreviated form of rational planning.

As one interviewee explained:

> We don't have the sort of data that we need to do it by the book, but we know enough from the market to get close enough that it does not make a strategic difference.

This, living with information imperfection, seems to be a trait necessary for good violet planning and, to a lesser extent, for all forms of rational planning. By way of contrast, those companies that failed to understand the market were characterized by an obsession with robust quantitative data. At best, those companies gave up trying to use the tools before they really started, citing lack of information as a reason. At worst, they twisted the planning process to use what information they had, usually internal rather than market data, to waste time doing analyses which felt good but added little to marketing understanding.

With violets, as with reds, strategy is not so much chosen as emergent, as different initiatives gradually gain success and others fall back. With red planning, this is an expensive and relatively slow process. It becomes more expensive and slow as the market becomes more complex and there are more options with which to experiment. Violet processes resolve this by using rational planning to simplify the options and prioritize those that might be attempted. Interviewees explained that even limited planning was useful in clarifying what the 'big unknowns' were. These could then be answered by gathering new data, meta-analysis of existing data or experiment. The result was a choice of strategy, in the face of some complexity, in a way that did not require more trial and error or formal planning than the company was capable of. When it failed to choose strategies well, there seemed to be the worst of both worlds. Both rational planning and incrementalism consumed time and resources. Both were inefficient, involving planning charades on the one hand and unthinking action on the other. Worse still, these two inefficient processes seemed to work in glorious isolation. Typically, marketing did the 'planning' and sales did the 'action plans'. Neither resulted in a clear strategic choice, and resolving the problem was made more difficult once it involved interdepartmental politics.

The application of violet strategic marketing planning to decide what actions to take showed an interesting combination of the equivalent strengths and weaknesses of red and blue planning. When it worked well, it produced complete and coherent action plans. These emerged as developments of incremental changes and limited experiments. They were guided by an abbreviated, loose, but professional use of the tools, which helped to spot any gaps and incoherence in the action plans. A happy coincidence developed in which the actions that seemed to be the obvious implication of the rational planning were similar or identical to those that emerged from the trial and error process. When violets failed, neither charades of rational planning nor ill-considered knee-jerk reactions to the market were able to suggest a clear priority of action.

The shorthand for effective violets was provided by an interviewee who said:

> We plan only as far as we think we can see and do only as much as we dare.

This usefully captures the spirit of violet strategic marketing planning and the way it results from the limitations and capabilities of each of its components.

Tolerating ambiguity – white planners balance incrementalism and rational planning within a visionary command framework to cope with transition markets

Although there is no set pattern in which companies develop, our research usually observed increasing complexity over time, and often increasing turbulence. In some, relatively rare cases, both turbulence and complexity increased at the same time. For example, technically based markets that were simultaneously globalizing showed this pattern. Whilst this eventually may lead to a market that is both complex and turbulent (as dealt with in the next section), we more frequently observed companies attempting macrocongruence with an intermediate stage of market development. In these cases, the market was somewhat complex and turbulent but the objective tests (see Chapter 9) suggested that it was not at the extremes of either. In this intermediate case, the macrocongruent colour of strategic marketing planning was white, a judicious mix of rational planning, incrementalism and visionary command processes. White had another advantage, too, in that it seemed to be easier for companies used to some other colour of planning to gain microcongruence with white processes.

Whites understand the market first by an element of visionary command, the leadership group intuiting the key issues in the market in an accurate but incomplete way. This is augmented by professional but abbreviated rational planning, and both are informed by the incrementalists' meta-analysis of current success and failure. To do so seems to require unusual ability to synthesize different kinds of knowledge and to avoid being too autocratic, analytical or experimental. This balancing act is a cultural trick that is hard to learn, which explains the comments of those companies in moderately complex and turbulent markets. They cited lack of ability to cope with turbulence or complexity, or both. This seems to indicate that the cultural artefacts that support white planning are in some way internally contradictory and hard to reconcile. One has only to consider the assumptions and values that fit with each colour (see Tables 11.1 and 11.2) to see that they could easily contradict each other.

The same balancing act is needed for whites in deciding strategy. At this stage they must balance the rigour of planning with the sometimes *ad hoc* nature of incrementalism, all within the guidance of a strategic vision. As before, the skill seems to lie in not getting too obsessive about any of the three primary approaches, and using what works from each. Hence, in effective whites, a strong but imprecise vision guides some professional but abbreviated rational planning and is informed by incremental meta-analysis to make a good strategy choice.

To use the words of one interviewee:

> We can't be too purist about anything, because we might be wrong.

When bad strategy choices are made by whites, or if the choice is unclear, this seems to be the result of balance being displaced by purist instincts. In other words, one of vision, planning or incrementalism has driven out the other two. Failing whites can show any or all of the faults of red, blue or yellow planners when it comes to strategy choice.

In the action-deciding stage, the failure or success of whites is sometimes hard to differentiate. Successful whites have action plans that are complete but not inflexible, and are coherent but not more complex than the market needs. By contrast, failing whites create a grey mush of actions that is so opaque as to be hard to test for completeness or coherence. It is only by assessing the overall strategy that it can be discerned whether or not whites have succeeded.

So the key to white planning is balance, using just enough of the three primary approaches to get their benefits, without overdoing it. When challenged about the apparent contradictions in his statements ('we tell them to plan but sometimes overrule it'), one successful white planner summed it up as:

> A bit of a split personality seems to help.

Enlightened dictatorships – green planners use rational planning to augment visionary command and *vice versa*

Markets that are both very complex and very turbulent are relatively rare. The only examples seen in the research were those sectors in which market maturity (and the associated complexity of segments, channels, etc.) was quite suddenly infused with turbulence due to regulatory or technical change. This was seen in some sectors of financial services, pharmaceutical and defence markets. When these extremes of market conditions apply, incrementalism is ineffective, except as a small contributor; it is simply too expensive to experiment with trial and error. Planning alone cannot cope with the market turbulence, and visionary command alone is overwhelmed by market complexity. Only a green blend of rational planning and visionary command can be macrocongruent.

Market understanding in such situations is very difficult. Those companies that achieve it seem to do so by using the tools and techniques of strategic planning to enhance the leaders' natural closeness to the market. The whole distinction between visioning and planning seems to disappear as strategic planning jargon and a deep understanding of strategic techniques permeates the leadership group. Effective white companies have very skilled planners feeding into boards who really value analysis. The contrast to this is not the eschewing of tools by the board, but rather pretence at their use. The same jargon and labels are used, but beneath the surface it is more yellow than green. The outcome is a gross oversimplification of the market situation, which undermines the rest of the strategy making process.

Strategy choice in complex, turbulent markets achieves the clever combination of nuanced decisiveness. Choices about customers and propositions are clear, but allow for subtle patterns of resource allocation that make provision for both today's and tomorrow's market. When green strategic marketing planning fails, it is either from too much decision-making (closing opportunities too soon) or too little (failing to focus efforts). It is hard to differentiate strong and weak strategy choices under these circumstances, making it especially important to test the end result via strategy diagnostics.

Deciding actions by green strategic marketing planning is done differently depending on the scale of the action. Very large investments, when needed, are selected by planning-informed leadership, while smaller investments and tactics arise from rational planning within the envisioned strategy. These may sound like semantic distinctions, but it is an illuminating distinction, illustrated by a quotation from one senior manager:

> It's probably true to say that smaller decisions are more planned than big ones. I realize that sounds silly, but the smaller choices are usually short term and we can plan them, while the big ones are usually long term and,

in an uncertain future, harder to plan. So we use planning where we can, and substitute intuitive assumptions where we have to.

Thus the key to dealing with complex turbulent markets is to be really good at both rational planning and visionary command. Even then, we must recognize the subtlety of shading from yellow-green for long-term strategic issues to blue-green for shorter-term ones, as dictated by the uncertainty of our knowledge.

Application point: What are the challenges of your current and intended strategic marketing planning process?

The lessons of practitioners described in the preceding section concern all of the seven stereotypical colours of strategic marketing planning. It follows that they will have a bearing on both your current practice and the process you intend to develop to achieve bicongruence. Before proceeding it is worth considering the following:

- Where, in the spectrum of strategic marketing planning behaviour, does your company currently sit?
- Are any of the positive or negative experiences of other practitioners, described above, reflected in your own experience?
- Where, in the spectrum of strategic marketing planning behaviour, does your company's intended, bicongruent process sit?
- Are any of the positive or negative experiences of other practitioners, described above, relevant to your intentions?

Pre-flight checks: How practitioners test their strategy before they execute it

As described in Chapter 8, translating the often unconscious competence of companies with strong strategies into a deliberate process leads us to a five-step process. The last of these five steps is to test the marketing strategy after it has been made by a bicongruent colour of strategic marketing planning. A comprehensive and rigorous set of tests for marketing strategy has been described in Chapter 5. These strategy diagnostics emerge from the results of forty-plus years of previous research. As such they are well founded but, being buried in academic research, have not been readily available to practitioners until the publication of this book. Hence the great companies studied in this research had to test their strategy without reference to strategy diagnostics, at least in their explicit, clarified form.

The best marketing practitioners did, of course, test their strategy, both as they made it and, after they made it, before and during execution. In effect, they used strategy diagnostics in an informal and continuous sense, of which even they were sometimes unaware until their behaviour was questioned and challenged by an inquisitive management researcher. Although the tests they applied did correlate closely to the strategy diagnostics described in Chapter 5, the marketers differed in the way they phrased the questions they asked of their own strategy and the order in which they applied the tests.

Although the different marketers interviewed did not all adopt exactly the same approach, it is possible to deduce a pattern and structure in what they did. As a guide to other practitioners trying to emulate them, this structure is perhaps best described as consisting of three fundamental questions about the marketing strategy under challenge, each composed of a small number of component questions. Presented in order of importance, as perceived by the practitioners, these questions and their components are given below.

Would this strategy create customer preference for any company?

Exemplar practitioners in our study first applied an acid test for their marketing strategy that tested the strength of the strategy, independent of which company was executing it. Most often, this was phrased something along the lines of: 'But will it create customer preference?' In other words, would the target customers want this offer more than that of the competitors? This simple but powerful question was used by senior marketers to cut through the detail of strategy presentations, the waffle about budgets and tactics, to create an honest critique of the marketing strategy. When probed about what answers to this fundamental question were indicative of future success, practitioners answered in terms that correlated closely to the first two strategy diagnostics of target definition and proposition flexibility.

How real and lifelike does this customer sound?

Respondents were positive about strategies that described target segments driven strongly by complex sets of higher needs, such as emotions, relationships and seeking overall value from an augmented proposition. They were equally negative about target market descriptions that gave little insight into customer motivations, such as when targets were described by industry categories, job roles or demographic labels. As one marketing director said:

> I feel more comfortable if we know the target is innovative, non-price sensitive, works in a technically based company, is identifiable by his other buying behaviour and speaks to us often than if all we have is his job title and SIC number.

How well does our offer fit this target?

Respondents were positive about strategies that described propositions in terms of benefits that were very specific to the target. They were equally negative about propositions described in terms of product features that were meant to be attractive to everyone. One interviewee articulated her instinct as:

> I go cold at technical specs and target product profiles. I'm looking for something in our offer which makes [the customer's] choice obvious and highly driven, such as, when our terms take away the risk that he's most frightened of.

These two tests describe the initial challenge of marketing strategy strength made by great marketers. If a strategy passes these, it is a strong strategy, but it may yet not be the best for a particular company.

The second criterion of strategy strength was captured in the second question asked by exemplary marketers.

Would this strategy work for us?

Having satisfied themselves that their marketing strategy was a strong one for someone to execute, our exemplar practitioners went on to assess the appropriateness of the strategy to their company. On close examination, these managers went on to describe components of appropriateness that were very similar to the three strategy diagnostics relating to SWOT alignment, strategy uniqueness and future anticipation.

Does this marketing strategy play to our strengths?

Interviewees were positive about strategies that considered tangible or intangible relative differences between the company and the competition. They were negative about strategies that considered only absolute resources, rather than relative ones, or which ignored either strengths or weaknesses. One telling quotation was illustrative:

> I look for the reason that we are better placed to do this than anyone else, because it means that if and when we are copied we will still win.

Will this strategy work by the time it gets to market?

The exemplars interviewed rated highly those strategies that allowed for the implications of macroenvironmental trends in the market and discounted those that did not. A board member dealing with a turbulent market said:

> For all the turmoil in the market, we are confident about a few key trends, like the convergence of digital technologies and the fragmentation of markets. If a marketing strategy doesn't build in those trends, it starts to fail before it is implemented.

What's different about this marketing strategy?

Good companies, especially market followers, sought to avoid head-on conflict with established competitors. They therefore demanded some uniqueness in either the targeting or the proposition or preferably both. One interviewee paraphrased Michael Porter to say:

> We get parity by copying, but advantage only by doing things differently. My killer question at strategy presentations is always: 'What are we doing differently from the other guys?' If the answer is only some detail of the product features, I start to worry; but if the answer is some fundamental difference in how we do things, then I feel confident.

The preceding three questions therefore challenge a strong strategy to be not only strong but appropriate to the company. If a marketing strategy gets through those tests, then it is known that the strategy can work. The challenge now is to maximize the chances that it will work by reducing to a practical minimum any risks associated with the strategy.

Can we make the strategy any less risky?

If the marketing strategy is proven, by challenge, to be both strong and appropriate, it usually gets to be executed. However, before that, the best companies test for risk. Because, of course, shareholder value creation is related strongly to risk, effective boards ask questions designed to minimize any risk associated with the marketing strategy. The questions they ask align closely to the last five strategy diagnostics about synergy, resources, tactics, objectives and risk.

Are we realizing any synergy?

Exemplar companies look to make the most of the interaction between different strategy components. They accept strategies that have identifiable internal synergies (e.g. share resources between strategies) or external synergies (e.g. interacting customer segments between strategies). They reject or modify those that have neither. One finance director justified this test in terms of the inadequacy of his accounting systems:

> We know the limitations of management accounting, especially when we have to account across product or market divisions. So we know that real synergies mean returns above and beyond what is in the P&L.

Are we giving the strategy enough resources?

Interestingly, the best companies in our study were as concerned with under-resourcing as with over-resourcing. They looked for a realistic correlation between what activity was planned and the resources used. One very experienced director described this as follows:

> Less experienced managers tend to be overly optimistic and underestimate the cost of change and the need for contingency plans. The job of us 'old heads' is to make sure a good strategy is not undermined for the want of sufficient muscle behind it.

Does the strategy add up?

Just as the correlation between resources applied and actions planned was challenged, the correlation between actions planned and objectives was also questioned. In particular, proportionality was sought between changes in marketing strategy and the results it was aiming for. The same experienced leader quoted above said:

> The same inexperienced optimism sometimes leads managers to underestimate market inertia. I have learned that large changes in market share only come from correspondingly large changes in strategy. If a strategy says we'll change a little and get a lot, I'm naturally sceptical.

Does the strategy translate into action?

Most senior marketers were conscious that implementation is the biggest part of strategy and therefore paid close attention to what tactics were implied by the strategy. They were positive about strategies that made tactics, such as pricing, promotion, etc., obviously sensible and others obviously not. They were less positive about strategies that left major tactical decisions open for debate. As one interviewee said:

> A good test of strategic thinking is what it implies for action. If the strategy makes the tactical decisions clearer, it gets my vote. If not, it often indicates a fuzzy strategy.

Have we done all we can to reduce risk?

The final challenge to marketing strategy by exemplar companies sought to reduce the chances of failure and optimize the probability of success, in terms of what was known and assumed about the market and the proposition. Hence, strategies with low market risk (e.g. known markets) and low-implementation risk (e.g. that made cautious allowances for pricing, costs and competitor impact) were welcomed. By contrast, marketing strategies with high-market risk (e.g. new markets) and high-implementation risk (e.g. large competitor impact and optimistic costing and pricing assumptions) were rejected or modified.

As with all the other aspects of making strong marketing strategy, from understanding the market to selecting the macrocongruent colour of strategic marketing planning to ensuring a microcongruent culture, testing the strategy is often an unconscious competence. However, the questions described in this section reflect that competence in action and provide guidance for others to achieve the same competence in a deliberate, and therefore learnable, manner.

Application point: How good is your marketing strategy and what are the sources of its weaknesses?

The practical expression and manifestation of the strategy diagnostics described above is useful in respect of both your current and future marketing strategies. Before proceeding it is worth considering the following.

- What are the principal weaknesses of your current marketing strategy?
- What, in terms of macrocongruence and microcongruence, do you think are the underlying causes of those weaknesses?
- How might you use the above questions to test your marketing strategy during development and both before and after its implementation?

Journey's end

With the questions that exemplar companies and their strategists ask to test their strategy, the five-step journey for emulating the best strategists comes to an end. If you have understood the history and research background of Part 1, grasped the lessons of the new research in Part 2 and followed the five-step process in Part 3, you are now better equipped to make strong marketing strategy. It is an important task for you, for your career, and ultimately for the economy and therefore our society. Please let me know how you get on.

Power points

- Having developed a bicongruent strategic marketing planning process, what remains is to implement it and then test the resultant marketing strategy.
- Each of the seven stereotypical colours of strategic marketing planning has characteristics of success and failure at each of the three stages of strategy making (understanding the market, choosing the strategy, deciding the actions).

- Having developed a marketing strategy, exemplar companies test it to see first if it is strong, secondly if it is appropriate, then finally if it is risky.

Reflection points for marketing practitioners

- Which of the lessons concerning the implementation of each colour of strategic marketing planning hold most relevance to you?
- What are the principal weaknesses in your current marketing strategy, and what causes them?
- How will you begin the process of improving your strategic marketing planning?

Afterword: a continuing journey

> There are risks and costs to a program of action, but they are far less than the long-range risks and costs of comfortable inaction.
>
> (John F. Kennedy)

Although this book has travelled from a historical survey of strategic marketing planning, via academic research, to prescriptive methods and tools, it was born in a very current and practical management problem. In my direct experience, corroborated by the observations of others, the huge amount of effort put into strategic marketing planning generally adds little value. Once the useful but small value of ordering and recording information and agreed actions is discounted, the value-add of what many marketing strategists do is very limited. If we measure it against our goal of creating distinct and sustainable competitive advantage, the contribution to our goals of all that analysis and preparation is often insignificantly small. That is not to dismiss the successes of the few or the good intentions of the many but, two generations after its conception, marketing mostly doesn't happen. It pretends to, but underneath a fur coat of jargon and PowerPoint there is little underwear, to steal a colloquialism from my regional origins. As reflective marketing practitioners, we need to do better – much better.

This book therefore is my contribution to that effort to improve the value-add of marketing. Whatever its many faults, it is carefully targeted at the reflective practitioner. My hope is that, with the help of such reflective practitioners, the ideas and tools in this book can be improved, developed and made still more practically useful. To that end, I warmly invite readers to submit comments, anecdotes, suggestions and criticisms to me. The more, and the more critical, the better. All will help to improve future editions of this book.

My final thought is inspired by the words of President Kennedy, above. What is advocated in this book is not easy. Keeping your head down and carrying on as before may seem a much more attractive option to most marketers. But if you've read this far, you're not like most marketers.

Dr Brian Smith
brian.smith@pragmedic.com

References

Abratt, R. and Bendixen, M. (1993). Marketing planning: an empirical analysis of practices in British companies. University of Melbourne Graduate School of Management Working Paper 4 (unpublished).

Albert, T. C. (2003). Need-based segmentation and customised communication strategies in a complex-commodity industry: a supply chain study. *Industrial Marketing Management*, **32**, 281–290.

Ames, B. C. (1970). Trappings versus substance in industrial marketing. *Harvard Business Review*, **48(4)**, 93–102.

Anderson, P. F. (1982). Marketing, strategic planning, and the theory of the firm. *Journal of Marketing*, **46(2)**, 15–26.

Andrews, K. R. (1971). *The Concept of Corporate Strategy*. Homewood, IL: Dow-Jones Irwin.

Ansoff, I. H. (1965). *Corporate Strategy*. London: Penguin.

Ansoff, I. H. (1991). Critique of Henry Mintzberg's 'The design school: reconsidering the basic premises of strategic management', *Strategic Management Journal*, **12(6)**, 449–461.

Appiah-Adu, K., Morgan, R. E. and Katsikeas, C. S. (1996). Diagnosing organizational planning benefits: the efficacy of planning formalization. *Journal of Strategic Marketing*, **4(4)**, 221–238.

Armstrong, J. S. (1982). The value of formal planning for strategic decisions: review of empirical research. *Strategic Management Journal*, **3(3)**, 197–211.

Bailey, A. and Johnson, G. (1995). The processes of strategy development. In: *The CIMA Handbook of Strategic Management* (J. L. Thompson, ed.). Oxford: Butterworth-Heinemann.

Barney, J. B. (1986). Organizational culture: can it be a source of competitive advantage? *Academy of Management Review*, **11(3)**, 656–665.

Barney, J. B. (2001a). *Gaining and Sustaining Competitive Advantage*, 2nd edn. Upple Saddle River, NJ: Prentice Hall.

Barney, J. B. (2001b). Resource-based theories of competitive advantage: a ten-year retrospective on the resource-based view. *Journal of Management*, **27**, 643–650.

Bartels, R. (1962). *The Development of Marketing Thought*, 1st edn. Homewood, IL: Richard D. Irwin.

Bell, L. and Emory, C. W. (1971). The faltering marketing concept. *Journal of Marketing Management*, **35(4)**, 37–42.

Bishop, R. C. and Bresser, R. K. (1983). Dysfunctional effects of formal planning: two theoretical explanations. *Academy of Management Review*, **8(4)**, 588–599.

Bracker, J. S. and Pearson, J. N. (1986). Planning and financial performance in small, mature, firms. *Strategic Management Journal*, **7(6)**, 503–522.

Brown, S. (1996). Art or science? Fifty years of marketing debate. *Journal of Marketing Management*, **12**, 243–267.

Burns, T. and Stalker, G. M. (1961). *The Management of Innovation*. London: Tavistock.

Burrell, G. and Morgan, G. (1979). *Sociological Paradigms and Organizational Analysis*, 1st edn. Beverley Hills, CA: Sage.

Buzzell, R. D. and Wiersema, F. D. (1981). Successful share-building strategies. *Harvard Business Review*, **59**, 135–144.

Cameron, K. S. (1986). Effectiveness as a paradox: consensus and conflict in conceptions of organizational effectiveness. *Management Science*, **32(5)**, 539–553.

Carson, D. and Cromie, S. (1989). Marketing planning in small enterprises: a model and some empirical evidence. *Journal of Marketing Management*, **1(4)**, 33–49.

Chakravarthy, B. S. (1986). Measuring strategic performance. *Strategic Management Journal*, **7(5)**, 437–458.

Claycomb, C., Germain, R. and Droge, C. (2000). The effects of formal strategic marketing planning on the industrial firm's configuration, structure, exchange patterns and performance. *Industrial Marketing Management*, **29**, 219–234.

Converse, P. D. (1921). *Marketing Methods and Policies*. New York, NY: MacMillan.

Converse, P. D. (1952). Notes on origin of the American Marketing Association. *Journal of Marketing (pre-1986)*, **17(000001)**, 65.

Covin, J. G., Slevin, D. P. and Heeley, M. B. (2001). Strategic decision making in an intuitive vs. technocratic mode: structural and environmental considerations. *Journal of Business Research*, **52(1)**, 51.

Cravens, D. W. (2000). *Strategic Marketing*, 6th edn. London: Irwin McGraw-Hill.

Curren, M., Folkes, V. and Steckel, J. (1992). Explanations of successful and unsuccessful marketing decisions. *Journal of Marketing*, **56(2)**, 18–31.

Cyert, R. B. and March, J. G. (1963). *A Behavioural Theory of the Firm*. Englewood Cliffs, NJ: Prentice Hall.

Denison, D. R. and Mishra, A. K. (1995). Towards a theory of organizational culture and effectiveness. *Organizational Science*, **6(2)**, 204–221.

DiMaggio, P. and Powell, W. (1983). The iron cage revisited: institutional isomorphism and collective rationality in organizational fields. *American Sociology Review*, **48(2)**, 147–160.

Drucker, P. F. (1954). *The Practice of Management*. New York, NY: Harper and Row.

Drucker, P. F. (1974). *Management: Tasks, Responsibilities, Practices*, 1st edn. Oxford: Butterworth-Heinemann.

Drucker, P. F. (1993). Corporate culture: use it, don't lose it. In: *Managing for the Future*, 1st edn (P. F. Drucker, ed.), pp. 150–154. Oxford: Butterworth-Heinemann.

Dunn, M. G., Norburn, D. and Birley, S. (1985). Corporate culture: a positive correlate with marketing effectiveness. *International Journal of Advertising*, **4**, 65–73.

Eastlack, J. O. and McDonald, P. R. (1970). The CEO's role in corporate growth. *Harvard Business Review*, **48(3)**, 150–163.

Eisenhardt, K. M. (1989). Making fast strategic decisions in high-velocity environments. *Academy of Management Journal*, **32(3)**, 543–576.

Eisenhardt, K. M. and Zbaracki, M. J. (1992). Strategic decision making. *Strategic Management Journal*, **13(Special Issue)**, 17–37.

Fitzgerald, T. H. (1988). Can change in organizational culture really be managed? *Organizational Dynamics*, **17(2)**, 5–15.

Flynn, F. J. and Staw, B. M. (2004). Lend me your wallets: the effect of charismatic leadership on external support for an organization. *Strategic Management Journal*, **25**, 309–330.

Fredrickson, J. W. (1984). The comprehensiveness of strategic decision processes: extension, observations, future directions. *Academy of Management Journal*, **27(3)**, 445–466.

Fredrickson, J. W. and Mitchell, T. R. (1984). Strategic decision processes: comprehensiveness and performance in an industry with an unstable environment. *Academy of Management Journal*, **27(2)**, 399–423.

Freytag, P. V. and Clarke, A. H. (2001). Business to business market segmentation. *Industrial Marketing Management*, **30(6)**, 473–486.

Glaister, K. W. and Falshaw, J. R. (1999). Strategic planning: still going strong. *Long Range Planning*, **32(1)**, 107–116.

Goold, M. and Campbell, A. (2000). Taking stock of synergy: a framework for assessing linkages between businesses. *Long Range Planning*, **33**, 72–96.

Greenley, G. E. (1985). Marketing plan utilisation. *Quarterly Review of Marketing*, **10**, 12–19.

Greenley, G. E. (1994). Strategic planning and company performance: an appraisal of the empirical evidence. *Scandinavian Journal of Management*, **10(4)**, 383–396.

Greenley, G. E. and Bayus, B. L. (1994). Marketing planning processes in UK and US companies. *Journal of Strategic Marketing*, **2(2)**, 140–154.

Hannan, M. T. and Freeman, J. H. (1984). Structural inertia and organizational change. *American Sociology Review*, **49(2)**, 149–164.

Harris, L. C. (1996). The anti-planner's tactics to thwart planning initiation. *Journal of Strategic Marketing*, **4(4)**, 239–253.

Harris, L. C. (1999a). A contingency approach to market orientation: distinguishing behaviours, systems, structures, strategies, and performance characteristics. *Journal of Marketing Management*, **15(7)**, 617–646.

Harris, L. C. (1999b). Initiating planning: the problem of entrenched cultural values. *Long Range Planning*, **32(1)**, 117–126.

Harris, L. C. (1999c). Management behavior and barriers to market orientation in retailing companies. *Journal of Services Marketing*, **13(2)**, 113–131.

Harris, L. C. (2000). Getting professionals to plan: pressures, obstacles and tactical responses. *Long Range Planning*, **33(6)**, 849–877.

Harris, L. C. (2002). Developing market orientation: an exploration of differences in management approaches. *Journal of Marketing Management*, **18**, 603–632.

Harris, L. C. and Ogbonna, E. (1999a). Developing a market oriented culture: a critical evaluation. *Journal of Management Studies*, **36(2)**, 177–196.

Harris, L. C. and Ogbonna, E. (1999b). The strategic legacy of company founders. *Long Range Planning*, **32(3)**, 333–343.

Harris, L. C. and Ogbonna, E. (2001). Strategic human resource management, market orientation, and organizational performance. *Journal of Business Research*, **51(2)**, 157–166.

Harris, L. C. and Ogbonna, E. (2002). The unintended consequences of culture interventions: a study of unexpected outcomes. *British Journal of Management*, **13**, 31–49.

Haspeslagh, P. (1982). Portfolio planning: uses and limits. *Harvard Business Review*, **60**, 58–73.

Hatch, M. J. (1999). The cultural dynamics of organizational change. In: *The Handbook of Organizational Culture and Climate* (N. M. Ashkanasy, W. Celest and M. F. Peterson, eds.). Thousand Oaks, CA: Sage.

Hendry, J. (2000). Strategic decision making, discourse and strategy as social practice. *Journal of Management Studies*, **37(7)**, 955–977.

Hendry, J. and Seidl, D. (2003). The structure and significance of strategic episodes: social systems theory and the routine practices of strategic change. *Journal of Management Studies*, **40(1)**, 175–197.

Herold, D. M. (1972). Long range planning and organizational performance: a cross-validation study. *Academy of Management Journal*, **15(1)**, 91–102.

Hickson, D. J., Butler, R., Cray, D. *et al.* (1986). *Top Decisions: Strategic Decision Making in Organizations*. San Francisco, CA: Jossey-Bass.

Hill, T. and Westbrook, R. (1997). SWOT analysis: it's time for a product recall. *Long Range Planning*, **30(1)**, 46–52.

Hinings, C. R., Hickson, D. J., Pennings, J. M. and Schneck, R. E. (1974). Structural conditions of intraorganizational power. *Administrative Science Quarterly*, **19(1)**, 22–44.

Hodgkinson, G. P. (2002). *The Competent Organization*, 1st edn. Maidenhead: Open University Press.

Hooley, G. J., West, C. J. and Lynch, J. E. (1981). *Marketing in the UK*. Maidenhead: The Institute of Marketing.

Hooley, G. J., Lynch, J. E. and Shepherd, J. (1990). The marketing concept: putting theory into practice. *European Journal of Marketing*, **24(9)**, 7–23.

Hopkins, D. S. (1981). *The Marketing Plan*. New York, NY: The Conference Board.

Jenkins, M. and McDonald, M. H. B. (1997). Market segmentation: organizational archetypes and research agenda. *European Journal of Marketing*, **31(1)**, 17–32.

Jensen, M. and Zajac, E. J. (2004). Corporate elites and corporate strategy: how demographic preferences and structural position shape the scope of the firm. *Strategic Management Journal*, **25**, 507–524.

Johnson, G. and Scholes, K. (2001). *Exploring Corporate Strategy*. London: Prentice Hall.

Kaplan, R. S. and Norton, D. P. (1992). The balanced scorecard – measures that drive performance. *Harvard Business Review*, **70(1)**, 71–79.

Karger, D. W. and Malik, Z. A. (1975). Long range planning and organizational performance. *Long Range Planning*, **8(6)**, 150–163.

Keats, B. W. and Hitt, M. T. (1988). A causal model of linkages among environmental dimensions, macro-organizational characteristics and performance. *Academy of Management Journal*, **31(3)**, 570–598.

Kleinman, M. (2004). Iceland hires Sun chief to halt slide. *Marketing*, 31 October, p. 1.

Kotler, P. (1991). *Marketing Management: Analysis, Planning and Control*, 7th edn. London: Prentice Hall.

Kotler, P. (2002). *Marketing Management*, 11th edn. New York, NY: Pearson.

Kotter, J. P. and Heskett, J. L. (1992). *Corporate Culture and Performance*, 1st edn. New York, NY: Free Press.

Lancaster, G. and Waddelow, I. (1998). An empirical investigation into the process of strategic marketing planning in SMEs: its attendant problems, and proposals towards a new practical paradigm. *Journal of Marketing Management*, **14(8)**, 853–878.

Lawrence, P. R. and Lorsch, J. W. (1967a). Differentiation and integration in complex organizations. *Administrative Science Quarterly*, **12(1)**, 1–47.

Lawrence, P. R. and Lorsch, J. W. (1967b). *Organization and Environment*. Boston, MA: Harvard University.

Legge, K. (1994). Managing culture: fact or fiction. In: *Personnel Management: A Comprehensive Guide to Theory and Practice in Britain*, 2nd edn (K. Sissons, ed.), pp. 397–432. Oxford: Blackwell.

Levitt, T. (1960). Marketing myopia. *Harvard Business Review*, **38**, 45–56.

Lindblom, C. E. (1959). The science of muddling through. *Public Administration Review*, **19(2)**, 79–88.

Lindblom, C. E. (1979). Still muddling, not yet through. *Public Administration Review*, **39(6)**, 517–527.

Liu, H. (1995). Market orientation and firm size: an empirical examination in UK firms. *European Journal of Marketing*, **29(1)**, 57–71.

Lorsch, J. W. (1986). Managing culture: the invisible barrier to strategic change. *California Management Review*, **28(2)**, 95–109.

Lysonski, S. and Percottich, A. (1992). Strategic marketing planning, environmental uncertainty and performance. *International Journal of Research in Marketing*, **9(3)**, 247–255.

Maitlis, S. and Lawrence, T. B. (2003). Orchestral manoeuvres in the dark: understanding failure in organizational strategizing. *Journal of Management Studies*, **40(1)**, 109–139.

March, J. G. and Simon, H. A. (1958). *Organizations*. New York, NY: Wiley.

Marginson, D. E. W. (2002). Management control systems and their effects on strategy formation at middle-management levels: evidence from a UK organization. *Strategic Management Journal*, **23**, 1019–1031.

Marketing Week (2004). Too little, too late, for fallen giants. *Marketing Week*, **27(43)**, 3–5 (21 October).

Marketwatch: Financial Services (2004). Tesco: barking about its own success. *Marketwatch: Financial Services*, **3(10)**, 14.

Martin, J. (1979). Business planning: the gap between theory and practice. *Long Range Planning*, **12(6)**, 2–10.

McColl-Kennedy, J. and Keil, G. (1990). Marketing planning practices in Australia: a comparison across company types. *Marketing Intelligence and Planning*, **8(4)**, 2–29.

McDonald, M. H. B. (1982). *Theory and Practice of Marketing Planning for Industrial Goods in International Markets*. Cranfield: Cranfield University School of Management.

McDonald, M. H. B. (1989). Ten barriers to marketing planning. *Journal of Marketing Management*, **5(1)**, 1–18.

McDonald, M. H. B. (1996). Strategic marketing planning: theory, practice, and research agendas. *Journal of Marketing Management*, **12**, 5–27.

McDonald, M. H. B. (2002). *Marketing Plans: How to Prepare Them, How to Use Them*, 5th edn. Oxford: Butterworth-Heinemann.

McDonald, M. H. B. and Wilson, H. N. (1999). Exploiting technique interrelationships: a model of strategic marketing planning. *Journal of Euromarketing*, **7(3)**, 1–26.

McKiernan, P. and Morris, C. (1994). Strategic planning and financial performance in UK SMEs. *British Journal of Management*, **5**, 531–541.

McNamara, C. P. (1972). The present status of the marketing concept. *Journal of Marketing*, **36(1)**, 50–57.

Miller, C. C. and Cardinal, L. B. (1994). Strategic planning and firm performance: a synthesis of more than two decades of research. *Academy of Management Journal*, **37(6)**, 1649–1665.

Mintzberg, H. (1990). The design school: reconsidering the basic premises of strategic management. *Strategic Management Journal*, **11(3)**, 171–195.

Mintzberg, H. (1994). *The Rise and Fall of Strategic Planning*, 1st edn. Hemel Hempstead: Prentice Hall.

Mintzberg, H. (1996). Musings on management. *Harvard Business Review*, **Jul–Aug**, 61–65.

Mintzberg, H. (2000). View from the top: Henry Mintzberg on strategy and management. *Academy of Management Review*, **14(3)**, 31–42.

Mintzberg, H., Ahlstrand, B. and Lampel, J. (1998). *Strategy Safari*, 1st edn. New York, NY: The Free Press.

Mitchell, V. W. (1996). Questioning the role of descriptor variables on market segmentation. *Journal of Targeting, Measurement and Analysis in Marketing*, **5(2)**, 95–103.

Mowen, J. and Gaeth, G. (1992). The evaluation stage in marketing decision making. *Journal of the Academy of Marketing Science*, **20(2)**, 177–187.

Mulcahy, A. (2004). Serving up Xerox. *eweek*, **21(38)**, 15 (20 September).

Neely, A. (1999). The performance measurement revolution: why now and what next? *International Journal of Operations and Production Management*, **19(2)**, 205–228.

Ogbonna, E. and Harris, L. C. (2002). The performance implications of management fads and fashions: an empirical study. *Journal of Strategic Marketing*, **10**, 47–68.

Ogbonna, E. and Wilkinson, B. (2003). The false promise of organizational culture change: a case study of middle managers in grocery retailing. *Journal of Management Studies*, **40(5)**, 1151–1178.

Owen, G. (2004). The leadership legacy that has kept GKN aloft. *Financial Times*, 6 January.

Pearce, J. A. II and Robbins, D. K. (1987). The impact of grand strategy and planning formality on financial performance. *Strategic Management Journal*, **8(2)**, 125–135.

Pearce, J. A. II, Freeman, E. B. and Robinson, R. B. Jr (1987). The tenuous link between formal strategic planning and financial performance. *Academy of Management Review*, **12(4)**, 658–676.

Pettigrew, A. M. (1973). *The Politics of Organizational Decision Making*. London: Tavistock.

Pettigrew, A. M. (1979). On studying organizational cultures. *Administrative Science Quarterly*, **24(4)**, 570–581.

Piercy, N. F. and Giles, W. (1989). Making SWOT analysis work. *Marketing Intelligence and Planning*, **7(5)**, 5–7.

Piercy, N. F. and Morgan, N. A. (1993). Strategic and operational market segmentation: a managerial analysis. *Journal of Strategic Marketing*, **1**, 123–140.

Porter, M. E. (1980). *Competitive Strategy*, 1st edn. New York, NY: Free Press.

Porter, M. E. (1996). What is strategy? *Harvard Business Review*, **74(6)**, 61–78.

Priem, R. L., Rasheed, A. M. A. and Kotulic, A. G. (1995). Rationality in strategic decision processes, environmental dynamism and firm performance. *Journal of Management*, **21(5)**, 913–929.

Pugh, D. S., Hickson, D. J., Hinings, C. R. and Turner, C. (1968). Dimensions of organization structure. *Administrative Science Quarterly*, **13**, 65–105.

Pulendran, S., Speed, R. and Widing, R. E. (2003). Marketing planning, market orientation and business performance. *European Journal of Marketing*, **37(3/4)**, 476.

Quinn, J. B. (1980). *Strategies for Change: Logical Incrementalism*. Homewood, IL: Irwin.

Reid, D. M. and Hinckley, I. C. (1989). Strategic planning: the cultural impact. *Marketing Intelligence and Planning*, **7(11/12)**, 4–12.

Rhyne, L. C. (1986). The relationship of strategic planning to financial performance. *Strategic Management Journal*, **7(5)**, 423–436.

Ross, J. E. and Silverblatt, R. (1987). Developing the strategic plan. *Industrial Marketing Management*, **16**, 103–108.

Rue, L. W. and Fulmer, R. M. (1973). Is long range planning profitable? *Academy of Management Proceedings*, 66–73.

Ruekert, R. W. (1992). Developing a market orientation: an organizational strategy perspective. *International Journal of Research in Marketing*, **9(3)**, 225–245.

Ruekert, R. W. and Walker, O. C. (1987). Marketing's interaction with other functional units: a conceptual approach and empirical evidence. *Journal of Marketing*, **51(1)**, 1–19.

Russell, B. (1935). *Sceptical Essays*. London: Allen.

Schein, E. H. (1984). Coming to a new awareness of organizational culture. *Sloan Management Review*, **25(2)**, 3–16.

Schein, E. H. (1991). What is culture? In: *Reframing Organizational Culture*, 1st edn (P. J. Frost *et al*., eds.), pp. 243–254. Newbury Park, CA: Sage.

Schein, E. H. (1999). *The Corporate Culture Survival Guide*, 1st edn. San Francisco, CA: Jossey-Bass Inc.

Schön, D. A. (1999). *The Reflective Practitioner: How Professionals Think in Action*, 1st edn. New York, NY: Perseus Books Group.

Schwenk, C. R. (1995). Strategic decision making. *Journal of Management*, **21(3)**, 471–493.

Schwenk, C. R. and Shrader, C. B. (1993). Effects of formal strategic planning on financial performance in small firms: a meta-analysis. *Entrepreneurship Theory and Practice*, **17(3)**, 53–64.

Shapiro, E. C. (1995). *Fad Surfing in the Boardroom*, 1st edn. Reading, MA: Addison-Wesley.

Shrader, C. B., Taylor, L. and Dalton, D. R. (1984). Strategic planning and organizational performance: a critical appraisal. *Journal of Management*, **10(2)**, 149–171.

Shrivastava, P. (1985). Integrating strategy formulation with organizational culture. *Journal of Business Strategy*, **5(3)**, 103–112.

Simon, H. A. (1947). *Administrative Behaviour*. New York, NY: MacMillan.

Slevin, D. P. and Covin, J. G. (1997). Strategy formation patterns, performance and the significance of context. *Journal of Management*, **32(2)**, 189–209.

Smirchich, L. (1983). Concepts of culture and organizational analysis. *Administrative Science Quarterly*, **28(3)**, 339–358.

Smirchich, L. and Calas, M. B. (1987). Organizational culture: a critical assessment. In: *Handbook of Organizational Communication* (F. M. Jablin, L. L. Putnam, K. H. Roberts and L. W. Porter, eds.). Newbury Park, NJ: Sage.

Smith, A. D. and Manna, D. R. (2004). Strategic *disintermediation* within the context of e-commerce: the effect on distributors and re-sellers. *Journal of the American Academy of Business, Cambridge*, **5(1/2)**, 374–384.

Smith, B. D. (1999). *Clinica's Guide to Successful Marketing Strategies for Medical Devices and Diagnostics*, 1st edn. Richmond: PJB Publications.

Smith, B. D. (2003). The effectiveness of marketing-strategy making processes: a critical literature review and a research agenda. *Journal of Targeting, Measurement and Analysis for Marketing*, **11(3)**, 273–290.

Speed, R. (1994). Environmental context and marketing planning processes. *Journal of Marketing Management*, **10(7)**, 667–677.

Stampfl, R. W. (1983). Structural analysis and the marketing concept: problems and solutions. In: *The Marketing Concept: Perspective and Viewpoints* (P. R. Varadarajan, ed.), pp. 95–107. College Station, TX: The Marketing Department, Texas A&M University.

Stone, M. (2004). Segmentation and competitive customer insight in retailing (unpublished).

Taylor, F. (1911). *The Principles of Scientific Management*. New York, NY: Harper and Row.

The Economist (2004). Has Kodak missed the moment? *The Economist*, 30 December.

Thune, S. S. and House, R. J. (1970). Where long range planning pays off: findings of a survey of formal, informal planners. *Business Horizons*, **13(4)**, 81–87.

Treacy, M. and Wiersema, M. (1995). *The Discipline of the Market Leaders*. London: Harper Collins.

Venkatraman, N. and Ramanujam, V. (1986). Measurement of business performance in strategy research: a comparison of approaches. *Academy of Management Review*, **11(4)**, 801–814.

Verhage, B. J. and Waarts, E. (1988). Marketing planning for improved performance: a comparative analysis. *International Marketing Review*, **5(2)**, 20–30.

Walker, O. C. and Ruekert, R. W. (1987). Marketing's role in the implementation of business strategies: a critical review and conceptual framework. *Journal of Marketing*, **51(3)**, 15–33.

Ward, K. R. (2003). *Marketing Finance*. Oxford: Elsevier.

Weick, K. E. (1995). *Sensemaking in Organizations*, 1st edn. Thousand Oaks, CA: Sage.

Westley, F. and Mintzberg, H. (1989). Visionary leadership and strategic management. *Strategic Management Journal*, **10(Special Issue)**, 17–32.

Wilkins, A. L. and Ouchi, W. G. (1983). Efficient cultures: exploring the relationship between culture and organizational performance. *Administrative Science Quarterly*, **28(3)**, 468–481.

Wittink, D. R. and Cattin, P. (1989). Commercial use of conjoint analysis: an update. *Journal of Marketing*, **53**, 91–96.

Wong, V., Saunders, J. and Doyle, P. (1989). *The Barriers to Achieving a Stronger Market Orientation in British Companies: An Exploratory Study*. Loughborough: Department of Management Studies, Loughborough University, pp. 35–64.

Wood, D. R. and LaForge, R. L. (1979). The impact of comprehensive planning on financial performance. *Academy of Management Journal*, **22(3)**, 516–526.

Wood, D. R. and LaForge, R. L. (1986). Lessons from strategic portfolio planning in large US banks. *SAM Advanced Management Journal*, **51**, 25–31.

Zeithaml, V. A., Parasuraman, A. and Berry, L. (1985). Problems and strategies in service marketing. *Journal of Marketing*, **49(2)**, 33–46.

Index